Philosophy Looks to the Future

CONFRONTATION, COMMITMENT, AND UTOPIA

WALTER L. FOGG
Northeastern University

PEYTON E. RICHTER
Boston University

HOLBROOK PRESS, INC.   BOSTON

PHOTO CREDITS: *Stock, Boston*

To

Mary Bell Richter
Edith and Walter M. Fogg
Jane Fogg
and to the memory of
Mary B. Richter

Contents

Preface

The purpose of this book is to introduce beginning students of philosophy to a number of problems which, we believe, are appropriate subjects for reflection. These problems relate to reliable beliefs, authority and freedom, the definition of the good and criteria of morality, the nature of man, the religious quest, and the definition of art and the value of aesthetic experience. We might have selected problems at a lower level of generality and have included readings on specific problems such as the new morality, the population explosion, and the ecological crisis. Instead we have chosen problems of greater generality which are not only relevant to the immediate interests of college students and their teachers but at the same time are of perennial and ultimate concern to all reflective men and women.

We believe that the beginning student's first contact with philosophical writing should not be the razor-sharp arguments of professional specialists. These should come later when the student sees the need for them. Rather, the central purpose of an introductory text should be to show philosophy as working toward an enlargement of the understanding in relation to human experience. Generality may be one of philosophy's greatest vices; but it may also be one of its greatest virtues.

The theme of confrontation and commitment, around which we have organized our topics and selections, hardly needs any justification either as a pedagogical schema or as an ideational choice. It is basically only another formulation of the central concern of the whole philosophical enterprise: the critical scrutiny of belief and of problematic situations as a basis for responsible decisions and defensible choices. The word "confrontation" has unfortunately recently gained currency in its sense of "meeting with hostility" rather than in the more positive sense in which we are using it here: "to bring face to face with" or "to encounter immediately." It is in this sense that we hope to promote a "confrontation" between students and basic issues. We propose to use "commitment" in the sense of "the binding together of agent and belief as a basis for action." As its dictionary meaning would suggest, a commitment is a pledge, something undertaken, but by no means is it to be construed as something pledged in ignorance or undertaken blindly. To the contrary, a commitment ideally should spring from a conviction, and a conviction, in turn, from reflection on values, not from mere happenstance and ignorance. The commited life is the life pledged to the realization and protection of certain values.

The philosopher raises the question: "Why be commited to one kind of life rather than another?"

In answering this question, philosophy must look to the future. However, modern readers often discern their own assumptions and values only by comparison with the assumptions and world views of the past. The editors have accepted the view of philosophy as a discipline which takes place in historical contexts, contexts which have meaningful continuities with the present. Accordingly, the various readings in the book are for the most part arranged chronologically and contain a good deal of traditional material.

Although most of the reading selections included are taken from the works of philosophers, we have drawn also upon the works of other thinkers, from novelists (Dostoyevsky), psychologists (Fromm), playwrights (Wilde) and poets (Morris) whenever their treatment of various problems have the merit of originality, profundity, or unusual interest. This will make the book of use, we hope, in enriching the content of introductory philosophy courses. In addition, it will also make available a philosophically oriented source book for general education courses in the humanities and the social sciences as well as provide an unusual adjunct text for particular courses in literature, religion, and psychology. We would like to hope, too, that this book may be of interest to those readers exploring philosophical questions for the first time on their own.

Finally, we believe that students today have practical and idealistic concerns with the future. They are very personally concerned with defining themselves through their commitments to careers and lifestyles. They also show concern with the lure of alternative social philosophies and communal ideals. At the end of the text we have therefore asked the reader to envisage an ideal society, a utopia, in which he or she confonts the future and tests the consequences of commitments, if only in imagination. Utopias, as working hypotheses, not only provide a survey of future possibilities, they also enable the student to coordinate and illustrate concretely social and philosophical commitments.

For having typed portions of the manuscript, we wish to thank Mrs. Charles Arman.

Walter L. Fogg

Peyton E. Richter

PART ONE

Confrontation with the Human Condition:
Commitment to Philosophical Inquiry

Whence? whither? why? how? — these
questions cover all philosophy.
Joseph Joubert

Ignorance never settles a question.
Benjamin Disraeli

An idea, to be suggestive, must come to the individual
with the force of a revelation.

William James

To strive, to seek, to find, and not to yield.
Alfred Tennyson

There are more things in heaven and earth, Horatio,
than is dreamt of in your philosophy.
Shakespeare's *Hamlet*

The man who cannot wonder . . . is but a
pair of spectacles behind which there is
no eye.

Thomas Carlyle

In philosophy, it is not the attainment of
the goal that matters, it is the things that
are met with by the way.

Havelock Ellis

Convictions are more dangerous enemies
of truth than lies.

Friedrich Nietzsche

Ofttimes the test of courage becomes
rather to live than to die.

Vittorio Alfieri

One life — a little gleam of Time between
two Eternities.

Thomas Carlyle

It hurts more to have a belief pulled than to have a tooth
pulled, and no intellectual novocain is available.

Elmer Davis

Introduction / Why Philosophy?

Many students approach the study of philosophy with the idea that it is a kind of game in which they will be required to take seriously such trivial questions as whether there is any sound when a tree falls in a forest when no person is around. Ambrose Bierce defined philosophy in his *Devil's Dictionary* as "a route of many roads leading from nowhere to nothing." Philosophy is, in fact, interested in puzzles and paradoxes, and in some seemingly trivial ones, when the analysis and resolution of these can aid in the resolution of more significant problems, such as the nature of matter and mind.

The source from which philosophical inquiry springs and to which it must return is the human condition. Each of us is acquainted with doubt, human suffering, the need for action, and the anguish of moral decision. Almost everyone experiences hope and fear, a feeling of what is right and wrong, a sense of beauty, a curiosity about unanswered questions, and a desire to exercise powers and continue to develop them. Each individual responds to the human condition in which these experiences occur and attempts to create a life that has meaning and value. In doing this, he or she reflects and speculates, especially when conflicts requiring resolution arise between beliefs, feelings, and actions.

Philosophy is never very far from ordinary reflection. The philosopher insists, however, on reflecting more thoroughly and with as much precision as possible. Consistency of argument, coherence of belief, and clarity of meaning are the hallmarks of philosophical reflection. "Philosophy," wrote Victor Hugo, "is the microscope of thought."

Philosophizing

The term *philosophy* literally means "love of wisdom" (*philein,* "to love"; *sophia,* "wisdom"). Philosophy may indeed love and aspire to wisdom, but it never gives its followers the satisfaction of permanent possession of its goal.

The philosopher examines beliefs and concepts the way a biologist does magnified cells, some of which may be harmless or healthy while others are dangerous. With his "microscope of thought" he submits them to his most concentrated scrutiny. He makes them give an account of themselves—of their origin, meaning, and value. Committed himself to the life of critical inquiry, he examines commitments in all areas of the human condition no matter how secular or sacred. If his conclusions leave him unhappy, even enraged, he is determined nevertheless to reach them and to make them his own.

Philosophy and Doubt

Philosophers have sometimes been referred to as "dutiful doubters." The spirit of scepticism has undoubtedly always been closely allied with philosophical reflection. "The first step toward philosophy is incredulity," said Diderot. More recently, Alfred North Whitehead has defined philosophy as "an attitude of mind toward doctrines ignorantly entertained."[1] Both of these statements are in the mainstream of Western philosophy, which goes back to the Greeks and Socrates who stressed the importance not only of knowing oneself but of knowing *for* oneself, of arguing and testing one's convictions, and of following the path of truth wherever it might lead. The person who defined philosophy as "a refined sense of one's own ignorance" was Socratic in his inspiration.

Several of the great doubters in the history of philosophy will be presented in the next part of this book: René Descartes, who doubted his way to certainty; David Hume, "the prince of philosophical sceptics"; Leo Tolstoy, whose doubts nearly drove him mad; and William James, who overcame the will to doubt with the will to believe. Different though they were, these thinkers would agree that one must confront one's doubts courageously rather than try to run away from them, and that the unflinching confrontation with doubt can lead to many benefits, focal as well as fringe. For only by testing one's beliefs in an air of philosophical scepticism, can one know if the beliefs are not just accepted but acceptable. "I respect faith," someone has said, "but doubt is what gets you an education."

Philosophy and Freedom

Beginning students of philosophy often wonder why philosophers get so excited over philosophical theories and why they resist so vehemently any attempt by authorities to interfere with their freedom of inquiry. Isn't philosophy only a matter of ideas, and do ideas really matter? Shouldn't we rely on expert opinion and on reliable authorities in all fields who know what they're talking about and can tell us exactly what to believe?

The answers to these questions will be given by various thinkers in Part Three. Feodor Dostoyevsky suggests in "The Legend of the Grand Inquisitor" that most people really don't want to be free to believe what is true and to do what they please. Among these is certainly not Henry David Thoreau, "the sage of Concord," who will argue for the individual's right and duty to defy all authority and to do his own thinking, insisting that "if I could not doubt, I should not believe." Thoreau's defense of freedom to doubt, to believe, and to act would be strongly supported by John Stuart Mill, who argues persuasively in *On Liberty* that freedom of philosophical reflection, among other forms of freedom, is not a luxury but an absolute necessity. Mill, like Clarence Darrow, would consider it a tragedy to teach children not to doubt, since they would in all probability become adults who lack the ability to think critically and to act creatively. They might be "true believers" but they would adhere to false beliefs. They would lack the spontaneity which Erich Fromm identified as the pulse of freedom. They would certainly fail to appreciate the importance of thinking for themselves and would not hesitate to impose, if necessary by force, their own prejudices and beliefs upon those who disagreed with them. Freedom and doubt cannot exist without one another. Neither can tyranny and fraud, for, as Bergen Evans points out:

> In the last analysis all tyranny rests on fraud, on getting someone to accept false assumptions, and any man who for one moment abandons or suspends the questioning spirit has for that moment betrayed humanity.[2]

Philosophers, then, are persons who put a premium on open-mindedness, who entertain interesting ideas as though they were honored guests, and who find the company of provocative questions far more engaging than that of pat answers. Bertrand Russell, himself a great sceptic, saw in this questioning spirit philosophy's chief value and ultimate justification. Philosophy should be studied, Russell believed, not for the sake of its answers, which can never be proved absolutely true, but for the sake of the questions it raises. These questions open and stretch the mind, stimulate the intellectual imagination, and undermine dogmatism and tyranny. Furthermore, Russell concluded, "through the greatness of the universe which philosophy contemplates, the mind also is rendered great, and becomes capable of that union with the universe which constitutes its highest end."[3]

Boundary Situations

Besides affording countless opportunities to doubt, the human condition has other sources from which philosophy springs. The German pessimist Arthur Schopenhauer held that "undoubtedly it is the knowledge of death, and therewith the consideration of the suffering and misery of life, that give the strongest impulse to philosophical reflection and metaphysical explanations of the world."[4] If our lives were painless and endless, Schopenhauer believed, we would never wonder why the world exists or question the meaning of our existence. We would simply take it all as a matter of course.

Another German philosopher, Karl Jaspers, traced one of the major sources of philosophy to man's sense of "forsakenness," to the anxiety he experiences when he confronts what Jaspers calls "ultimate" or "boundary situations."[5] These are situations that arise from the very nature of the human condition. They are inescapable, insurmountable, and insoluble by ordinary practical or rational means. Struggle, chance, guilt, death—to mention only four of these unique situations—face all of us no matter how hard we may try to avoid them or discount them. Only by confronting them directly and courageously can we become, Jaspers believes, truly human beings. Although these boundary situations can shatter us, causing us to founder, in the process we can commit ourselves to what Paul Tillich calls our "ultimate concern" (see Part Six). Unless we are committed to something, there can no more be meaning to life than there can be intimacy in love without a total personal commitment. As Nietzsche put it, "If one can find a *why* to live for, one can live with almost any *how*." If we can find no meaning to human existence and no end to strive for under the shadow of death, our sufferings would seem horrifying and our predicament absurd. In light of such considerations, Albert Camus argued that the most fundamental philosophical problem is suicide and tried to develop a philosophy of life that would justify creative involvement rather than self-destruction (see Part Seven).

Philosophy for Action

In addition to doubt and boundary situations, another source from which philosophical reflection has developed is the desire to formulate a theoretical basis for action or practice. One of the best exemplifications of this is Karl Marx, who said that whereas previous philosophers had been concerned with understanding the world, he and his fellow communists were concerned with changing it. Confronted with a capitalistic society, first Marx and later William Morris committed themselves to a revolutionary program that would lead eventually, they were convinced, to a classless society. Following this tradition, the contemporary philosopher Herbert Marcuse has brought Marxism up to date, reinterpreting its implications for American society and presenting a powerfully charged image of a "one-dimensional man" that continues to haunt twentieth-century capitalism (see Part Five).

Like Marx, Morris, and Marcuse, the pragmatists William James and John Dewey also stressed the intimate relationship between ideas and consequences and theory and practice. Theory, they held, was valuable only insofar as it clarified and guided practice, and practice, properly observed, should modify and verify theory. Doing and undergoing, observing and reflecting, theorizing and experimenting are continuous not separate activities, and philosophy, therefore, should never be separated from concrete human experience.

Among the other proponents of a philosophy that transforms man and his world, one of the most controversial is the behavioral psychologist B. F. Skinner. Skinner's defense of scientific methods in solving problems, his rejection of the concepts of consciousness, freedom, and human dignity, and his utopian vision of a world ruled by the principles of behavioral engineering are presented far more dispassionately than the doctrines of either the Marxists or the pragmatists. His approach is, however, no less radical and, according to his critics, fraught with as many difficulties (see Part Five).

Philosophy and Life

Despite Marx's strictures against speculative philosophy, philosophers have never really thought merely in order to think. They have always had to think also in order to act. Socrates, when he taught that the unexamined life was not worth living, certainly did not mean that one should spend one's life constantly examining one's life without living it. Philosophy's relationship to life is intimate and complex. A philosophy of life inspires action and guides conduct; it also permeates a person's attitude toward himself, toward other people, and ultimately toward the universe. He is not only committed to it, it commits him to a certain stance, a certain perspective, and usually to a certain life style. A person's philosophy of life gives him a base from which to evaluate reflectively past experience, both personal and historical, and a vantage point from which to survey the reality, both physical and mental, in which he lives. It provides him with principles by which he can answer the central moral question, What ought I to do?, thus allowing for resolution of moral conflict and a commitment to acting so as to promote and to attain the good (see Part Four).

From Wonder to Wisdom

After contemplating the human condition, the French mathematician and mystic Blaise Pascal observed:

> When I consider the short duration of my life, swallowed up in the eternity before and after, the little space which I fill, and even can see, engulfed in the infinite immensity of spaces of which I am ignorant, and which know me not, I am frightened, and am astonished at being here rather than there; for there is no reason why here rather than there, why now rather than then. Who has put me here? By whose order and direction have this place and time been allotted to me?[6]

Out of such attempts to fathom and cope with the condition of being human have sprung a wide variety of activities including work and play, education and politics, moral conduct and religious worship, artistic creation and scientific inquiry, and philosophizing. For philosophy, as Socrates once said, begins in wonder. It springs from the same source as science and religion and, like these activities, it attempts to map a previously unexplored territory. As the reflective appraisal of life's meanings and values, philosophy is one of the chief means by which we try to make ourselves feel a little more at home on a tiny planet whirling around a sun in a solar system adrift in a vast and mysterious universe. A philosopher, it has been said, is a person who has waked up to wonder.

1 / The Committed Philosopher
Socrates

Any discussion of the nature of philosophy will seem quite abstract until one considers such a philosopher as Socrates. He lived and died by his commitment to self-examination, which was to him the essence of philosophizing. Socrates is the very paradigm of the committed philosopher. He encountered doubt and questioned authority. He confronted human nature and faced moral conflict. But while confrontation was the beginning, true commitment was the end of his practical vocation as a philosopher.

The current distinction between analytic and speculative philosophy can be traced to Socrates. He was analytic in that he distinguished clearly the meanings of terms and formulated carefully his definitions and assumptions; he was speculative in that he reflected upon the highest ends of moral conduct and attempted to relate the parts of experience within a larger coherent framework of meaning. A study of Socrates' life, methods, and beliefs (such as he admitted to) can therefore present to the beginning student the basic problems that must be grappled with as he or she strives toward a rationally and morally justifiable commitment.

In understanding Socrates' commitments, one should keep in mind that Socrates was convinced that he had an obligation to search for truth himself as well as to sting others into an awareness of the importance of the search. "I am that gadfly which God has attached to the state," he told the Athenians, "and all day long and in all places am always fastening upon you, arousing and persuading and reproaching you."[7] Not that Socrates claimed to know it all. To the contrary, he claimed that he knew nothing. He was astonished at first when he was told that the oracle at Delphi, when asked who was the wisest man in Greece, had replied, "Socrates." But finally, after searching throughout Athens for men who could give him convincing answers to the questions he raised, who really *knew* what they were talking about, whether it was politics, poetry, or carpentry, the oracle's meaning became clear to Socrates. As he told his fellow citizens when some of them eventually brought their gadfly to trial:

> The truth is, O men of Athens, that God only is wise; and by his answer he intends to show that the wisdom of men is worth little or nothing; he is not speaking of Socrates, he is only using my name by way of illustration, as if he said, He, O men, is the wisest, who, like Socrates, knows that his wisdom is in truth worth nothing.[8]

Socratic Convictions

But long before Socrates had to defend his beliefs and his life in a court of law, many Athenians misunderstood his methods and his aim completely. They considered him to be either a dangerous sceptic and atheist, an underminer of the state's traditions and beliefs, or a calculating Sophist who hoped to profit materially from his teachings.

Socrates was none of these. To be sure, he was sceptical in that he doubted that most men knew what they were talking about when they spoke of such things as justice and injustice, beauty and ugliness, truth and falsehood. Socrates felt that he had a moral obligation to confront such men with his doubt. He challenged them to examine the convictions upon which they were acting by asking questions that provoked them to think more deeply about their basic beliefs. For to *be* good, one must *know* precisely what goodness is; virtue *is* knowledge. One has a moral obligation to examine carefully his personal commitments to be sure that they are worthy of the highest human aspiration and conducive to the best possible life. One must discover to what extent he is living up to the potentialities—rational, moral, and aesthetic—with which he has been endowed. The unexamined life, Socrates was convinced, is not worth living.

Socratic Method

Only a superficial or malicious observer could have mistaken Socrates' dialectical method, which consisted of his asking questions of his interlocutors and of raising objections to the answers they gave, for a purely sceptical method the aim of which was to stir up doubt for its own sake or to encourage the suspension of belief. The reliable first-hand reports that we have on Socrates' life and teaching agree that his intention was not to undermine the state but to improve it. He always showed respect for the religious institutions of Athens. While he claimed to be guided by an inner sign, a divine *daemon,* he taught no secret doctrines, sought no disciples, and, unlike some of the earlier Greek philosophers, made no attempt to explain the nature of the universe scientifically. He pursued what he considered to be his divinely appointed mission of helping others to see by the light of reason, and he did this publicly and freely. Xenophon reported,

Socrates lived ever in the open; for early in the morning he went to the public promenades and training grounds; in the forenoon he was seen in the market; and the rest of the day he passed just where most people were to be met: he was generally talking, and anyone might listen.[9]

His interest was in human not heavenly phenomena. To his admirers it seemed incredible that such a man, so open, conscientious, and dedicated to truth and goodness could be accused, as he later was, of rejecting the gods of Athens and of teaching strange deities.

It was perhaps even more incredible to such friends of Socrates as Xenophon and Plato that he could also be accused, as he was in the later charges brought against him, of corrupting the youth of the Athenian city-state. For Socrates valued youth. He admired its enthusiasm, its resoluteness, its moral earnestness, and its sense of wonder. He spoke to young men, not as to unequals, but as to fellow searchers after truth. He realized that they were considerably less adept than he in asking and answering the right questions and that they conceived of the search for knowledge to be a far easier undertaking that it actually was. But, nevertheless, Socrates believed that young people were usually much more sincere than their elders in their desire to distinguish appearance from reality, truth from falsehood, and sham learning from authentic wisdom. The example that he set for them to follow seemed irreproachable to Xenophon and Plato. His self-control, his courage, his good humor, and his intellectual honesty made him a captivating figure to his admirers but, at the same time, a constant threat to his enemies who despised and feared the intellectual and moral discipline for which he stood. "To be sure, he never professed to teach this," Xenophon writes, "but, by letting his own light shine, he led his disciples to hope that they through imitation of him would attain to such excellence."[10]

Aim and Impact of Socrates

Some who at first followed Socrates, later drifted away to settle down to a life of complacent dogmatism and comfortable conformity. Others, such as Critias and Alcibiades, quickly learned the Socratic method of argumentation and applied it, or rather a travesty of it, for their own selfish political ends, thus contributing to the ruin of Athens and the death of Socrates. Such young men, the defenders of Socrates hasten to point out, were not corrupted by Socrates; they became corrupt because they failed to emulate the Socratic example of impartial and critical inquiry. Even some of those who failed to measure up to the high standards that Socrates held up to them recognized that the fault was their own. For example, Alcibiades, his former admirer who went astray, had this to say in praise of Socrates, according to Plato's *Symposium*:

For he makes me confess that I ought not to live as I do, neglecting the wants of my own soul and busying myself with the concerns of the Athenians. . . . And he is the only person who ever made me ashamed. . . . For I know I cannot answer him or say that I ought not to do as he bids, but when I leave his presence the love of popularity gets the better of me. And therefore I run away and fly from him, and when I see him I am ashamed of what I have confessed to him. Many a time have I wished that he was dead, and yet I know that I should be much more sorry than glad, if he were to die.[11]

Fortunately, Socrates was often more successful than he was with Alcibiades in his efforts to help young people follow through in examining their convictions. He would have agreed with Nietzsche that we must have, beyond the courage of our convictions, the courage to examine our convictions. The Socratic method submits convictions to rigorous critical scrutiny in order to clarify, test, and revise them. Intellectual and moral growth in the person should, Socrates believed, follow as a consequence of the examination and reappraisal of his convictions or beliefs. Socrates attempted to make all of this clear in the defense of his method as reported by Plato in his *Apology*.

Plato's Apology

In 399 B.C. Socrates was brought to trial before a court composed of 501 Athenian citizens. In his defense he spoke as follows:

How you, O Athenians, have been affected by my accusers, I cannot tell; but I know that they almost made me forget who I was—so persuasively did they speak; and yet they have hardly uttered a word of truth. But of the many falsehoods told by them, there was one which quite amazed me;—I mean when they said that you should be upon your guard and not allow yourselves to be deceived by the force of my eloquence. To say this, when they were certain to be detected as soon as I opened my lips and proved myself to be anything but a great speaker, did indeed appear to me most shameless—unless by the force of eloquence they mean the force of truth; for if such is their meaning, I admit that I am eloquent. But in how different a way from theirs! Well, as I was saying, they have scarcely spoken the truth at all; but from me you shall hear the whole truth: not, however, delivered after their manner in a set oration duly ornamented with words and phrases. No, by heaven! but I shall use the words and arguments which occur to me at the moment; for I am confident in the justice of my cause: at my time of life I ought not to be appearing before you, O men of Athens, in the character of a juvenile orator—let no one expect it of me. And I must beg of you to grant me a favour:—If I defend

Plato, "Apology," from *The Dialogues of Plato,* trans. Benjamin Jowett, 3d ed., Vol. I (New York: Oxford University Press, 1892).

myself in my accustomed manner, and you hear me using the words which I have been in the habit of using in the agora, at the tables of the money-changers, or anywhere else, I would ask you not to be surprised, and not to interrupt me on this account. For I am more than seventy years of age, and appearing now for the first time in a court of law, I am quite a stranger to the language of the place; and therefore I would have you regard me as if I were really a stranger, whom you would excuse if he spoke in his native tongue, and after the fashion of his country:—Am I making an unfair request of you? Never mind the manner, which may or may not be good; but think only of the truth of my words, and give heed to that: let the speaker speak truly and the judge decide justly.

And first, I have to reply to the older charges and to my first accusers, and then I will go on to the later ones. For of old I have had many accusers, who have accused me falsely to you during many years; and I am more afraid of them than of Anytus and his associates, who are dangerous, too, in their own way. But far more dangerous are the others, who began when you were children, and took possession of your minds with their falsehoods, telling of one Socrates, a wise man, who speculated about the heaven above, and searched into the earth beneath, and made the worse appear the better cause. The disseminators of this tale are the accusers whom I dread; for their hearers are apt to fancy that such enquirers do not believe in the existence of the gods. And they are many, and their charges against me are of ancient date, and they were made by them in the days when you were more impressible than you are now—in childhood, or it may have been in youth—and the cause when heard went by default, for there was none to answer. And hardest of all, I do not know and cannot tell the names of my accusers; unless in the chance case of a comic poet. All who from envy and malice have persuaded you—some of them having first convinced themselves—all this class of men are most difficult to deal with; for I cannot have them up here, and cross-examine them, and therefore I must simply fight with shadows in my own defence, and argue when there is no one who answers. I will ask you then to assume with me, as I was saying, that my opponents are of two kinds; one recent, the other ancient: and I hope that you will see the propriety of my answering the latter first, for these accusations you heard long before the others, and much oftener.

Well, then, I must make my defence, and endeavour to clear away in a short time, a slander which has lasted a long time. May I succeed, if to succeed be for my good and yours, or likely to avoid me in my cause! The task is not an easy one; I quite understand the nature of it. And so leaving the event with God, in obedience to the law I will now make my defence.

I will begin at the beginning, and ask what is the accusation which has given rise to the slander of me, and in fact has encouraged Meletus to prefer this charge against me. Well, what do the slanderers say? They shall be my prosecutors, and I will sum up their words in an affidavit: "Socrates is an evildoer, and a curious person, who searches into things under the earth and in heaven, and he makes the worse appear the better cause; and he teaches the aforesaid doctrines to others." Such is the nature of the accusation: it is just what you have yourselves seen in the comedy of Aristophanes, who has introduced a man whom he calls Socrates, going about and saying that he walks in air, and talking a deal of nonsense concerning matters of which I do not pretend to know either much or little—not that I mean to speak disparagingly of any one who is a student of natural philosophy. I should be very sorry if Meletus could bring so grave a charge against me. But the simple truth is, O Athenians, that I have nothing to do with physical speculations. Very many of those here present are witnesses to the truth of this, and to them I appeal. Speak then, you who have heard me, and tell your neighbours whether any of you have ever known me hold forth in few words or in many upon such matters. . . . You hear their answer. And from what they say of this part of the charge you will be able to judge of the truth of the rest.

As little foundation is there for the report that I am a teacher, and take money; this accusation has no more truth in it than the other. Although, if a man were really able to instruct mankind, to receive money for giving instruction would, in my opinion, be an honour to him. There is Gorgias of Leontium, and Prodicus of Ceos, and Hippias of Elis, who go the round of the cities, and are able to persuade the young men to leave their own citizens by whom they might be taught for nothing, and come to them whom they not only pay, but are thankful if they may be allowed to pay them. There is at this time a Parian philosopher residing in Athens, of whom I have heard; and I came to hear of him in this way:—I came across a man who has spent a world of money on the Sophists, Callias, the son of Hipponicus, and knowing that he had sons, I asked him: "Callias," I said, "if your two sons were foals or calves, there would be no difficulty in finding some one to put over them; we should hire a trainer of horses, or a farmer, probably, who would improve and perfect them in their own proper virtue and excellence; but as they are human beings, whom are you thinking of placing over them? Is there any one who understands human and political virtue? You must have thought about the matter, for you have sons; is there any one?" "There is," he said. "Who is he?" said I; "and of what country? and what does he charge?" "Evenus the Parian," he replied; "he is the man, and his charge is five minae." Happy is Evenus, I said to myself, if he really has this wisdom, and teaches at such a moderate charge. Had I the same, I should have been very proud and conceited; but the truth is that I have no knowledge of the kind.

I dare say, Athenians, that some one among you will reply, "Yes, Socrates, but what is the origin of these accusations which are brought against you; there must have been something strange which you have been doing? All these rumours and this talk about you would never have arisen if you had been like other men: tell us, then, what is the cause of them, for we should be sorry to judge hastily of you." Now, I regard this as a fair challenge, and I will endeavour to explain to you the reason why I am called wise and have such an evil fame. Please to attend then. And although some of you may think that I am joking, I declare that I will tell you the entire truth. Men of Athens, this reputation of mine has come of a certain sort of wisdom which I possess. If you ask me what kind of wisdom, I reply, wisdom such as may perhaps be attained by man, for to that extent I am inclined to believe that I am wise; whereas the persons of whom I was speaking have a super-human wisdom, which I may fail to describe, because I have it not myself; and he who says that I have, speaks falsely, and is taking away my character. And here, O men of Athens, I must beg you not to interrupt me, even if I seem to say something extravagant. For the word which I will speak is not mine. I will refer you to a witness who is worthy of credit; that witness shall be the god of Delphi—he will tell you about my wisdom, if I have any, and of what sort it is. You must have known Chaerephon; he was early a friend of mine, and also a friend of yours, for he shared in the recent exile of the people, and returned with you. Well, Chaerephon, as you know, was very impetuous in all his doings, and he went to Delphi and boldly asked the oracle to tell him whether —as I was saying, I must beg you not to interrupt—he asked the oracle to tell him whether any one was wiser than I was, and the Pythian prophetess answered, that there was no man wiser. Chaerephon is dead himself; but his brother, who is in court, will confirm the truth of what I am saying.

Why do I mention this? Because I am going to explain to you why I have such an evil name. When I heard the answer, I said to myself, What can the god mean? and what is the interpretation of his riddle? for I know I have no wisdom, small or great. What then can he mean when he says that I am the wisest of men? And yet he is a god, and cannot lie; that would be against his nature. After long consideration, I thought of a method of trying the question. I reflected that if I could only find a man wiser than myself, then I might go to the god with a refutation in my hand. I should say to him, "Here is a man who is wiser than I am; but you said that I was the wisest." Accordingly I went to one who had the reputation of wisdom, and observed him— his name I need not mention; he was a politician whom I selected for examination—and the result was as follows: When I began to talk with him, I could not help thinking that he was not really wise, although he was thought wise by many, and still wiser by himself; and thereupon I tried to explain to him that he thought himself wise, but was not really wise; and the consequence was that he hated me, and his enmity was shared by several who were present and heard me. So I left him, saying to myself, as I went away: Well, although I do not suppose that either of us knows anything really beautiful and good, I am better off than he is,—for he knows nothing, and thinks that he knows; I neither know nor think that I know. In this latter particular, then, I seem to have slightly the advantage of him. Then I went to another who had still higher pretentions to wisdom, and my conclusion was exactly the same. Whereupon I made another enemy of him, and many others besides him.

Then I went to one man after another, being

not unconscious of the enmity which I provoked, and I lamented and feared this: but necessity was laid upon me,—the word of God, I thought, ought to be considered first. And I said to myself, Go I must to all who appear to know, and find out the meaning of the oracle. And I swear to you, Athenians, by the dog I swear!—for I must tell you the truth—the result of my mission was just this: I found that the men most in repute were all but the most foolish; and that others less esteemed were really wiser and better. I will tell you the tale of my wanderings and of the "Herculean" labours, as I may call them, which I endured only to find at last the oracle irrefutable. After the politicians, I went to the poets; tragic, dithyrambic, and all sorts. And there, I said to myself, you will be instantly detected; now you will find out that you are more ignorant than they are. Accordingly I took them some of the most elaborate passages in their own writings, and asked what was the meaning of them—thinking that they would teach me something. Will you believe me? I am almost ashamed to confess the truth, but I must say that there is hardly a person present who would not have talked better about their poetry than they did themselves. Then I knew that not by wisdom do poets write poetry, but by a sort of genius and inspiration; they are like diviners or soothsayers who also say many fine things, but do not understand the meaning of them. The poets appeared to me to be much in the same case; and I further observed that upon the strength of their poetry they believed themselves to be the wisest of men in other things in which they were not wise. So I departed, conceiving myself to be superior to them for the same reason that I was superior to the politicians.

At last I went to the artisans. I was conscious that I knew nothing at all, as I may say, and I was sure that they knew many fine things; and here I was not mistaken, for they did know many things of which I was ignorant, and in this they certainly were wiser than I was. But I observed that even the good artisans fell into the same error as the poets;—because they were good workmen they thought that they also knew all sorts of high matters, and this defect in them overshadowed their wisdom; and therefore I asked myself on behalf of the oracle, whether I would like to be as I was, neither having their knowledge nor their ignorance, or like them in both; and I made answer to myself and to the oracle that I was better off as I was.

This inquisition has led to my having many enemies of the worst and most dangerous kind, and has given occasion also to many calumnies. And I am called wise, for my hearers always imagine that I myself possess the wisdom which I find wanting in others: but the truth is, O men of Athens, that God only is wise; and by his answer he intends to show that the wisdom of men is worth little or nothing; he is not speaking of Socrates, he is only using my name by way of illustration, as if he said, He, O men, is the wisest, who, like Socrates, knows that his wisdom is in truth worth nothing. And so I go about the world obedient to the god, and search and make enquiry into the wisdom of any one, whether citizen or stranger, who appears to be wise; and if he is not wise, then in vindication of the oracle I show him he is not wise; and my occupation quite absorbs me, and I have no time to give either to any public matter of interest or to any concern of my own, but I am in utter poverty by reason of my devotion to the god.

There is another thing:—young men of the richer classes, who have not much to do, come about me of their own accord; they like to hear the pretenders examined, and they often imitate me, and proceed to examine others; there are plenty of persons, as they quickly discover, who think that they know something, but really know little or nothing; and then those who are examined by them instead of being angry with themselves are angry with me: This confounded Socrates, they say; this villainous misleader of youth!—and then if somebody asks them, Why, what evil does he practise or teach? they do not know, and cannot tell; but in order that they may not appear to be at a loss, they repeat the ready-made charges which are used against all philosophers about teaching things up in the clouds and under the earth, and having no gods, and making the worse appear the better cause; for they do not like to confess that their pretence of knowledge has been detected—which is the truth; and as they are numerous and ambitious and energetic, and are drawn up in battle array and have persuasive tongues, they have filled your ears with their loud and inveterate calumnies. And this is the reason why my three accusers, Meletus and Anytus and Lycon, have set upon me; Meletus, who has a quarrel with me on behalf of the poets; Anytus, on behalf of the craftsmen and politicians; Lycon, on behalf of the rhetoricians: and, as I said at the beginning, I cannot expect to get rid of such a mass of calumny all in a moment. And this, O men of Athens, is the truth and the whole truth; I have concealed nothing, I have dissembled nothing. And yet, I know that my plainness of speech makes them hate me, and what is their hatred but a proof that I am speaking the truth? Hence has arisen the prejudice against me; and this is the reason of it, as you will find out either in this or in any future enquiry.

I have said enough in my defence against the first class of my accusers; I turn to the second class. They are headed by Meletus, that good man and true lover of his country, as he calls himself. Against these, too, I must try to make a defence:—Let their affidavit be read: it contains something of this kind: It says that Socrates is a doer of evil, who corrupts the youth; and who does not believe in the gods of the State, but has other new divinities of his own. Such is the charge; and now let us examine the particular counts. He says that I am a doer of evil, and corrupt the youth; but I say, O men of Athens, that Meletus is a doer of evil, in that he pretends to be in earnest when he is only in jest, and is so eager to bring men to trial from a pretended zeal and interest about matters in which he really never had the smallest interest. And the truth of this I will endeavour to prove to you.

Come hither, Meletus, and let me ask a question of you. You think a great deal about the improvement of youth?

Yes, I do.

Tell the judges, then, who is their improver; for you must know, as you have taken the pains to discover their corrupter, and are citing and accusing me before them. Speak, then, and tell the judges who their improver is.—Observe, Meletus, that you are silent, and have nothing to say. But is not this rather disgraceful, and a very considerable proof of what I was saying, that you have no interest in the matter? Speak up, friend, and tell us who their improver is.

The laws.

But that, my good sir, is not my meaning. I want to know who the person is, who, in the first place, knows the laws.

The judges, Socrates, who are present in court.

What, do you mean to say, Meletus, that they are able to instruct and improve youth?

Certainly they are.

What, all of them, or some only and not others?

All of them.

By the goddess. Here, that is good news! There are plenty of improvers, then. And what do you say of the audience,—do they improve them?

Yes, they do.

And the senators?

Yes, the senators improve them.

But perhaps the members of the assembly corrupt them?—or do they improve them?

They improve them.

Then every Athenian improves and elevates them; all with the exception of myself; and I alone am their corrupter? Is that what you affirm?

That is what I stoutly affirm.

I am very unfortunate if you are right. But suppose I ask you a question: How about horses? Does one man do them harm and all the world good? Is not the exact opposite the truth? One man is able to do them good, or at least not many;—the trainer of horses, that is to say, does them good, and others who have to do with them rather injure them? Is not that true, Meletus, of horses, or of any other animals? Most assuredly it is; whether you and Anytus say yes or no. Happy indeed would be the condition of youth if they had one corrupter only, and all the rest of the world were their improvers. But you, Meletus, have sufficiently shown that you never had a thought about the young: your carelessness is seen in your not caring about the very things which you bring against me.

And now, Meletus, I will ask you another question—by Zeus I will: Which is better, to live among bad citizens, or among good ones? Answer, friend, I say; the question is one which may be easily answered. Do not the good do their neighbours good, and the bad do them evil?

Certainly.

And is there any one who would rather be injured than benefited by those who live with him? Answer, my good friend, the law requires you to answer—does any one like to be injured?

Certainly not.

And when you accuse me of corrupting and deteriorating the youth, do you allege that I corrupt them intentionally or unintentionally?

Intentionally, I say.

But you have just admitted that the good do their neighbours good, and the evil do them evil. Now, is that a truth which your superior wisdom has recognized thus early in life, and am I, at my age, in such darkness and ignorance as not to know that if a man with whom I have to live is corrupted by me, I am very likely to be harmed by him; and yet I corrupt him, and intentionally, too—so you say, although neither I nor any other human being is ever likely to be convinced by you. But either I do not corrupt them, or I corrupt them unintentionally; and on either view of the case you lie. If my offence is unintentional, the law has no cognizance of unintentional offences: you ought to have taken me privately, and warned and admonished me; for if I had been better advised, I should have left off doing what I only did unintentionally—no doubt I should; but you would have nothing to say to me and refused to teach me. And now you bring me up in this court, which is a place not of instruction, but of punishment.

It will be very clear to you, Athenians, as I was saying, that Meletus has no care at all, great or small, about the matter. But still I should like to know, Meletus, in what I am affirmed to corrupt the young. I suppose you mean, as I infer from your indictment, that I teach them not to acknowledge the gods which the State acknowledges, but some other new divinities or spiritual agencies in their stead. These are the lessons by which I corrupt the youth, as you say.

Yes, that I say emphatically.

Then, by the gods, Meletus, of whom we are speaking, tell me and the court, in somewhat plainer terms, what you mean! For I do not as yet understand whether you affirm that I teach other men to acknowledge some gods, and therefore that I do believe in gods, and am not an entire atheist—this you do not lay to my charge,—but only you say that they are not the same gods which the city recognizes—the charge is that they are different gods. Or, do you mean that I am an atheist simply, and a teacher of atheism?

I mean the latter—that you are a complete atheist.

What an extraordinary statement! Why do you think so, Meletus? Do you mean that I do not believe in the godhead of the sun or moon, like other men?

I assure you, judges, that he does not: for he says that the sun is stone, and the moon earth.

Friend Meletus, you think that you are accusing Anaxagoras: and you have but a bad opinion of the judges, if you fancy them illiterate to such a degree as not to know that these doctrines are found in the books of Anaxagoras the Clazomenian, which are full of them. And so, forsooth, the youth are said to be taught them by Socrates, when there are not infrequently exhibitions of them at the theatre (price of admission one drachma at the most); and they might pay their money, and laugh at Socrates if he pretends to father these extraordinary views. And so, Meletus, you really think that I do not believe in any god?

I swear by Zeus that you believe absolutely in none at all.

Nobody will believe you, Meletus, and I am pretty sure that you do not believe yourself. I cannot help thinking, that he has written this indictment in a spirit of mere wantonness and youthful bravado. Has he not compounded a riddle, thinking to try me? He said to himself;—I shall see whether the wise Socrates will discover my facetious contradiction, or whether I shall be able to deceive him and the rest of them. For he certainly does appear to me to contradict himself in the indictment as much as if he said that Socrates is guilty of not believing in the gods, and yet of believing in them —but this is not like a person who is in earnest.

I should like you, O men of Athens, to join me in examining what I conceive to be his inconsistency; and do you, Meletus, answer. And I must remind the audience of my request that they would not make a disturbance if I speak in my accustomed manner:

Did ever man, Meletus, believe in the existence of human things, and not of human beings? . . . I wish, men of Athens, that he would answer, and not be always trying to get up an interruption. Did ever any man believe in horsemanship, and not in horses, or in flute-playing, and not in flute-players? No, my friend; I will answer to you and to the court, as you refuse to answer for yourself. There is no man who ever did. But now please to answer the next question: Can a man believe in spiritual and divine agencies, and not in spirits or demigods?

He cannot.

How lucky I am to have extracted that answer, by the assistance of the court! But then you swear in the indictment that I teach and believe in divine or spiritual agencies (new or old, no matter for that); at any rate, I believe in spiritual agencies—so you say and swear in the affidavit; and yet if I believe in divine beings, how can I help believing in spirits or demigods; —must I not? To be sure I must; and therefore I may assume that your silence gives consent. Now what are spirits or demigods? are they not either gods or the sons of gods?

Certainly they are.

But this is what I call the facetious riddle invented by you: the demigods or spirits are gods, and you say first that I do not believe in gods, and then again that I do believe in gods; that is, if I believe in demigods. For if the demigods are the illegitimate sons of gods, whether by the nymphs or by any other mothers, of whom they are said to be the sons—what human being will ever believe that there are no gods if they are the sons of gods? You might as well affirm the existence of mules, and deny that of horses and asses. Such nonsense, Meletus, could only have been intended by you to make trial of me. You have put this into the indictment because you had nothing real of which to accuse me. But no one who has a particle of understanding will ever be convinced by you that the same men can believe in divine and superhuman things, and yet not believe that there are gods and demigods and heroes.

I have said enough in answer to the charge of Meletus: any elaborate defence is unnecessary; but I know only too well how many are the enmities which I have incurred, and this is what will be my destruction if I am destroyed; —not Meletus, nor yet Anytus, but the envy and detraction of the world, which has been the death of many good men, and will probably be the death of many more; there is no danger of my being the last of them.

Some one will say: And are you not ashamed,

Socrates, of a course of life which is likely to bring you to an untimely end? To him I may fairly answer: There you are mistaken: a man who is good for anything ought not to calculate the chance of living or dying; he ought only to consider whether in doing anything he is doing right or wrong—acting the part of a good man or a bad. Whereas, upon your view, the son of Thetis above all, who altogether despised danger in comparison with disgrace; and when he was so eager to slay Hector, his goddess mother said to him, that if he avenged his companion Patroclus, and slew Hector, he would die himself— "Fate," she said, in these or the like words, "waits for you next after Hector"; he, receiving this warning, utterly despised danger and death, and instead of fearing them, feared rather to live in dishonour, and not to avenge his friend. "Let me die forthwith," he replies, "and be avenged of my enemy, rather than abide here by the beaked ships, a laughing stock and a burden of the earth." Had Achilles any thought of death and danger? For wherever a man's place is, whether the place which he has chosen or that in which he has been placed by a commander, there he ought to remain in the hour of danger; he should not think of death or of anything but of disgrace. And this, O men of Athens, is a true saying.

Strange, indeed, would be my conduct, O men of Athens, if I, who, when I was ordered by the generals whom you chose to command me at Potidaea and Amphipolis and Delium, remained where they placed me, like any other man, facing death—if now, when, as I conceive and imagine, God orders me to fulfil the philosopher's mission of searching into myself and other men, I were to desert my post through fear of death, or any other fear; that would indeed be strange, and I might justly be arraigned in court for denying the existence of the gods, if I disobeyed the oracle because I was afraid of death, fancying that I was wise when I was not wise. For the fear is indeed the pretence of wisdom, and not real wisdom, being a pretence of knowing the unknown; and no one knows whether death, which men in their fear apprehend to be the greatest evil, may not be the greatest good. Is not this ignorance of a disgraceful sort, the ignorance which is the conceit that a man knows what he does not know? And in this respect only I believe myself to differ from men in general, and may perhaps claim to be wiser than they are:—that whereas I know but little of the world below, I do not suppose that I know: but I do know that injustice and disobedience to a better, whether God or man, is evil and dishonourable, and I will never fear or avoid a possible good rather than a certain evil. And therefore if you let me go now, and are not convinced by Anytus, who said that since I had been prosecuted I must be put to death; (or if not that I ought never to have been prosecuted at all); and that if I escape now, your sons will all be utterly ruined by listening to my words—if you say to me, Socrates, this time we will not mind Anytus, and you shall be let off, but upon one condition, that you are not to enquire and speculate in this way any more, and that if you are caught doing so again you shall die;—if this was the condition on which you let me go, I should reply: Men of Athens, I honour and love you; but I shall obey God rather than you, and while I have life and strength I shall never cease from the practice and teaching of philosophy, exhorting any one whom I meet and saying to him after my manner: You, my friend,—a citizen of the great and mighty and wise city of Athens,—are you not ashamed of heaping up the greatest amount of money and honour and reputation, and caring so little about wisdom and truth and the greatest improvement of the soul, which you never regard or heed at all? And if the person with whom I am arguing, says: Yes, but I do care; then I do not leave him or let him go at once; but I proceed to interrogate and examine him, and if I think that he has no virtue in him, but only says that he has, I reproach him with undervaluing the greater, and overvaluing the less. And I shall repeat the same words to every one whom I meet, young and old, citizen and alien, but especially to the citizens, inasmuch as they are my brethren. For know that this is the command of God; and I believe that no greater good has ever happened in the State than my service to the God. For I do nothing but go about persuading you all, old and young alike, not to take thought for your persons or your properties, but first and chiefly to care about the greatest improvement of the soul. I tell you that virtue is not given by money, but that from virtue comes money and every other good of man, public as well as private. This is my teaching, and if this is the doctrine which corrupts the youth, I am a mischievous person. But if any one says that this is not my teaching, he is speaking an untruth. Wherefore, O men of Athens, I say to you, do as Anytus bids or not as Anytus bids, and either acquit me or not; but whichever you do, understand that I shall never alter my ways, not even if I have to die many times.

Men of Athens, do not interrupt, but hear me; there was an understanding between us that you should hear me to the end: I have something more to say, at which you may be inclined to cry out; but I believe that to hear me will be good for you, and therefore I beg that you will not cry out. I would have you know, that if you kill such an one as I am, you will injure yourselves more than you will injure me. Nothing will injure me, not Meletus nor yet Anytus—they cannot, for a bad man is not permitted to injure a better than himself. I do not deny that Anytus may, perhaps, kill him, or drive him into exile, or deprive him of civil rights; and he may imagine, and others may imagine, that he is inflicting a great injury upon him: but there I do not agree. For the evil of doing as he is doing—the evil of unjustly taking away the life of another—is greater far.

And, now, Athenians, I am not going to argue for my own sake, as you may think, but for yours, that you may not sin against the God by condemning me, who am his gift to you. For if you kill me you will not easily find a successor to me, who, if I may use such a ludicrous figure of speech, am a sort of gadfly, given to the State by God; and the State is a great and noble steed who is tardy in his motions owing to his very size, and requires to be stirred into life. I am that gadfly which God has attached to the State, and all day long and in all places am always fastening upon you, arousing and persuading and reproaching you. You will not easily find another like me, and therefore I would advise you to spare me. I dare say that you may feel out of temper (like a person who is suddenly awakened from sleep), and you think that you might easily strike me dead as Anytus advises, and then you would sleep on for the remainder of your lives, unless God in his care of you sent you another gadfly. When I say that I am given to you by God, the proof of my mission is this:—if I had been like other men, I should not have neglected all my own concerns or patiently seen the neglect of them during all these years, and have been doing yours, coming to you individually like a father or elder brother, exhorting you to regard virtue; such conduct, I say, would be unlike human nature. If I had gained anything, or if my exhortations had been paid, there would have been some sense in my doing so; but now, as you will perceive, not even the impudence of my accusers dares to say that I have ever extracted or sought pay of any one; of that they have no witness. And I have a sufficient witness to the truth of what I say—my poverty.

Some one may wonder why I go about in private giving advice and busying myself with the concerns of others, but do not venture to come forward in public and advise the State. I will tell you why. You have heard me speak at sundry times and in divers places of an oracle or sign which comes to me, and is the divinity which Meletus ridicules in the indictment. This sign, which is a kind of voice, first began to come to me when I was a child; it always forbids but never commands me to do anything which I am going to do. This is what deters me from being a politician. And rightly, as I think. For I am certain, O men of Athens, that if I had engaged in politics, I should have perished long ago, and done no good either to you or to myself. And do not be offended at my telling you the truth; for the truth is, that no man who goes to war with you or any other multitude, honestly striving against the many lawless and unrighteous deeds which are done in a State, will save his life; he who will fight for the right, if he would live even for a brief space, must have a private station and not a public one.

I can give you convincing evidence of what I say, not words only, but what you value far more —actions. Let me relate to you a passage of my own life which will prove to you that I should never have yielded to injustice from any fear of death and that "as I should have refused to yield" I must have died at once. I will tell you a tale of the courts, not very interesting perhaps, but nevertheless true. The only office of State which I ever held, O men of Athens, was that of senator: the tribe Antiochis, which is my tribe, had the presidency at the trial of the generals who had not taken up the bodies of the slain after the battle of Arginusae; and you proposed to try them in a body, contrary to law, as you all thought afterwards; but at the time I was the only one of the Prytanes who was opposed to the illegality, and I gave my vote against you; and when the orators threatened to impeach and arrest me, and you called and shouted, I made up my mind that I would run the risk, having law and justice with me, rather than take part in your injustice because I feared imprisonment and death. This happened in the days of the democracy. But when the oligarchy of the Thirty was in power, they sent for me and four others into the rotunda, and bade us bring Leon the Salaminian from Salamis, as they wanted to put him to death. This was a specimen of the sort of commands which they were always giving with the view of implicating as many as possible in their crimes; and then I showed, not in word

only but in deed, that, if I may be allowed to use such an expression, I cared not a straw for death, and that my great and only care was lest I should do an unrighteous or unholy thing. For the strong arm of that oppressive power did not frighten me into doing wrong; and when we came out of the rotunda the other four went to Salamis and fetched Leon, but I went quietly home. For which I might have lost my life, had not the power of the Thirty shortly afterwards come to an end. And many will witness to my words.

Now, do you really imagine that I could have survived all these years, if I had led a public life, supposing that like a good man I had always maintained the right and had made justice, as I ought, the first thing? No, indeed, men of Athens, neither I nor any other man. But I have been always the same in all my actions, public as well as private, and never have I yielded any base compliance to those who are slanderously termed my disciples, or to any other. Not that I have any regular disciples. But if any one likes to come and hear me while I am pursuing my mission, whether he be young or old, he is not excluded. Nor do I converse only with those who pay; but any one, whether he be rich or poor, may ask and answer me and listen to my words; and whether he turns out to be a bad man or a good one, neither result can be justly imputed to me; for I never taught or professed to teach him anything. And if any one says that he has ever learned or heard anything from me in private which all the world has not heard, let me tell you that he is lying.

But I shall be asked, Why do people delight in continually conversing with you? I have told you already, Athenians, the whole truth about this matter: they like to hear the cross-examination of the pretenders to wisdom; there is amusement in it. Now, this duty of cross-examining other men has been imposed upon me by God; and has been signified to me by oracles, visions, and in every way in which the will of divine power was ever intimated to any one. This is true, O Athenians; or, if not true, would be soon refuted. If I am or have been corrupting the youth, those of them who are now grown up and have become sensible that I gave them bad advice in the days of their youth should come forward as accusers, and take their revenge; or if they do not like to come themselves, some of their relatives, fathers, brothers, or other kinsmen, should say what evil their families have suffered at my hands. Now is their time. Many of them I see in the court. There is Crito, who is of the same age of the same deme with myself, and there is Critobulus his son, whom I also see. Then again there is Lysanias of Sphettus, who is the father of Aeschines—he is present; and also there is Antiphon of Cephisus, who is the father of Epigenes; and there are the brothers of several who have associated with me. There is Nicostratus the son of Theosdotides, and the brother of Theodotus (now Theodotus himself is dead, and therefore he, at any rate, will not seek to stop him); and there is Paralus the son of Demodocus, who had a brother Theages; and Adeimantus the son of Ariston, whose brother Plato is present; and Aeantodorus, who is the brother of Apollodorus, whom I also see. I might mention a great many others, some of whom Meletus should have produced as witnesses in the course of his speech; and let him still produce them, if he has forgotten—I will make way for him. And let him say, if he has any testimony of the sort which he can produce. Nay, Athenians, the very opposite is the truth. For all these are ready to witness on behalf of the corrupter, of the injurer of their kindred, as Meletus and Anytus call me; not the corrupted youth only—there might have been a motive for that— but their uncorrupted elder relatives. Why should they too support me with their testimony? Why, indeed, except for the sake of truth and justice, and because they know that I am speaking the truth, and that Meletus is a liar.

Well, Athenians, this and the like of this is all the defence which I have to offer. Yet a word more. Perhaps there may be some one who is offended at me, when he calls to mind how he himself on a similar, or even a less serious occasion, prayed and entreated the judges with many tears, and how he produced his children in court, which was a moving spectacle, together with a host of relations and friends; whereas I, who am probably in danger of my life, will do none of these things. The contrast may occur to his mind, and he may be set against me, and vote in anger because he is displeased at me on this account. Now, if there be such a person among you,—mind, I do not say that there is,—to him I may fairly reply: My friend, I am a man, and like other men, a creature of flesh and blood, and not "of wood or stone," as Homer says; and I have a family, yes, and sons, O Athenians, three in number, one almost a man, and two others who are still young; and yet I will not bring any of them hither in order to petition you for an acquittal. And why not? Not from any self-assertion or want of respect for you. Whether I am or am not afraid of death is another question, of which I will not now speak. But, having regard to public opinion, I feel that such conduct would be discreditable to myself, and to you, and to the whole State. One who has reached my years, and who has a name for wisdom, ought not to demean himself. Whether this opinion of me be deserved or not, at any rate the world has decided that Socrates is in some way superior to other men. And if those among you who are said to be superior in wisdom and courage, and any other virtue, demean themselves in this way, how shameful is their conduct! I have seen men of reputation, when they have been condemned, behaving in the strangest manner: they seemed to fancy that they were going to suffer something dreadful if they died, and that they could be immortal if you only allowed them to live; and I think that such are a dishonour to the State, and that any stranger coming in would have said of them that the most eminent men of Athens, to whom the Athenians themselves give honour and command, are no better than women. And I say that these things ought not to be done by those of us who have a reputation; and if they are done, you ought not to permit them; you ought rather to show that you are far more disposed to condemn the man who gets up a doleful scene and makes the city ridiculous, than him who holds his peace.

But, setting aside the question of public opinion, there seems to be something wrong in asking a favour of a judge, and thus procuring an acquittal, instead of informing and convincing him. For his duty is, not to make a present of justice, but to give judgment; and he has sworn that he will judge according to the laws, and not according to his own good pleasure; and we ought not to encourage you, nor should you allow yourselves to be encouraged, in this habit of perjury—there can be no piety in that. Do not then require me to do what I consider dishonourable and impious and wrong, especially now, when I am being tried for impiety on the indictment of Meletus. For if, O men of Athens, by force of persuasion and entreaty I could overpower your oaths, then I should be teaching you to believe that there are no gods, and in defending should simply convict myself of the charge of not believing in them. But that is not so—far otherwise. For I do believe that there are gods, and in a sense higher than that in which any of my accusers believe in them. And to you and to God I commit my cause, to be determined by you as is best for you and me. . . .

A majority of the jurors then found Socrates guilty: 281 votes against 220. The condemned man was allowed to propose a penalty in lieu of the death penalty proposed by Meletus. Socrates again spoke:

There are many reasons why I am not grieved, O men of Athens, at the vote of condemnation. I expected it, and am only surprised that the votes are so nearly equal; for I had thought that the majority against me would have been far larger; but now, had thirty votes gone over to the other side, I should have escaped Meletus. I may say more; for without the assistance of Anytus and Lycon, any one may see that he would not have had a fifth part of the votes, as the law requires, in which case he would have incurred a fine of a thousand drachmae.

And so he proposes death as the penalty. And what shall I propose on my part, O men of Athens? Clearly that which is my due. And what is my due? What returns shall be made to the man who has never had the wit to be idle during his whole life; but has been careless of what the many care for—wealth, and family interests, and military offices, and speaking in the assembly, and magistracies, and plots, and parties. Reflecting that I was really too honest a man to be a politician and live, I did not go where I could do no good to you or to myself; but where I could do the greatest good privately to every one of you, thither I went, and sought to persuade every man among you that he must look to himself, and seek virtue and wisdom before he looks to his private interests, and look to the State before he looks to the interests of the State; and that this should be the order which he observes in all his actions. What shall be done to such an one? Doubtless some good thing, O men of Athens, if he has his reward; and the good should be of a kind suitable to him. What would be a reward suitable to a poor man who is your benefactor, and who desires leisure that he may instruct you? There can be no reward so fitting as maintenance in the Prytaneum, O men of Athens, a reward which he deserves far more than the citizen who has won the prize at Olympia in the horse or chariot race, whether the chariots were drawn by two horses or by many. For I am in want, and he has enough; and he only gives you the appearance of happiness, and I give you the reality. And if I am to estimate the penalty fairly, I should say that maintenance in the Prytaneum is the just return.

Perhaps you think that I am braving you in what I am saying now, as in what I said before about the tears and prayers. But this is not so. I speak rather because I am convinced that I never intentionally wronged any one, although I cannot convince you—the time has been too short; if there were a law at Athens, as there is in other cities, that a capital cause should not be decided in one day, then I believe that I should have convinced you. But I cannot in a moment refute great slanders; and, as I am convinced that I never wronged another, I will assuredly not wrong myself. I will not say of myself that I serve any evil, or propose any penalty. Why should I? Because I am afraid of the penalty of death which Meletus proposes? When I do not know whether death is a good or an evil, why should I propose a penalty which would certainly be an evil? Shall I say imprisonment? And why should I live in prison, and be the slave of the magistrate of the year—of the Eleven? Or shall the penalty be a fine, and imprisonment until the fine is paid? There is the same objection. I should have to lie in prison, for money I have none, and cannot pay. And if I say exile (and this may possibly be the penalty which you will affix), I must indeed be blinded by the love of life, if I am so irrational as to expect that when you, who are my own citizens, cannot endure my discourses and words, and have found them so grievous and odious that you will have no more of them, others are likely to endure me. No, indeed, men of Athens, that is not very likely. And what a life should I lead, at my age, wandering from city to city, ever changing my place of exile, and always being driven out! For I am quite sure that wherever I go, there, as here, the young men will flock to me; and if I drive them away, their elders will drive me out at their request; and if I let them come, their fathers and friends will drive me out for their sakes.

Some one will say: Yes, Socrates, but cannot you hold your tongue, and then you may go into a foreign city, and no one will interfere with you? Now, I have great difficulty in making you understand my answer to this. For if I tell you that to do as you say would be a disobedience to the God, and therefore that I cannot hold my tongue, you will not believe that I am serious; and if I say again that daily to discourse about virtue, and of those other things about which you hear me examining myself and others, is the greatest good of man, and that the unexamined life is not worth living, you are still less likely to believe me. Yet I say what is true, although a thing of which it is hard for me to persuade you. Also, I have never been accustomed to think that I deserve to suffer any harm. Had I money I might have estimated the offence at what I was able to pay, and not have been much the worse. But I have none, and therefore I must ask you to proportion the fine to my means. Well, perhaps I could afford a mina, and therefore I propose that penalty: Plato, Crito, Critobulus, and Apollodorus, my friends here, bid me say thirty minae, and they will be the sureties. Let thirty minae be the penalty; for which sum they will be ample security to you. . . .

Another vote was taken and the death penalty was passed. Socrates then made his final statement:

Not much time will be gained, O Athenians, in return for the evil name which you will get from the detractors of the city, who will say that you killed Socrates, a wise man; for they will call me wise, even although I am not wise, when they want to reproach you. If you had waited a little while, your desire would have been fulfilled in the course of nature. For I am far advanced in years, as you may perceive, and not far from death. I am speaking now not to all of you, but only to those who have condemned me to death. And I have another thing to say to them: You think that I was convicted because I had not words of the sort which would have procured my acquittal—I mean, if I had thought fit to leave nothing undone or unsaid. Not so; the deficiency which led to my conviction was not of words—certainly not. But I had not the boldness or impudence or inclination to address you as you would have liked me to do, weeping and wailing and lamenting, and saying and doing many things which you have been accustomed to hear from others, and which, as I maintain, are unworthy of me. I thought at the time that I ought not to do anything common or mean when in danger: nor do I now repent of the style of my defence; I would rather die having spoken after my manner, than speak in your manner and live. For neither in war nor yet at law ought I or any man to use every way of escaping death. Often in battle there can be no doubt that if a man will throw away his arms, and fall on his knees before his pursuers, he may escape death; and in other dangers there are other ways of escaping death, if a man is willing to say and do anything. The difficulty, my friends, is not to avoid death, but to avoid unrighteousness; for that runs faster than death. I am old and move slowly, and the slower runner has overtaken me, and my accusers are keen and quick, and the faster runner, who is unrighteousness, has overtaken them. And now I depart hence condemned by you to suffer the penalty of death,—they too go their ways condemned by the truth to suffer the penalty of villainy and wrong; and I must abide by my award—let them abide by my award—let them abide by theirs. I suppose that these things may be regarded as fated,—and I think that they are well.

And now, O men who have condemned me, I would fain prophesy to you; for I am about to die, and in the hour of death men are gifted with prophetic power. And I prophesy to you who are my murderers, that immediately after my departure punishment far heavier than you have inflicted on me will surely await you. Me you have killed because you wanted to escape the accuser, and not to give an account of your lives. But that will not be as you suppose: far otherwise. For I say that there will be more accusers of you than there are now; accusers whom hitherto I have restrained: and as they are younger they will be more inconsiderate with

you, and you will be more offended at them. If you think that by killing men you can prevent some one from censuring your evil lives, you are mistaken; that is not a way of escape which is either possible or honorable; the easiest and the noblest way is not to be disabling others, but to be improving yourselves. This is the prophecy which I utter before my departure to the judges who have condemned me.

Friends, who would have acquitted me, I would like also to talk with you about the thing which has come to pass, while the magistrates are busy, and before I go to the place at which I must die. Stay then a little, for we may as well talk with one another while there is time. You are my friends, and I should like to show you the meaning of this event which has happened to me. O my judges—for you I may truly call judges—I should like to tell you a wonderful circumstance. Hitherto the divine faculty of which the internal oracle is the source has constantly been in the habit of opposing me even about trifles, if I was going to make a slip or error in any matter; and now as you see there has come upon me that which may be thought, and is generally belived to be, the last and worst evil. But the oracle made no sign of opposition, either when I was leaving my house in the morning, or when I was on my way to the court, or while I was speaking, at anything which I was going to say; and yet I have often been stopped in the middle of a speech, but now in nothing I either said or did touching the matter in hand has the oracle opposed me. What do I take to be the explanation of this silence? I will tell you. It is an intimation that what has happened to me is a good, and that those of us who think that death is an evil are in error. For the customary sign would surely have opposed me had I been going to evil and not to good.

Let us reflect in another way, and we shall see that there is great reason to hope that death is a good; for one of two things—either death is a state of nothingness and utter unconsciousness, or, as men say, there is a change and migration of the soul from this world to another. Now, if you suppose that there is no consciousness, but a sleep like the sleep of him who is undisturbed even by dreams, death will be an unspeakable gain. For if a person were to select the night in which his sleep was undisturbed even by dreams, and were to compare with this the other days and nights of his life, and then were to tell us how many days and nights he had passed in the course of his life better and more pleasantly than this one, I think that any man, I will not say a private man, but even the great king will not find many such days or nights, when compared with the others. Now, if death be of such a nature, I say that to die is gain; for eternity is then only a single night. But if death is the journey to another place, and there, as men say, all the dead abide, what good, O my friends and judges, can be greater than this? If, indeed, when the pilgrim arrives in the world below, he is delivered from the professors of justice in this world, and finds the true judges who are said to give judgment there, Minos and Rhadamanthus and Aeacus and Triptolemus, and other sons of God who were righteous in their own life, that pilgrimage will be worth making. What would not a man give if he might converse with Orpheus and Musaeus and Hesiod and Homer? Nay, if this be true, let me die again and again. I myself, too, shall have a wonderful interest in there meeting and conversing with Palamedes, and Ajax the son of Telamon, and any other ancient hero who has suffered death through an unjust judgment; and there will be no small pleasure, as I think, in comparing my own sufferings with theirs. Above all, I shall then be able to continue my search into true and false knowledge; as in this world, so also in the next; and I shall find out who is wise, and who pre-

tends to be wise, and is not. What would not a man give, O judges, to be able to examine the leader of the great Trojan expedition; or Odysseus or Sisyphus, or numberless others, men and women too! What infinite delight would there be in conversing with them and asking them questions! In another world they do not put a man to death for asking questions: assuredly not. For besides being happier than we are, they will be immortal, if what is said is true.

Wherefore, O judges, be of good cheer about death, and know of a certainty, that no evil can happen to a good man, either in life or after death. He and his are not neglected by the gods; nor has my own approaching end happened by mere chance. But I see clearly that the time had arrived when it was better for me to die and be released from trouble; wherefore the oracle gave no sign. For which reason, also, I am not angry with my condemners, or with my accusers; they have done me no harm, although they did not mean to do me any good; and for this I may gently blame them.

Still, I have a favour to ask of them. When my sons are grown up, I would ask you, O my friends, to punish them; and I would have you trouble them, as I have troubled you, if they seem to care about riches, or anything, more than about virtue; or if they pretend to be something when they are really nothing,—then reprove them, as I have reproved you, for not caring about that for which they ought to care, and thinking that they are something when they are really nothing. And if you do this, both I and my sons will have received justice at your hands.

The hour of departure has arrived, and we go our ways—I to die, and you to live. Which is better God only knows.

Afterword / Socratic Commitment

Plato's *Apology* can be read and appreciated from several different perspectives. As drama, it depicts the moving clash of personalities: the uncompromising, just philosopher against his unjust and rather stupid accusers. As history, it reports the postwar trial of an important Athenian philosopher whose teaching and influence had stirred controversy in the minds of his fellow citizens during a certain stage in the deterioration of the Athenian Empire. As personal testimony, it presents eloquently and persuasively not only Socrates' own defense of his character and justification of his style of living and thinking but also Plato's love of the man and his loyalty to the ideals for which Socrates lived and died. And, finally, his *Apology* can be read from the perspective of the collision of doctrines and ideas. It presents in high relief the conflict of different conceptions of what it means to be a good citizen and to lead a good life.

Significance of the Trial of Socrates

To Plato and to others who agreed with his way of life, it must have seemed that freedom itself was on trial when the aged philosopher Socrates rose to defend himself against charges that he had corrupted the youth of Athens and had taught false gods. As an Athenian citizen, Socrates took for granted all the privileges and duties that went with living in the freest and most highly civilized of all the Greek city-states. The Athenian general Pericles had summed up the Athenian ideal in the funeral oration that he delivered in the midst of the war with Sparta, which was to end with the defeat of Athens three years before the trial of Socrates:

> It is true that we are called a democracy, for the administration is in the hands of the many and not of the few. But while the law secures equal justice to all alike in their private disputes, the claim of excellence is also recognized; and when a citizen is in any way distinguished, he is

preferred to the public service, not as a matter of privilege, but as the reward of merit. Neither is poverty a bar, but a man may benefit his country whatever be the obscurity of his condition. There is no exclusiveness in our public life, and in our private intercourse we are not suspicious of one another, nor angry with our neighbor if he does what he likes; we do not put on sour looks at him which, though harmless, are not pleasant. While we are thus unconstrained in our private intercourse, a spirit of reverence pervades our public acts; we are prevented from doing wrong by respect for the authorities and for the laws, having an especial regard to those which are ordained for the protection of the injured as well as to those unwritten laws which bring upon the transgressor of them the reprobation of the general sentiment.[12]

Pericles also made the following remark later in his speech:

> The great impediment to action is, in our opinion, not discussion, but the want of that knowledge which is gained by discussion preparatory to action. For we have a peculiar power of thinking before we act and of acting too, whereas other men are courageous from ignorance but hesitate upon reflection.[13]

Philosophy and the Pursuit of Excellence

Nothing could be more in accord with the Socratic spirit, as it is preserved in Xenophon and in Plato, than these typically Athenian beliefs that were expressed by the leader under whom Athens attained its golden age. Socrates pursued his mission in the agora, the market place of Athens, where ideas as well as commodities were exchanged. His mission was basically carried on through free and open discussion aimed at attaining the knowledge which is, he believed, virtue. How could men be sure they were acting rightly, Socrates asked, if they did not first inquire what rightness or moral goodness or justice is? How could they be sure they were acting courageously if they did not know what the virtue of courage is? Socrates agreed with Pericles that philosophical reflection should not stymie action but clarify the very basis for acting and thus liberate the individual to act always knowingly and rightly. Freedom to discuss, to inquire, to follow the path of truth wherever it might lead were duties of Athenian citizenship as Socrates and Pericles conceived it. The excellence of the state would always depend upon the excellence of its citizens, and they could only achieve and maintain excellence—of character, judgment, and action—through freedom of thought and speech.

Another aspect of Pericles' speech was of equal importance to him, to Socrates, and to Greek thinkers, whether philosophers or common men. "The law," Pericles pointed out, "secures equal justice to all alike in their private disputes," and that is what Socrates, the members of the jury, and the observers at his trial expected (or at least hoped) would be the outcome. But, as Pericles also pointed out, the claim of excellence is equally recognized and rewarded. Thus, after Socrates was condemned and was allowed to make a counterproposal, he felt justified in proposing, to the astonishment of those who had voted against him if not to others, that he be supported comfortably at public expense for the rest of his life in recognition of the excellence of his service as gadfly to the state.

Reverence and Reflection

Pericles made another statement that is of importance in understanding why Socrates said what he did in his defense and expected it to be relevant and persuasive. "A spirit of reverence pervades our public acts," Pericles had said of the Athenian citizens. In the *Apology,* Socrates denied the charges that he had taught false gods, claiming that he had never taught disrespect for the gods or for the state religion. On the contrary, his whole mission, he argued, had been inspired and carried out in a spirit of reverence. It had been inspired, Socrates said, even before the oracle of Apollo at Delphi declared him to be the wisest man in Greece, by his typically Greek passion for knowledge and social well-being.

Finally, there is the crucial point upon which Socrates' whole defense rests. "We are prevented from doing wrong," Pericles had continued, "by respect for the authorities and for the laws both written and unwritten." Socrates claims he has shown proper respect for the authorities and for the laws. He holds he has been a good citizen and a good man. As he stands confronting his accusers and the authorities who will judge him guilty or innocent and who have the legal power to condemn him to death, he demands that he be given his freedom to pursue his philosophical mission.

Socrates is not the only one on trial. The jury of his peers, the authority of Athens, the principle of authority itself are on trial. What constitutes a good authority? By what criteria should an authority be judged? In cases of conflicting authorities, which authority should take precedence and be obeyed? These and many other questions as important to the American as to the Athenian citizen are raised and examined, first in the *Apology* and later in the *Crito.*

Socrates and the Future of Philosophy

Finally, and less obviously, the *Apology* is a document that deals not just with the past (the trial and defense of Socrates) or with the present (Plato's temporal perspective within which he was living and writing), but also with the future. Socrates expresses this concern, not just in his final reference to death, but throughout his defense. He is not as concerned with his own future as with the fate of what he loves more than life itself: philosophy. What is to be the fate of the life of rational inquiry when he is no longer around to pursue, improve, and defend it? Will other gadflies arise and dare to buzz around and at times to deliver stings once their chief exemplar has been killed? As Socrates' chief disciple, Plato shared his master's concern and, in looking to the future, did his utmost to see that philosophy would be promulgated through his own writings, teachings, and other endeavors. Plato's most lasting contribution to the future of philosophy was his magnificent *Dialogues* in which he captured the spirit of the Socratic method and applied it as a means for presenting his own (and partly Socrates') philosophy. Alfred North Whitehead once remarked that the whole history of European philosophy was a series of footnotes to Plato. Although this may be an exaggeration, it suggests philosophy's enormous debt to Plato and to Socrates, who awakened his great disciple to the wonder of a life guided by reason and instilled in him an insatiable appetite for goodness, beauty, and truth.

Notes

1. Alfred North Whitehead, *Modes of Thought* (New York: Capricorn Books, Macmillan, 1958), p. 233.

2. Bergen Evans, *The Natural History of Nonsense* (New York: Vintage Book, Knopf, 1960), p. 262.

3. Bertrand Russell, *The Problems of Philosophy* (New York: Henry Holt, n.d.), p. 249.

4. Arthur Schopenhauer, *The World as Will and Representation,* trans. E. F. J. Payne (Indian Hills, Colorado: The Falcon's Wing Press, 1958), p. 161.

5. See Karl Jaspers, *Way to Wisdom* (New Haven: Yale University Press, 1954), chap. 2.

6. Pascal, *Pensées, trans.* W. F. Trotter (New York: Modern Library, Random House, 1941), sec. III, no. 205, pp. 74–75.

7. Plato, "Apology," in *The Dialogues of Plato,* trans. Benjamin Jowett, 3d ed. (Oxford: Clarendon Press, 1892), Vol. I.

8. Ibid.

9. Xenophon, *Memorabilia,* trans. E. C. Marchant (Cambridge, Mass.: Harvard University Press, 1918), bk. 1, chap. 1, sec. 10, p. 7.

10. Ibid., bk. I, chap. 2, sec. 4, p. 15.

11. Plato, "Symposium," in *Dialogues,* Jowett translation.

12. Thucydides, *History of the Peloponnesian War,* trans. Benjamin Jowett (Boston: D. Lothrop & Co., 1883), bk. 11, sec. 37, pp. 117–118.

13. Ibid., sec. 40, p. 119.

Related Reading

(Works marked * are available in paperbound editions)

Bartley, William W. *The Retreat to Commitment*. New York: Knopf, 1962.

Bugental, J. F. T. *The Search for Authenticity*. New York: Holt, Rinehart and Winston, 1965.

*Camus, Albert. *The Stranger*. New York: Knopf, 1960.

Commitment and Human Development, vol. VIII (February, 1972) of *Humanitas*.

Edman, Irwin. *Four Ways of Philosophy*. New York: Henry Holt, 1937.

————. *Philosopher's Quest*. New York: Viking Press, 1947.

*Erikson, Erik. *Identity, Youth and Crisis*. New York: W. W. Norton, 1968.

*Frankl, Viktor. *Man's Search for Meaning*. New York: Washington Square Press, 1963.

*Fromm, Erich. *The Sane Society*. New York: Fawcett, 1955.

Gabor, Dennis. *Inventing the Future*. New York: Knopf, 1964.

Gardner, John W. *Self-renewal*. New York: Harper and Row, 1963.

Hamalian, Leo and Frederick R. Karl, eds. *The Radical Vision: Essays for the Seventies*. New York: Crowell, 1970.

*Hesse, Hermann. *Siddhartha*. New York: New Directions, 1951.

*Jaspers, Karl. *Socrates, Buddha, Confucius, Jesus: The Paradigmatic Individuals,* ed. Hannah Arendt. New York: Harcourt, Brace & World, 1962.

*————. *Way to Wisdom*. New Haven: Yale, 1954.

Jungk, Robert. *Tomorrow Is Already Here*. New York: Simon & Schuster, 1954.

Keeton, Morris. *Values Men Live By*. New York: Abingdon, 1960.

*Keniston, Kenneth. *The Uncommitted: Alienated Youth in American Society*. New York: Harcourt, Brace and World, 1965.

Kiesler, Charles A. *The Psychology of Commitment*. New York: Academe Press, 1971.

Koch, Adrienne, ed. *Philosophy for a Time of Crisis*. New York: Dutton, 1959.

Lin, Yutang, *The Importance of Living*. New York: John Day, 1940.

*May, Rollo. *Man's Search for Himself*. New York: Signet, 1953.

McGreal, Ian. *The Art of Making Choices*. Dallas, Texas: Southern Methodist University Press, 1953.

*Mead, Margaret. *Culture and Commitment: a Study of the Generation Gap*. New York: Doubleday, 1970.

*Muller, Herbert. *The Uses of the Past*. New York: Oxford, 1952.

*Ortega y Gasset, José. *What Is Philosophy?* New York: Norton, 1960.

Paul, Leslie A. *Alternatives to Christian Belief*. New York: Doubleday, 1967.

Rahner, Karl. *The Christian Commitment*. New York: Sheed and Ward, 1963.

Ramsey, Paul. *Basic Christian Ethics*. New York: Scribner's, 1952.

Rumke, H. C. *The Psychology of Unbelief.* New York: Sheed and Ward, 1962.

*Smith, Huston. *The Religions of Man.* New York: Harper and Row, 1958.

*Stapledon, Olaf. *Last and First Men and Star Maker.* New York: Dover, 1968.

Stark, Rodney and Charles Y. Glock: *American Piety: The Nature of Religious Commitment.* Berkeley, Calif.: University of California Press, 1968.

*Tillich, Paul. *The Courage to Be.* New Haven: Yale, 1952.

*Watts, Alan. *The Book: On the Taboo Against Knowing Who You Are.* New York: Pantheon, 1966.

Wertheimer, Michael, ed. *Confrontation: Psychology and the Problems of Today.* New York: Scott, Foresman, 1970.

*Whitehead, Alfred North. *The Aims of Education.* New York: New American Library, 1949.

*Wieman, Henry Nelson. *Man's Ultimate Commitment.* Carbondale: Southern Illinois University Press, 1958.

PART TWO

Confrontation with Doubt:
Commitment to Belief

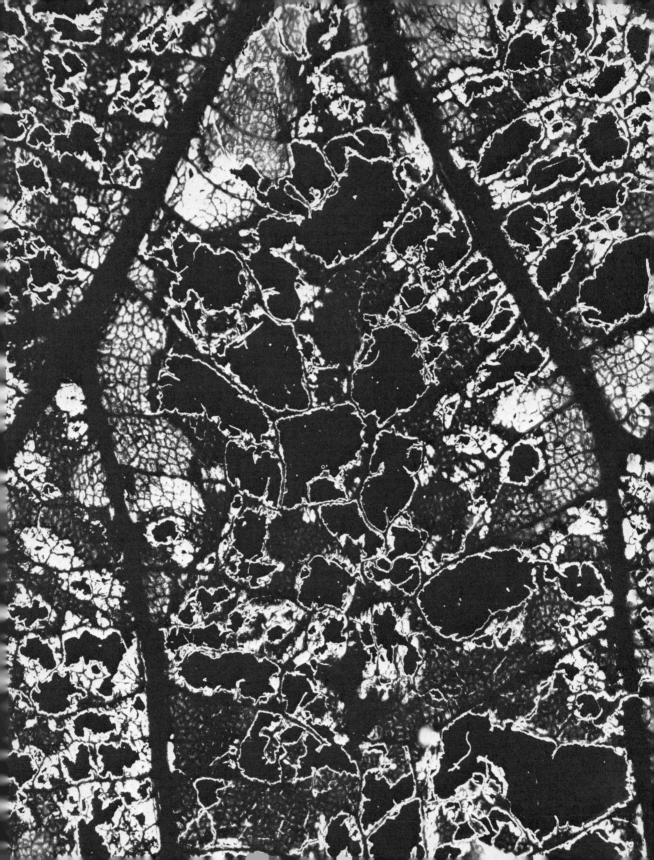

Seek and ye shall find.
Jesus Christ

Que sais-je? ("What do I know?")
Michel de Montaigne

Comfort is no criterion of truth.
Anonymous

Be ye lamps unto yourselves.
Gautama, the Buddha

Philosophy begins in wonder.
Socrates

Philosophy takes nothing for granted.
Anonymous

Questions, questions, questions!
Anonymous

The unexamined life is not worth living.
Socrates

You will not learn philosophy from me but how to philosophize—not thoughts to repeat, but how to think. Think for yourselves, inquire for yourselves, stand on your own feet.

Immanuel Kant

Like archers, we stand a better chance of hitting upon the right if we can see it.

Aristotle

A little philosophy inclines a man's mind to atheism, but depth of philosophy leads back to religion.

Francis Bacon

It is better to be a human being dissatisfied than a pig satisfied; better to be a Socrates dissatisfied than a fool satisfied.

John Stuart Mill

No caterpillar could be a sceptic — and walk.
Anonymous

Myself when young did eagerly frequent
Doctor and Saint, and heard great argument
About it and about: but evermore
Came out by the same door wherein I went.
Omar Khayam

Introduction / The Courage of One's Doubts

Living today means confronting perpetual and often unprecedented changes. Scientific discoveries, technological innovations, new life-styles, and shifts in values are constantly making new demands upon our attention and adaptability. Unless we can find adequate ways of coping with these challenges and develop better means of directing, modifying, and even decreasing the speed of change, we may eventually be traumatized by an overload of novel stimuli which Alvin Toffler has called "future shock."

Confronting such disturbing prospects, many people today are doubting the traditions of the past, questioning the values of the present, and are uncertain about the promise of the future. Very little may seem certain in a century in which two world wars have been waged at the cost of millions of lives and genocide has been practiced on the largest scale in history; in which the spaceship earth is threatened with an environmental pollution that may soon make it uninhabitable; and in which the outbreak of a third world war could mean the destruction of mankind. Some people cling tenaciously to the old traditions and cherished beliefs of their culture, accepting them without question. Others throw over all beliefs, rejecting the search for certainty, and live as well as they can with a day-to-day existence that is bearable only so long as they don't think or bother to ask questions. Still others claim we must seek radically different alternatives.

To confront such uncertainty and to make some kind of commitment is by no means easy, but if we expect to do so, we must be willing to reflect and to doubt. Someone has said that if we wish to dispel doubt, we can only do so by further doubting. Philosophy can be considered as systematic and controlled doubting. Its intense and intensive questioning sometimes can issue in satisfying and satisfactory beliefs. Without this radical doubt, the existentialist Karl Jaspers holds, there can be no genuine philosophy. Philosophy begins in doubt.

Radical doubt is not only doubt, questioning, but doubt that is radical: it tries to get down to the very root (*radicus*) of problems. It can either cut a way through a jungle of false beliefs and foolish dogmas, or it can cut the ground out from under us. Thinking can forge ahead or, as Camus pointed out, it can undermine. Thus philosophers need courage as well as intelligence in order to accomplish their goal. They need, as Nietzsche emphasized, not just the courage of their convictions, but the courage to question their convictions. Socrates is perhaps the best example of courageous self-examination.

In this part you will become acquainted with several thinkers who exhibit this kind of courage. They are some of the great doubters in the history of philosophy, each displaying a different mode of doubting or scepticism. Socrates, who can be credited with having launched the method of methodological doubting, conceived of himself, as he made clear in the *Apology*, primarily as a gadfly (today we would say a catalyst) whose method of intensive interrogation aimed at eliciting clearer and sounder ideas. We can call his type of scepticism *catalytic scepticism*, a kind of doubting that, when successful, can lead to radical changes in the beliefs and attitudes of those who have engaged in it. The first philosopher in this part, René Descartes, used scepticism primarily as a means to an end in order to show that particular beliefs could be accepted as indubitably certain. His scepticism was not all-encompassing. Before he started, he exempted specific beliefs, such as his moral code, from the range of scrutiny. His scepticism has thus been called *methodological scepticism*.

In contrast to Descartes', David Hume's scepticism seems more authentic, more radical, and possibly more devastating. The analytical tools that Hume forged, his radical empirical attitude, and his delight in clarity and consistency contributed to a genuine commitment to continuing doubt and questioning. His is *analytical scepticism*.

Leo Tolstoy exemplifies another kind of scepticism. For a long and agonizing period in his life, Tolstoy was confronted with the problems of death and other human predicaments that Jaspers called "boundary situations." He asked himself the question that Camus later raised in *The Myth of Sisyphus:* Why live if life is meaningless, absurd? Later he found his way through to a commitment to primitive Christianity. But during the period he describes so movingly in *My Confession,* Tolstoy adhered to what we may call *existential scepticism*.

Finally, William James developed and defended his view that in certain situations, in which one is faced with what he calls "live options" and yet lacks adequate empirical and rational grounds for choosing either, one is justified in committing himself to that option which is emotionally most satisfying. One wills to believe. Insofar as doubt or questioning precedes this commitment or pragmatic belief, we can call it *pragmatic scepticism*.

These, then, are five different varieties of scepticism that have played important roles in arriving at answers to some of the questions that matter most. As you become acquainted with them, you will be encountering the spirit of philosophy.

2 / Doubting One's Way to Certainty
Descartes

Descartes "consecrated Doubt," wrote the nineteenth-century English evolutionist, Thomas Huxley. Descartes, "the father of modern philosophy," had introduced a way of thinking that revolutionized the ideas of his own time and those of generations to come.[1] This way of thinking commenced by entertaining not ideas but doubts. In Huxley's words, "it removed Doubt from the seat of penance among the grievous sins to which it had long been condemned, and enthroned it in that high place among the primary duties, which is assigned to it by the scientific conscience of these latter days."[2]

It would be a mistake, however, to think of René Descartes (1596–1650) as a sceptic of the ancient Greek variety who often seemed to doubt for the sake of doubting and was content to live with uncertainty. Scepticism for Descartes was always a means to an end, a method by which he hoped to attain indubitable truth. "My design," he wrote, "was singly to find ground of assurance, and cast aside the loose earth and sand, that I might reach the rock or the clay."[3] Before launching his philosophical investigations, he had carefully delineated, as he reports in his *Discourse on Method* (1637), the limits within which he would allow himself to doubt. Within these limits, Descartes provided himself with a "provisory code of Morals" which, he believed, would keep him from losing his bearings as he proceeded to apply his methodological scepticism to the various fields of knowledge.[4] According to the first of his maxims, Descartes obliged himself to obey the laws and customs of his country, to act with judiciousness and moderation, and to adhere firmly to the religious faith (Catholicism) in which he had been educated. The second maxim required him to be as "firm and resolute" as possible in his actions and not to vacillate in supporting his opinions once he had adopted them. The third maxim stressed that he should always try to conquer himself rather than the world.

Reflecting on the way of life he had chosen, which, as he put it, consisted "in devoting my whole life to the culture of my Reason, and in making the greatest progress I was able in the knowledge of truth, on the principles of the Method which I had prescribed to myself,"[5] Descartes convinced himself that no way could possibly have suited him better. He was filled with intense satisfaction and enthusiasm as he continued to examine himself and probed into the various spheres of knowledge in hope of discovering important new truths. And, like Socrates before him, he believed that the life of the philosopher was divinely sanctioned. "For since God has endowed each of us with some light of Reason by which to distinguish truth from error," he wrote in his *Discourse,* "I could not have believed that I ought for a single moment to rest satisfied with the opinions of another, unless I had resolved to exercise my own judgment in examining these whenever I should be duly qualified for the task."[6]

The method which Descartes formulated and for which he showed such enthusiasm and devotion was basically the rationalistic method of mathematics rather than the empirical method of the natural sciences. Intuition and deduction, rather than observation and induction, were its basic elements. Absolute certainty rather than probable truth was its aim. The method upon which he relied may be summed up in his own words as follows:

1. Never to accept anything for true which I did not clearly know to be such, that is to say, carefully to avoid precipitance and prejudice, and to comprise nothing more in my judgment than what was presented to my mind so clearly and distinctly as to exclude all ground of doubt.
2. To divide each of the difficulties under examination into as many parts as possible, and as might be necessary for its adequate solution.
3. To conduct my thoughts in such order that, by commencing with objects the simplest and easiest to know, I might ascend little and little, and, as it were, step by step, to the knowledge of the more complex; assigning in thought a certain order even to those obejcts which in their own nature do not stand in a relation of antecedence and sequence.
4. In every case to make enumerations so complete, and reviews so general, that I might be assured that nothing was omitted.[7]

The method thus requires of its practitioners clarity and distinctness of ideas, the utmost care and precision in making deductions, an orderly and analytical procedure, and a coherent and systematic approach. How Descartes applied it to arrive at his basic indubitable premise, the famous *cogito ergo sum* ("I think, therefore I am"), from which he could advance to solve the problems of the nature of mind, the existence of God, and the constitution of the universe will be suggested by the following selections from his *Meditations* and his *Discourse on Method.*

What Can Be Doubted

Several years have now elapsed since I first became aware that I had accepted, even from my youth, many false opinions for true, and that consequently what I afterwards based on such principles was highly doubtful; and from that time I was convinced of the necessity of undertaking once in my life to rid myself of all the opinions I had adopted, and of commencing anew the work of building from the foundation, if I desired to establish a firm and abiding superstructure in the sciences. But as this enterprise appeared to me to be one of great magnitude, I waited until I had attained an age so mature as to leave me no hope that at any stage of life more advanced I should be better able to execute my design. On this account, I have delayed so long that I should henceforth consider I was doing wrong were I still to consume in deliberation any of the time that now remains for action. Today, then, since I have opportunely freed my mind from all cares, [and am happily disturbed by no passions],* and since I am in the secure possession of leisure in a peaceable retirement, I will at length apply myself earnestly and freely to the general overthrow of all my former opinions. But, to this end, it will not be necessary for me to show that the whole of these are false—a point, perhaps, which I shall never reach; but as even now my reason convinces me that I ought not the less carefully to withhold belief from what is not entirely certain and indubitable, than from what is manifestly false, it will be sufficient to justify the rejection of the whole if I shall find in each some ground for doubt. Nor for this purpose will it be necessary even to deal with each belief individually, which would be truly an endless labour; but, as the removal from below of the foundation necessarily involves the downfall of the whole edifice, I will at once approach the criticism of the principles on which all my former beliefs rested.

All that I have, up to this moment, accepted as possessed of the highest truth and certainty, I received either from or through the senses. I observed, however, that these sometimes misled us; and it is the part of prudence not to place absolute confidence in that by which we have even once been deceived.

But it may be said, perhaps, that, although the senses occasionally mislead us respecting minute objects, and such as are so far removed from us as to be beyond the reach of close observation, there are yet many other of their informations (presentations), of the truth of which it is manifestly impossible to doubt; as for example, that I am in this place, seated by the fire, clothed in a winter dressing-gown, that I hold in my hands this piece of paper, with other intimations of the same nature. But how could I deny that I possess these hands and this body, and withal escape being classed with persons in a state of insanity, whose brains are so disordered and clouded by dark bilious vapours as to cause them pertinaciously to assert that they are monarchs when

From René Descartes, "Meditation I" in *The Method, Meditations and Philosophy of Descartes,* trans. John Veitch (New York: Tudor Publishing Co., 1901), pp. 219–24.

*Bracketed passages are additions to the original revised French translation.—EDS.

they are in the greatest poverty; or clothed [in gold] and purple when destitute of any covering; or that their head is made of clay, their body of glass, or that they are gourds? I should certainly be not less insane than they, were I to regulate my procedure according to examples so extravagant.

Though this be true, I must nevertheless here consider that I am a man, and that, consequently, I am in the habit of sleeping, and representing to myself in dreams those same things, or even sometimes others less probable, which the insane think are presented to them in their waking moments. How often have I dreamt that I was in these familiar circumstances,—that I was dressed, and occupied this place by the fire, when I was lying undressed in bed? At the present moment, however, I certainly look upon this paper with eyes wide awake; the head which I now move is not asleep; I extend this hand consciously and with express purpose, and I perceive it; the occurrences in sleep are not so distinct as all this. But I cannot forget that, at other times, I have been deceived in sleep by similar illusions; and, attentively considering those cases, I perceive so clearly that there exist no certain marks by which the state of waking can ever be distinguished from sleep, that I feel greatly astonished; and in amazement I almost persuade myself that I am now dreaming.

Let us suppose, then, that we are dreaming, and that all these particulars—namely, the opening of the eyes, the motion of the head, the forth-putting of the hands—are merely illusions; and even that we really possess neither an entire body nor hands such as we see. Nevertheless, it must be admitted at least that the objects which appear to us in sleep are, as it were, painted representations which could not have been formed unless in the likeness of realities; and, therefore, that those general objects, at all events, —namely, eyes, a head, hands, and an entire body—are not simply imaginary, but really existent. For, in truth, painters themselves, even when they study to represent sirens and satyrs by

forms the most fantastic and extraordinary, cannot bestow upon them natures absolutely new, but can only make a certain medley of the members of different animals; or if they chance to imagine something so novel that nothing at all similar has ever been seen before, and such as is, therefore, purely fictitious and absolutely false, it is at least certain that the colours of which this is composed are real.

And on the same principle, although these general objects, viz. [a body], eyes, a head, hands, and the like, be imaginary, we are nevertheless absolutely necessitated to admit the reality at least of some other objects still more simple and universal than these, of which, just as of certain real colours, all those images of things, whether true and real, or false and fantastic, that are found in our consciousness, are formed.

To this class of objects seem to belong corporeal nature in general and its extension; the figure of extended things, their quantity or magnitude, and their number, as also the place in, and the time during, which they exist, and other things of the same sort. We will not, therefore, perhaps reason illegitimately if we conclude from this that Physics, Astronomy, Medicine, and all the other sciences that have for their end the consideration of composite objects, are indeed of a doubtful character; but that Arithmetic, Geometry, and the other sciences of the same class, which regard merely the simplest and most general objects, and scarcely inquire whether or not these are really existent, contain somewhat that is certain and indubitable: for whether I am awake or dreaming, it remains true that two and three make five, and that a square has but four sides; nor does it seem possible that truths so apparent can ever fall under a suspicion of falsity [or incertitude].

Nevertheless, the belief that there is a God who is all-powerful, and who created me, such as I am, has, for a long time, obtained steady possession of my mind. How, then, do I know that he has not arranged that there should be neither earth, nor sky, nor any extended thing, nor figure, nor magnitude, nor place, providing at the same time, however, for [the rise in me of the perceptions of all these objects, and] the persuasion that these do not exist otherwise than as I perceive them? And further, as I sometimes think that others are in error respecting matters of which they believe themselves to possess a perfect knowledge, how do I know that I am not also deceived each time I add together two and three, or number the sides of a square, or form some judgment still more simple, if more simple indeed can be imagined? But perhaps Deity has not been willing that I should be thus deceived, for He is said to be supremely good. If, however, it were repugnant to the goodness of Deity to have created me subject to constant deception, it would seem likewise to be contrary to his goodness to allow me to be occasionally deceived; and yet it is clear that this is permitted. Some, indeed, might perhaps be found who would be disposed rather to deny the existence of a Being so powerful than to believe that there is nothing certain. But let us for the present refrain from opposing this opinion, and grant that all which is here said of a Deity is fabulous: nevertheless in whatever way it be supposed that I reached the state in which I exist, whether by fate, or chance, or by an endless series of antecedents and consequents, or by any other means, it is clear (since to be deceived and to err is a certain defect) that the probability of my being so imperfect as to be the constant victim of deception, will be increased exactly in proportion as the power possessed by the cause, to which they assign my origin, is lessened. To these reasonings I have assuredly nothing to reply, but am constrained at last to avow that there is nothing of all that I formerly believed to be true of which it is impossible to doubt, and that not through thoughtlessness or levity, but from cogent and maturely considered reasons; so that henceforward, if I desire to discover anything certain, I ought not the less carefully to refrain from assenting to those same opinions than to what might be shown to be manifestly false.

But it is not sufficient to have made these observations; care must be taken likewise to keep them in remembrance. For those old and customary opinions perpetually recur—long and familiar usage giving them the right of occupying my mind, even almost against my will, and subduing my belief; nor will I lose the habit of deferring to them and confiding in them so long as I shall consider them to be what in truth they are, viz., opinions to some extent doubtful, as I have already shown, but still highly probable, and such as it is much more reasonable to believe than deny. It is for this reason I am persuaded that I shall not be doing wrong, if, taking an opposite judgment of deliberate design, I become my own deceiver, by supposing, for a time, that all those opinions are entirely false and imaginary, until at length, having thus balanced my old by my new prejudices, my judgment shall no longer be turned aside by perverted usage from the path that may conduct to the perception of truth. For I am assured that, meanwhile, there will arise neither peril nor error from this course, and that I cannot for the present yield too much to distrust, since the end I now seek is not action but knowledge.

I will suppose, then, not that Deity, who is sovereignly good and the fountain of truth, but that some malignant demon, who is at once exceedingly potent and deceitful, has employed all his artifice to deceive me; I will suppose that the sky, the air, the earth, colours, figures, sounds, and all external things, are nothing better than the illusions of dreams, by means of which this being has laid snares for my credulity; I will consider myself as without hands, eyes, flesh, blood, or any of the senses, and as falsely believing that I am possessed of these; I will continue resolutely fixed in this belief, and if indeed by this means it be not in my power to arrive at the knowledge of truth, I shall at least do what is in my power, viz., [suspend my judgment], and guard with settled purpose against giving my assent to what is false, and being imposed upon by this deceiver, whatever be his power and artifice.

But this undertaking is arduous, and a certain indolence insensibly leads me back to my ordinary course of life; and just as the captive, who, perchance, was enjoying in his dreams an imaginary liberty, when he begins to suspect that it is but a vision, dreads awakening, and conspires with the agreeable illusions that the deception may be prolonged; so I, of my own accord, fall back into the train of my former beliefs, and fear to arouse myself from my slumber, lest the time of laborious wakefulness that would succeed this quiet rest, in place of bringing any light of day, should prove inadequate to dispel the darkness that will arise from the difficulties that have now been raised.

What Is Indubitable

I am in doubt as to the propriety of making my first meditations, in the place above mentioned, matter of discourse; for these are so metaphysical, and so uncommon, as not, perhaps, to be acceptable to everyone. And yet, that it may be determined whether the foundations that I have laid are sufficiently secure, I find myself in a measure constrained to advert to them. I had long before remarked that, in relation to practice, it is sometimes necessary to adopt, as if above doubt, opinions which we discern to be highly uncertain, as has been already said; but as I then desired to give my attention solely to the search after truth, I thought that a procedure exactly the opposite was called for, and that I ought to reject as absolutely false all opinions in regard to which I could suppose the least ground for doubt, in order to ascertain whether after that there remained aught in my belief that was wholly indubitable. Accordingly, seeing that our senses sometimes deceive us, I was willing to suppose that there existed nothing really such as they presented to us; and because some men err in reasoning, and fall into paralogisms, even on the simplest matters of Geometry, I, convinced that I was as open to error as any other, rejected as false all the reasonings I had hitherto taken for demonstrations; and finally, when I considered that the very same thoughts (presentations) which we experience when awake may also be experienced when we are asleep, while there is

From René Descartes, "The Discourse on Method," Part IV, in *The Method, Meditations and Philosophy of Descartes,* trans. John Veitch (New York: Tudor Publishing Co., 1901), pp. 170–72.

at that time not one of them true, I supposed that all the objects (presentations) that had ever entered into my mind when awake, had in them no more truth than the illusions of my dreams. But immediately upon this I observed that, whilst I thus wished to think that all was false, it was absolutely necessary that I, who thus thought, should be somewhat; and as I observed that this truth, I THINK, HENCE I AM, was so certain and of such evidence, that no ground of doubt, however extravagant, could be alleged by the Sceptics capable of shaking it, I concluded that I might, without scruple, accept it as the first principle of the philosophy of which I was in search.

In the next place, I attentively examined what I was, and as I observed that I could suppose that I had no body, and that there was no world nor any place in which I might be; but that I could not therefore suppose that I was not; and that, on the contrary, from the very circumstance that I thought to doubt of the truth of all things, it most clearly and certainly followed that I was; while, on the other hand, if I had only ceased to think, although all the other objects which I had ever imagined had been in reality existent, I would have had no reason to believe that I existed; I thence concluded that I was a substance whose whole essence or nature consists only in thinking, and which, that it may exist, has need of no place, nor is dependent on any material thing; so that "I", that is to say, the mind by which I am what I am, is wholly distinct from the body, and is even more easily known than the latter, and is such, that although the latter were not, it would still continue to be all that it is.

After this I inquired in general into what is essential to the truth and certainty of a proposition; for since I had discovered one which I knew to be true, I thought that I must likewise be able to discover the ground of this certitude. And as I observed that in the words I THINK, HENCE I AM, there is nothing at all which gives me assurance of their truth beyond this, that I see very clearly that in order to think it is necessary to exist. I concluded that I might take, as a general rule, the principle, that all the things which we very clearly and distinctly conceive are true, only observing, however, that there is some difficulty in rightly determining the objects which we distinctly conceive.

In the next place, from reflecting on the circumstance that I doubted, and that consequently my being was not wholly perfect (for I clearly saw that it was a greater perfection to know than to doubt), I was led to inquire whence I had learned to think of something more perfect than myself; and I clearly recognized that I must hold this notion from some Nature which in reality was more perfect. As for the thoughts of many other objects external to me, as of the sky, the earth, light, heat, and a thousand more, I was less at a loss to know whence these came; for since I remarked in them nothing which seemed to render them superior to myself, I could believe that, if these were true, they were dependencies on my own nature, in so far as it possessed a certain perfection, and, if they were false, that I held them from nothing, that is to say, that they were in me because of a certain imperfection of my nature. But this could not be the case with the idea of a Nature more perfect than myself; for to receive it from nothing was a thing manifestly impossible; and, because it is not less repugnant that the more perfect should be an effect of, and dependence on the less perfect, than that something should proceed from nothing, it was equally impossible that I could hold it from myself; accordingly, it but remained that it had been placed in me by a Nature which was in reality more perfect than

mine, and which even possessed within itself all the perfections of which I could form any idea: that is to say, in a single word, which was God. And to this I added that, since I knew some perfections which I did not possess, I was not the only being in existence, (I will here, with your permission, freely use the terms of the Schools); but on the contrary, that there was of necessity some other more perfect Being upon whom I was dependent, and from whom I had received all that I possessed; for if I had existed alone, and independently of every other being, so as to have had from myself all the perfection, however little, which I actually possessed, I should have been able, for the same reason, to have had from myself the whole remainder of perfection, of the want of which I was conscious, and thus could of myself have become infinite, eternal, immutable, omniscient, all-powerful, and, in fine, have possessed all the perfections which I could recognize in God. For in order to know the nature of God (whose existence has been established by the preceding reasonings), as far as my own nature permitted, I had only to consider in reference to all the properties of which I found in my mind some idea, whether their possession was a mark of perfection; and I was assured that no one which indicated any imperfection was in him, and that none of the rest was awanting. Thus I perceived that doubt, inconstancy, sadness, and such like, could not be found in God, since I myself would have been happy to be free from them. Besides, I had ideas of many sensible and corporeal things; for although I might suppose that I was dreaming, and that all which I saw or imagined was false, I could not, nevertheless, deny that the ideas were in reality in my thoughts. But because I had already very clearly recognized in myself that the intelligent nature is distinct from the corporeal, and as I observed that all composition is an evidence of dependency, and that a state of dependency is manifestly a state of imperfection, I therefore determined that it could not be a perfection in God to be compounded of these two natures, and that consequently he was not so compounded; but that if there were any bodies in the world, or even any intelligences, or other natures that were not wholly perfect, their existence depended on his power in such a way that they could not subsist without him for a single moment.

I was disposed straightway to search for other truths; and when I had represented to myself the object of the geometers, which I conceived to be a continuous body, or a space indefinitely extended in length, breadth, and height or depth, divisible into divers parts which admit of different figures and sizes, and of being moved or transposed in all manner of ways (for all this the geometers suppose to be in the object they contemplate), I went over some of their simplest demonstrations. And, in the first place, I observed that the great certitude which by common consent is accorded to these demonstrations, is founded solely upon this, that they are clearly conceived in accordance with the rules I have already laid down. In the next place, I perceived that there was nothing at all in these demonstrations which could assure me of the existence of their object; thus, for example, supposing a triangle to be given, I distinctly perceived that its three angles were necessarily equal to two right angles, but I did not on that account perceive anything which could assure me that any triangle existed; while, on the contrary, recurring to the examination of the idea of a Perfect Being, I found that the existence of the Being was comprised in the idea in the same way that the equality of its three angles to two right angles is comprised in the idea of a triangle, or as in the idea of a sphere, the equidistance of all points on its surface from the center, or even still more clearly; and that consequently it is at least as certain that God, who is this Perfect Being, is, or exists, as any demonstration of Geometry can be.

But the reason which leads many to persuade themselves that there is a difficulty in knowing this truth, and even also in knowing what their mind really is, is that they never raise their thoughts above sensible objects, and are so accustomed to consider nothing except by way of imagination, which is a mode of thinking limited to material objects, that all that is not imaginable seems to them not intelligible. The truth of this is sufficiently manifest from the single circumstance, that the philosophers of the Schools accept as a maxim that there is nothing in the Understanding which was not previously in the Senses, in which however it is certain that the ideas of God and of the Soul have never been; and it appears to me that they who make use of their imagination to comprehend these ideas do exactly the same thing as if, in order to hear sounds or smell odors, they strove to avail themselves of their eyes; unless indeed that there is this difference, that the sense of sight does not afford us an inferior assurance to those of smell or hearing; in place of which, neither our imagination nor our senses can give us assurance of anything unless our Understanding intervene.

Finally, if there be still persons who are not sufficiently persuaded of the existence of God and of the soul, by the reasons I have adduced, I am desirous that they should know that all the other propositions, of the truth of which they deem themselves perhaps more assured, as that we have a body, and that there exist stars and an earth, and such like, are less certain; for, although we have a moral assurance of these things, which is so strong that there is an appearance of extravagance in doubting of their existence, yet at the same time no one, unless his intellect is impaired, can deny, when the question relates to a metaphysical certitude, that there is sufficient reason to exclude entire assurance, in the observation that when asleep we can in the same way imagine ourselves possessed of another body and that we see other stars and another earth, when there is nothing of the kind. For how do we know that the thoughts which occur in dreaming are false rather than those other which we experience when awake, since the former are often not less vivid and distinct than the latter? And though men of the highest genius study this question as long as they please, I do not believe that they will be able to give any reason which can be sufficient to remove this doubt, unless they presuppose the existence of God. For, in the first place, even the principle which I have already taken as a rule, viz., that all the things which we clearly and distinctly conceive are true, is certain only because God is or exists, and because he is a Perfect Being, and because all that we possess is derived from him; whence it follows that our ideas or notions, which to the extent of their clearness and distinctness are real, and proceed from God, must to that extent be true. Accordingly, whereas we not unfrequently have ideas or notions in which some falsity is contained, this can only be the case with such as are to some extent confused and obscure, and in this proceed from nothing, (participate of negation), that is, exist in us thus confused because we are not wholly perfect. And it is evident that it is not less repugnant that falsity or imperfection, insofar as it is imperfection, should proceed from God, than that truth or perfection should proceed from nothing. But if we did not know that all which we possess of real and true proceeds from a Perfect and Infinite Being, however clear and distinct our ideas might be, we should have no ground on that account for the assurance that they possessed the perfection of being true.

But after the knowledge of God and of the soul has rendered us certain of this rule, we can easily understand that the truth of the thoughts we experience when awake, ought not in the slightest degree to be called in question on account of the illusions of our dreams. For if it happened that an individual, even when asleep, had some very distinct idea, as, for example, if a geometer should discover some new demonstra-

tion, the circumstance of his being asleep would not militate against its truth; and as for the most ordinary error of our dreams, which consists in their representing to us various objects in the same way as our external senses, this is not prejudicial, since it leads us very properly to suspect the truth of the ideas of sense; for we are not unfrequently deceived in the same manner when awake; as when persons in the jaundice see all objects yellow, or when the stars or bodies at a great distance appear to us much smaller than they are. For, in fine, whether awake or asleep, we ought never to allow ourselves to be persuaded of the truth of anything unless on the evidence of our Reason. And it must be noted that I say of our REASON, and not of our imagination or of our senses: thus, for example, although we very clearly see the sun, we ought not therefore to determine that it is only of the size which our sense of sight presents; and we may very distinctly imagine the head of a lion joined to the body of a goat, without being therefore shut up to the conclusion that a chimera exists; for it is not a dictate of Reason that what we thus see or imagine is in reality existent; but it plainly tells us that all our ideas or notions contain in them some truth; for otherwise it could not be that God, who is wholly perfect and veracious, should have placed them in us. And because our reasonings are never so clear or so complete during sleep as when we are awake, although sometimes the acts of our imagination are then as lively and distinct, if not more so than in our waking moments, Reason further dictates that, since all our thoughts cannot be true because of our partial imperfection, those possessing truth must infallibly be found in the experience of our waking moments rather than in that of our dreams.

Notes

1. Thomas H. Huxley, *Methods and Results* (New York: D. Appleton, 1897), p. 169.

2. Ibid., pp. 169–70.

3. René Descartes, *The Discourse on Method,* part III, in *The Method, Meditations, and Philosophy of Descartes,* trans. John Veitch (New York: Tudor Publishing Co., n.d.), p. 168.

4. Ibid., pp. 164–67.

5. Ibid., p. 167.

6. Ibid.

7. Ibid., part II, p. 161.

3 / Sensible Scepticism
Hume

David Hume (1711–1776) has the reputation of being one of the greatest sceptics in the history of philosophy. By keen analysis and consistent inference he showed the inadequacy and absurdity of traditional concepts of cause and effect, substance, self-identity, and undermined belief in miracles, in a universal moral law, in a soul, and in an all-powerful and all-loving Divine Being. Despite this reputation, and despite the fact that he often paid tribute to extreme scepticism or Pyrrhonism and brilliantly employed its arguments when they suited his purpose, Hume disclaimed such total scepticism. "Should it here be asked me," he wrote in his *Treatise of Human Nature* (1739), after having used sceptical arguments to attack the dependency on reason, "whether I sincerely assent to this argument, which I seem to take such pains to inculcate, and whether I be really one of those sceptics who hold that all is uncertain. . . . I should reply that this question is entirely superfluous, and that neither I, nor any person, was ever sincerely and constantly of that opinion."[1] Hume went on to explain that to adhere to and to practice total scepticism would make life not only intolerable but impossible. We feel and breathe as well as judge, he pointed out, and we have to act whether we can rationally justify our actions or not.[2] Beliefs relate not just to our rational, cognitive nature but to our sensitive, instinctive nature. Custom and habit determine our actions and beliefs far more strongly than do reason and reflection. At the purely speculative level, the sceptic may reach the conclusion that he cannot rationally support his adherence to certain beliefs (for example, the law of cause and effect), but he immediately recognizes that he is quite willing to take such beliefs for granted in his day-to-day action. The senses may at times deceive us and may fail to support what our reason tells us must be the case, but while the recognition of this fact may make us more cautious—seeing is *not* believing—it does not prevent us from having confidence in the reports of our senses and from relying upon them constantly.

However, this does not mean that, because man must constantly refer to common sense and instinct in order to live, he can do without philosophy and scepticism. Philosophy would be worthwhile, Hume held, even if it provided nothing beyond "the gratification of an innocent curiosity" about the nature of things, one of "those few safe and harmless pleasures which are bestowed on the human race."[3] The value of philosophical reflection, Hume continued, can also be justified on other grounds. Only by engaging in it can we learn to distinguish superstitions from knowledge, metaphysical jargon from meaningful discourse, and pseudo from genuine philosophical questions. "The only way of freeing learning, at once, from these abstruse questions," Hume wrote in his *Enquiry*, "is to inquire seriously into the nature of human understanding, and show, from an exact analysis of its powers and capacity, that it is by no means fitted for such remote and abstruse subjects. We must submit to this fatigue, in order to live at ease ever after: And must cultivate true metaphysics with some care, in order to destroy the false and adulterate."[4] Hume also was hopeful that the careful pursuit of philosophy could someday provide a fuller and more concrete understanding of human nature by uncovering "the secret springs and principles by which the human mind is actuated in its operations."[5] In presenting his own philosophy he hoped to reconcile "profound inquiry with clearness, and truth with novelty." In this respect at least he succeeded admirably.

In discussing the importance of philosophy, Hume attempted to place philosophical reflection within the larger sphere of human life. "Be a philosopher," he urged, "but, amidst all your philosophy, be still a man."[6] Unrelieved by practical activity and diversion, philosophizing can eventually lead to despair.

> Where am I, or what? From what causes do I derive my existence, and to what condition shall I return? Whose favour shall I court, and whose anger must I dread? What beings surround me? and on whom have I any influence, or who have any influence on me? I am confounded with all these questions, and begin to fancy myself in the most deplorable condition imaginable, environed with the deepest darkness, and utterly deprived of the use of every member and faculty.[7]

In this predicament, the philosopher, Hume believed, would be wise to follow his example and learn when to leave reflection aside for other, less weighty concerns.

> I dine, I play a game of backgammon, I converse, am merry with my friends; and when, after three or four hours' amusement, I would return to these speculations, they appear so cold, so strained, and ridiculous that I cannot find in my heart to enter into them any further.[8]

Yet Hume was always able to resume his philosophizing with enthusiasm. If at times his sceptical reflections led him to despair or to error, he was well-balanced and good-tempered enough soon to recover his equilibrium. To be sure, philosophy made its demands upon him, but these demands were moderate and agreeable. Unlike religious enthusiasm, he argued, enthusiasm for philosophy arouses only "mild and moderate sentiments" and seldom leads to an interruption of natural inclinations and to a radical modification of ordinary conduct. And "generally speaking," he added, "the errors in religion are dangerous; those of philosophy only ridiculous."[9]

Throughout his works and to the end of his life, Hume retained his enthusiasm for philosophy, especially for sceptical philosophy. He admired its stress on doubt rather than dogma and its willingness to suspend judgment rather than to make a judgment carelessly, rashly, or in haste. He admired scepticism because its practitioners were content to undertake inquiries within clearly defined and reasonably narrow boundaries, and renounced lofty metaphysical speculations having little or no relationship to real life. Better than any kind of philosophy, scepticism, Hume believed, could oppose "the supine indolence of mind, its rash arrogance, its lofty pretensions, and its superstitious credulity."[10] Scepticism mortifies every human passion, "except the love of truth, and that passion," Hume held, "never is, nor can be, carried to too high a degree."[11] Considering its usefulness, scepticism certainly would not seem to deserve the widespread hatred and resentment it has incurred. But, as Hume pointed out, its characteristics are precisely those which would make a philosophy unpopular and provoke hostility. "By flattering no irregular passion, it gains few partisans: By opposing so many vices and follies, it raises to itself abundance of enemies, who stigmatize it as libertine, profane, and irreligious."[12]

In the first of the following selections, Hume presents his own defense of doubt and commits himself to a "mitigated" rather than an "excessive" scepticism. The second selection contains an important example of Hume's analytical method in operation: his analysis and appraisal, from a sceptical point of view, of the concept of personal identity.

Varieties of Scepticism

The *sceptic* is another enemy of religion, who naturally provokes the indignation of all divines and graver philosophers; though it is certain, that no man ever met with any such absurd creature, or conversed with a man, who had no opinion or principle concerning any subject, either of action or speculation. This begets a very natural question; What is meant by a sceptic? And how far is it possible to push these philosophical principles of doubt and uncertainty?

There is a species of scepticism, *antecedent* to all study and philosophy, which is much inculcated by Descartes and others, as a sovereign preservative against error and precipitate judgment. It recommends an universal doubt, not only of all our former opinions and principles, but also of our very faculties; of whose veracity, say they, we must assure ourselves, by a chain of reasoning, deduced from some original principle, which cannot possibly be fallacious or deceitful. But neither is there any such original principle, which has a prerogative above others, that are self-evident and convincing: or if there were, could we advance a step beyond it, but by the use of those very faculties, of which we are supposed to be already diffident. The Cartesian doubt, therefore, were it ever possible to be attained by any human creature (as it plainly is not) would be entirely uncurable; and no reasoning could ever bring us to a state of assurance and conviction upon any subject.

It must, however, be confessed, that this species of scepticism, when more moderate, may be understood in a very reasonable sense, and is a necessary preparative to the study of philosophy, by preserving a proper impartiality in our judgments, and weaning our mind from all those prejudices, which we may have imbibed from education or rash opinion. To begin with clear and self-evident principles, to advance by timorous and sure steps, to review frequently our conclusions, and examine accurately all their consequences; though by these means we shall make both a slow and a short progress in our systems; are the only methods by which we can ever hope to reach truth, and attain a proper stability and certainty in our determinations.

There is another species of scepticism, *consequent* to science and inquiry, when men are supposed to have discovered either the absolute fallaciousness of their mental faculties, or their unfitness to reach any fixed determination in all those curious subjects of speculation, about which they are commonly employed. Even our very senses are brought into dispute, by a certain species of philosophers; and the maxims of common life are subjected to the same doubt as the most profound principles or conclusions of metaphysics and theology. As these paradoxical tenets (if they may be called tenets) are to be met with in some philosophers, and the refutation of them in several, they naturally excite our curiosity, and make us inquire into the arguments, on which they may be founded.

I need not insist upon the more trite topics,

From David Hume, *An Enquiry Concerning Human Understanding* in *Essays: Moral, Political and Literary,* ed. T. H. Green and T. H. Grose (London: Longmans, Green, 1882), sec. XII, part I–III, pp. 122–33.

employed by the sceptics in all ages, against the evidence of the *sense;* such as those which are derived from the imperfection and fallaciousness of our organs, on numberless occasions; the crooked appearance of an oar in water; the various aspects of objects, according to their different distances; the double images which arise from the pressing one eye; with many other appearances of a like nature. These sceptical topics, indeed, are only sufficient to prove, that the senses alone are not implicitly to be depended on; but that we must correct their evidence by reason, and by considerations, derived from the nature of the medium, the distance of the object, and the disposition of the organ, in order to render them, within their sphere, the proper *criteria* of truth and falsehood. There are other more profound arguments against the senses, which admit not of so easy a solution.

It seems evident, that men are carried, by a natural instinct or prepossession, to repose faith in their senses; and that, without any reasoning, or even almost before the use of reason, we always suppose an external universe, which depends not on our perception, but would exist, though we and every sensible creature were absent or annihilated. Even the animal creation are governed by a like opinion, and preserve this belief in external objects, in all their thoughts, designs, and actions.

It seems also evident, that, when men follow this blind and powerful instinct of nature, they always suppose the very images, presented by the senses, to be the external objects, and never entertain any suspicion, that the one are nothing but representations of the other. This very table, which we see white, and which we feel hard, is believed to exist, independent of our perception, and to be something external to our mind, which perceives it. Our presence bestows not being on it; our absence does not annihilate it. It preserves its existence uniform and entire, independent of the situation of intelligent beings, who perceive or contemplate it.

But this universal and primary opinion of all men is soon destroyed by the slightest philosophy, which teaches us, that nothing can ever be present to the mind but an image or perception, and that the senses are only the inlets, through which these images are conveyed, without being able to produce any immediate intercourse between the mind and the object. The table, which we see, seems to diminish, as we remove farther from it; but the real table, which exists independent of us, suffers no alteration: it was, therefore, nothing but its image, which was present to the mind. These are the obvious dictates of reason; and no man, who reflects, ever doubted, that the existences, which we consider, when we say, *this house* and *that tree,* are nothing but perceptions in the mind, and fleeting copies or representations of other existences, which remain uniform and independent.

So far, then, are we necessitated by reasoning to contradict or depart from the primary instincts of nature, and to embrace a new system with regard to the evidence of our senses. But here philosophy finds herself extremely embarrassed, when she would justify this new system, and obviate the cavils and objections of the sceptics. She can no longer plead the infallible and irresistible instinct of nature: for that led us to a quite different system, which is acknowledged fallible and even erroneous. And to justify this pretended philosophical system, by a chain of clear and convincing argument, or even any appearance of argument, exceeds the power of all human capacity.

By what argument can it be proved, that the perceptions of the mind must be caused by external objects, entirely different from them, though resembling them (if that be possible) and could not arise either from the energy of the mind itself, or from the suggestion of some invisible and unknown spirit, or from some other cause still more unknown to us? It is acknowledged, that, in fact, many of these perceptions arise not from anything external, as in dreams, madness, and other diseases. And nothing can be more inexplicable than the manner, in which body should so operate upon mind as ever to convey an image of itself to a substance, supposed of so different, and even contrary a nature.

It is a question of fact, whether the perceptions of the senses be produced by external objects, resembling them: how shall this question be determined? By experience surely; as all other questions of a like nature. But here experience is, and must be entirely silent. The mind has never anything present to it but the perceptions, and cannot possibly reach any experience of their connections with objects. The supposition of such a connection is, therefore, without any foundation in reasoning.

To have recourse to the veracity of the supreme Being, in order to prove the veracity of our senses, is surely making a very unexpected circuit. If his veracity were at all concerned in this matter, our senses would be entirely infallible; because it is not possible that he can ever deceive. Not to mention, that, if the external world be once called in question, we shall be at a loss to find arguments, by which we may prove the existence of that Being or any of his attributes.

This is a topic, therefore, in which the profounder and more philosophical sceptics will always triumph, when they endeavor to introduce an universal doubt into all subjects of human knowledge and inquiry. Do you follow the instincts and propensities of nature, may they say, in assenting to the veracity of sense? But these lead you to believe that the very perception or sensible image is the external object. Do you disclaim this principle, in order to embrace a more rational opinion, that the perceptions are only representations of something external? You here depart from your natural propensities and more obvious sentiments; and yet are not able to satisfy your reason, which can never find any convincing argument from experience to prove, that the perceptions are connected with any external objects.

There is another sceptical topic of a like nature, derived from the most profound philosophy; which might merit our attention, were it requisite to dive so deep, in order to discover arguments and reasonings, which can so little serve to any serious purpose. It is universally allowed by modern inquirers, that all the sensible qualities of objects, such as hard, soft, hot, cold, white, black, etc. are merely secondary, and exist not in the objects themselves, but are perceptions of the mind, without any external archetype or model, which they represent. If this be allowed, with regard to secondary qualities, it must also follow, with regard to the supposed primary qualities of extension and solidity; nor can the latter be any more entitled to that denomination than the former. The idea of extension is entirely acquired from the senses of sight and feeling; and if all the qualities, perceived by the senses, be in the mind, not in the object, the same conclusion must reach the idea of extension, which is wholly dependent on the sensible ideas or the ideas of secondary qualities. Nothing can save us from this conclusion, but the asserting, that the ideas of those primary qualities are attained by *abstraction,* an opinion, which, if we examine it accurately, we shall find to be unintelligible, and even absurd. An extension, that is neither tangible nor visible, cannot possibly be conceived; and a tangible or visible extension, which is neither hard nor soft, black or white, is equally beyond the reach of human conception. Let any man try to conceive a triangle in general, which is neither *isosceles* nor *scalenum,* nor has any particular length or proportion of sides; and he will soon perceive the absurdity of all the scholastic notions with regard to abstraction and general ideas.

Thus the first philosophical objection to the evidence of sense or to the opinion of external existence consists in this, that such an opinion, if rested on natural instinct, is contrary to reason, and if referred to reason, is contrary to natural instinct, and at the same time carries no rational evidence with it, to convince an impartial inquirer. The second objection goes farther, and represents this opinion as contrary to reason; at least, if it be a principle of reason, that all sensible qualities are in the mind, not in the object. Bereave matter of all its intelligible qualities, both primary and secondary, you in a manner annihilate it, and leave only a certain unknown, inexplicable *something,* as the cause of our perceptions; a notion so imperfect, that no sceptic will think it worth while to contend against it. . . .

The sceptical objections to *moral* evidence, or to the reasonings concerning matter of fact, are either *popular* or *philosophical.* The popular objections are derived from the natural weakness of human understanding; the contradictory opinions, which have been entertained in different ages and nations; the variations of our judgment in sickness and health, youth and old age, prosperity and adversity; the perpetual contradiction of each particular man's opinions and sentiments; with many other topics of that kind. It is needless to insist farther on this head. These objections are but weak. For as, in common life, we reason every moment concerning fact and existence, and cannot possibly subsist, without continually employing this species of argument, any popular objections, derived from thence, must be insufficient to destroy that evidence. The great subverter of *Pyrrhonism* or the excessive principles of scepticism is action, and employment, and the occupations of common life. These principles may flourish and triumph in the schools, where it is, indeed, difficult, if not impossible, to refute them. But as soon as they leave the shade, and by the presence of the real objects, which actuate our passions and sentiments, are put in opposition to the more powerful principles of our nature, they vanish like smoke, and leave the most determined sceptic in the same conditions as other mortals.

The sceptic, therefore, had better keep within his proper sphere, and display those *philosophical* objections, which arise from more profound researches. Here he seems to have ample matter of triumph, while he justly insists, that all

our evidence for any matter of fact, which lies beyond the testimony of sense or memory, is derived entirely from the relation of cause and effect; that we have no other idea of this relation than that of two objects, which have been frequently *conjoined* together; that we have no argument to convince us, that objects, which have, in our experience, been frequently conjoined, will likewise, in other instances, be conjoined in the same manner; and that nothing leads us to this inference but custom or a certain instinct of our nature; which it is indeed difficult to resist, but which, like other instincts, may be fallacious and deceitful. While the sceptic insists upon these topics, he shows his force, or rather, indeed, his own and our weakness; and seems, for the time at least, to destroy all assurance and conviction. These arguments might be displayed at greater length, if any durable good or benefit to society could ever be expected to result from them.

For here is the chief and most confounding objection to *excessive* scepticism, that no durable good can ever result from it; while it remains in its full force and vigor. We need only ask such a sceptic, *What his meaning is? And what he proposes by all these curious researches?* He is immediately at a loss, and knows not what to answer. A Copernican or Ptolemaic, who supports each his different system of astronomy, may hope to produce a conviction, which will remain constant and durable, with his audience. A Stoic or Epicurean displays principles, which may not be durable, but which have an effect on conduct and behavior. But a Pyrrhonian cannot expect, that his philosophy will have any constant influence on the mind: or if it had, that its influence would be beneficial to society. On the contrary, he must acknowledge, if he will acknowledge anything, that all human life must perish, were his principles universally and steadily to prevail. All discourse, all action would immediately cease; and men remain in a total lethargy, till the necessities of nature, unsatisfied, put an end to their miserable existence. It is true; so fatal an event is very little to be dreaded. Nature is always too strong for principle. And though a Pyrrhonian may throw himself or others into a momentary amazement and confusion by his profound reasonings; the first and most trivial event in life will put to flight all his doubts and scruples, and leave him the same, in every point of action and speculation, with the philosophers of every sect, or with those who never concerned themselves in any philosophical researches. When he awakes from his dream, he will be the first to join in the laugh against himself, and to confess, that all his objections are mere amusement, and can have no other tendency than to show the whimsical condition of mankind, who must act and reason and believe; though they are not able, by their most diligent inquiry, to satisfy themselves concerning the foundation of these operations, or to remove the objections, which may be raised against them. . . .

There is, indeed, a more *mitigated* scepticism or *academical* philosophy, which may be both durable and useful, and which may, in part, be the result of this Pyrrhonism, or *excessive* scepticism, when its undistinguished doubts are, in some measure, corrected by common sense and reflection. The greater part of mankind are naturally apt to be affirmative and dogmatical in their opinions; and while they see objects only on one side, and have no idea of any counterpoising argument, they throw themselves precipitately into the principles, to which they are inclined; nor have they any indulgence for those who entertain opposite sentiments. To hesitate or balance perplexes their understanding, checks their passion, and suspends their action. They are, therefore, impatient till they escape from a state, which to them is so uneasy: and they think, that they could never remove themselves far enough from it, by the violence of their affirmations and obstinacy of their belief. But could such dogmatical reasoners become sensible of the strange infirmities of human understanding, even in its most perfect state, and when most

accurate and cautious in its determinations; such a reflection would naturally inspire them with more modesty and reserve, and diminish their fond opinion of themselves, and their prejudice against antagonists. The illiterate may reflect on the disposition of the learned, who, admidst all the advantages of study and reflection, are commonly still diffident in their determinations: and if any of the learned be inclined, from their natural temper, to haughtiness and obstinacy, a small tincture of Pyrrhonism might abate their pride, by showing them, that the few advantages, which they may have attained over their fellows, are but inconsiderable, if compared with the universal perplexity and confusion, which is inherent in human nature. In general, there is a degree of doubt, and caution, and modesty, which, in all kinds of scrutiny and decision, ought forever to accompany a just reasoner.

Another species of *mitigated* scepticism which may be of advantage to mankind, and which may be the natural result of the Pyrrhonian doubts and scruples, is the limitation of our inquiries to such subjects as are best adapted to the narrow capacity of human understanding. The *imagination* of man is naturally, sublime, delighted with whatever is remote and extraordinary, and running, without control, into the most distant parts of space and time in order to avoid the objects, which custom has rendered too familiar to it. A correct *judgment* observes a contrary method, and avoiding all distant and high inquiries, confines itself to common life, and to such subjects as fall under daily practice and experience; leaving the more sublime topics to the embellishment of poets and orators, or to the arts of priests and politicians. To bring us to so salutary a determination, nothing can be more serviceable, than to be once thoroughly convinced of the force of the Pyrrhonian doubt, and of the impossibility, that anything, but the strong power of natural instinct, could free us from it. Those who have a propensity to philosophy, will still continue their researches; because they reflect, that, besides the immediate pleasure, attending such an occupation, philosophical decisions are nothing but the reflections of common life, methodized and corrected. But they will never be tempted to go beyond common life, so long as they consider the imperfection of those faculties which they employ, their narrow reach, and their inaccurate operations. While we cannot give a satisfactory reason, why we believe, after a thousand experiments, that a stone will fall, or fire burn; can we ever satisfy ourselves concerning any determination, which we may form, with regard to the origin of worlds, and the situation of nature, from, and to eternity?

This narrow limitation, indeed, of our inquiries, is, in every respect, so reasonable, that it suffices to make the slightest examination into the natural powers of the human mind and to compare them with their objects, in order to recommend it to us. We shall then find what are the proper subjects of science and inquiry.

A Sceptical Examination of Personal Identity

There are some philosophers who imagine we are every moment intimately conscious of what we call our *self;* that we feel its existence and its continuance in existence; and are certain, beyond the evidence of a demonstration, both of its perfect identity and simplicity. The strongest sensation, the most violent passion, say they, instead of distracting us from this view, only fix it the more intensely, and makes us consider their influence on *self* either by their pain or pleasure. To attempt a further proof of this were to weaken its evidence; since no proof can be derived from any fact of which we are so intimately conscious; nor is there anything of which we can be certain if we doubt of this.

Unluckily all these positive assertions are contrary to that very experience which is pleaded for them; nor have we any idea of *self,* after the manner it is here explained. For, from what impression could this idea be derived? This question it is impossible to answer without a manifest contradiction and absurdity; and yet it is a question which must necessarily be answered, if we would have the idea of self pass for clear and intelligible. It must be some one impression that gives rise to every real idea. But self or person is not any one impression, but that to which our several impressions and ideas are supposed to have a reference. If any impression gives rise to

From David Hume, *A Treatise of Human Nature,* ed. by T. H. Green and T. H. Grose (London: Longmans, Green, 1886), part IV, sec. VI, pp. 533–43.

the idea of self, that impression must continue invariably the same, through the whole course of our lives; since self is supposed to exist after that manner. But there is no impression constant and invariable. Pain and pleasure, grief and joy, passions and sensations succeed each other, and never all exist at the same time. It cannot therefore be from any of these impressions, or from any other, that the idea of self is derived; and consequently there is no such idea.

But further, what must become of all our particular perceptions upon this hypothesis? All these are different, and distinguishable, and separable from each other, and may be separately considered, and may exist separately, and have no need of anything to support their existence. After what manner therefore do they belong to self, and how are they connected with it? For my part, when I enter most intimately into what I call *myself,* I always stumble on some particular perception or other, of heat or cold, light or shade, love or hatred, pain or pleasure. I never can catch *myself* at any time without a perception, and never can observe anything but the perception. When my perceptions are removed for any time, as by sound sleep, so long am I insensible of *myself,* and may truly be said not to exist. And were all my perceptions removed by death, and could I neither think, nor feel, nor see, nor love, nor hate, after the dissolution of my body, I should be entirely annihilated, nor do I conceive what is further requisite to make me a perfect nonentity. If any one, upon serious and unprejudiced reflection, thinks he has a different notion of *himself,* I must confess I can reason no longer with him. All I can allow him is, that he may be in the right as well as I, and that we are essentially different in this particular. He may, perhaps, perceive something simple and continued, which he calls *himself;* though I am certain there is no such principle in me.

But setting aside some metaphysicians of this kind, I may venture to affirm of the rest of mankind, that they are nothing but a bundle or collection of different perceptions, which succeed each other with an inconceivable rapidity, and are in a perpetual flux and movement. Our eyes cannot turn in their sockets without varying our perceptions. Our thought is still more variable than our sight; and all our other senses and faculties contribute to this change; nor is there any single power of the soul, which remains unalterably the same, perhaps for one moment. The mind is a kind of theatre, where several perceptions successively make their appearance; pass, repass, glide away, and mingle in an infinite variety of postures and situations. There is properly no *simplicity* in it at one time, nor *identity* in different; whatever natural propension we may have to imagine that simplicity and identity. The comparison of the theatre must not mislead us. They are the successive perceptions only, that constitute the mind; nor have we the most distant notion of the place where these scenes are represented, or of the materials of which it is composed.

What then gives us so great a propension to ascribe an identity to these successive perceptions, and to suppose ourselves possessed of an invariable and uninterrupted existence through the whole course of our lives? In order to answer this question we must distinguish betwixt personal identity, as it regards our thought or imagination, and as it regards our passions or the concern we take in ourselves. The first is our present subject; and to explain it perfectly we must take the matter pretty deep, and account for that identity, which we attribute to plants and animals; there being a great analogy betwixt it and the identity of a self or person.

We have a distinct idea of an object that remains invariable and uninterrupted through a supposed variation of time; and this idea we call that of *identity* or *sameness.* We have also a distinct idea of several different objects existing in succession, and connected together by a close relation; and this to an accurate view affords as perfect a notion of *diversity* as if there was no manner of relation among the objects. But though these two ideas of identity, and a succession of related objects, be in themselves perfectly distinct, and even contrary, yet it is certain that, in our common way of thinking, they are generally confounded with each other. That action of the imagination, by which we consider the uninterrupted and invariable object, and that by which we reflect on the succession of related objects, are almost the same to the feeling; nor is there much more effort of thought required in the latter case than in the former. The relation facilitates the transition of the mind from one object to another, and renders its passage as smooth as if it contemplated one continued object. This resemblance is the cause of the confusion and mistake, and makes us substitute the notion of identity, instead of that of related objects. However at one instant we may consider the related succession as variable or interrupted, we are sure the next to ascribe to it a perfect identity, and regard it as invariable and uninterrupted. Our propensity to this mistake is so great from the resemblance above mentioned, that we fall into it before we are aware; and though we incessantly correct ourselves by reflection; and return to a more accurate method of thinking, yet we cannot long sustain our philosophy, or take off this bias from the imagination. Our last resource is to yield to it, and boldly assert that these different related objects are in effect the same, however interrupted and variable. In order to justify to ourselves this absurdity, we often feign some new and unintelligible principle, that connects the objects together, and prevents their interruption or variation. Thus we feign the continued existence of the perceptions of our senses, to remove the interruption; and run into the notion of a *soul,* and *self,* and *substance,* to disguise the variation. But, we may further observe, that where we do not give rise to such a fiction, our propension to confound identity with relation is so great, that we are apt to imagine something unknown and mysterious, connecting the parts, beside their relation; and this I take to be the case with regard to the identity we ascribe to plants and vegetables. And even when this does not take place, we still feel a propensity to confound these ideas, though we are not able fully to satisfy ourselves in that particular, nor find anything invariable and uninterrupted to justify our notion of identity.

Thus the controversy concerning identity is not merely a dispute of words. For when we attribute identity, in an improper sense, to variable or interrupted objects, our mistake is not confined to the expression, but is commonly attended with a fiction, either of something invariable and uninterrupted, or of something mysterious and inexplicable, or at least with a propensity to such fictions. What will suffice to prove this hypothesis to the satisfaction of every fair inquirer, is to show, from daily experience and observation, that the objects which are variable or interrupted, and yet are supposed to continue the same, are such only as consist of a succession of parts, connected together by resemblance, contiguity, or causation. For as such a succession answers evidently to our notion of diversity, it can only be by mistake we ascribe to it an identity; and as the relation of parts, which leads us into this mistake, is really nothing but a quality, which produces an association of ideas, and an easy transition of the imagination from one to another, it can only be from the resemblance, which this act of the mind bears to that by which we contemplate one continued object, that the error arises. Our chief business, then, must be to prove that all objects to which we ascribe identity, without observing their invariableness and uninterruptedness, are such as consist of a succession of related objects. . . .

Notes

1. David Hume, *A Treatise of Human Nature,* ed. T. H. Green and T. H. Grose (London: Longmans, Green, 1886), vol. I, part IV, sec. I, p. 474.

2. Ibid.

3. David Hume, *An Enquiry Concerning Human Understanding* in *Essays; Moral, Political and Literary,* ed. T. H. Green and T. H. Grose (London: Longmans, Green, 1882), vol. II, sec. I, p. 7.

4. Ibid., p. 9.

5. Ibid., p. 11.

6. Ibid., p. 6.

7. Hume, *Treatise,* part IV, sec. VII, p. 549.

8. Ibid., pp. 548–49.

9. Ibid., p. 551.

10. Hume, *Enquiry,* sec. V, part I, p. 35.

11. Ibid.

12. Ibid., p. 36.

4 / Agonizing Doubt
Tolstoy

Up to the point when despair almost drove him to end it, the life of Leo Tolstoy (1828–1910) seemed to have been one of self-fulfillment and satisfaction. His noble birth and inherited wealth had given him the opportunities and leisure to develop his inner resources and talents, as well as a wide range of freedom to explore and observe his outer environment. The brilliance of his intellect, the intensity of his responses, and the fertility of his imagination contributed to his early success as a writer of realistic fiction that was saturated with poetic feeling. His sensual appetites had certainly not gone unsatiated. His passionate idealism had found social objectives upon which to focus, such as the education of the peasants on his family estate. He was adored by his wife and children, admired by his fellow artists, and idolized by his increasingly large reading audience for his greatest literary achievements, the novels *War and Peace* (1864–69) and *Anna Karenina* (1873–77), which were to place him among the literary geniuses of all time.

But instead of finding himself happy at the apex of his career, Tolstoy at fifty found himself completely miserable. In his relentless drive to perfect his literary art, to achieve widespread recognition and perpetual fame, and to reach personal fulfillment in love, marriage, and family life, he had avoided facing certain questions that now could not remain unanswered. Questions about the value of his life and art arose in his mind to plague him. The more he reflected on his predicament as a human being, the more he was confronted with doubt and uncertainty. The questions to which he now required answers were no longer questions related to beauty and ugliness, love and hate, war and peace, but the more fundamental existential questions relating in the most personal way to his own life and death. During this period of his life, which he later described in *My Confession* (1872–82), he one day listed on a sheet of paper the following six "unknown questions" to which he must find answers:

1. Why am I living?
2. What is the cause for my existence and that of everyone else?

3. What purpose has my existence or any other?
4. What does the division which I feel within me into good and evil signify, and for what purpose is it there?
5. How must I live?
6. What is death—how can I save myself? [1]

In the course of pondering such questions, the once happy Russian novelist eventually found the peace of mind he craved by achieving a final transformation in which he became a practicing primitive Christian and a world-famous religious sage. Part of Tolstoy's account of his confrontation with doubt and of the conversion that allowed him to vanquish it is given below. It begins after he has just finished describing his marriage and the fifteen years of happy family life that had caused him to postpone his soul-searching.

This remarkable document lends itself to a number of different interpretations. From the psychological point of view, it reveals Tolstoy's strong guilt feelings over his past impulsive acts of violence, greed, and sensuality and his great need to resolve the unconscious conflicts that continued to trouble him. Also revealed is his intense fear of death, which later was to be expressed so powerfully in his short story "The Death of Ivan Ilych" (1886). From the religious point of view that Tolstoy held, the experiences described have a universal human significance. They are to be understood in light of man's sinful nature and his search for salvation. The need for forgiveness, for atonement, and for peace of soul through a loving and harmonious relationship with a Divine Being are, to Tolstoy, the essential and uniquely human needs. To meet these needs, Tolstoy was willing to renounce his reason and to identify with the mass of sincere but uncritical believers who loved their God and their fellowmen unquestioningly. Eventually he was excommunicated from the Orthodox Church, but this did not bother him. He had found another, more personal faith by which to live and die.

Finally, from the philosophical point of view, Tolstoy's account is of interest in that in it he formulates clearly and vividly one of the broadest and most crucial questions with which speculative philosophy has traditionally been concerned: What is the nature of man and the meaning of human existence? Tolstoy suffered his problems and tried to render his thoughts and feelings as concretely as possible. He expressed beautifully the experience of doubt, uncertainty, fear, anxiety, and despair, and acted freely and completely to dispel his doubts by committing himself to a way of believing and acting. Tolstoy thus became, along with Kierkegaard, Nietzsche, and Dostoyevsky, an important nineteenth-century precursor of existentialism and an invaluable illuminator of the human predicament.

Doubts about the Meaning of Life

Thus I lived; but, five years ago, a strange state of mind began to grow upon me: I had moments of perplexity, of a stoppage, as it were, of life, as if I did not know how I was to live, what I was to do, and I began to wander, and was a victim to low spirits. But this passed, and I continued to live as before. Later, these periods of perplexity began to return more and more frequently, and invariably took the same form. These stoppages of life always presented themselves to me with the same questions: "Why?" and "What after?"

At first it seemed to me that these were aimless, unmeaning questions; it seemed to me that all they asked about was well known, and that if at any time when I wished to find answers to them I could do so without much trouble—that just at that time I could not be bothered with this, but whenever I should stop to think them over I should find an answer. But these questions presented themselves to my mind with ever-increasing frequency, demanding an answer with still greater and greater persistence, and like dots grouped themselves into one black spot.

It was with me as it happens in the case of every mortal internal ailment—at first appear the insignificant symptoms of indisposition, disregarded by the patient; then these symptoms are repeated more and more frequently, till they merge in uninterrupted suffering. The sufferings increase, and the patient is confronted with the fact that what he took for a mere indisposition has become more important to him than anything else on earth, that it is <u>death</u>!

This is exactly what happened to me. I became aware that this was not a chance indisposition, but something very serious, and that if all these questions continued to recur, I should have to find an answer to them. And I tried to answer them. The questions seemed so foolish, so simple, so childish; but no sooner had I taken hold of them than I was convinced, first, that they were neither childish nor silly, but were concerned with the deepest problems of life; and, in the second place, that I could not decide them—could not decide them, however I put my mind upon them.

Before occupying myself with my Samara estate, with the education of my son, with the writing of books, I was bound to know why I did these things. As long as I do not know the reason "why" I cannot do anything. I cannot live. While thinking about the management of my household and estate, which in these days occupied much of my time, suddenly this question came into my head:

"Well and good, I have now six thousand desyatins in the government of Samara, and three hundred horses—what then?"

I was perfectly disconcerted, and knew not what to think. Another time, dwelling on the thought of how I should educate my children, I ask myself *"Why?"* Again, when considering

From Leo Tolsoy, *My Confession* in *Tolstoi's Works,* trans. Nathan H. Dole (New York: T. Y. Crowell Co., 1899), pp. 12–57 (with omissions).

by what means the well-being of the people might best be promoted, I suddenly exclaimed, "But what concern have I with it?" When I thought of the fame which my works were gaining me, I said to myself:

"Well, what if I should be more famous than Gogol, Pushkin, Shakespeare, Molière—than all the writers of the world—well, and what then?" . . .

I could find no reply. Such questions will not wait: they demand an immediate answer; without one it is impossible to live; but answer there was none.

I felt that the ground on which I stood was crumbling, that there was nothing for me to stand on, that what I had been living for was nothing, that I had no reason for living . . .

My life had come to a stop. I was able to breathe, to eat, to drink, to sleep, and I could not help breathing, eating, drinking, sleeping; but there was no real life in me because I had not a single desire, the fulfilment of which I could feel to be reasonable. If I wished for anything, I knew beforehand that, were I to satisfy the wish, or were I not to satisfy it, nothing would come of it. Had a fairy appeared and offered me all I desired, I should not have known what to say. If I had, in moments of excitement, I will not say wishes, but the habits of former wishes, at calmer moments I knew that it was a delusion, that I really wished for nothing. I could not even wish to know the truth, because I guessed in what it consisted.

The truth was, that life was meaningless. Every day of life, every step in it, brought me, as it were, nearer the precipice, and I saw clearly that before me there was nothing but ruin. And to stop was impossible; and it was impossible to shut my eyes so as not to see that there was nothing before me but suffering and actual death, absolute annihilation.

Thus, I, a healthy and a happy man, was brought to feel that I could live no longer,—some irresistible force was dragging me onward to escape from life. I do not mean that I wanted to kill myself.

The force that drew me away from life was stronger, fuller, and more universal than any wish; it was a force like that of my previous attachment to life, only in a contrary direction. With all my force I struggled away from life. The idea of suicide came as naturally to me as formerly that of bettering my life. This thought was so attractive to me that I was compelled to practise upon myself a species of self-deception in order to avoid carrying it out too hastily. I was unwilling to act hastily, only because I wanted to employ all my powers in clearing away the confusion of my thoughts; if I should not clear them away, I could at any time kill myself. And here was I, a man fortunately situated, hiding away a cord, to avoid being tempted to hang myself by it to the transom between the closets of my room, where I undressed alone every evening; and I ceased to go hunting with a gun because it offered too easy a way of getting rid of life. I knew not what I wanted; I was afraid of life; I struggled to get away from it, and yet there *was* something I hoped for from it.

Such was the condition I had to come to, at a time when all the circumstances of my life were pre-eminently happy ones, and when I had not reached my fiftieth year. I had a good, loving, and beloved wife, good children, and a large estate, which, without much trouble on my part, was growing and increasing; I was more than ever respected by my friends and acquaintances; I was praised by strangers, and could lay claim to having made my name famous without much self-deception. Moreover, I was not mad or in an unhealthy mental state; on the contrary, I enjoyed a mental and physical strength which I have seldom found in men of my class and pursuits; I could keep up with a peasant in mowing, and could continue mental labor for eight or ten hours at a stretch, without any evil consequences. And in this state of things it came to this,—that I could not live, and as I feared death I was obliged to employ ruses against myself so as not to put an end to my life.

The mental state in which I then was seemed to me summed up in the following: My life was a foolish and wicked joke played on me by some one. Notwithstanding the fact that I did not recognize a "Some one," who may have created me, this conclusion that some one had wickedly and foolishly made a joke of me in bringing me into the world seemed to me the most natural of all conclusions.

It was this that was terrible! And to get free from this horror of what awaited me; I knew that this horror was more horrible than the position itself, but I could not patiently await the end. However persuasive the argument might be that all the same a blood-vessel in the heart would be ruptured or something would burst and all be over, still I could not patiently await the end. The horror of the darkness was too great to bear, and I longed to free myself from it as speedily as possible by a rope or a pistol ball. This was the feeling that, above all, drew me to think of suicide . . .

"But is it possible that I have overlooked something, that I have failed to understand something," I asked myself; "may it not be that this state of despair is common among men?"

And in every branch of human knowledge I sought an explanation of the questions that tormented me; I sought that explanation painfully and long, not out of mere curiosity; I did not seek it indolently, but painfully, obstinately, day and night; I sought it as a perishing man seeks safety, and I found nothing.

I sought it in all branches of knowledge, and not only did I fail, but, moreover, I convinced myself that all those who had searched like myself had likewise found nothing; and not only had found nothing, but had come, as I had, to the despairing conviction, that the only absolute knowledge man can possess is this,—that life is without meaning.

I sought in all directions, and thanks to a life spent in study, and also to my connections with the learned world, the most accomplished scholars in all the various branches of knowledge were accessible to me, and they did not refuse to open to me all the sources of knowledge both in books and through personal intercourse. I knew all that learning could answer to the question, "What is life?" . . .

I had lost my way in the forest of human knowledge, in the light of the mathematical and experimental sciences which opened out for me clear horizons where there could be no house, and in the darkness of philosophy, plunging me into a greater gloom with every step I took, until I was at last persuaded that there was, and could be, no issue.

When I followed what seemed the bright light of learning, I saw that I had only turned aside from the real question. However alluring and clear were the horizons unfolded before me, however alluring it was to plunge into the infinity of these kinds of knowledge, I saw that the clearer they were the less did I need them, the less did they give me an answer to my question.

Thus my wanderings over the fields of knowledge not only failed to cure me of my despair, but increased it. One branch of knowledge gave no answer at all to the problem of life; another gave a direct answer which confirmed my despair, and showed that the state to which I had come was not the result of my going astray, of any mental disorder, but, on the contrary, it assured me that I was thinking rightly, that I was in agreement with the conclusions of the most powerful intellects among mankind.

I could not be deceived. All is vanity. A misfortune to be born. Death is better than life; life's burden must be got rid of.

My position was terrible. I knew that from the knowledge which reason has given man, I could get nothing but the denial of life, and from faith nothing but the denial of reason, which last was even more impossible than the denial of life. By the knowledge founded on reason it was proved that life is an evil and that men know it to be so, that men may cease to live if they will, but that they have lived and they go on living—I myself lived on, though I had long known that life was meaningless and evil. If I went by faith it resulted that, in order to understand the meaning of life, I should have to abandon reason, the very part of me that required a meaning in life! ...

When I had come to this conclusion, I understood that it was useless to seek an answer to my question from knowledge founded on reason, and that the answer given by this form of knowledge is only an indication that no answer can be obtained till the question is put differently—till the question be made to include the relation between the finite and the infinite. I also understood that, however unreasonable and monstrous the answers given by faith, they have the advantage of bringing into every question the relation of the finite to the infinite, without which there can be no answer.

However I may put the question, How am I to live? the answer is, "By the law of God."

Will anything real and positive come of my life, and what?

Eternal torment, or eternal bliss.

What meaning is there not to be destroyed by death?

Union with an infinite God, paradise.

In this way I was compelled to admit that, besides the reasoning knowledge, which I once thought the only true knowledge, there was in every living man another kind of knowledge, an unreasoning one,—faith,—which gives a possibility of living ...

I was now ready to accept any faith that did not require of me a direct denial of reason, for that would be to act a lie; and I studied Buddhism and Mohammedanism in their books, and especially also Christianity, both in its writings and in the lives of its professors around me.

I naturally turned my attention at first to the believers in my own immediate circle, to learned men, to orthodox divines, to the older monks, to the orthodox divines of a new shade of doctrine, the so-called New Christians, who preach salvation through faith in a Redeemer. I seized upon these believers, and asked them what they believed in, and what for them gave a meaning to life.

No arguments were able to convince me of the sincerity of the faith of these men. Only actions, proving their conception of life to have destroyed the fear of poverty, illness, and death, so strong in myself, could have convinced me, and such actions I could not see among the various believers of our class. Such actions I saw, indeed, among the open infidels of my own class in life, but never among the so-called believers of our class.

I understood, then, that the faith of these men was not the faith which I sought; that it was no faith at all, but only one of the Epicurean consolations of life. I understood that this faith, if it could not really console, could at least soothe the repentant mind of a Solomon on his deathbed; but that it could not serve the enormous majority of mankind, who are born, not to be comforted by the labors of others, but to create a life for themselves. For mankind to live, for it to continue to live and be conscious of the meaning of its life, all these milliards must have another and a true conception of faith. It was not, then, the fact that Solomon, Schopenhauer, and I had not killed ourselves, which convinced me that faith existed, but the fact that these milliards have lived and are now living, carrying along with them on the impulse of their life both Solomon and ourselves.

I began to draw nearer to the believers among the poor, the simple, and the ignorant, the pilgrims, the monks, the raskolniks, and the peasants. The doctrines of these men of the people, like those of the pretended believers of my own class, were Christian. Here also much that was superstitious was mingled with the truths of Christianity, but with this difference, that the superstition of the believers of our class was entirely unnecessary to them, and never influenced their lives beyond serving as a kind of Epicurean distraction; while the superstition of the believing laboring class was so interwoven with their lives that it was impossible to conceive them without it—it was a necessary condition of their living at all. The whole life of the believers of our class was in flat contradiction with their faith, and the whole life of the believers of the people was a confirmation of the meaning of life which their faith gave them.

Thus I began to study the lives and the doctrines of the people, and the more I studied the more I became convinced that a true faith was among them, that their faith was for them a necessary thing, and alone gave them a meaning in life and a possibility of living. In direct opposition to what I saw in our circle—where life without faith was possible, and where not one in a thousand professed himself a believer— amongst the people there was not a single unbeliever in a thousand. In direct opposition to what I saw in our circle—where a whole life is spent in idleness, amusement, and dissatisfaction with life—I saw among the people whole lives passed in heavy labor and unrepining content. In direct opposition to what I saw in our circle —men resisting and indignant with the privations and sufferings of their lot—the people unhesitatingly and unresistingly accepting illness and sorrow, in the quiet and firm conviction that all these must be and could not be otherwise, and that all was for the best. In contradiction to the theory that the less learned we are the less we understand the meaning of life, and see in our sufferings and death but an evil joke, these men of the people live, suffer, and draw near to death, in quiet confidence and oftenest with joy. In contradiction to the fact that an easy death, without terror or despair, is a rare exception in our class, a death which is uneasy, rebellious, and sorrowful is among the people the rarest exception of all.

These people, deprived of all that for us and for Solomon makes the only good in life, and experiencing at the same time the highest happiness, form the great majority of mankind. I looked more widely around me, I studied the lives of the past and contemporary masses of humanity, and I saw that, not two or three, or ten, but hundreds, thousands, millions had so understood the meaning of life that they were able both to live and to die. All these men, infinitely divided by manners, powers of mind, education, and position, all alike in opposition to my ignorance, were well acquainted with the meaning of life and of death, quietly labored, endured privation and suffering, lived and died, and saw in all this, not a vain, but a good thing.

I began to grow attached to these men. The more I learned of their lives, the lives of the living and of the dead of whom I read and heard, the more I liked them, and the easier I felt it so to live. I lived in this way during two years, and then there came a change which had long been preparing in me, and the symptoms of which I had always dimly felt: the life of our circle of rich and learned men, not only became repulsive, but lost all meaning. All our actions, our reasoning, our science and art, all appeared to me in a new light. I understood that it was all child's play, that it was useless to seek a meaning in it. The life of the working classes, of the whole of mankind, of those that create life, appeared to me in its true significance. I understood that this was life itself, and that the meaning given to this life was true, and I accepted it. . . .

When I remembered how these very doctrines had repelled me, how senseless they had seemed when professed by men whose lives were spent in opposition to them, and how these same doctrines had attracted me and seemed reasonable when I saw men living in accordance with them, I understood why I had once rejected them and thought them unmeaning, why I now adopted them and thought them full of meaning. I understood that I had erred, and how I had erred. I had erred, not so much through having thought incorrectly, as through having lived ill. I understood that the truth had been hidden from me, not so much because I had erred in my reasoning, as because I had led the exceptional life of an epicure bent on satisfying the lusts of the flesh. I understood that my question, "What is my life," and the answer, "An evil," were in accordance with the truth of things. The mistake lay in my having applied to life in general an answer which only concerned myself. I had asked what my own life was, and the answer was "An evil and absurdity." Exactly so, my life— a life of indulgence, of sensuality—was an absurdity and an evil, and the answer, "Life is meaningless and evil," therefore, referred only to my own life, and not to human life in general.

I understood the truth which I afterwards found in the Gospel: "That men loved darkness rather than light because their deeds were evil. For every man that doeth evil hateth the light, neither cometh to the light, lest his deeds should be reproved."

I understood that, for the meaning of life to be understood, it was necessary first that life should be something more than evil and meaningless, and afterwards that there should be the light of reason to understand it. I understood why I had so long been circling round this self-evident truth without apprehending it, and that if we would think and speak of the life of mankind, we must think and speak of that life as a whole, and not merely of the life of certain parasites on it.

This truth was always a truth, as $2+2=4$, but I had not accepted it, because, besides acknowledging $2+2=4$, I should have been obliged to acknowledge that I was evil. It was of more importance to me to feel that I was good, more binding on me, than to believe $2+2=4$. I loved good men, I hated myself, and I accepted truth. Now it was all clear to me. . . .

My conviction of the error into which all knowledge based on reason must fall assisted me in freeing myself from the seductions of idle reasoning. The conviction that a knowledge of truth can be gained only by living, led me to doubt the justness of my own life; but I had only to get out of my own particular groove, and look around me, to observe the simple life of the real working-class, to understand that such a life was the only real one. I understood that, if I wished to understand life and its meaning, I must live, not the life of a parasite, but a real life; and, accepting the meaning given to it by the combined lives of those that really form the great human whole, submit it to a close examination.

At the time I am speaking of, the following was my position:

During the whole of that year, when I was asking myself almost every minute whether I should or should not put an end to it all with a cord or a pistol, during the time my mind was occupied with the thoughts which I have described, my heart was oppressed by a tormenting feeling. This feeling I cannot describe otherwise than as a searching after God.

This search after a God was not an act of my reason, but a feeling, and I say this advisedly, because it was opposed to my way of thinking; it came from the heart. It was a feeling of dread, of orphanhood, of isolation amid things all apart from me, and of hope in a help I knew not from whom.

I remember one day in the early springtime I was alone in the forest listening to the woodland sounds, and thinking only of one thing, the same of which I had constantly thought for two years—I was again seeking for a God.

I said to myself:

"Very good, there is no God, there is none with a reality apart from my own imaginings, none as real as my own life—there is none such. Nothing, no miracles can prove there is, for miracles only exist in my own unreasonable imagination."

And then I asked myself:

"But my idea of the God whom I seek, whence comes it?"

And again at this thought arose the joyous

billows of life. All around me seemed to revive, to have a new meaning. My joy, though, did not last long. Reason continued its work:

"The idea of a God is not God. The idea is what goes on within myself; the idea of God is an idea which I am able to rouse in my mind or not as I choose; it is not what I seek, something without which life could not be."

Then again all seemed to die around and within me, and again I wished to kill myself.

After this I began to retrace the process which had gone on within myself, the hundred times repeated discouragement and revival. I remembered that I had lived only when I believed in a God. As it was before, so it was now; I had only to know God, and I lived; I had only to forget Him, not to believe in Him, and I died.

What was this discouragement and revival? I do not live when I lose faith in the existence of a God; I should long ago have killed myself, if I had not had a dim hope of finding Him. I really live only when I am conscious of Him and seek Him. "What more, then, do I seek?" A voice seemed to cry within me, "This is He, He without whom there is no life. To know God and to live are one. God is life."

Live to seek God, and life will not be without God. And stronger than ever rose up life within and around me, and the light that then shone never left me again.

Note

1. Quoted in Stephan Zweig, *The Living Thoughts of Tolstoy* (Philadelphia: David McKay Co., 1939), p. 4.

5 / Beyond Scepticism
James

In developing a philosophy to live by, the American philosopher William James (1841–1910) confronted the most extreme scepticism and found his own way of meeting it. The traditional rationalist attempts to meet sceptical arguments with logical refutations. This approach has never succeeded in reducing the amount of general scepticism, James pointed out, because scepticism is not a purely logical affair but rather, in his words, "the live mental attitude of refusing to conclude."[1] The consistent sceptic is no fool or ignoramus. He is usually shrewd enough not to commit himself to a dogmatic position which asserts that "there is nothing certain" or "I know nothing." Instead, like Montaigne, he may refuse to commit himself to an affirmative position. He may merely sum up his sceptical attitude in a question such as, What do I know? or, Who knows anything? The true sceptic, James realized, simply chooses his scepticism as a habit. It thus becomes "a permanent torpor of the will, renewing itself in detail toward each successive thesis."[2] This torpor can never be dispelled by clear and distinct ideas, dissipated by rational argument, or destroyed by force. The nature of scepticism is such that rational argument cannot logically defeat it.

Is there no way then to deal with scepticism? James asserted that there is, but this way necessitates assuming a new concept of the task of philosophy, a new approach to thinking about the nature of the universe, and a new method of arriving at truth.

First, James urged that we should not expect from philosophy final answers to life's problems, a universal truth to believe in, or an absolutely certain system by which we may explain everything. What we can expect is help in developing "the habit of always seeing an alternative, of not taking the usual for granted, of making conventionalities fluid again, of imagining foreign states of mind."[3] James held that philosophy "means the possession of mental perspective."[4] A study of philosophy can instill in us a flexible, open-minded frame of mind that will not be unduly disturbed by scepticism; in fact, it is vitally imbued with the best sceptical spirit. Rejecting both dogmatism and excessive scepticism, it is free to venture.

In his own philosophical venturing, James developed a new way of thinking about the universe. He called it *radical empiricism*. As *empiricism*, this viewpoint considers beliefs about matters of fact to be simply "hypotheses liable to modification in the course of future experience."[5] It is *radical* because it rejects philosophical monism or the explanation of reality as a complete, self-contained system or absolute unity. Instead, radical empiricism emphasizes the multiplicity of things, the complexity, the manifoldness, even the crudity of the world of real, experienced things. Unlike other philosophic approaches, it can do justice to, not distort, dismiss, or rationalize life as it appears to the ordinary man. Rejecting monistic explanations, it is able to take into account "real possibilities, real indeterminations, real beginnings, real ends, real evil, real crises, catastrophes, and escapes, a real God, and a real moral life just as common sense conceives these things."[6] James's radical empiricism aimed at creating a "mosaic philosophy, a philosophy of plural facts,"[7] which starts with parts rather than with wholes and universals in building up a conception of reality. It is thus basically pluralistic rather than monistic in its orientation.

Finally, James proposed and developed a method of defining and testing the truth of a concept, idea, or proposition that had been formulated by one of his contemporaries, the mathematician and philosopher Charles S. Peirce. This is the method of *pragmatism* (from the Greek *pragma,* practice). "True ideas," according to James's pragmatic method, "are those that we can assimilate, validate, corroborate, and verify." "False ideas," on the other hand, "are those that we cannot."[8] Thus truth is not some static inherent property of an idea. "Truth *happens* to an idea."[9] An idea becomes true if and only if it is made true by the events or consequences by which it is verified. "The true," James wrote, summing up his view, "is only the expedient in the way of our thinking, just as the right is only the expedient in the way of our behaving."[10]

James's will to believe can best be understood against the background of his dynamic conception of philosophy, his radical empiricism, and, above all, his pragmatic approach to the definition and test of truth.

Notes

1. William James, *The Meaning of Truth* (London: Longmans, Green & Co., 1912), p. 180.

2. Ibid.

3. Quoted in Horace M. Kallen, ed., *The Philosophy of William James* (New York: Random House, n.d.), p. 58.

4. Ibid.

5. Ibid., p. 60.

6. Ibid., p. 61.

7. William James, *Essays in Radical Empiricism* (London: Longmans, Green & Co., 1912), pp. 41–42).

8. James, *The Meaning of Truth,* v–viii.

9. Ibid.

10. Ibid., p. 166.

The Will to Believe

In the recently published Life by Leslie Stephen of his brother, Fitz-James, there is an account of a school to which the latter went when he was a boy. The teacher, a certain Mr. Guest, used to converse with his pupils in this wise: "Gurney, what is the difference between justification and sanctification?—Stephen, prove the omnipotence of God!" etc. In the midst of our Harvard free-thinking and indifference we are prone to imagine that here at your good old orthodox College conversation continues to be somewhat upon this order; and to show you that we at Harvard have not lost all interest in these vital subjects, I have brought with me tonight something like a sermon on justification by faith to read to you,—I mean an essay in justification *of* faith, a defense of our right to adopt a believing attitude in religious matters, in spite of the fact that our merely logical intellect may not have been coerced. "The Will to Believe," accordingly, is the title of my paper.

I have long defended to my own students the lawfulness of voluntary adopted faith; but as soon as they have got well imbued with the logical spirit, they have as a rule refused to admit my contention to be lawful philosophically, even though in point of fact they were personally at the time chock-full of some faith or other themselves. I am all the while, however, so profoundly convinced that my own position is correct, that your invitation has seemed to me a

From William James, *The Will to Believe and Other Essays in Popular Philosophy* (London: Longmans, Green & Co., 1897), pp. 1–31 (with omissions).

good occasion to make my statements more clear. Perhaps your minds will be more open than those with which I have hitherto had to deal. I will be as little technical as I can, though I must begin by setting up some technical distinctions that will help us in the end. . . .

Let us give the name of *hypothesis* to anything that may be proposed to our belief; and just as the electricians speak of live and dead wires, let us speak of any hypothesis as either *live* or *dead*. A live hypothesis is one which appeals as a real possibility to him to whom it is proposed. If I ask you to believe in the Mahdi, the notion makes no electric connection with your nature— it refuses to scintillate with any credibility at all. As an hypothesis it is completely dead. To an Arab, however (even if he be not one of the Mahdi's followers), the hypothesis is among the mind's possibilities: it is alive. This shows that deadness and liveness in an hypothesis are not intrinsic properties, but relations to the individual thinker. They are measured by his willingness to act. The maximum of liveness in an hypothesis means willingness to act irrevocably. Practically, that means belief; but there is some believing tendency wherever there is willingness to act at all.

Next, let us call the decision between two hypotheses an *option*. Options may be of several kinds. They may be—1. *living* or *dead;* 2. *forced* or *avoidable;* 3. *momentous* or *trivial;* and for our purposes we may call an option a *genuine* option when it is of the forced, living, and momentous kind.

1. A living option is one in which both

hypotheses are live ones. If I say to you: "Be a theosophist or be a Mohammedan," it is probably a dead option, because for you neither hypothesis is likely to be alive. But if I say: "Be an agnostic or be a Christian," it is otherwise: trained as you are, each hypothesis makes some appeal, however small, to your belief.

2. Next, if I say to you: "Choose between going out with your umbrella or without it," I do not offer you a geninue option, for it is not forced. You can easily avoid it by not going out at all. Similarly, if I say, "Either love me or hate me," "Either call my theory true or call it false," your option is avoidable. You may remain indifferent to me, neither loving nor hating, and you may decline to offer any judgment as to my theory. But if I say, "Either accept this truth or go without it," I put on you a forced option, for there is no standing place outside of the alternative. Every dilemma based on a complete logical disjunction, with no possibility of not choosing, is an option of this forced kind.

3. Finally, if I were Dr. Nansen and proposed to you to join my North Pole expedition, your option would be momentous; for this would probably be your only similar opportunity, and your choice now would either exclude you from the North Pole sort of immortality altogether or put at least the chance of it into your hands. He who refuses to embrace a unique opportunity loses the prize as surely as if he tried and failed. *Per contra,* the option is trivial when the opportunity is not unique, when the stake is insignificant, or when the decision is reversible if it later prove unwise. Such trivial options abound in the scientific life. A chemist finds an hypothesis live enough to spend a year in its verification: he believes in it to that extent. But if his experiments prove inconclusive either way, he is quit for his loss of time, no vital harm being done.

It will facilitate our discussion if we keep all these distinctions in mind. . . .

In Pascal's *Thoughts* there is a celebrated passage known in literature as Pascal's wager. In it he tries to force us into Christianity by reasoning as if our concern with truth resembled our concern with the stakes in a game of chance. Translated freely his words are these: You must either believe or not believe that God is—which will you do? Your human reason cannot say. A game is going on between you and the nature of things which at the day of judgment will bring out either heads or tails. Weigh what your gains and your losses would be if you should stake all you have on heads, or God's existence: if you win in such case, you gain eternal beatitude; if you lose, you lose nothing at all. If there were an infinity of changes, and only one for God in this wager, still you ought to stake your all on God; for though you surely risk a finite loss by this procedure, any finite loss is reasonable, even a certain one is reasonable, if there is but the possibility of infinite gain. Go, then, and take holy water, and have masses said; belief will come and stupefy your scruples,—*Cela vous fera croire et vous abêtira.* Why should you not? At bottom, what have you to lose? . . .

The thesis I defend is, briefly stated, this: *Our passional nature not only lawfully may, but must, decide an option between propositions, whenever it is a genuine option that cannot by its nature be decided on intellectual grounds; for to say, under such circumstances, "Do not decide, but leave the question open," is itself a passional decision,—just like deciding yes or no,—and is attended with the same risk of losing the truth.* The thesis thus abstractly expressed will, I trust, soon become quite clear. . . .

And now, after all this introduction, let us go straight at our question. I have said, and now repeat it, that not only as a matter of fact do we find our passional nature influencing us in our opinions, but that there are some options between opinions in which this influence must be regarded both as an inevitable and as a lawful determinant of our choice.

I fear here that some of you my hearers will begin to scent danger, and lend an inhospitable ear. Two first steps of passion you have indeed had to admit as necessary,—we must think so as to avoid dupery, and we must think so as to gain truth; but the surest path to those ideal consummations, you will probably consider, is from now onwards to take no further passional step.

Well, of course, I agree as far as the facts will allow. Wherever the option between losing truth and gaining it is not momentous, we can throw the chance of *gaining truth* away, and at any rate save ourselves from any chance of *believing falsehood,* by not making up our minds at all till objective evidence has come. In scientific questions, this is almost always the case; and even in human affairs in general, the need of acting is seldom so urgent that a false belief to act on is better than no belief at all. Law courts, indeed, have to decide on the best evidence attainable for the moment, because a judge's duty is to make law as well as to ascertain it, and (as a learned judge once said to me) few cases are worth spending much time over: the great thing is to have them decided on *any* acceptable principle, and got out of the way. But in our dealings with objective nature we obviously are recorders, not makers, of the truth; and decisions for the mere sake of deciding promptly and getting on to the next business would be wholly out of place. Throughout the breadth of physical nature facts are what they are quite independently of us, and seldom is there any such hurry about them that the risks of being duped by believing a premature theory need be faced. The questions here are always trivial options, the hypotheses are hardly living (or any rate not living for us spectators), the choice between believing truth or falsehood is seldom forced. The attitude of sceptical balance is therefore the absolutely wise one if we would escape mistakes. What difference, indeed, does it make to most of us whether we have or have not a theory of the Röntgen rays, whether we believe or not in mind-stuff, or have a conviction about the causality of conscious states? It makes no difference. Such options are not forced on us. On every account it is better not to make them, but still keep weighing reasons *pro et contra* with an indifferent hand.

I speak, of course, here of the purely judging mind. For purposes of discovery such indifference is to be less highly recommended, and science would be far less advanced than she is if the passionate desires of individuals to get their own faiths confirmed had been kept out of the game. See for example the sagacity which Spencer and Weismann now display. On the other hand, if you want an absolute duffer in an investigation, you must, after all, take the man who has no interest whatever in its results: he is the warranted incapable, the positive fool. The most useful investigator, because the most sensitive observer, is always he whose eager interest in one side of the question is balanced by an equally keen nervousness lest he become deceived. Science has organized this nervousness into a regular *technique,* her so-called method of verification; and she has fallen so deeply in love with the method that one may even say she has ceased to care for truth by itself at all. It is only truth as technically verified that interests her. The truth of truths might come in merely affirmative form, and she would decline to touch it. Such truth as that, she might repeat with Clifford, would be stolen in defiance of her duty to mankind. Human passions, however, are stronger than technical rules. *Le coeur a ses raisons,* as Pascal says, *que la raison ne connait pas;* and however indifferent to all but the bare rules of the game the umpire, the abstract intellect, may be, the concrete players who furnish him the materials to judge of are usually, each one of them, in love with some pet 'live hypothesis' of his own. Let us agree, however, that wherever there is no forced option, the dispassionately judicial intellect with no pet hypothesis, saving us, as it does, from dupery at any rate, ought to be our ideal.

The question next arises: Are there not somewhere forced options in our speculative questions, and can we (as men who may be interested at least as much in positively gaining truth as in merely escaping dupery) always wait with impunity till the coercive evidence shall have arrived? It seems *a priori* improbable that the truth should be so nicely adjusted to our needs and powers as that. In the great boarding-house of nature, the cakes and the butter and the syrup seldom come out so even and leave the plates so clean. Indeed, we should view them with scientific suspicion if they did. . . .

Moral questions immediately present themselves as questions whose solution cannot wait for sensible proof. A moral question is a question not of what sensibly exists, but of what is good, or would be good if it did exist. Science can tell us what exists; but to compare the *worths,* both of what exists and of what does not exist, we must consult not science, but what Pascal calls our heart. Science herself consults her heart when she lays it down that the infinite ascertainment of fact and correction of false beliefs are the supreme goods for man. Challenge the statement, and science can only repeat it oracularly, or else prove it by showing that such ascertainment and correction bring man all sorts of other goods which man's heart in turn declares. The question of having moral beliefs at all or not having them is decided by our will. Are our moral preferences true or false, or are they only odd biological phenomena, making things good or bad for *us,* but in themselves indifferent? How can your pure intellect decide? If your heart does not *want* a world of moral reality, your head will assuredly never make you believe in one. Mephistophelian scepticism, indeed, will satisfy the head's play-instincts much better than any rigorous idealism can. Some men (even at the student age) are so naturally cool-hearted that the moralistic hypothesis never has for them any pungent life, and in their supercilious presence the hot young moralist always feels strangely ill at ease. The appearance of

knowingness is on their side, of naïveté and gullibility on his. Yet, in the inarticulate heart of him, he clings to it that he is not a dupe, and that there is a realm in which (as Emerson says) all their wit and intellectual superiority is no better than the cunning of a fox. Moral scepticism can no more be refuted or proved by logic than intellectual scepticism can. When we stick to it that there *is* truth (be it of either kind), we do so with our whole nature, and resolve to stand or fall by the results. The sceptic with his whole nature adopts the doubting attitude; but which of us is the wiser, Omniscience only knows.

Turn now from these wide questions of good to a certain class of questions of fact, questions concerning personal relations, states of mind between one man and another. *Do you like me or not?*—for example. Whether you do or not depends, in countless instances, on whether I meet you half-way, am willing to assume that you must like me, and show you trust and expectation. The previous faith on my part in your liking's existence is in such cases what makes your liking come. But if I stand aloof, and refuse to budge an inch until I have objective evidence, until you shall have done something apt, as the absolutists say, *ad extorquendum assensum meum,* ten to one your liking never comes. How many women's hearts are vanquished by the mere sanguine insistence of some man that they *must* love him! He will not consent to the hypothesis that they cannot. The desire for a certain kind of truth here brings about that special truth's existence; and so it is in innumerable cases of other sorts. Who gains promotions, boons, appointments, but the man in whose life they are seen to play the part of live hypotheses, who discounts them, sacrifices other things for their sake before they have come, and takes risks for them in advance? His faith acts on the powers above him as a claim, and creates its own verification.

A social organism of any sort whatever, large or small, is what it is because each member proceeds to his own duty with a trust that the other members will simultaneously do theirs. Wherever a desired result is achieved by the co-operation of many independent persons, its existence as a fact is a pure consequence of the precursive faith in one another of those immediately concerned. A Government, an army, a commercial system, a ship, a college, an athletic team, all exist on this condition, without which not only is nothing achieved, but nothing is even attempted. A whole train of passengers (individually brave enough) will be looted by a few highwaymen, simply because the latter can count on one another, while each passenger fears that if he makes a movement of resistance, he will be shot before any one else backs him up. If we believed that the whole car-full would rise at once with us, we should each severally rise, and train-robbing would never even be attempted. There are, then, cases where a fact cannot come at all unless a preliminary faith exists in its coming. *And where faith in a fact can help create the fact,* that would be an insane logic which should say that faith running ahead of scientific evidence is the 'lowest kind of immorality' into which a thinking being can fall. Yet such is the logic by which our scientific absolutists pretend to regulate our lives! ...

In truths dependent on our personal action, then, faith based on desire is certainly a lawful and possibly an indispensable thing.

But now, it will be said, these are all childish human cases, and have nothing to do with great cosmical matters, like the question of religious faith. Let us then pass on to that. Religions differ so much in their accidents that in discussing the religious question we must make it very generic and broad. What then do we now mean by the religious hypothesis? Science says things are; morality says some things are better than other things; and religion says essentially two things.

First, she says that the best things are the more eternal things, the overlapping things, the things

in the universe that throw the last stone, so to speak, and say the final word. "Perfection is eternal,"—this phrase of Charles Secrétan seems a good way of putting this first affirmation of religion, an affirmation which obviously cannot yet be verified scientifically at all.

The second affirmation of religion is that we are better off even now if we believe her first affirmation to be true.

Now, let us consider what the logical elements of this situation are *in case the religious hypothesis in both its branches be really true.* (Of course, we must admit that possibility at the outset. If we are to discuss the question at all, it must involve a living option. If for any of you religion be a hypothesis that cannot, by any living possibility be true, then you need go no farther. I speak to the 'saving remnant' alone.) So proceeding, we see, first, that religion offers itself as a *momentous* option. We are supposed to gain, even now, by our belief, and to lose by our non-belief, a certain vital good. Secondly, religion is a *forced* option, so far as that good goes. We cannot escape the issue by remaining sceptical and waiting for more light, because, although we do avoid error in that way *if religion be untrue,* we lose the good, *if it be true,* just as certainly as if we positively chose to disbelieve. It is as if a man should hesitate indefinitely to ask a certain woman to marry him because he was not perfectly sure that she would prove an angel after he brought her home. Would he not cut himself off from that particular angel-possibility as decisively as if he went and married some one else? Scepticism, then, is not avoidance of option; it is option of a certain particular kind of risk. *Better risk loss of truth than chance of error,*—that is your faith-vetoer's exact position. He is actively playing his stake as much as the believer is; he is backing the field against the religious hypothesis, just as the believer is backing the religious hypothesis against the field. To preach scepticism to us as a duty until 'sufficient evidence' for religion be found, is tantamount therefore to telling us, when in presence of the religious hypothesis, that to yield to our fear of its being error is wiser and better than to yield to our hope that it may be true. It is not intellect against all passions, then; it is only intellect with one passion laying down its law. And by what, forsooth, is the supreme wisdom of this passion warranted? Dupery for dupery, what proof is there that dupery through hope is so much worse than dupery through fear? I, for one, can see no proof; and I simply refuse obedience to the scientist's command to imitate his kind of option, in a case where my own stake is important enough to give me the right to choose my own form of risk. If religion be true and the evidence for it be still insufficient, I do not wish, by putting your extinguisher upon my nature (which feels to me as if it had after all some business in this matter), to forfeit my sole chance in life of getting upon the winning side,— that chance depending, of course, on my willingness to run the risk of acting as if my passional need of taking the world religiously might be prophetic and right.

All this is on the supposition that it really may be prophetic and right, and that, even to us who are discussing the matter, religion is a live hypothesis which may be true. Now, to most of us religion comes in a still further way that makes a veto on our active faith even more illogical. The more perfect and more eternal aspect of the universe is represented in our religions as having personal form. The universe is no longer a mere *It* to us, but a *Thou,* if we are religious; and any relation that may be possible from person to person might be possible here. For instance, although in one sense we are passive portions of the universe, in another we show a curious autonomy, as if we were small active centers on our own account. We feel, too, as if the appeal of religion to us were made to our own active good-will, as if evidence might be forever withheld from us unless we met the hypothesis half-way. To take a trivial illustration: just as a man who in a company of gentlemen made no advances, asked a warrant for

every concession, and believed no one's word without proof, would cut himself off by such churlishness from all the social rewards that a more trusting spirit would earn,—so here, one who should shut himself up in snarling logicality and try to make the gods extort his recognition willy-nilly, or not get it at all, might cut himself off forever from his only opportunity of making the gods' acquaintance. This feeling, forced on us we know not whence, that by obstinately believing that there are gods (although not to do so would be so easy both for our logic and our life) we are doing the universe the deepest service we can, seems part of the living essence of the religious hypothesis. If the hypothesis *were* true in all its parts, including this one, then pure intellectualism, with its veto on our making willing advance, would be an absurdity; and some participation of our sympathetic nature would be logically required. I, therefore, for one, cannot see my way to accepting the agnostic rules for truth-seeking, or wilfully agree to keep my willing nature out of the game. I cannot do so for this plain reason, that *a rule of thinking which would absolutely prevent me from acknowledging certain kinds of truth if those kinds of truth were really there, would be an irrational rule.* That for me is the long and short of the formal logic of the situation, no matter what the kinds of truth might materially be.

I confess I do not see how this logic can be escaped. But sad experience makes me fear that some of you may still shrink from radically saying with me, *in abstracto,* that we have the right to believe at our own risk any hypothesis that is live enough to tempt our will. I suspect, however, that if this is so, it is because you have got away from the abstract logical point of view altogether, and are thinking (perhaps without realizing it) of some particular religious hypothesis which for you is dead. The freedom to 'believe what we will' you apply to the case of some patent superstition; and the faith you think of is the faith defined by the schoolboy when he said, "Faith is when you believe something that you know ain't true." I can only repeat that this is misapprehension. *In concreto,* the freedom to believe can only cover living options which the intellect of the individual cannot by itself resolve; and living options never seem absurdities to him who has them to consider. When I look at the religious question as it really puts itself to concrete men, and when I think of all the possibilities which both practically and theoretically it involves, then this command that we shall put a stopper on our heart, instincts, and courage, and *wait*—acting of course meanwhile more or less as if religion were *not* true—till* doomsday, or till such time as our intellect and senses working together may have raked in evidence enough, —this command, I say, seems to me the queerest idol ever manufactured in the philosophic cave. Were we scholastic absolutists, there might be more excuse. If we had an infallible intellect with its objective certitudes, we might feel ourselves disloyal to such a perfect organ of knowledge in not trusting to it exclusively, in not waiting for its releasing word. But if we are empiricists, if we believe that no bell in us tolls to let us know for certain when truth is in our grasp, then it seems a piece of idle fantasticality to preach so solemnly our duty of waiting for the bell. Indeed we *may* wait if we will,—I hope you do not think that I am denying that,—but if we do so, we do so at our peril as much as if we believed. In either case we *act,* taking our

*Since belief is measured by action, he who forbids us to believe religion to be true, necessarily also forbids us to act as we should if we did believe it to be true. The whole defence of religious faith hinges upon action. If the action required or inspired by the religious hypothesis is in no way different from that dictated by the naturalistic hypothesis, then religious faith is a pure superfluity, better pruned away, and controversy about its legitimacy is a piece of idle trifling, unworthy of serious minds. I myself believe, of course, that the religious hypothesis gives to the world an expression whch specifically determines our reactions, and makes them in a large part unlike what they might be on a purely naturalistic scheme of belief.

life in our hands. No one of us ought to issue vetoes to the other, nor should we bandy words of abuse. We ought, on the contrary, delicately and profoundly to respect one another's mental freedom: then only shall we bring about the intellectual republic; then only shall we have that spirit of inner tolerance without which all our outer tolerance is soulless, and which is empiricism's glory; then only shall we live and let live, in speculative as well as in practical things.

I began by a reference to Fitz-James Stephen; let me end by a quotation from him. "What do you think of yourself? What do you think of the world? . . . These are questions with which all must deal as it seems good to them. They are riddles of the Sphinx, and in some way or other we must deal with them. . . . In all important transactions of life we have to take a leap in the dark. . . . If we decide to leave the riddles unanswered, that is a choice; if we waver in our answer, that, too, is a choice: but whatever choice we make, we make it at our peril. If a man chooses to turn his back altogether on God and the future, no one can prevent him; no one can show beyond reasonable doubt that he is mistaken. If a man thinks otherwise and acts as he thinks, I do not see that any one can prove that *he* is mistaken. Each must act as he thinks best; and if he is wrong, so much the worse for him. We stand on a mountain pass in the midst of whirling snow and blinding mist, through which we get glimpses now and then of paths which may be deceptive. If we stand still we shall be frozen to death. If we take the wrong road we shall be dashed to pieces. We do not certainly know whether there is any right one. What must we do? 'Be strong and of a good courage.' Act for the best, hope for the best, and take what comes. . . . If death ends all, we cannot meet death better."*

*Fitz-James Stephen, *Liberty, Equality, Fraternity,* 2d ed. (London, 1874), p. 353.

Afterword   /   The Will to Doubt

Examining the doubts that the various thinkers in this part confronted in order to reach commitments to reliable beliefs, what can we conclude? What have these thinkers accomplished? Of what value is scepticism?

Let us begin again with Socrates who taught by means of his actions and questions. It is difficult to arrive at a set of doctrines that he expounded and accepted. Not that he lacked convictions; a man who was willing to die rather than to recant beliefs or relinquish practices certainly was profoundly committed to beliefs. But since Socrates never set them down in writing, we have limited and varying reports as to what he said, and the passage of time has elevated him, like Jesus and the Buddha, to such a high level of significance that he is enshrouded in mystery and myth. But the Socrates of Xenophon and of Plato is still very much alive and perennially awakens intense curiosity in the minds of readers, testifying to the value of the examined life. Socrates' scepticism is provocative and evocative. He provokes us to think about what we have always taken for granted, and he evokes in us the desire to achieve more rationally justifiable beliefs.

Like Socrates and Jesus, Tolstoy asks us to examine our beliefs and to consider our ultimate commitments. But as a follower of Jesus rather than of Socrates and Descartes, Tolstoy would object to the rationalism of the earlier thinkers. Thinking, for him, is not an abstract process that we can do according to strictly logical laws and arrive at purely cognative answers. Thinking is adjoined with feeling; we know the truth of propositions intuitively, not just abstractly. Faith more than reason determines whether or not a life is worth living. The important thing, for Tolstoy, is to be commited to one's beliefs in an existential sense, to be willing to live and die by one's authentic convictions. Tolstoy would not disagree with Socrates that examining life is of great importance, but to remain content with scepticism would be, from Tolstoy's point of view, intolerable, and even immoral.

Descartes was careful to see that his brand of scepticism was chastely moral. Historically, his approach marked a move away from scholasticism and an impetus to the reawakening of the true Socratic spirit in modern philosophy. Descartes, with his rational, methodical approach to solving problems and his concern with proofs of God and arguments for the immortality of the soul, remained in many respects a scholastic. Yet his willingness to venture, his promotion of the method of doubt, and his arrival at his central certainty, the intuited truth that "I think, therefore I am," remain landmarks for every explorer of the fields of philosophy as well as stimulants to further reflection. Descartes may, as one student put it, have "copped out when it came to God," but as long as people are concerned with the questions of what can I know for sure, who am I, and what am I, Descartes will continue to speak to the human condition.

William James's concept of "the will to believe," like Pascal's famous wager, has frequently been criticized. Bertrand Russell said that if he were God and knew that a person had simply willed to believe in him to be on the safe side, he would unhesitatingly condemn such a person to Hell and save an honest but unbelieving atheist. Although James's argument may not be convincing, can we reject it so cavalierly? He is careful to set down the limiting conditions under which he considers it justifiable to will to believe. He certainly isn't advocating believing or disbelieving whatever one wants despite evidence to the contrary. James advocates intelligent, responsible commitment, not blind faith or deaf doubt.

James's purpose, unlike Hume's, is not to advocate scepticism but an alternative to it. Hume, however, would support the sceptical and agnostic thinkers W. K. Clifford and T. H. Huxley, to whom James was partly responding. He could well have written these lines by Clifford:

> It is wrong always, everywhere, and for any one, to believe anything upon insufficient evidence. Habitual want of care about what I believe leads to habitual want of care in others about the truth of what is told to me. The credulous man is father to the liar and the cheat.[1]

The fascination in reading Hume derives not so much from reaching or accepting his conclusions as in following him while he formulates problems, proceeds to solve them by demolishing previous answers to them, and, in the process, clarifies ideas. Perhaps this is why of all the great philosophers of the past, David Hume is probably held in highest esteem by analytic philosophers of today.

Scepticism has aroused violent controversy as well as high praise. Doubt has often been held to be dangerous, self-defeating, immoral, and illegal. Men have been put to death not just because of their beliefs, but also because of their doubts. Yet, as George Santayana remarked, while scepticism may be more of an exercise and discipline to purify the mind of prejudice rather than a life and an end in itself, it is "the chastity of the intellect which should not too quickly be surrendered."[2] "The will to doubt," to use Bertrand Russell's phrase, needs at times to be as much exerted and appreciated as "the will to believe." It may be as essential to our sanity and survival sometimes to say, "Don't believe, doubt," as it is sometimes essential to our sanity and survival to say, "Don't doubt, believe." It takes a philosopher to know when to say one or the other.

Notes

1. Quoted in Alburey Castell, *An Introduction to Modern Philosophy,* 2d. ed., (New York: Macmillan, 1963), p. 64.
2. George Santayana, *Scepticism and Animal Faith* (New York: Charles Scribner's Sons, 1923), p. 69.

Related Reading

(Works marked * are available in paperbound editions)

Ammerman, Robert R. and Marcus G. Singer, eds. *Belief, Knowledge and Truth.* New York: Scribner, 1970.

*Ayer, A. J. *Language, Truth, and Logic,* 2d rev. ed. London: Gollancz, 1946.

*Camus, Albert. *The Myth of Sisyphus and Other Essays,* trans. Justin O'Brien. New York: Vintage Books, 1955.

Cohen, Morris R. *Reason and Nature,* 2d ed. New York: Free Press, 1964.

*Douglas, Norman. *South Wind.* New York: Bantam Books, 1946.

*Evans, Bergen. *The Natural History of Nonsense.* New York: Vintage, 1958.

*Gardner, Martin. *Fads and Fallacies in the Name of Science,* 2d ed. New York: Dover, 1957.

*————. *Great Essays in Science.* New York: Pocket Books, 1957.

*Hume, David. *Dialogues Concerning Natural Religion,* ed. Norman Kemp Smith, 2d ed. London: Thomas Nelson and Sons, 1947.

Huxley, Thomas Henry. *Selections from the Essays of T. H. Huxley,* ed. Alburey Castell. New York: Appleton, 1948.

*James, William. *Pragmatism.* New York: Longmans, Green, 1907.

*Kaplan, Abraham. *The New World of Philosophy.* New York: Collier Books, 1962.

*Kaufman, Walter. *Critique of Religion and Philosophy.* New York: Harper and Brothers, 1958.

Kemp Smith, Norman. *The Philosophy of David Hume.* London: Macmillan and Co., 1941.

Lavrin, Janko. *Tolstoy: An Approach.* New York: Macmillan, 1946.

Montague, William P. *The Ways of Knowing.* New York: Macmillan, 1925.

Montaigne. *Complete Essays.* New York: Modern Library, n. d.

Novak, Michael. *The Experience of Nothingness.* New York: Harper and Row, 1970.

*Plato. *The Dialogues of Plato,* trans. Benjamin Jowett, 5 vols. New York: Oxford University Press, 1892.

Russell, Bertrand. *Sceptical Essays.* New York: W. W. Norton and Co., 1928.

———. *The Scientific Outlook.* New York: W. W. Norton and Co., 1962.

———. *The Will to Doubt.* New York: Philosophical Library, 1958.

Santayana, George. *Scepticism and Animal Faith, Introduction to a System of Philosophy.* New York: Charles Scribner's Sons, 1923.

*Simmons, Ernest J. *Leo Tolstoy.* Boston: Little Brown and Co., 1946.

Sprague, Elmer. *What Is Philosophy?* New York: Oxford University Press, 1951.

*Stebbing, L. S. *Thinking to Some Purpose.* London: Penguin Books, 1948.

*Taylor, A. E. *Socrates: The Man and His Thought.* New York: Doubleday and Co., 1954.

*Voltaire. *Candide,* trans. Tobias Smollett. New York: Washington Square Press, 1966.

PART THREE

Confrontation with Authority:
Commitment to Freedom

. . . That this nation, under God, shall have a new birth of freedom.

Abraham Lincoln

Eternal vigilance is the price of liberty.

J. P. Curran

And ye shall know the truth and the truth shall make you free.

Jesus Christ

I would rather sit on a pumpkin, and have it all to myself, than to be crowded on a velvet cushion.

Henry David Thoreau

In a free country there is much clamour, with little suffering; in a despotic state there is little complaint, with much grievance.

Lazare Carnot

O liberty! How many crimes are committed in thy name!

Mme. Jeanne Roland

Liberty is the only thing you cannot have unless you are willing to give it to others.

William Allen White

No amount of political freedom will satisfy the hungry masses.

Lenin

The people never give up their liberties but under some delusion.

Edmund Burke

Give me the liberty to know, to think, to believe, and to utter freely according to conscience, above all other liberties.

John Milton

Those who give up essential liberty to purchase a little temporary safety deserve neither liberty nor safety.

Benjamin Franklin

Since the general civilization of mankind I believe there are more instances of the abridgement of the freedom of the people by gradual and silent encroachments of those in power than by violent and sudden usurpations.

James Madison

Introduction / What Price Freedom?

Aldous Huxley's *Brave New World* and George Orwell's *1984* are two very frightening and thought-provoking visions of the world of the future. The first envisages a society dedicated to the ideals of "Community, Identity, and Stability." Everyone in this society has been made completely happy through advances in science and technology. All suffering has been eliminated. People are no longer born but hatched in test tubes. Sexual promiscuity has replaced romantic love; orgies have taken the place of religion. A wonder drug *soma* keeps everyone high and contented. The world is at peace under a totalitarian state administered by twelve world controllers. Freedom, individuality, and dignity have disappeared.

In the second work, *1984,* totalitarianism is again envisaged as triumphant. Wars are still pursued, however, as instruments of policy. The proliferation of propaganda and the imposition of rigid censorship have made possible a "double-think" that conceives of war as peace, freedom as slavery, love as hate, and poverty as plenty. Personal relations are severely restricted, actions and thoughts of every citizen are monitored by Big Brother and his henchmen, and any lack of conformity is prohibited and punished. Here, too, freedom, individualism, and dignity have disappeared and, as in *Brave New World,* a hero is destroyed when he dares to reassert them. Orwell joins Huxley in warning man that if certain trends in the present go unchecked he may in the near future find himself in a collectivized utopia and in a new form of Hell.

Such a philosopher as Socrates would also be revolted by the societies projected by Huxley and Orwell and undoubtedly would do his best to subvert them. Surely he would reject the easy hedonism of *Brave New World* that would divert persons away from the difficult but more rewarding path of philosophical searching. Since Brave New Worlders do not examine their drug-controlled lives, they would not be living lives that are worthwhile according to Socratic doctrine. Socrates, like Huxley's hero John Savage, would definitely opt out of the hedonistic paradise if he were unable to pursue his philosophical mission, just as, in a democracy, he chose to die rather than to recant his beliefs or relinquish what was to him a divinely inspired mission. Certainly he would have gotten into trouble quickly in a society such as Orwell depicted in *1984*. Loving truth, freedom, and goodness, Socrates would have renounced and opposed the ignorance that masqueraded as knowledge, the crushing authoritarianism, and the malevolence that permeated the entire society.

Socrates' *Apology*, like Huxley's and Orwell's dystopias, can be read as a powerful indictment of all institutions and persons that would, in theory or in fact, curtail human freedom and stymie individual spontaneity and self-actualization. But what is freedom? Are there no limits or conditions imposed upon the individual? Can we even conceive of freedom without restrictions? If not, what are the restrictions and who—what authority—is to have the right to impose them?

Reflecting on what Henry David Thoreau has to say about freedom may help us to answer such fundamental questions. "Simplify" was to Thoreau a moral maxim. He would most likely observe that today we are so lost in complexities we have lost sight of the simplicities; in reading the Times, as he would say, we miss the Eternities. Thoreau asserts and defends the primacy of the individual. State authority is, to him, artificial; personal freedom is natural. Only individuals create values; collective entities create nothing. That government is best, according to his anarchistic view, that governs least or not at all.

In his quest for simplicity, Thoreau, from John Stuart Mill's viewpoint, could be accused of oversimplifying. Mill, too, appreciated the values of individuality and personal initiative but, as a socialist and a utilitarian, he recognized that these values could only be nurtured and protected under a government that had as its aim the realization of the greatest happiness of the greatest number. Mill, therefore, tried to strike a balance between individualism and collectivism, with the scales, at least in his "Essay on Liberty," tipped toward individualism where, he believed, freedom rested.

In his strong desire to defend and preserve freedom, Mill did not sufficiently emphasize a consideration that Feodor Dostoyevsky and later Erich Fromm stressed: some people don't want to be free. Dostoyevsky's magnificent vision of the Grand Inquisitor, with which this part opens, argues that humanity apparently cannot rise above its craving, irrational though it may be, for miracle, authority, and mystery. Fromm, witnessing the rise and temporary triumph of totalitarian regimes in Europe before the Second World War, analyzed the motives and behavior of the supporters of absolute authoritarianism. These people willingly relinquished their freedom in order to overcome their anxieties and to gain a sense of identity and power. Later existentialists, such as Jean Paul Sartre, also recognized freedom as anxiety-provoking. Like Fromm, they stressed the importance of facing and using constructively the freedom that one has, both within oneself and in social and political relations with others, instead of cowardly fleeing from it.

Fortunately, *Brave New World* and *1984* are still only fictions, but for some of the following thinkers they are taking on the qualities of prophecy and nightmare. As more and more people grow tired or fearful of their freedom of choice, are they becoming more willing to exchange it for the promise of security, certainty, and comfort held out by advocates of political panaceas or technological control?

6 / Flight from Freedom
Dostoyevsky

Through the characters in his fiction, the Russian novelist Feodor Dostoyevsky (1821—1881) portrays with remarkable clarity and power many of the basic conflicts within the human psyche. He depicts those that arise between passion and reason, raw impulse and ideal aspiration, self-hatred and self-love, desire to withdraw from others and need to unite with them. Believing that these and other such conflicts are inherent in the nature of man, Dostoyevsky thinks that they must be taken into account in any discussion of freedom.

The hero or anti-hero of *Notes from Underground* (1864) exemplifies man's complexity and self-contradiction. He points out that man is more than a mere rational animal. He also possesses some irrational and anti-rational elements that he must give vent to and satisfy in order to fulfill himself. Reason analyzes, dissects, reflects, and appraises. These functions are useful and necessary in solving many human problems, but reason often fails to take into account those aspects of human nature which are self-contradictory and mysterious. Freedom entails more than willing what is rational and doing it; it also entails willing and doing the irrational. For what purpose would a man voluntarily choose not to follow reason? For the sake of passion, from depravity, or simply for no purpose at all, says the Underground man. The human psyche does not feel obliged to obey the laws of thought, such as the law of noncontradiction. Unconscious impulses, which well up from the depths of a human being, are nonrational but nonetheless real. Dostoyevsky would not agree with Socrates' view that no man intentionally does wrong. More often than not man sees the right and refuses to choose it; instead, he willfully goes toward the evil, the self-destructive, even the diabolical.

Reflection on the nature of man and on what it means to be human leads Dostoyevsky's hero (and Dostoyevsky himself) to stress, against the views of all optimists, rationalists, and scientific-minded utopian socialists, the unfathomed, unexplored, murky depths of human nature. Because of his inherent nature, man desires more than sheer enjoyment, well-being, perfect utopian bliss. Man also craves and needs suffering, not only to satisfy the irrational aspects of human nature, but also in order to contrast it with enjoyment, in order to learn, to teach, and, ultimately, to transcend human existence, to sanctify life, and to redeem it. "Man is sometimes extraordinarily, passionately in love with suffering, and that is a fact," says the Underground man.[1] Christianity owes a good part of its appeal to its presenting to man a suffering man-god who holds out to man salvation, not through science and reason but through suffering.

In light of such considerations, Dostoyevsky believes that the goal of human aspiration and the ultimate good for man should be more than a utopian ant-hill in which each human ant does its bit for the welfare of the whole. To attain such a goal—and with increased scientific knowledge it does seem more and more feasible—may not be desirable. Perhaps, says Dostoyevsky's Underground man, the value of the goal that man strives for lies in the process of his striving for it, not in his attaining it. Attaining utopia would bring boredom, frustration, and despair to man, not the satiation of desire and the fulfillment of human potentialities and aspirations.

Also concerned with the problem of freedom, another of Dostoyevsky's characters, Shigalov in *The Possessed* (1871), proposes a system of world organization that he believes is based on the realities of human nature.[2] Mankind is divided into two unequal categories, one-tenth being granted individual freedom and ruling the remaining nine-tenths who have lost all freedom and individuality. Through conditioning and a series of mutations the larger group has been gradually transformed into a happy human herd living in primeval innocence and paradisiacal happiness. Although he cannot conceive of any better workable solution to social problems, Shigalov is in despair over the outcome of his utopian speculation. Having started out envisaging a social order in which there would be unrestricted freedom, he has ended up proposing an anti-utopia of unrestrained despotism.

In his final and greatest novel *The Brothers Karamazov* (1880), Dostoyevsky again confronts his readers with the problem of freedom. Here he does so in the form of a legend, "The Grand Inquisitor," which is narrated by one of the novel's heroes, the atheistic Ivan Karamazov, to his saintly brother Alyosha.

The Legend of the Grand Inquisitor

"My story is laid in Spain, in Seville, in the most terrible time of the Inquisition, when fires were lighted every day to the glory of God, and 'in the splendid *auto da fé* the wicked heretics were burnt.' Oh, of course, this was not the coming in which He will appear according to His promise at the end of time in all His heavenly glory, and which will be sudden 'as lightning flashing from east to west.' No, He visited His children only for a moment, and there where the flames were crackling round the heretics. In His infinite mercy He came once more among men in that human shape in which He walked among men for three years fifteen centuries ago. He came down to the 'hot pavement' of the southern town in which on the day before almost a hundred heretics had, *ad majorem gloriam Dei,* been burnt by the cardinal, the Grand Inquisitor, in a magnificent *auto da fé,* in the presence of the king, the court, the knights, the cardinals, the most charming ladies of the court, and the whole population of Seville.

"He came softly, unobserved, and yet, strange to say, everyone recognized Him. That might be one of the best passages in the poem. I mean, why they recognized Him. The people are irresistibly drawn to Him, they surround Him, they flock about Him, follow Him. He moves silently in their midst with a gentle smile of infinite

From Feodor Dostoyevsky, *The Brothers Karamazov,* trans. Constance Garnett (New York: Random House, 1937), bk. V, chap. 5 ("The Grand Inquisitor"), pp. 305–25.

compassion. The sun of love burns in His heart, light and power shine from His eyes, and their radiance, shed on the people, stirs their hearts with responsive love. He holds out His hands to them, blesses them, and a healing virtue comes from contact with Him, even with His garments. An old man in the crowd, blind from childhood, cries out, 'O Lord, heal me and I shall see Thee!' and, as it were, scales fall from his eyes and the blind man sees Him. The crowd weeps and kisses the earth under His feet. Children throw flowers before Him, sing, and cry hosannah. 'It is He—it is He!' all repeat. 'It must be He, it can be no one but Him!' He stops at the steps of the Seville cathedral at the moment when the weeping mourners are bringing in a little open white coffin. In it lies a child of seven, the only daughter of a prominent citizen. The dead child lies hidden in flowers. 'He will raise your child,' the crowd shouts to the weeping mother. The priest, coming to meet the coffin, looks perplexed, and frowns, but the mother of the dead child throws herself at His feet with a wail. 'If it is Thou, raise my child!' she cries, holding out her hands to Him. The procession halts, the coffin is laid on the steps at His feet. He looks with compassion, and His lips once more softly pronounce, 'Maiden, arise!' and the maiden arises. The little girl sits up in the coffin and looks around, smiling with wide-open wondering eyes, holding a bunch of white roses they had put in her hand.

"There are cries, sobs, confusion among the people, and at that moment the cardinal himself, the Grand Inquisitor, passes by the cathedral. He is an old man, almost ninety, tall and erect, with a withered face and sunken eyes, in which there is still a gleam of light. He is not dressed in his gorgeous cardinal's robes, as he was the day before, when he was burning the enemies of the Roman Church—at that moment he was wearing his coarse, old, monk's cassock. At a distance behind him come his gloomy assistants and slaves and the 'holy guard.' He stops at the sight of the crowd and watches it from a distance. He sees everything; he sees them set the coffin down at His feet, sees the child rise up, and his face darkens. He knits his thick grey brows and his eyes gleam with a sinister fire. He holds out his finger and bids the guards take Him. And such is his power, so completely are the people cowed into submission and trembling obedience to him, that the crowd immediately make way for the guards, and in the midst of deathlike silence they lay hands on Him and lead Him away. The crowd instantly bows down to the earth, like one man, before the old inquisitor. He blesses the people in silence and passes on. The guards lead their prisoner to the close, gloomy vaulted prison in the ancient palace of the Holy Inquisition and shut Him in it. The day passes and is followed by the dark, burning 'breathless' night of Seville. The air is 'fragrant with laurel and lemon.' In the pitch darkness the iron door of the prison is suddenly opened and the Grand Inquisitor himself comes in with a light in his hand. He is alone; the door is closed at once behind him. He stands in the doorway and for a minute or two gazes into His face. At last he goes up slowly, sets the light on the table and speaks.

" 'Is it Thou? Thou?' but receiving no answer, he adds at once, 'Don't answer, be silent. What canst Thou say, indeed? I know too well what Thou wouldst say. And Thou hast no right to add anything to what Thou hadst said of old. Why, then, art Thou come to hinder us? For Thou hast come to hinder us, and Thou knowest

that. But dost Thou know what will be tomorrow? I know not who Thou art and care not to know whether it is Thou or only a semblance of Him, but tomorrow I shall condemn Thee and burn Thee at the stake as the worst of heretics. And the very people who have today kissed Thy feet, tomorrow at the faintest sign from me will rush to heap up the embers of Thy fire. Knowest Thou that? Yes, maybe Thou knowest it,' he added with thoughtful penetration, never for a moment taking his eyes off the Prisoner."

"I don't quite understand, Ivan. What does it mean?" Alyosha, who had been listening in silence, said with a smile. "Is it simply a wild fantasy, or a mistake on the part of the old man —some impossible *quid pro quo?*"

"Take it as the last," said Ivan, laughing, "if you are so corrupted by modern realism and can't stand anything fantastic. If you like it to be a case of mistaken identity, let it be so. It is true," he went on, laughing, "the old man was ninety, and he might well be crazy over his set idea. He might have been struck by the appearance of the Prisoner. It might, in fact, be simply his ravings, the delusion of an old man of ninety, over-excited by the *auto da fé* of a hundred heretics the day before. But does it matter to us after all whether it was a mistake of identity or a wild fantasy? All that matters is that the old man should speak out, should speak openly of what he had thought in silence for ninety years."

"And the Prisoner too is silent? Does He look at him and not say a word?"

"That's inevitable in any case," Ivan laughed again. "The old man has told Him He hasn't the right to add anything to what He has said of old. One may say it is the most fundamental feature of Roman Catholicism, in my opinion at least. 'All has been given by Thee to the Pope,' they say, 'and all, therefore, is still in the Pope's hands, and there is no need for Thee to come now at all. Thou must not meddle for the time, at least.' That's how they speak and write too —the Jesuits, at any rate. I have read it myself in the works of their theologians. 'Hast Thou the right to reveal to us one of the mysteries of that world from which Thou has come?' my old man asks Him, and answers the question for Him. 'No, Thou hast not; that Thou mayest not add to what has been said of old, and mayest not take from men the freedom which Thou didst exalt when Thou wast on earth. Whatsoever Thou revealest anew will encroach on men's freedom of faith; for it will be manifest as a miracle, and the freedom of their faith was dearer to Thee than anything in those days fifteen hundred years ago. Didst Thou not often say then, "I will make you free"? But now Thou hast seen these "free" men,' the old man adds suddenly, with a pensive smile. 'Yes, we've paid dearly for it,' he goes on, looking sternly at Him, 'but now it is ended and over for good. Dost Thou not believe that it's over for good? Thou lookest meekly at me and deignest not even to be wroth with me. But let me tell Thee that now, today, people are more persuaded than ever that they have perfect freedom, yet they have brought their freedom to us and laid it humbly at our feet. But that has been our doing. Was this what Thou didst? Was this Thy freedom?' "

"I don't understand again," Alyosha broke in. "Is he ironical, is he jesting?"

"Not a bit of it! He claims it as a merit for himself and his Church that at last they have vanquished freedom and have done so to make men happy. 'For now' (he is speaking of the Inquisition, of course) 'for the first time it has become possible to think of the happiness of men. Man was created a rebel; and how can rebels be happy? Thou was warned,' he says to Him. 'Thou hast had no lack of admonitions and warnings, but Thou didst not listen to those warnings; Thou didst reject the only way by which men might be made happy. But, fortunately, departing Thou didst hand on the work to us. Thou hast promised, Thou hast established by Thy word, Thou hast given to us the right to bind and to unbind, and now, of course, Thou canst not think of taking it away. Why, then, hast Thou come to hinder us?' "

"And what's the meaning of 'no lack of admonitions and warnings'?" asked Alyosha.

"Why, that's the chief part of what the old man must say."

" 'The wise and dread spirit, the spirit of self-destruction and non-existence,' the old man goes on, 'the great spirit talked with Thee in the wilderness, and we are told in the books that he "tempted" Thee. Is that so? And could anything truer be said than what he revealed to Thee in three questions and what Thou didst reject, and what in the books is called "the temptation"? And yet if there has ever been on earth a real stupendous miracle, it took place on that day, on the day of the three temptations. The statement of those three questions was itself the miracle. If it were possible to imagine simply for the sake of argument that those three questions of the dread spirit had perished utterly from the books, and that we had to restore them and to invent them anew, and to do so had gathered together all the wise men of the earth—rulers, chief priests, learned men, philosophers, poets—and had set them the task to invent three questions, such as would not only fit the occasion, but express in three words, three human phrases, the whole future history of the world and of humanity—dost Thou believe that all the wisdom of the earth united could have invented anything in depth and force equal to the three questions which were actually put to Thee then by the wise and mighty spirit in the wilderness? From those questions alone, from the miracle of their statement, we can see that we have here to do not with the fleeting human intelligence, but with the absolute and eternal. For in those three questions the whole subsequent history of mankind is, as it were, brought together into one whole, and foretold, and in them are united all the unsolved historical contradictions of human nature. At the time it could not be so clear, since the future was unknown; but now that fifteen hundred years have passed, we see that everything in those three questions was so justly divined and foretold, and has been so truly fulfilled, that nothing can be added to them or taken from them.

"'Judge Thyself who was right—Thou or he who questioned Thee then? Remember the first question; its meaning, in other words, was this: "Thou wouldst go into the world, and art going with empty hands, with some promise of freedom which men in their simplicity and their natural unruliness cannot even understand, which they fear and dread—for nothing has ever been more insupportable for a man and a human society than freedom. But seest Thou these stones in this parched and barren wilderness? Turn them into bread, and mankind will run after Thee like a flock of sheep, grateful and obedient, though for ever trembling, lest Thou withdraw Thy hand and deny them Thy bread." But Thou wouldst not deprive man of freedom and didst reject the offer, thinking, what is that freedom worth, if obedience is bought with bread? Thou didst reply that man lives not by bread alone. But does Thou know that for the sake of that earthly bread the spirit of the earth will rise up against Thee and will strive with Thee and overcome Thee, and all will follow him, crying, "Who can compare with this beast? He has given us fire from heaven!" Dost Thou know that the ages will pass, and humanity will proclaim by the lips of their sages that there is no crime, and therefore no sin; there is only hunger? "Feed men, and then ask of them virtue!" that's what they'll write on the banner, which they will raise against Thee, and with which they will destroy Thy temple. Where Thy temple stood will rise a new building; the terrible tower of Babel will be built again, and though, like the one of old, it will not be finished, yet Thou mightest have prevented that new tower and have cut short the sufferings of men for a thousand years; for they will come back to us after a thousand years of agony with their tower. They will seek us again, hidden underground in the catacombs, for we shall be again persecuted and tortured. They will find us and cry to us, "Feed us, for those who have promised us fire from heaven haven't given it!" And then we shall finish building their tower, for he finishes the building who feeds them. And we alone shall feed them in Thy name, declaring falsely that it is in Thy name. Oh, never, never can they feed themselves without us! No science will give them bread so long as they remain free. In the end they will lay their freedom at our feet, and say to us, "Make us your slaves, but feed us." They will understand themselves, at last, that freedom and bread enough for all are inconceivable together, for never, never will they be able to share between them! They will be convinced, too, that they can never be free, for they are weak, vicious, worthless and rebellious. Thou didst promise them the bread of Heaven, but, I repeat again, can it compare with earthly bread in the eyes of the weak, ever sinful and ignoble race of man? And if for the sake of the bread of Heaven thousands and tens of thousands shall follow Thee, what is to become of the millions and tens of thousands of millions of creatures who will not have the strength to forego the earthly bread for the sake of the heavenly? Or dost Thou care only for the tens of thousands of the great and strong, while the millions, numerous as the sands of the sea, who are weak but love Thee, must exist only for the sake of the great and strong? No, we care for the weak too. They are sinful and rebellious, but in the end they too will become obedient. They will marvel at us and look on us as gods, because we are ready to endure the freedom which they have found so dreadful and to rule over them— so awful it will seem to them to be free. But we shall tell them that we are Thy servants and rule them in Thy name. We shall deceive them again, for we will not let Thee come to us again. That deception will be our suffering, for we shall be forced to lie.

" 'This is the significance of the first question in the wilderness, and this is what Thou hast rejected for the sake of that freedom which Thou hast exalted above everything. Yet in this question lies hid the great secret of this world. Choosing "bread," Thou wouldst have satisfied the universal and everlasting craving of humanity—to find some one to worship. So long as man remains free he strives for nothing so incessantly and so painfully as to find some one to worship. But man seeks to worship what is established beyond dispute, so that all men would agree at once to worship it. For these pitiful creatures are concerned not only to find what one or the other can worship, but to find something that all would believe in and worship; what is essential is that all may be *together* in it. This craving for *community* of worship is the chief misery of every man individually and of all humanity from the beginning of time. For the sake of common worship they've slain each other with the sword. They have set up gods and challenged one another, "Put away your gods and come and worship ours, or we will kill you and your gods!" And so it will be to the end of the world, even when gods disappear from the earth; they will fall down before idols just the same. Thou didst know, Thou couldst not but have known, this fundamental secret of human nature, but Thou didst reject the one infallible banner which was offered Thee to make all men bow down to Thee alone—the banner of earthly bread; and Thou hast rejected it for the sake of freedom and the bread of Heaven. Behold what Thou didst further. And all again in the name of freedom! I tell Thee that man is tormented by no greater anxiety than to find some one quickly to whom he can hand over that gift of freedom with which the ill-fated creature is born. But only one who can appease their conscience can take over their freedom. In bread there was offered Thee an invincible banner; give bread, and man will worship Thee, for nothing is more certain than bread. But if some one else gains possession of his conscience—oh! then he will cast away Thy bread and follow after him who has ensnared his conscience. In that Thou wast right. For the secret of man's being is not only to live but to have something to live for. Without a stable conception of the object of life, man would not consent to go on living, and would rather destroy himself than remain on earth, though he had bread in abundance. That is true. But what happened? Instead of taking men's freedom from them, Thou didst make it greater than ever! Didst Thou forget that man prefers peace, and even death, to freedom of choice in the knowledge of good and evil? Nothing is more seductive for man than his freedom of conscience, but nothing is a greater cause of suffering. And behold, instead of giving a firm foundation for setting the conscience of man at rest for ever, Thou didst choose all that is exceptional, vague and enigmatic; Thou didst choose what was utterly beyond the strength of men, acting as though Thou didst not love them at all —Thou who didst come to give Thy life for them! Instead of taking possession of men's freedom, Thou didst increase it, and burdened the spiritual kingdom of mankind with its sufferings forever. Thou didst desire man's free love, that he should follow Thee freely, enticed and taken captive by Thee. In place of the rigid ancient law, man must hereafter with free heart decide for himself what is good and what is evil, having only Thy image before him as his guide. But didst Thou not know he would at last reject even Thy image and Thy truth, if he is weighed down with the fearful burden of free choice? They will cry aloud at last that the truth is not in Thee, for they could not have been left in greater confusion and suffering than Thou hast caused, laying upon them so many cares and unanswerable problems.

" 'So that, in truth, Thou didst Thyself lay the foundation for the destruction of Thy kingdom, and no one is more to blame for it. Yet what was offered Thee? There are three powers, three powers alone, able to conquer and to hold captive for ever the conscience of these impotent rebels for their happiness—those forces are miracle, mystery and authority. Thou hast rejected all three and hast set the example for doing so. When the wise and dread spirit set Thee on the pinnacle of the temple and said to Thee, "If Thou wouldst know whether Thou art the Son of God then cast Thyself down, for it is written: the angels shall hold him up lest he fall and bruise himself, and Thou shalt know then whether Thou art the Son of God and shall prove then how great is Thy faith in Thy Father." But Thou didst refuse and wouldst not cast Thyself down. Oh! of course, Thou didst proudly and well, like God; but the weak, unruly race of men, are they gods? Oh, Thou didst know then that in taking one step, in making one movement to cast Thyself down, Thou wouldst be tempting God and have lost all Thy faith in Him, and wouldst have been dashed to pieces against that earth which Thou didst come to save. And the wise spirit that tempted Thee would have rejoiced. But I ask again, are there many like Thee? And couldst Thou believe for one moment that men, too, could face such a temptation? Is the nature of men such, that they can reject miracle, and at the great moments of their life, the moments of their deepest, most agonising spiritual difficulties, cling only to the free verdict of the heart? Oh, Thou didst know that Thy deed would be recorded in books, would be handed down to remote times and the utmost ends of the earth, and Thou didst hope that man, following Thee, would cling to God and not ask for a miracle. But Thou didst not know that when man rejects miracle he rejects God too; for man seeks not so much God as the miraculous. And as man cannot bear to be without the miraculous, he will create new miracles of his own for himself, and will worship deeds of sorcery and witchcraft, though he might be a hundred times over a rebel, heretic and infidel. Thou didst not come down from the Cross when they shouted

to Thee, mocking and reviling Thee, "Come down from the cross and we will believe that Thou art He." Thou didst not come down, for again Thou wouldst not enslave man by a miracle, and didst crave faith given freely, not based on miracle. Thou didst crave for free love and not the base raptures of the slave before the might that has overawed him for ever. But Thou didst think too highly of men therein, for they are slaves, of course, though rebellious by nature. Look round and judge; fifteen centuries have passed, look upon them. Whom hast Thou raised up to Thyself? I swear, man is weaker and baser by nature than Thou hast believed him! Can he, can he do what Thou didst? By showing him so much respect, Thou didst, as it were, cease to feel for him, for Thou didst ask far too much from him—Thou who hast loved him more than Thyself! Respecting him less, Thou wouldst have asked less of him. That would have been more like love, for his burden would have been lighter. He is weak and vile. What though he is everywhere now rebelling against our power, and proud of his rebellion? It is the pride of a child and a schoolboy. They are little children rioting and barring out the teacher at school. But their childish delight will end; it will cost them dear. They will cast down temples and drench the earth with blood. But they will see at last, the foolish children, that, though they are rebels, they are impotent rebels, unable to keep up their own rebellion. Bathed in their foolish tears, they will recognise at last that He who created them rebels must have meant to mock at them. They will say this in despair, and their utterance will be a blasphemy which will make them more unhappy still, for man's nature cannot bear blasphemy, and in the end always avenges it on itself. And so unrest, confusion and unhappiness—that is the present lot of man after Thou didst bear so much for their freedom! Thy great prophet tells in vision and in image, that he saw all those who took part in the first resurrection and that they were of each tribe twelve thousand But if there were so many of them, they must have been not men but gods. They had borne Thy cross, they had endured scores of years in the barren, hungry wilderness, living upon locusts and roots—and Thou mayest indeed point with pride at those children of freedom, of free love, of free and splendid sacrifice for Thy name. But remember that they were only some thousands; and what of the rest? And how are the other weak ones to blame, because they could not endure what the strong have endured? How is the weak soul to blame that it is unable to receive such terrible gifts? Canst Thou have simply come to the elect and for the elect? But if so, it is a mystery and we cannot understand it. And if it is a mystery, we too have a right to preach a mystery, and to teach them that it's not the free judgment of their hearts, not love that matters, but a mystery which they must follow blindly, even against their conscience. So we have done. We have corrected Thy work and have founded it upon *miracle, mystery* and *authority*. And men rejoiced that they were again led like sheep, and that the terrible gift that had brought them such suffering, was, at last, lifted from their hearts. Were we right teaching them this? Speak. Did we not love mankind, so meekly acknowledging their feebleness, lovingly lightening their burden, and permitting their weak nature even sin with our sanction? Why hast Thou come now to hinder us? And why dost Thou look silently and searchingly at me with Thy mild eyes? Be angry. I don't want Thy love, for I love Thee not. And what use is it for me to hide anything from Thee? Don't I know to Whom I am speaking? All that I can say is known to Thee already. And is it for me to conceal from Thee our mystery? Perhaps it is Thy will to hear it from my lips. Listen, then. We are not working with Thee, but with *him*—that is our mystery. It's long— eight centuries—since we have been on *his* side and not on Thine. Just eight centuries ago, we

took from him what Thou didst reject with scorn, that last gift he offered Thee, showing Thee all the kingdoms of the earth. We took from him Rome and the sword of Caesar, and proclaimed ourselves sole rulers of the earth, though hitherto we have not been able to complete our work. But whose fault is that? Oh, the work is only beginning, but it has much to suffer, but we shall triumph and shall be Caesars, and then we shall plan the universal happiness of man. But Thou mightest have taken even then the sword of Caesar. Why didst Thou reject that last gift? Hadst Thou accepted that last counsel of the mighty spirit, Thou wouldst have accomplished all that man seeks on earth—that is, some one to worship, some one to keep his conscience, and some means of uniting all in one unanimous and harmonious antheap, for the craving for universal unity is the third and last anguish of men. Mankind as a whole has always striven to organise a universal state. There have been many great nations with great histories, but the more highly they were developed the more unhappy they were, for they felt more acutely than other people the craving for worldwide union. The great conquerors, Timours and Ghenghis-Khan, whirled like hurricanes over the face of the earth striving to subdue its people, and they too were but the unconscious expression of the same craving for universal unity. Hadst Thou taken the world and Caesar's purple, Thou wouldst have founded the universal state and have given universal peace. For who can rule men if not he who holds their conscience and their bread in his hands? We have taken the sword of Caesar, and in taking it, of course, have rejected Thee and followed *him*. Oh, ages are yet to come of the confusion of free thought, of their science and cannibalism. For having begun to build their tower of Babel without us, they will end, of course, with cannibalism. But then the beast will crawl to us and lick our feet and spatter them with tears of blood. And we shall sit upon the beast and raise the cup, and on it will be written, "Mystery." But then, and only then, the reign of peace and happiness will come for men. Thou art proud of Thine elect, but Thou hast only the elect, while we give rest to all. And besides, how many of those elect, those mighty ones who could become elect, have grown weary waiting for Thee, and have transferred and will transfer the powers of their spirit and the warmth of their heart to the other camp, and end by raising their *free* banner against Thee. Thou didst Thyself lift up that banner. But with us all will be happy and will no more rebel nor destroy one another as under Thy freedom. Oh, we shall persuade them that they will only become free when they renounce their freedom to us and submit to us. And shall we be right or shall we be lying? They will be convinced that we are right, for they will remember the horrors of slavery and confusion to which Thy freedom brought them. Freedom, free thought and science, will lead them into such straits and will bring them face to face with such marvels and insoluble mysteries, that some of them, the fierce and rebellious, will destroy themselves, others, rebellious but weak, will destroy one another, while the rest, weak and unhappy, will crawl fawning to our feet and whine to us: "Yes, you were right, you alone possess His mystery, and we come back to you, save us from ourselves!"

" 'Receiving bread from us, they will see clearly that we take the bread made by their hands from them, to give it to them, without any miracle. They will see that we do not change the stones to bread, but in truth they will be more thankful for taking it from our hands than for the bread itself! For they will remember only too well that in old days, without our help, even the bread they made turned to stones in their hands, while since they have come back to us, the very stones have turned to bread in their hands. Too, too well they know the value of complete submission! And until men know that, they will be unhappy. Who is most to blame for

their not knowing it, speak? Who scattered the flock and sent it astray on unknown paths? But the flock will come together again and will submit once more, and then it will be once for all. Then we shall give them the quiet humble happiness of weak creatures such as they are by nature. Oh, we shall persuade them at last not to be proud, for Thou didst lift them up and thereby taught them to be proud. We shall show them that they are weak, that they are only pitiful children, but that childlike happiness is the sweetest of all. They will become timid and will look to us and huddle close to us in fear, as chicks to the hen. They will marvel at us and will be awestricken before us, and will be proud at our being so powerful and clever, that we have been able to subdue such a turbulent flock of thousands of millions. They will tremble impotently before our wrath, their minds will grow fearful, they will be just as ready at a sign from us to pass to laughter and rejoicing, to happy mirth and childish song. Yes, we shall set them to work, but in their leisure hours we shall make their life like a child's game, with children's songs and innocent dance. Oh, we shall allow them even sin, they are weak and helpless, and they will love us like children because we allow them to sin. We shall tell them that every sin will be expiated, if it is done with our permission, that we allow them to sin because we love them, and the punishment for these sins we take upon ourselves. And we shall take it upon ourselves, and they will adore us as their saviours, who have taken on themselves their sins before God. And they will have no secrets from us. We shall allow or forbid them to live with their wives and mistresses, to have or not to have children—according to whether they have been obedient or disobedient—and they will submit to us gladly and cheerfully. The most painful secrets of their conscience, all, all they will bring to us, and we shall have an answer for all. And they will be glad to believe our answer, for it will save them from the great anxiety and terrible agony they endure at present in making a free decision for themselves. And all will be happy, all the millions of creatures except the hundred thousand who rule over them. For only we, we who guard the mystery, shall be unhappy. There will be thousands of millions of happy babes, and a hundred thousand sufferers who have taken upon themselves the curse of the knowledge of good and evil. Peacefully they will die, peacefully they will expire in Thy name, and beyond the grave they will find nothing but death. But we shall keep the secret, and for their happiness we shall allure them with the reward of heaven and eternity. Though if there were anything in the other world, it certainly would not be for such as they. It is prophesied that Thou wilt come again in victory, Thou wilt come with Thy chosen, the proud and strong, but we will say that they have only saved themselves, but we have saved all. We are told that the harlot who sits upon the beast, and holds in her hands the *mystery,* shall be put to shame, that the weak will rise up again, and will rend her royal purple and will strip naked her loathsome body. But then I will stand up and point out to Thee the thousand millions of happy children who have known no sin. And we who have taken their sins upon us for their happiness will stand up before Thee and say: "Judge us if Thou canst and darest." Know that I too have been in the wilderness, I too have lived on roots and locusts, I too prized the freedom with which Thou hast blessed men, and I too was striving to stand among Thy elect, among the strong and powerful, thirsting "to make up the number." But I awakened and would not serve madness. I turned back and joined the ranks of those *who have corrected Thy work.* I left the proud and went back to the humble, for the happiness of the humble. What I say to Thee will come to pass, and our dominion will be built up. I repeat, tomorrow Thou shalt see that obedient flock who at a sign from me will hasten to heap up the hot cinders about the pile on which I shall burn Thee for coming to hinder us. For if any one has ever de-

served our fires, it is Thou. Tomorrow I shall burn Thee. Dixi.' "

Ivan stopped. He was carried away as he talked and spoke with excitement; when he had finished, he suddenly smiled.

Alyosha had listened in silence; towards the end he was greatly moved and seemed several times on the point of interrupting, but restrained himself. Now his words came with a rush.

"But . . . that's absurd!" he cried, flushing. "Your poem is in praise of Jesus, not in blame of Him—as you meant it to be. And who will believe you about freedom? Is that the way to understand it? That's not the idea of it in the Orthodox Church . . . That's Rome, and not even the whole of Rome, it's false—those are the worst of the Catholics, the Inquisitors, the Jesuits. . . . And there could not be such a fantastic creature as your Inquisitor. What are these sins of mankind they take on themselves? Who are these keepers of the mystery who have taken some curse upon themselves for the happiness of mankind? When have they been seen? We know the Jesuits, they are spoken ill of, but surely they are not what you describe? They are not that at all, not at all. . . . They are simply the Romish army for the earthly sovereignty of the world in the future, with the Pontiff of Rome for Emperor . . . that's their ideal, but there's no sort of mystery or lofty melancholy about it. . . . It's simple lust of power, of filthy earthly gain, of domination—something like a universal serfdom with them as masters—that's all they stand for. They don't even believe in God perhaps. Your suffering inquisitor is a mere fantasy."

"Stay, stay," laughed Ivan, "how hot you are! A fantasy you say, let it be so! Of course it's a fantasy. But allow me to say: do you really think that the Roman Catholic movement of the last centuries is actually nothing but the lust of power, of filthy earthly gain? Is that Father Païssy's teaching?"

"No, no, on the contrary, Father Païssy did once say something rather the same as you . . . but of course it's not the same, not a bit the same," Alyosha hastily corrected himself.

"A precious admission, in spite of your 'not a bit the same.' I ask you why your Jesuits and Inquisitors have united simply for vile material gain? Why can there not be among them one martyr oppressed by great sorrow and loving humanity? You see, only suppose that there was one such man among all those who desire nothing but filthy material gain—if there's only one like my old inquisitor, who had himself eaten roots in the desert and made frenzied efforts to subdue his flesh to make himself free and perfect. But yet all his life he loved humanity, and suddenly his eyes were opened, and he saw that it is no great moral blessedness to attain perfection and freedom, if at the same time one gains the conviction that millions of God's creatures have been created as a mockery, that they will never be capable of using their freedom, that these poor rebels can never turn into giants to complete the tower, that it was not for such geese that the great idealist dreamt his dream of harmony. Seeing all that he turned back and joined—the clever people. Surely that could have happened?"

"Joined whom, what clever people? cried Alyosha, completely carried away. "They have no such great cleverness and no mysteries and secrets. . . . Perhaps nothing but Atheism, that's all their secret. Your inquisitor does not believe in God, that's his secret!"

"What if it is so! At last you have guessed it. It's perfectly true that that's the whole secret, but isn't that suffering, at least for a man like that, who has wasted his whole life in the desert and yet could not shake off his incurable love of humanity? In his old age he reached the clear conviction that nothing but the advice of the great dread spirit could build up any tolerable sort of life for the feeble, unruly, 'incomplete, empirical creatures created in jest.' And so, convinced of this, he sees that he must follow the counsel of the wise spirit, the dread spirit of death and destruction, and therefore accept lying and deception, and lead men consciously to death and destruction, and yet deceive them all the way so that they may not notice where they are being led, that the poor blind creatures may at least on the way think themselves happy. And note, the deception is in the name of Him in Whose ideal the old man had so fervently believed all his life long. Is not that tragic? And if only one such stood at the head of the whole army 'filled with the lust of power only for the sake of filthy gain'—would not one such be enough to make a tragedy? More than that, one such standing at the head is enough to create the actual leading idea of the Roman Church with all its armies and Jesuits, its highest idea. I tell you frankly that I firmly believe that there has always been such a man among those who stood at the head of the movement. Who knows, there may have been some such even among the Roman Popes. Who knows, perhaps the spirit of that accursed old man who loves mankind so obstinately in his own way, is to be found even now in a whole multitude of such old men, existing not by chance but by agreement, as a secret league formed long ago for the guarding of the mystery, to guard it from the weak and the unhappy, so as to make them happy. No doubt it is so, and so it must be indeed. I fancy that even among the Masons there's something of the same mystery at the bottom, and that that's why the Catholics so detest the Masons as their rivals breaking up the unity of the idea, while it is so essential that there should be one flock and one shepherd. . . . But from the way I defend my idea I might be an author impatient of your criticism. Enough of it."

"You are perhaps a Mason yourself!" broke suddenly from Alyosha. "You don't believe in God," he added, speaking this time very sorrowfully. He fancied besides that his brother was looking at him ironically. "How does your poem end?" he asked, suddenly looking down. "Or was it the end?"

"I meant to end it like this. When the Inquisitor ceased speaking he waited some time for his Prisoner to answer him. His silence weighed down upon him. He saw that the Prisoner had listened intently all the time, looking gently in his face and evidently not wishing to reply. The old man longed for Him to say something, however bitter and terrible. But He suddenly approached the old man in silence and softly kissed him on his bloodless aged lips. That was all his answer. The old man shuddered. His lips moved. He went to the door, opened it, and said to Him: 'Go, and come no more. . . . come not at all, never, never!' And he let Him out into the dark alleys of the town. The Prisoner went away."

"And the old man?"

"The kiss glows in his heart, but the old man adheres to his idea."

"And you with him, you too?" cried Alyosha, mournfully.

Ivan laughed.

"Why, it's all nonsense, Alyosha. It's only a senseless poem of a senseless student, who could never write two lines of verse. Why do you take it so seriously? Surely you don't suppose I am going straight off to the Jesuits, to join the men who are correcting His work? Good Lord, it's no business of mine. I told you, all I want is to live on to thirty, and then . . . dash the cup to the ground!"

"But the little sticky leaves, and the precious tombs, and the blue sky, and the woman you love! How will you live, how will you love them?" Alyosha cried sorrowfully. "With such a hell in your heart and your head, how can you? No, that's just what you are going away for, to join them . . . if not, you will kill yourself, you can't endure it."

"There is a strength to endure everything," Ivan said with a cold smile.

"What strength?"

"The strength of the Karamazov—the strength of the Karamazov baseness."

"To sink into debauchery, to stifle your soul with corruption, yes?"

"Possibly even that . . . only perhaps till I am thirty I shall escape it, and then."

"How will you escape it? By what will you escape it? That's impossible with your ideas."

"In the Karamazov way, again."

" 'Everything is lawful,' you mean? Everything is lawful, is that it?"

Ivan scowled, and all at once turned strangely pale.

"Ah, you've caught up yesterday's phrase, which so offended Miusov—and which Dmitri pounced upon so naively and paraphrased!" he smiled queerly.

"Yes, if you like, 'everything is lawful' since the word has been said. I won't deny it. And Mitya's version isn't bad."

Alyosha looked at him in silence.

"I thought that going away from here I have you at least," Ivan said suddenly, with unexpected feeling; "but now I see that there is no place for me even in your heart, my dear hermit. The formula, 'all is lawful,' I won't renounce—will you renounce me for that, yes?"

Alyosha got up, went to him and softly kissed him on the lips.

"That's plagiarism," cried Ivan, highly delighted. "You stole that from my poem. Thank you though. Get up, Alyosha, it's time we were going, both of us." . . .

Notes

1. Feodor Dostoyevsky, *Notes from Underground* in *White Nights and Other Stories,* trans. Constance Garnett (New York: Macmillan, 1923), p. 77.

2. See Feodor Dostoyevsky, *The Possessed,* part II, chap. 7.

7 / The Free Individual
Thoreau

Like Socrates, Henry David Thoreau (1817—1862) urges us to examine not only our convictions but also the kind of life that these convictions, whether consciously formulated or not, have directed us to follow. How do we spend our lives? In what sorts of activities are we engaged? What are our deepest hopes and our strongest aspirations? To what extent are we able to fulfill these hopes and aspirations?

The vast majority of men, Thoreau believes, live lives of quiet desperation. They find themselves living in a world that is considered to be merely a place of business, where men are preoccupied with buying and selling things, with fitting means to ends and, frequently, with justifying the means used to attain the ends without examining carefully the value of those ends. Practicality and usefulness are appreciated in only the crudest, most materialistic, and selfish sense. Hoarding of material things, exploitation of men and nature, and ruthless competition, in which the least worthy specimens of the human race seem to survive are the inevitable results of this mistaken system of values, which Erich Fromm was later to call the "marketing orientation."

In light of this orientation, it is not surprising to Thoreau that genuine human beings in such a world are made to feel that they are antisocial eccentrics and misfits. "If a man walk in the woods for love of them half of each day, he is in danger of being regarded as a loafer," Thoreau writes in "Life without Principle," "but if he spends his whole day as a speculator, shearing these woods and making earth bald before her time, he is esteemed an industrious and enterprising citizen. As if a town had no interest in its forests but to cut them down!"[1] Everyone is expected to make a living but not to live, and making a living means, of course, making money. And the ways by which men make money lead them downward, away from any realization of what it really means to be a human being. No matter what you do to make a living, to make money, you are usually being paid "for being something less than a man."[2] Under such a system, inefficient and incompetent human beings often prosper although they do so because they have sold their birthright as free individuals for a mess of pottage.

Unlike the mass of men, Thoreau's ideal man refuses to sell himself, "both his forenoons and afternoons," to the society in which he happens to live. He has learned to be as self-reliant, as self-supporting as possible. He gets down to the real business of living; he lives by loving. He is willing to follow a solitary path, to defend an unpopular cause, and to take a controversial position without fear of losing his livelihood. "A man had better starve at once than lose his innocence in the process of getting his bread."[3] Inwardness, honesty, sincerity, intellectual chastity—these are virtues that the wise man values above anything material. He listens to his heart and to nature rather than to the gossiping of his fellow men. His heightened awareness makes it possible for him to feel enriched by the mere contemplation of the things that ordinary men take for granted—the sun, the clouds, the snow, the trees. Every day wisely lived brings forth its own minor miracles and "it requires more than a day's devotion to know and possess the wealth of a day."[4]

Although Thoreau is sometimes called a "transcendentalist," he (again, like Socrates) made no attempt to construct a system of philosophy or to preach a gospel of salvation. Usually he suggested his viewpoints in prose and poetry; sometimes, as in the situation described in his essay on civil disobedience, his actions testified to the firmness and sincerity of his beliefs. His transcendentalism was a living experience. A commitment to Goodness, Truth, and Beauty, as knowledge, he believed, "does not come to us by details, but in flashes of light from heaven."[5]

The following essay shows Thoreau's profound commitment to freedom. While he loved and defended some aspects of his country, he did not believe it was yet truly a land of the free. America might have freed itself of a political tyrant, he pointed out, but it was still enslaved by economic and moral tyranny. "What is it to be free from King George and continue the slaves of King Prejudice? What is it to be born free and not to live free? What is the value of any political freedom, but as a means to moral freedom? Is it a freedom to be slaves, or a freedom to be free, of which we boast?"[6] Thoreau believed it to be the free individual's moral obligation under certain circumstances to practice civil disobedience, because he was convinced that this could bring into existence more freedom for more individuals. To fail to stand up against the often morally unjustifiable authority of the state and to confront the persons who work its bureaucratic machinery with resistance to their sometimes unjust decrees and arbitrary decisions is to countenance authoritarianism and to weaken the always necessary defences against tyranny.

Civil Disobedience

I heartily accept the motto,—"That government is best which governs least;" and I should like to see it acted up to more rapidly and systematically. Carried out, it finally amounts to this, which also I believe,—"That government is best which governs not at all;" and when men are prepared for it, that will be the kind of government which they will have. Government is at best but an expedient; but most governments are usually, and all governments are sometimes, inexpedient. The objections which have been brought against a standing army, and they are many and weighty, and deserve to prevail, may also at last be brought against a standing government. The government itself, which is only the mode which the people have chosen to execute their will, is equally liable to be abused and perverted before the people can act through it. Witness the present Mexican war, the work of comparatively a few individuals using the standing government as their tool; for, in the outset, the people would not have consented to this measure.

This American government,—what is it but a tradition, though a recent one, endeavoring to transmit itself unimpaired to posterity, but each instant losing some of its integrity? It has not the vitality and force of a single living man; for a single man can bend it to his will. It is a sort of wooden gun to the people themselves. But it is not the less necessary for this; for the people must have some complicated machinery or

From "Civil Disobedience," *The Writings of* Henry David Thoreau, vol. IV (Boston: Houghton Mifflin & Co., 1906), pp. 356–87 (with omissions).

other, and hear its din, to satisfy that idea of government which they have. Governments show thus how successfully men can be imposed on, even impose on themselves, for their own advantage. It is excellent, we must all allow. Yet this government never of itself furthered any enterprise, but by the alacrity with which it got out of its way. *It* does not keep the country free. *It* does not settle the West. *It* does not educate. The characer inherent in the American people has done all that has been accomplished; and it would have done somewhat more, if the government had not sometimes got in its way. For government is an expedient by which men would fain succeed in letting one another alone; and, as has been said, when it is most expedient, the governed are most let alone by it. Trade and commerce, if they were not made of India-rubber, would never manage to bounce over the obstacles which legislators are continually putting in their way; and, if one were to judge these men wholly by the effects of their actions and not partly by their intentions, they would deserve to be classed and punished with those mischievous persons who put obstructions on the railroads.

But, to speak practically and as a citizen, unlike those who call themselves no-government men, I ask for, not at once no government, but *at once* a better government. Let every man make known what kind of government would command his respect, and that will be one step toward obtaining it.

After all, the practical reason why, when the power is once in the hands of the people, a majority are permitted, and for a long period continue, to rule is not because they are most likely to be in the right, nor because this seems fairest to the minority, but because they are physically the strongest. But a government in which the majority rule in all cases cannot be based on justice, even as far as men understand it. Can there not be a government in which majorities do not virtually decide right and wrong, but conscience?—in which majorities decide only those questions to which the rule of expediency is applicable? Must the citizen ever for a moment, or in the least degree, resign his conscience to the legislator? Why has every man a conscience, then? I think that we should be men first, and subjects afterward. It is not desirable to cultivate a respect for the law, so much as for the right. The only obligation which I have a right to assume is to do at any time what I think right. It is truly enough said, that a corporation has no conscience; but a corporation of conscientious men is a corporation *with* a conscience. Law never made men a whit more just; and, by means of their respect for it, even the well-disposed are daily made the agents of injustice. A common and natural result of an undue respect for law is, that you may see a file of soldiers, colonel, captain, corporal, privates, powder-monkeys, and all, marching in admirable order over hill and dale to the wars, against their wills, ay, against their common sense and consciences, which makes it very steep marching indeed, and produces a palpitation of the heart. They have no doubt that it is a damnable business in which they are concerned; they are all peaceably inclined. Now, what are they? Men at all? or small moveable forts and magazines, at the service of some unscrupulous man in power? Visit the Navy-Yard, and behold a marine, such a man as an American government can make, or such as it can make a man with its black arts,— a mere shadow and reminiscence of humanity, a man laid out alive and standing, and already, as one may say, buried under arms with funeral accompaniments, though it may be,—

Not a drum was heard, not a funeral note,
  As his corse to the rampart we hurried;
Not a soldier discharged his farewell shot
  O'er the grave where our hero we buried.

The mass of men serve the state thus, not as men mainly, but as machines, with their bodies. They are the standing army, and the militia, jailors, constables, posse comitatus, etc. In most cases there is no free exercise whatever of the judgment or of the moral sense; but they put themselves on a level with wood and earth and stones; and wooden men can perhaps be manufactured that will serve the purpose as well. Such command no more respect than men of straw or a lump of dirt. They have the same sort of worth only as horses and dogs. Yet such as these even are commonly esteemed good citizens. Others— as most legislators, politicians, lawyers, ministers, and office-holders—serve the state chiefly with their heads; and, as they rarely make any moral distinctions, they are as likely to serve the Devil, without *intending* it, as God. A very few, as heroes, patriots, martyrs, reformers in the great sense, and *men,* serve the state with their consciences also, and so necessarily resist it for the most part; and they are commonly treated as enemies by it. A wise man will only be useful as a man, and will not submit to be "clay," and "stop a hole to keep the wind away," but leave that office to his dust at least. . . .

How can a man be satisfied to entertain an opinion merely, and enjoy *it*? Is there any enjoyment in it, if his opinion is that he is aggrieved? If you are cheated out of a single dollar by your neighbor, you do not rest satisfied with knowing that you are cheated, or with saying that you are cheated, or even with petitioning him to pay you your due; but you take effectual steps at once to obtain the full amount, and see that you are never cheated again. Action from principle, the perception and the performance of right, changes things and relations; it is essentially revolutionary, and does not consist wholly with anything which was. It not only divides states and churches, it divides families; ay, it divides the *individual,* separating the diabolical in him from the divine.

Unjust laws exist: shall we be content to obey them, or shall we endeavor to amend them, until we have succeeded, or shall we transgress them at once? Men generally, under such a government as this, think that they ought to wait until they have persuaded the majority to alter them. They think that, if they should resist, the remedy would be worse than the evil. But it is the fault of the government itself that the remedy *is* worse than the evil. *It* makes it worse. Why is it not more apt to anticipate and provide for reform? Why does it not cherish its wise minority? Why does it cry and resist before it is hurt? Why does it not encourage its citizens to be on the alert to point out its faults, and *do* better than it would have them? Why does it always crucify Christ, and excommunicate Copernicus and Luther, and pronounce Washington and Franklin rebels?

One would think, that a deliberate and practical denial of its authority was the only offense never contemplated by government; else, why has it not assigned its definite, its suitable and proportionate penalty? If a man who has no property refuses but once to earn nine shillings for the state, he is put in prison for a period unlimited by any law that I know, and determined only by the discretion of those who placed him there; but if he should steal ninety times nine shillings from the state, he is soon permitted to go at large again.

If the injustice is part of the necessary friction of the machine of government, let it go, let it go: perchance it will wear smooth,—certainly the machine will wear out. If the injustice has a spring, or a pulley, or a rope, or a crank, exclusively for itself, then perhaps you may consider whether the remedy will not be worse than the evil; but if it is of such a nature that it requires you to be the agent of injustice to another, then,

I say, break the law. Let your life be a counter friction to stop the machine. What I have to do is to see, at any rate, that I do not lend myself to the wrong which I condemn.

As for adopting the ways which the state has provided for remedying the evil, I know not of such ways. They take too much time, and a man's life will be gone. I have other affairs to attend to. I came into this world, not chiefly to make this a good place to live in, but to live in it, be it good or bad. A man has not everything to do, but something; and because he cannot do *everything,* it is not necessary that he should do *something* wrong. It is not my business to be petitioning the Governor or the Legislature any more than it is theirs to petition me; and if they should not hear my petition, what should I do then? But in this case the state has provided no way: its very Constitution is the evil. This may seem to be harsh and stubborn and unconciliatory; but it is to treat with the utmost kindness and consideration the only spirit that can appreciate or deserves it. So is all change for the better, like birth and death, which convulse the body.

I do not hesitate to say that those who call themselves Abolitionists should at once effectually withdraw their support, both in person and property, from the government of Massachusetts and not wait till they constitute a majority of one, before they suffer the right to prevail through them. I think that it is enough if they have God on their side, without waiting for that other one. Moreover, any man more right than his neighbors constitutes a majority of one already....

Under a government which imprisons any unjustly, the true place for a just man is also a prison. The proper place today, the only place which Massachusetts has provided for her freer and less desponding spirits, is in her prisons, to be put out and locked out of the State by her own act, as they have already put themselves out by their principles. It is there that the fugitive slave, and the Mexican prisoner on parole, and the Indian come to plead the wrongs of his race should find them; on that separate, but more free and honorable ground, where the State places those who are not *with* her, but *against* her,—the only house in a slave State in which a free man can abide with honor. If any think that their influence would be lost there, and their voices no longer afflict the ear of the State, that they would not be as an enemy within its walls, they do not know by how much truth is stronger than error, nor how much more eloquently and effectively he can combat injustice who has experienced a little in his own person. Cast your whole vote, not a strip of paper merely, but your whole influence. A minority is powerless while it conforms to the majority; it is not even a minority then; but it is irresistible when it clogs by its whole weight. If the alternative is to keep all just men in prison, or give up war and slavery, the State will not hesitate which to choose. If a thousand men were not to pay their tax-bills this year, that would not be a violent and bloody measure, as it would be to pay them, and enable the State to commit violence and shed innocent blood. This is, in fact, the definition of a peaceable revolution, if any such is possible. If the tax-gatherer, or any other public officer, asks me, as one has done, "But what shall I do?" my answer is, "If you really wish to do anything, resign your office." When the subject has refused allegiance, and the officer has resigned his office, then the revolution is accomplished. But even suppose blood should flow. Is there not a sort of blood shed when the conscience is wounded? Through this wound a man's real manhood and immortality flow out, and he bleeds to an everlasting death. I see this flood flowing now.

I have contemplated the imprisonment of the offender, rather than the seizure of his goods,—though both will serve the same purpose,—because they who assert the purest right, and consequently are most dangerous to a corrupt State,

commonly have not spent much time in accumulating property. To such the State renders comparatively small service, and a slight tax is wont to appear exorbitant, particularly if they are obliged to earn it by special labor with their hands. If there were one who lived wholly without the use of money, the State itself would hesitate to demand it of him. But the rich man—not to make any invidious comparison—is always sold to the institution which makes him rich. Absolutely speaking, the more money, the less virtue; for money comes between a man and his objects, and obtains them for him; and it was certainly no great virtue to obtain it. It puts to rest many questions which he would otherwise be taxed to answer; while the only new question which it puts is the hard but superfluous one, how to spend it. Thus his moral ground is taken from under his feet. The opportunities of living are diminished in proportion as what are called the "means" are increased. The best thing a man can do for his culture when he is rich is to endeavor to carry out those schemes which he entertained when he was poor. Christ answered the Herodians according to their condition. "Show me the tribute-money," said he;—and one took a penny out of his pocket;—if you use money which has the image of Caesar on it and which he has made current and valuable, that is, *if you are men of the State,* and gladly enjoy the advantages of Caesar's government, then pay him back some of his own when he demands it. "Render therefore to Caesar that which is Caesar's, and to God those things which are God's,"—leaving them no wiser than before as to which was which; for they did not wish to know.

When I converse with the freest of my neighbors, I perceive that, whatever they may say about the magnitude and seriousness of the question, and their regard for the public tranquillity, the long and the short of the matter is, that they cannot spare the protection of the existing government, and they dread the consequences to their property and families of disobedience to it. For my own part, I should not like to think that I ever rely on the protection of the State. But, if I deny the authority of the State when it presents its tax-bill, it will soon take and waste all my property, and so harass me and my children without end. This is hard. This makes it impossible for a man to live honestly, and at the same time comfortably, in outward respects. It will not be worth the while to accumulate property; that would be sure to go again. You must hire or squat somewhere, and raise but a small crop, and eat that soon. You must live within yourself, and depend upon yourself always tucked up and ready for a start, and not have many affairs. A man may grow rich in Turkey even, if he will be in all respects a good subject of the Turkish government. Confucius said: "If a state is governed by the principles of reason, poverty and misery are subjects of shame; if a state is not governed by the principles of reason, riches and honors are the subjects of shame." No: until I want the protection of Massachusetts to be extended to me in some distant Southern port, where my liberty is endangered, or until I am bent solely on building up an estate at home by peaceful enterprise, I can afford to refuse allegiance to Massachusetts, and her right to my property and life. It costs me less in every sense to incur the penalty of disobedience to the State than it would be to obey. I should feel as if I were worth less in that case.

Some years ago, the State met me in behalf of the Church, and commanded me to pay a certain sum toward the support of a clergyman whose preaching my father attended, but never I myself. "Pay," it said, "or be locked up in the jail." I declined to pay. But, unfortunately, another man saw fit to pay it. I did not see why the schoolmaster should be taxed to support the priest, and not the priest the schoolmaster; for I was not the State's schoolmaster, but I supported myself by voluntary subscription. I did not see why the lyceum should not present its tax-bill, and have the State to back its de-

mand, as well as the Church. However, at the request of the selectmen, I condescended to make some such statement as this in writing:—"Know all men by these presents, that I, Henry Thoreau, do not wish to be regarded as a member of any incorporated society which I have not joined." This I gave to the town clerk; and he has it. The State, having thus learned that I did not wish to be regarded as a member of that church, has never made a like demand on me since; though it said that I must adhere to its original presumption that time. If I had known how to name them, I should then have signed off in detail from all the societies which I never signed on to; but I did not know where to find a complete list.

I have paid no poll-tax for six years. I was put into a jail once on this account, for one night; and, as I stood considering the walls of solid stone, two or three feet thick, the door of wood and iron, a foot thick, and the iron grating which strained the light, I could not help being struck with the foolishness of that institution which treated me as if I were mere flesh and blood and bones, to be locked up. I wondered that it should have concluded at length that this was the best use it could put me to, and had never thought to avail itself of my services in some way. I saw that, if there was a wall of stone between me and my townsmen, there was a still more difficult one to climb or break through before they could get to be as free as I was. I did not for a moment feel confined, and the walls seemed a great waste of stone and mortar. I felt as if I alone of all my townsmen had paid my tax. They plainly did not know how to treat me, but behaved like persons who are underbred. In every threat and in every compliment there was a blunder; for they thought that my chief desire was to stand the other side of that stone wall. I could not but smile to see how industriously they locked the door on my meditations, which followed them out again without let or hindrance, and *they* were really all that was dangerous. As they could not reach me, they had resolved to punish my body; just as boys, if they cannot come at some person against whom they have a spite, will abuse his dog. I saw that the State was half-witted, that it was timid as a lone woman with her silver spoons, and that it did not know its friends from its foes, and I lost all my remaining respect for it, and pitied it.

Thus the State never intentionally confronts a man's sense, intellectual or moral, but only his body, his senses. It is not armed with superior wit or honesty, but with superior physical strength. I was not born to be forced. I will breathe after my own fashion. Let us see who is the strongest. What force has a multitude? They only can force me who obey a higher law than I. They force me to become like themselves. I do not hear of *men* being *forced* to live this way or that by masses of men. What sort of life were that to live? When I meet a government which says to me, "Your money or your life," why should I be in haste to give it my money? It may be in a great strait, and not know what to do: I cannot help that. It must help itself; do as I do. It is not worth the while to snivel about it. I am not responsible for the successful working of the machinery of society. I am not the son of the engineer. I perceive that, when an acorn and a chestnut fall side by side, the one does not remain inert to make way for the other, but both obey their own laws, and spring and grow and flourish as best they can, till one, perchance, overshadows and destroys the other. If a plant cannot live according to its nature, it dies; and so a man. . . .

When I came out of prison,—for some one interfered, and paid that tax,—I did not perceive that great changes had taken place on the common, such as he observed who went in a youth and emerged a tottering and grey-headed man; and yet a change has to my eyes come over the scene,—the town, and State, and country,—greater than any that mere time could effect. I saw yet more distinctly the State in which I lived. I saw to what extent the people among whom I lived could be trusted as good neighbors and friends; that their friendship was for summer weather only; that they did not greatly propose to do right; that they were a distinct race from me by their prejudices and superstitions, as the Chinamen and Malays are; that in their sacrifices to humanity they ran no risks, not even to their property; that after all they were not so noble but they treated the thief as he had treated them, and hoped, by a certain outward observance and a few prayers, and by walking in a particular straight though useless path from time to time, to save their souls. This may be to judge my neighbors harshly; for I believe that many of them are not aware that they have such an institution as the jail in their village.

It was formerly the custom in our village, when a poor debtor came out of jail, for his acquaintances to salute him, looking through their fingers, which were crossed to represent the grating of a jail window, "How do ye do?" My neighbors did not thus salute me, but first looked at me, and then at one another, as if I had returned from a long journey. I was put into jail as I was going to the shoemaker's to get a shoe which was mended. When I was let out the next morning, I proceeded to finish my errand, and, having put on my mended shoe, joined a huckleberry party, who were impatient to put themselves under my conduct; and in half an hour,—for the horse was soon tackled,—was in the midst of a huckleberry field, on one of our highest hills, two miles off, and then the State was nowhere to be seen.

This is the whole history of "My Prisons."

I have never declined paying the highway tax, because I am as desirous of being a good neighbor as I am of being a bad subject; and as for supporting schools, I am doing my part to educate my fellow-countrymen now. It is for no particular item in the tax-bill that I refuse to pay it. I simply wish to refuse allegiance to the State, to withdraw and stand aloof from it effectually. I do not care to trace the course of my dollar, if I could, till it buys a man or a musket to shoot with,—the dollar is innocent,—but I am concerned to trace the effects of my allegiance. In fact, I quietly declare war with the State, after my fashion, though I will still make what use and get what advantage of her I can, as is usual in such cases.

If others pay the tax which is demanded of me, from a sympathy with the State, they do but what they have already done in their own case, or rather they abet injustice to a greater extent than the State requires. If they pay the tax from a mistaken interest in the individual taxed, to save his property, or prevent his going to jail, it is because they have not considered wisely how far they let their private feelings interfere with the public good.

This, then, is my position at present. But one cannot be too much on his guard in such a case, lest his action be biased by obstinacy or an undue regard for the opinions of men. Let him see that he does only what belongs to himself and to the hour. . . .

I do not wish to quarrel with any man or nation. I do not wish to split hairs, to make fine distinctions, or set myself up as better than my neighbors. I seek rather, I may say, even an excuse for conforming to the laws of the land. I am but too ready to conform to them. Indeed, I have reason to suspect myself on this head; and each year, as the tax-gatherer comes round, I find myself disposed to review the acts and position of the general and State governments, and the spirit of the people to discover a pretext for conformity.

> We must affect our country as our parents,
> And if at any time we alienate
> Our love or industry from doing it honor,
> We must respect effects and teach the soul
> Matter of conscience and religion,
> And not desire of rule or benefit.

I believe that the State will soon be able to take all my work of this sort out of my hands, and then I shall be no better a patriot than my fellow-countrymen. Seen from a lower point of view, the Constitution, with all its faults, is very good; the law and the courts are very respectable; even this State and this American government are, in many respects, very admirable, and rare things, to be thankful for, such as a great many have described them; but seen from a point of view a little higher, they are what I have described them; seen from a higher still, and the highest, who shall say what they are, or that they are worth looking at or thinking of at all?

However, the government does not concern me much, and I shall bestow the fewest possible thoughts on it. It is not many moments that I live under a government, even in this world. If a man is thought-free, fancy-free, imagination-free, that which *is not* never for a long time appearing *to be* to him, unwise rulers or reformers cannot fatally interrupt him. . . .

The authority of government, even such as I am willing to submit to,—for I will cheerfully obey those who know and can do better than I, and in many things even those who neither know nor can do so well,—is still an impure one: to be strictly just, it must have the sanction and consent of the governed. It can have no pure right over my person and property but what I concede to it. The progress from an absolute to a limited monarchy, from a limited monarchy to a democracy, is a progress toward a true respect for the individual. Even the Chinese philosopher was wise enough to regard the individual as the basis of the empire. Is a democracy, such as we know it, the last improvement possible in government? Is it not possible to take a step further towards recognizing and organizing the rights of man? There will never be a really free and enlightened State until the State comes to recognize the individual as a higher and independent power, from which all its own power and authority are derived, and treats him accordingly. I please myself with imagining a State at last which can afford to be just to all men, and to treat the individual with respect as a neighbor; which even would not think it inconsistent with its own repose if a few were to live aloof from it, not meddling with it, nor embraced by it, who fulfilled all the duties of neighbors and fellow-men. A State which bore this kind of fruit, and suffered it to drop off as fast as it ripened, would prepare the way for a still more perfect and glorious State, which also I have imagined, but not yet anywhere seen.

Notes

1. "Life without Principle," *The Writings of Henry David Thoreau,* (Boston: Houghton Mifflin & Co., 1906), vol. IV, p. 457.

2. Ibid., p. 459.

3. Ibid., p. 468.

4. Ibid., p. 471.

5. Ibid., pp. 475–76.

6. Ibid., pp. 476–77.

Why Freedom Pays
Mill

A liberal thinker, John Stuart Mill (1806—1873) was opposed to forms of political tyranny that restrict freedom of thought, discussion, and action. He was also opposed to the "tyranny of the majority," which he felt was characteristic of his times. Under this kind of tyranny, which can flourish under the pretense of democratic government, society itself becomes a tyrant; collective opinions exert tremendous pressures upon individuals to conform, and those who dissent suffer from powerful social sanctions that make them feel isolated, rejected, and ostracized. Those moral standards which are approved by the majority are not to be questioned by individuals, since such questioning undermines the customary and traditional values that support the social order. Customary beliefs and not philosophically examined ideas must guide human behavior. Those who question such beliefs are often seen as threats to the status quo and as enemies of the people.

Such substitutes for rational inquiry, Mill believes, result in placing prejudice above reasoning, dogmatism above research, and in bestowing infallibility upon individuals and institutions whose interest may be in applying sanctions, including physical punishment, upon dissenting persons. Consequently, often the highest exemplars of human virtue suffer gross social injustice. Socrates is condemned as a corrupter of youth and forced to drink hemlock; Jesus is accused of blasphemy and crucified. Despite their unjust fates, such individuals nevertheless usually do succeed in rendering great service to the society that mistreats and condemns them. Mill is convinced that "to discover to the world something which deeply concerns it, and of which it was previously ignorant; to prove to it that it had been mistaken on some vital point of temporaral or spiritual interest, is as important a service as a human being can render to his fellow creatures."[1]

This service to society is often overlooked, ignored, or underestimated. In fact, some excuse their own lack of courage or lack of interest in preserving and furthering freedom of expression by repeating the dictum that truth always triumphs over persecution in the long run or, as Dr. Samuel Johnson believed, that truth even requires persecution in order to triumph. Mill rejects such beliefs as contrary to experience, citing numerous historical instances of truths that were put down by persecution.[2] Men can be as zealous to perpetuate error as truth, and, in Mill's view, "it is a piece of idle sentimentality that truth, merely as truth, has any inherent power denied to error of prevailing against the dungeon and the stake."[3] In our own time, heretics are seldom put to death in civilized countries, but they are often victims of methods no less effective and insidious. Under the pretense of maintaining a so-called healthy society, whether communist, fascist, or capitalist, dissent is often stigmatized and silenced, thus destroying the possibility of critical judgment and social change.

Not only heretics suffer from restrictions on freedom of thought and discussion, Mill points out; ordinary men do, too. A "closed society" eventually cramps everyone's mental development, atrophies creative faculties, and poisons human aspirations at their source. A few great intellects may rise above the mental stagnation but an intellectually active people can never emerge. Only in the free exchange of ideas can men develop their intellectual resources and awaken a desire to realize more fully their potentialities as unique individuals.

Individuality, in Mill's view, is one of the basic elements of well-being. Unless a person is free to follow his own interests, to develop his own life style, and to act spontaneously when and howsoever he chooses—insofar as his actions do not harm others or restrict their individuality—a person is not genuinely free. In fact, to grow more free is to grow more individualized and to become more of a unique person. Uniformity, standardization, and conformity may sometimes make life easier and more efficient to manage and, in certain situations, may even be necessary, but they are nonetheless enemies of individuality and must be guarded against if life is to become richer, more diversified, and challenging. For, in Mill's words, "whatever crushes individuality is despotism."[4]

Mill believes that, even from a purely selfish point of view, we should encourage others to develop their individuality as freely and fully as possible. First of all, as more people develop their individuality, there are more fulfilled and thus more happy people in the world manifesting more happiness in which others can share. Furthermore, individuality is the principle of innovation and originality. Without it, beliefs would become ossified and practices mechanical. Traditions would remain unchallenged. Life would become a bore. Mankind would be robbed of its geniuses, the most individual and creative of all people, for they "can only breathe freely in an atmosphere of freedom."[5]

For these and other reasons which he elaborated upon in *On Liberty*, Mill believes that all wise men and women will encourage individuality and not just tolerate but appreciate eccentricity. Only in this way can the despotism of custom be overthrown and the cult of conformity be dispersed.

Mill catalogues a mass of influences which he considers hostile to individuality in his time and foresees their strengthening rather than weakening in the future. The growth of government bureaucracies, the leveling down of classes, the extension of education to the masses, the expansion of public services, the industrial system with its regimentation of people and its standardization of products, and the increased influence of mass media are some of the major influences that Mill mentions as having strengthened "the tyranny of opinion."[6] "In this age," Mill writes in the midst of the Victorian age in England, "the mere example of non-conformity, the mere refusal to bend a knee to custom, is itself a service."[7] Eccentricity is not a sign of decadence in a society, Mill concludes, but is symptomatic of a free, tolerant, and vigorous environment in which geniuses can be spawned and the greatest happiness of the greatest number of individuals becomes a realizable ideal.

On Liberty

The object of this Essay is to assert one very simple principle, as entitled to govern absolutely the dealings of society with the individual in the way of compulsion and control, whether the means used be physical force in the form of legal penalties, or the moral coercion of public opinion. That principle is, that the sole end for which mankind are warranted, individually or collectively, in interfering with the liberty of action of any of their number, is self-protection. That the only purpose for which power can be rightfully exercised over any member of a civilised community, against his will, is to prevent harm to others. His own good, either physical or moral, is not a sufficient warrant. He cannot rightfully be compelled to do or forbear because it will be better for him to do so, because it will make him happier, because, in the opinions of others, to do so would be wise, or even right. These are good reasons for remonstrating with him, or reasoning with him, or persuading him, or entreating him, but not for compelling him, or visiting him with any evil in case he do otherwise. To justify that, the conduct from which it is desired to deter him must be calculated to produce evil to someone else. The only part of the conduct of anyone, for which he is amenable to society, is that which concerns others. In the part which merely concerns himself, his independence is, of right, absolute. Over himself, over his own body and mind, the individual is sovereign.

It is, perhaps, hardly necessary to say that this doctrine is meant to apply only to human beings in the maturity of their faculties. We are not speaking of children, or of young persons below the age which the law may fix as that of manhood or womanhood. Those who are still in a state to require being taken care of by others, must be protected against their own actions as well as against external injury. For the same reason, we may leave out of consideration those backward states of society in which the race itself may be considered as in its nonage. The early difficulties in the way of spontaneous progress are so great, that there is seldom any choice of means for overcoming them; and a ruler full of the spirit of improvement is warranted in the use of any expedients that will attain an end, perhaps otherwise unattainable. Despotism is a legitimate mode of government in dealing with barbarians, provided the end be their improvement, and the means justified by actually effecting that end. Liberty, as a principle, has no application to any state of things anterior to the time when mankind have become capable of being improved by free and equal discussion. Until then, there is nothing for them but implicit obedience to an Akbar or a Charlemagne, if they are so fortunate to find one. But as soon as mankind have attained the capacity of being guided to their own improvement by conviction or persuasion (a period long since reached in all nations with whom we need here concern ourselves), compulsion, either in the direct form or in that of pains and penalties for non-compliance, is no longer admissible as a means to their own good, and justifiable only for the security of others.

From John Stuart Mill, *On Liberty* (New York: John W. Lovell, n.d.), chaps. 1–2, pp. 20–93 (with omissions).

It is proper to state that I forego any advantage which could be derived to my argument from the idea of abstract right, as a thing independent of utility. I regard utility as the ultimate appeal on all ethical questions; but it must be utility in the largest sense, grounded on the permanent interests of a man as a progressive being. Those interests, I contend, authorize the subjection of individual spontaneity to external control, only in respect to those actions of each which concern the interest of other people. If any one does an act hurtful to others, there is a *prima facie* case for punishing him, by law, or, where legal penalties are not safely applicable, by general disapprobation. There are also many positive acts for the benefit of others, which he may rightfully be compelled to perform; such as to give evidence in a court of justice; to bear his fair share in the common defence, or in any other joint work necessary to the interest of the society of which he enjoys the protection; and to perform certain acts of individual beneficence, such as saving a fellow-creature's life, or interposing to protect the defenceless against ill-usage, things which whenever it is obviously a man's duty to do, he may rightfully be made responsible to society for not doing. A person may cause evil to others not only by his actions but by his inaction, and in either case he is justly accountable to them for the injury. The latter case, it is true, requires a much more cautious exercise of compulsion than the former. To make any one answerable for doing evil to others is the rule; to make him answerable for not preventing evil is, comparatively speaking, the exception. Yet there are many cases clear enough and grave enough to justify that exception. In all things which regard the external relations of the individual, he is *de jure* amenable to those whose interests are concerned, and, if need be, to society as their protector. There are often good reasons for not holding him to the responsibility; but these reasons must arise from the special expediencies of the case: either because it is a kind of case in which he is on the whole likely to act better, when left to his own discretion, than when controlled in any way in which society have it in their power to control him; or because the attempt to exercise control would produce other evils, greater than those which it would prevent. When such reasons as these preclude the enforcement of responsibility, the conscience of the agent himself should step into the vacant judgment seat, and protect those interests of others who have no external protection; judging himself all the more rigidly, because the case does not admit of his being made accountable to the judgment of his fellow-creatures.

But there is a sphere of action in which society, as distinguished from the individual, has, if any, only an indirect interest; comprehending all that portion of a person's life and conduct which affects only himself, or if it also affects others, only with their free, voluntary, and undeceived consent and participation. When I say only himself, I mean directly, and in the first instance; for whatever affects himself, may affect others through himself; and the objection which may be grounded on this contingency, will receive consideration in the sequel. This, then, is the appropriate region of human liberty. It comprises, first, the inward domain of consciousness; demanding liberty of conscience in the most comprehensive sense; liberty of thought and feeling; absolute freedom of opinion and sentiment on all subjects, practical or speculative, scientific, moral, or theological. The liberty of expressing and publishing opinions may seem to fall under a different principle, since it belongs to that part of the conduct of an individual which concerns other people; but, being almost of as much importance as the liberty of thought itself, and resting in great part on the same reasons, is practically inseparable from it. Secondly, the principle requires liberty of tastes and pursuits; of framing the plan of our life to suit our character; of doing as we like, subject to such consequences as may follow: without impediment from our fellow-creatures, so long as what we do does not harm them, even though they should think our conduct foolish, perverse, or wrong. Thirdly, from this liberty of each individual, follows the liberty, within the same limits, of combination among individuals; freedom to unite, for any purpose not involving harm to others: the persons combining being supposed to be of full age, and not forced or deceived.

No society in which these liberties are not, on the whole, respected, is free, whatever may be its form of government; and none is completely free in which they do not exist absolute and unqualified. The only freedom which deserves the name, is that of pursuing our own good in our own way, so long as we do not attempt to deprive others of theirs, or impede their efforts to obtain it. Each is the proper guardian of his own health, whether bodily, *or* mental and spiritual. Mankind are greater gainers by suffering each other to live as seems good to themselves, than by compelling each to live as seems good to the rest. . . .

Apart from the peculiar tenets of individual thinkers, there is also in the world at large an increasing inclination to stretch unduly the powers of society over the individual, both by the force of opinion, and even by that of legislation; and as the tendency of all the changes taking place in the world is to strengthen society, and diminish the power of the individual, this encroachment is not one of the evils which tend spontaneously to disappear, but, on the contrary, to grow more and more formidable. The disposition of mankind, whether as rulers or as fellow-citizens, to impose their own opinions and inclinations as a rule of conduct on others, is so energetically supported by some of the best and by some of the worst feelings incident to human nature, that it is hardly ever kept upon restraint by anything but want of power; and as the power is not declining, but growing, unless a strong barrier of moral conviction can be raised against the mischief, we must expect, in the present circumstances of the world to see it increase.

It will be convenient for the argument, if, instead of at once entering upon the general thesis, we confine ourselves in the first instance to a single branch of it, on which the principle here stated is, if not fully, yet to a certain point, recognised by the current opinions. This one branch is the Liberty of Thought: from which it is impossible to separate the cognate liberty of speaking and of writing. Although these liberties, to some considerable amount, form part of the political morality of all countries which profess religious toleration and free institutions, the grounds, both philosophical and practical, on which they rest, are perhaps not so familiar to the general mind, nor so thoroughly appreciated by many even of the leaders of opinion, as might have been expected. Those grounds, when rightly understood, are of much wider application than to only one division of the subject, and a thorough consideration of this part of the question will be found the best introduction to the remainder. Those to whom nothing which I am about to say will be new, may therefore, I hope, excuse me, if on a subject which for now three centuries has been so often discussed, I venture on one discussion more. . . .

The time, it is to be hoped, is gone by, when any defence would be necessary of the "liberty of the press" as one of the securities against corrupt or tyrannical government. No argument, we may suppose, can now be needed, against permitting a legislature or an executive, not identified in interest with the people, to prescribe opinions to them, and determine what doctrines or what arguments they shall be allowed to hear. This aspect of the question, besides, has been so often and so triumphantly enforced by preceding writers, that it needs not be specially insisted on in this place. Though the law of England, on the subject of the press, is as servile to this day as it was in the time of the Tudors, there is little danger of its being actually put in force against political discussion, except during some temporary panic, when fear of insurrection drives ministers and judges from their propriety; and, speaking generally, it is not, in constitutional countries, to be apprehended, that the government, whether completely responsible to the people or not, will often attempt to control the expression of opinion, except when in doing so it makes itself the organ of the general intolerance of the public. Let us suppose, therefore, that the government is entirely at one with the people, and never thinks of exerting any power of coercion unless in agreement with what it conceives to be their voice. But I deny the right of the people to exercise such coercion, either by themselves or by their government. The power itself is illegitimate. The best government has no more title to it than the worst. It is as noxious, or more noxious, when exerted in accordance with public opinion, than when in opposition to it. If all mankind minus one were of one opinion, and only one person were of the contrary opinion, mankind would be no more justified in silencing that one person, than he, if he had the power, would be justified in silencing mankind. Were an opinion a personal possession of no value except to the owner; if to be obstructed in the enjoyment of it were simply a private injury, it would make some difference whether the injury was inflicted only on a few persons or on many. But the peculiar evil of silencing the expression of an opinion is, that it is robbing the human race: posterity as well as the existing generation; those who dissent from the opinion, still more than those who hold it. If the opinion is right, they are deprived of the opportunity of exchanging error for truth: if wrong, they lose, what is almost as great a benefit, the clearer perception and livelier impression of truth, produced by its collision with error.

It is necessary to consider separately these two hypotheses, each of which has a distinct branch of the argument corresponding to it. We can never be sure that the opinion we are endeavouring to stifle is a false opinion; and if we were sure, stifling it would be an evil still.

First, the opinion which it is attempted to suppress by authority may possibly be true. Those who desire to suppress it, of course deny its truth; but they are not infallible. They have no authority to decide the question for all mankind, and exclude every other person from the means of judging. To refuse a hearing to an opinion, because they are sure that it is false, is to assume that *their* certainty is the same thing as *absolute* certainty. All silencing of discussion is an assumption of infallibility. Its condemnation may be allowed to rest on this common argument, not the worse for being common.

Unfortunately for the good sense of mankind, the fact of their fallibility is far from carrying the weight in their practical judgment which is always allowed to it in theory; for while every one well knows himself to be fallible, few think it necessary to take any precautions against their own fallibility, or admit the supposition that any opinion, of which they feel very certain, may be one of the examples of the error to which they acknowledge themselves to be liable. Absolute princes, or others who are accustomed to unlimited deference, usually feel this complete confidence in their own opinions on nearly all subjects. People more happily situated, who sometimes hear their opinions disputed, and are not wholly unused to be set right when they are wrong, place the same unbounded reliance only on such of their opinions as are shared by all who surround them, or to whom they habitually defer; for in proportion to a man's want of confidence in his own solitary judgment, does he usually repose, with implicit trust, on the infallibility of "the world" in general. And the world, to each individual, means the part of it with which he comes in contact: his party, his sect, his church, his class of society; the man may be called, by comparison, almost liberal and large-minded to whom it means anything so comprehensive as his own country or his own age. Nor is his faith in this collective authority at all shaken by his being aware that other ages, countries, sects, churches, classes, and parties have thought, and even now think, the exact reverse. He devolves upon his own world the responsibility of being in the right against the dissentient worlds of other people; and it never troubles him that mere accident has decided which of these numerous worlds is the object of his reliance, and that the same causes which make him a Churchman in London, would have made him a Buddhist or a Confucian in Pekin. Yet it is as evident in itself, as any amount of argument can make it, that ages are no more infallible than individuals; every age having held many opinions which subsequent ages have deemed not only false but absurd; and it is as certain that many opinions now general will be rejected by future ages, as it is that many, once general, are rejected by the present.

The objection likely to be made to this argument would probably take some such form as the following. There is no greater assumption of infallibility in forbidding the propagation of error, than in any other thing which is done by public authority on its own judgment and responsibility. Judgment is given to men that they may use it. Because it may be used erroneously, are men to be told that they ought not to use it all? To prohibit what they think pernicious, is not claiming exemption from error, but fulfilling the duty incumbent on them, although fallible, of acting on their conscientious conviction. If we were never to act on our opinions, because those opinions may be wrong, we should leave all our interest uncared for, and all our duties unperformed. An objection which applies to all conduct can be no valid objection to conduct in particular. It is the duty of governments and of individuals, to form the truest opinions they can; to form them carefully, and never impose them upon others unless they are quite sure of being right. But when they are sure (such reasoners may say), it is not conscientiousness but cowardice to shrink from acting on their opinions, and allow doctrines which they honestly think dangerous to the welfare of mankind, either in this life or in another, to be scattered abroad without restraint, because other people, in less en-

lightened times, have persecuted opinions now believed to be true. Let us take care, it may be said, not to make the same mistake; but governments and nations have made mistakes in other things, which are not denied to be fit subjects for the exercise of authority: they have laid on bad taxes, made unjust wars. Ought we therefore to lay on no taxes, and, under whatever provocation, make no wars: Men, and governments, must act to the best of their ability. There is no such thing as absolute certainty, but there is assurance sufficient for the purposes of human life. We may, and must, assume our opinion to be true for the guidance of our own conduct: and it is assuming no more when we forbid bad men to pervert society by the propagation of opinions which we regard as false and pernicious.

I answer, that it is assuming very much more. There is the greatest difference between presuming an opinion to be true, because, with every opportunity for contesting it, it has not been refuted, and assuming its truth for the purpose of not permitting its refutation. Complete liberty of contradicting and disproving our opinion is the very condition which justifies us in assuming its truth for purposes of action; and on no other terms can a being with human faculties have any rational assurance of being right.

When we consider either the history of opinion, or the ordinary conduct of human life, to what is it to be ascribed that the one and the other are no worse than they are? Not certainly to the inherent force of the human understanding; for, on any matter not self-evident, there are ninety-nine persons totally incapable of judging of it for one who is capable; and the capacity of the hundredth person is only comparative; for the majority of the eminent men of every past generation held many opinions now known to be erroneous, and did or approved numerous things which no one will now justify. Why is it, then, that there is on the whole a preponderance among mankind of rational opinions and rational conduct? If there really is this preponderance—which there must be unless human affairs are, and have always been, in an almost desperate state—it is owing to a quality of the human mind, the source of everything respectable in man either as an intellectual or as a moral being, namely, that his errors are corrigible. He is capable of rectifying his mistakes, by discussion and experience. Not by experience alone. There must be discussion, to show how experience is to be interpreted. Wrong opinions and practices gradually yield to fact and argument; but facts and arguments, to produce any effect on the mind, must be brought before it. Very few facts are able to tell their own story, without comments to bring out their meaning. The whole strength and value, then, of human judgment, depending on the one property, that it can be set right when it is wrong, reliance can be placed on it only when the means of setting it right are kept constantly at hand. In the case of any person whose judgment is really deserving of confidence, how has it become so? Because he has kept his mind open to criticism of his opinions and conduct. Because it has been his practice to listen to all that could be said against him; to profit by as much of it as was just, and expound to himself, and upon occasion to others, the fallacy of what was fallacious. Because he has felt, that the only way in which a human being can make some approach to knowing the whole of a subject, is by hearing what can be said about it by persons of every variety of opinion, and studying all modes in which it can be looked at by every character of mind. No wise man ever acquired his wisdom in any mode but this; nor is it in the nature of human intellect to become wise in any other manner. The steady habit of correcting and completing his own opinion by collating it with those of others, so far from causing doubt and hesitation in carrying it into practice, is the only stable foundation for a just reliance on it: for, being cognisant of all that can, at least obviously, be said against him, and having taken up his position against all gainsayers—knowing that he has sought for objections and difficulties, instead of avoiding them, and has shut out no light

which can be thrown upon the subject from any quarter—he has a right to think his judgment better than that of any person or any multitude, who have not gone through a similar process. . . .

Let us now pass to the second division of the argument, and dismissing the supposition that any of the received opinions may be false, let us assume them to be true, and examine into the worth of the manner in which they are likely to be held, when their truth is not freely and openly canvassed. However unwillingly a person who has a strong opinion may admit the possibility that his opinion may be false, he ought to be moved by the consideration that, however true it may be, if it is not fully, frequently, and fearlessly discussed, it will be held as a dead dogma, not a living truth.

There is a class of persons (happily not quite so numerous as formerly) who think it enough if a person assents undoubtingly to what they think true, though he has no knowledge whatever of the grounds of the opinion, and could not make a tenable defence of it against the most superficial objections. Such persons, if they can once get their creed taught from authority, naturally think that no good, and some harm, comes of its being allowed to be questioned. Where their influence prevails, they make it nearly impossible for the received opinion to be rejected wisely and considerately, though it may still be rejected rashly and ignorantly; for to shut out discussion entirely is seldom possible, and when it once gets in, beliefs not grounded on convictions are apt to give way before the slightest semblance of an argument. Waiving, however, this possibility—assuming that the true opinion abides in the mind, but abides as a prejudice, a belief independent of, and proof against, argument—this is not the way in which truth ought to be held by a rational being. This is not knowing the truth. Truth, thus held, is but one superstition the more, accidently clinging to the words which enunciate a truth.

If the intellect and judgment of mankind ought to be cultivated, a thing which Protestants at least do not deny, on what can these faculties be more appropriately exercised by any one, than on the things which concern him so much that it is considered necessary for him to hold opinions on them? If the cultivation of the understanding consists in one thing more than in another, it is surely in learning the grounds of one's own opinions. Whatever people believe, on subjects on which it is of the first importance to believe rightly, they ought to be able to defend against at least the common objections. But, some one may say, "Let them be *taught* the grounds of their opinions. It does not follow that opinions must be merely parroted because they are never heard controverted. Persons who learn geometry do not simply commit the theorems to memory, but understand and learn likewise the demonstrations; and it would be absurd to say that they remain ignorant of the grounds of geometrical truths, because they never hear any one deny, and attempt to disprove them." Undoubtedly: and such teaching suffices on a subject like mathematics, where there is nothing at all to be said on the wrong side of the question. The peculiarity of the evidence of mathematical truths is that all the argument is on one side. There are no objections, and no answers to objections. But on every subject on which difference of opinion is possible, the truth depends on a balance to be struck between two sets of conflicting reasons. Even in natural philosophy, there is always some other explanation possible of the same facts: some geocentric theory instead of heliocentric, some phlogiston instead of oxygen; and it has to be shown why that other theory cannot be the true one; and until this is shown, and until we know how it is shown, we do not understand the grounds of our opinion. But when we turn to subjects infinitely more complicated, to morals, religion, politics, social relations, and the business of life, three-fourths of the arguments for every disputed opinion consists in dispelling the appearances which favour some opinion different from it. The greatest orator, save one, of antiquity, has left it on record that

he always studied his adversary's case with as great, if not still greater, intensity than even his own. What Cicero practised as the means of forensic success requires to be imitated by all who study any subject in order to arrive at the truth. He who knows only his own side of the case, knows little of that. His reasons may be good, and no one may have been able to refute them. But if he is equally unable to refute the reasons on the opposite side; if he does not so much as know what they are, he has no ground for preferring either opinion. The rational position for him would be suspension of judgment, and unless he contents himself with that, he is either led by authority, or adopts, like the generality of the world, the side to which he feels most inclination. Nor is it enough that he should hear the arguments of adversaries from his own teachers, presented as they state them, and accompanied by what they offer as refutations. That is not the way to do justice to the arguments, or bring them into real contact with his own mind. He must be able to hear them from persons who actually believe them; who defend them in earnest, and do their very most for them. He must know them in their most plausible and persuasive form; he must feel the whole force of the difficulty which the true view of the subject has to encounter and dispose of; else he will never really possess himself of the portion of truth which meets and removes that difficulty. Ninety-nine in a hundred of what are called educated men are in this condition; even of those who can argue fluently for their opinions. Their conclusion may be true, but it might be false for anything they know: they have never thrown themselves into the mental position of those who think differently from them, and considered what such persons may have to say; and consequently they do not, in any proper sense of the word, know the doctrine which they themselves profess. They do not know those parts of it which explain and justify the remainder; the considerations which show that a fact which seemingly conflicts with another is reconcilable with it, or that, of two apparently strong reasons, one and not the other ought to be preferred. All that part of the truth which turns the scale, and decides the judgment of a completely informed mind, they are strangers to; nor is it ever really known, but to those who have attended equally and impartially to both sides, and endeavoured to see the reasons of both in the strongest light. So essential is this discipline to a real understanding of moral and human subjects, that if opponents of all important truths do not exist, it is indispensable to imagine them, and supply them with the strongest arguments which the most skillful devil's advocate can conjure up. . . .

It still remains to speak of one of the principal causes which make diversity of opinion advantageous, and will continue to do so until mankind shall have entered a stage of intellectual advancement which at present seems at an incalculable distance. We have hitherto considered only two possibilities: that the received opinion may be false, and some other opinion, consequently, true; or that, the received opinion being true, a conflict with the opposite error is essential to a clear apprehension and deep feeling of its truth. But there is a commoner case than either of these; when the conflicting doctrines, instead of being one true and the other false, share the truth between them; and the nonconforming opinion is needed to supply the remainder of the truth, of which the received doctrine embodies only a part. Popular opinions, on subjects not palpable to sense, are often true, but seldom or never the whole truth. They are a part of the truth; sometimes a greater, sometimes a smaller part, but exaggerated, distorted, and disjointed from the truths by which they ought to be accompanied and limited. Heretical opinions, on the other hand, are generally some of these suppressed and neglected truths, bursting the bonds which kept them down, and either seeking reconciliation with the truth contained in the common opinion, or fronting it as enemies, and setting themselves up, with similar exclusiveness, as the whole truth. The latter case

is hitherto the most frequent, as in the human mind, one sidedness has always been the rule, and many-sidedness the exception. Hence, even in revolutions of opinion, one part of the truth usually sets while another rises. Even progress, which ought to superadd, for the most part only substitutes one partial and incomplete truth for another; improvement consisting chiefly in this, that the new fragment of truth is more wanted, more adapted to the needs of the time, than that which it displaces. Such being the partial character of prevailing opinions, even when resting on a true foundation; every opinion which embodies somewhat of the portion of truth which the common opinion omits, ought to be considered precious, with whatever amount of error and confusion that truth may be blended. No sober judge of human affairs will feel bound to be indignant because those who force on our notice truths which we should otherwise have overlooked, overlook some of those which we see. Rather, he will think that so long as popular truth is one-sided, it is more desirable than otherwise that unpopular truth should have one-sided assertors too; such being usually the most energetic, and the most likely to compel reluctant attention to the fragment of wisdom which they proclaim as if it were the whole.

Thus, in the eighteenth century, when nearly all the instructed, and all those of the uninstructed who were led by them, were lost in admiration of what is called civilisation, and of the marvels of modern science, literature, and philosophy, and while greatly overrating the amount of unlikeness between the men of modern and those of ancient times, indulged the belief that the whole of the difference was in their own favour; with what a salutary shock did the paradoxes of Rousseau explode like bombshells in the midst, dislocating the compact mass of one-sided opinion, and forcing its elements to recombine in a better form and with additional ingredients. Not that the current opinions where on the whole farther from the truth than to it; they contained more of positive truth, and very much less of error. Nevertheless there lay in Rousseau's doctrine, and has floated down the stream of opinion along with it, a considerable amount of exactly those truths which the popular opinion wanted; and these are the deposit which was left behind when the flood subsided. The superior worth of simplicity of life, the enervating and demoralising effect of the trammels and hypocrisies of artificial society, are ideas which have never been entirely absent from cultivated minds since Rousseau wrote; and they will in time produce their due effect, though at present needing to be asserted as much as ever, and to be asserted by deeds, for words, on this subject have nearly exhausted their power.

In politics, again, it is almost a commonplace, that a party of order or stability, and a party of progress or reform, are both necessary elements of a healthy state of political life; until the one or the other shall have so enlarged its mental grasp as to be a party equally of order and of progress, knowing and distinguishing what is fit to be preserved from what ought to be swept away. Each of these modes of thinking derives its utility from the deficiencies of the other; but it is in a great measure the opposition of the other that keeps each within the limits of reason and sanity. Unless opinions favourable to democracy and to aristocracy, to property and to equality, to co-operation and to competition, to luxury and to abstinence, to sociality and individuality, to liberty and discipline, and all the other standing antagonisms of practical life, are expressed with equal freedom, and enforced and defended with equal talent and energy, there is no chance of both elements obtaining their due; one scale is sure to go up, and the other down. Truth, in the great practical concerns of life, is so much a question of the reconciling and combining of opposites that very few have minds sufficiently capacious and impartial to make the adjustments with an approach to correctness, and it has to be made by the rough process of a struggle between combatants fighting under hostile banners. On any of the great open questions just enumerated, if either of the two opinions has a better claim than the other, not merely to be tolerated, but to be encouraged and countenanced, it is the one which happens at the particular time and place to be in a minority. That is the opinion which, for the time being, represents the neglected interests, the side of human well-being which is in danger of obtaining less than its share. I am aware that there is not, in this country, any intolerance of differences of opinion on most of these topics. They are adduced to show, by admitted and multiplied examples, the universality of the fact, that only through diversity of opinion is there, in the existing state of human intellect, a chance of fair play to all sides of the truth. When there are persons to be found who form an exception to the apparent unanimity of the world on any subject, even if the world is in the right, it is always probable that dissentients have something worth hearing to say for themselves, and that truth would lose something by their silence. . . .

Notes

1. John Stuart Mill, *On Liberty* (New York: John W. Lovell, n.d.), chap. 2, pp. 48–49.
2. Ibid., chap. 2, p. 50.
3. Ibid.
4. Ibid., chap. 3, p. 107.
5. Ibid., p. 109.
6. Ibid., pp. 112–13.
7. Ibid., p. 112.

9 / Positive Freedom
Fromm

Erich Fromm's *Escape from Freedom* (1941) can be viewed as a psychologist's commentary on the text of Dostoyevsky's "Legend of the Grand Inquisitor." Why, Fromm asks, after centuries of human effort to abolish the external domination of men by nature, by the church, and by power of absolute rulers, have new authoritarian systems appeared, restricting the freedom of millions of human beings and demanding (and getting) almost complete submission of masses of men to a few powerful leaders?

In attempting to answer this question, Fromm traces the emergence of individual freedom during the Renaissance and Reformation and studies the psychological basis of human freedom (and submission) in human needs. There are "physiologically conditioned needs" (for example, the need for food) and uniquely human needs (for example, the need for relatedness) that distinguish man from the so-called lower animals. Man seeks to achieve a sense of belonging, tries to commune with others, and strives to avoid, at any cost, a feeling of complete isolation. Insofar as religious and nationalistic systems can help human beings satisfy this need for relatedness to one another and to a higher being or reality, they can get and maintain a power hold upon individuals.

Mature and free human beings, as Fromm conceives of them, realize that to become free means to grow beyond the original state of being one with mother nature and one's own mother. They relate to the world productively and are capable of spontaneity of feeling and action; in other words, they can work and love. Immature persons, on the other hand, are unable or unwilling to undergo the anxiety and exert the effort to reach the high and frequently difficult level of freedom and spontaneity. It is as though the immature person's umbilical cord has never been severed; he retains his dependency on a parental figure. He is afraid of launching out in what appears to be a foreign and threatening environment. He fails, in Fromm's view, to achieve individuation. Freedom, because it demands of him that he be born completely, that he learn to become his own mother and father, child and creator, he finds frightening. He prefers to be submissive rather than independent, to regress rather than progress, and to do this he must find an escape from freedom.

The urgency of this desire to escape from freedom has been intensified, Fromm believes, by the characteristics of modern Western civilization, which developed with the triumph of capitalism. A marketing orientation by which man sells himself like any other commodity has become prevalent; human beings have been "employed" as though they were machines. Through assemblyline production, workers have increasingly become alienated from the products they produce; they have been robbed of the enjoyment of the fruits of their labor. Modern expert advertising and political propaganda have bombarded and deadened men's sensory awareness, making them less feeling and at the same time less rational creatures. Wars and rumors of wars make the individual feel his life is uncertain; the increasing pollution of his environment makes life itself seem less worthwhile. It is no wonder that he longs to find a panacea and that he is too frightened by his human predicament to gain positive freedom, "freedom to," along with negative freedom, "freedom from." Instead, he flees from all freedom and responsibility.

The mechanisms of escape that modern man has resorted to in order to overcome his intense feelings of insecurity and anxiety when confronted with the frightening prospects of being on one's own—of being free to fail or succeed—are brilliantly delineated and discussed in Fromm's *Escape from Freedom*.

Authoritarianism, the first of these mechanisms, has as its psychological bases a masochistic striving, or a striving for submission, and a sadistic striving, or a striving for domination. Both of these strivings are neurotic. They arise from the same psychological effort to overcome aloneness and achieve security by the borrowed strength that comes from identifying with an external authority whether a human being or a social institution.

A second mechanism, destructiveness, Fromm considers to be "the outcome of unlived life."[1] Feeling thwarted in satisfying his desires, the individual achieves self-transcendence not through creative but through destructive activities. By destroying the objects or persons to which he feels inferior, such an individual achieves through his action at least the illusion of having overcome his isolation and powerlessness. Hitler's attempt to destroy his Third Reich along with himself in the last days of the Second World War is a good example of extreme destructiveness.

The third mechanism by which man attempts to escape from freedom Fromm calls Automation Conformity.[2] This is a kind of protective coloration that permits the individual to lose himself by conforming to mass norms or cultural patterns. He becomes an automaton among millions of other automatons, a mere number, a faceless entity who has lost his powerlessness and isolation by merging himself with a crowd. He thus becomes a pseudoself who can only deal with his insecurity and anxiety by seeking approval and recognition from others whom he hopes will thus give him back the sense of identity which he has not so much lost as never sufficiently developed.

In this context Fromm proceeds to develop his own conception of what it means to be a free and spontaneous person.

Freedom and Spontaneity

So far this book has dealt with one aspect of freedom: the powerlessness and insecurity of the isolated individual in modern society who has become free from all bonds that once gave meaning and security to life. We have seen that the individual cannot bear this isolation; as an isolated being he is utterly helpless in comparison with the world outside and therefore deeply afraid of it; and because of his isolation, the unity of the world has broken down for him and he has lost any point of orientation. He is therefore overcome by doubts concerning himself, the meaning of life, and eventually any principle according to which he can direct his actions. Both helplessness and doubt paralyze life, and in order to live man tries to escape from freedom, negative freedom. He is driven into new bondage. This bondage is different from the primary bonds, from which, though dominated by authorities or the social group, he was not entirely separated. The escape does not restore his lost security, but only helps him to forget his self as a separate entity. He finds new and fragmented security at the expense of sacrificing the integrity of his individual self. He chooses to lose his self since he cannot bear to be alone. Thus freedom—as freedom from— leads into new bondage.

Does our analysis lend itself to the conclusion that there is an inevitable circle that leads from freedom into new dependence? Does freedom

From *Escape from Freedom* by Erich Fromm. Copyright 1941, © 1969 by Erich Fromm. Reprinted by permission of Holt, Rinehart and Winston, Inc.

from all primary ties make the individual so alone and isolated that inevitably he must escape into new bondage? Are *independence* and freedom identical with *isolation* and fear? Or is there a state of positive freedom in which the individual exists as an independent self and yet is not isolated but united with the world, with other men, and nature?

We believe that there is a positive answer, that the process of growing freedom does not constitute a vicious circle, and that man can be free and yet not alone, critical and yet not filled with doubts, independent and yet an integral part of mankind. This freedom man can attain by the realization of his self, by being himself. What is realization of the self? Idealistic philosophers have believed that self-realization can be achieved by intellectual insight alone. They have insisted upon splitting human personality, so that man's nature may be suppressed and guarded by his reason. The result of this split, however, has been that not only the emotional life of man but also his intellectual faculties have been crippled. Reason, by becoming a guard set to watch its prisoner, nature, has become a prisoner itself; and thus both sides of human personality, reason and emotion, were crippled. We believe that the realization of the self is accomplished not only by an act of thinking but also by the realization of man's total personality, by the active expression of his emotional and intellectual potentialities. These potentialities are present in everybody; they become real only to the extent to which they are expressed. In other words, *positive freedom consists in the spontaneous activity of the total, integrated personality.*

We approach here one of the most difficult problems of psychology: the problem of spontaneity. An attempt to discuss this problem adequately would require another volume. However, on the basis of what we have said so far, it is possible to arrive at an understanding of the essential quality of spontaneous activity by means of contrast. Spontaneous activity is not compulsive activity, to which the individual is driven by his isolation and powerlessness; it is not the activity of the automaton, which is the uncritical adoption of patterns suggested from the outside. Spontaneous activity is free activity of the self and implies, psychologically, what the Latin root of the word, *sponte,* means literally: of one's free will. By activity we do not mean "doing something," but the quality of creative activity that can operate in one's emotional, intellectual, and sensuous experiences and in one's will as well. One premise for this spontaneity is the acceptance of the total personality and the elimination of the split between "reason" and "nature"; for only if man does not repress essential parts of his self, only if he has become transparent to himself, and only if the different spheres of life have reached a fundamental integration, is spontaneous activity possible.

While spontaneity is a relatively rare phenomenon in our culture, we are not entirely devoid of it. In order to help in the understanding of this point, I should like to remind the reader of some instances where we all catch a glimpse of spontaneity.

In the first place, we know of individuals who are—or have been—spontaneous, whose thinking, feeling, and acting were the expression of their selves and not of an automaton. These individuals are mostly known to us as artists. As a matter of fact, the artist can be defined as an individual who can express himself spontaneously. If this were the definition of an artist—Balzac defined him just in that way—then certain philosophers and scientists have to be called artists too, while others are as different from them as an old-fashioned photographer from a creative painter. There are other individuals who, though lacking the ability—or perhaps merely the training—for expressing themselves in an objective medium as the artist does, possess the same spontaneity. The position of the artist is vulnerable, though, for it is really only the successful artist whose individuality or spontaneity is respected; if he does not succeed in selling his art, he remains to his contemporaries a crank, a "neurotic." The artist in this matter is in a similar position to that of the revolutionary throughout history. The successful revolutionary is a statesman, the unsuccessful one a criminal.

Small children offer another instance of spontaneity. They have an ability to feel and think that which is really theirs; this spontaneity shows in what they say and think, in the feelings that are expressed in their faces. If one asks what makes for the attraction small children have for most people I believe that, aside from sentimental and conventional reasons, the answer must be that it is this very quality of spontaneity. It appeals profoundly to everyone who is not so dead himself that he has lost the ability to perceive it. As a matter of fact, there is nothing more attractive and convincing than spontaneity whether it is to be found in a child, in an artist, or in those individuals who cannot thus be grouped according to age or profession.

Most of us can observe at least moments of our own spontaneity which are at the same time moments of genuine happiness. Whether it be the fresh and spontaneous perception of a landscape, or the dawning of some truth as the result of our thinking, or a sensuous pleasure that is not stereotyped, or the welling up of love for another person—in these moments we all know what a spontaneous act is and may have some vision of what human life could be if these experiences were not such rare and uncultivated occurrences.

Why is spontaneous activity the answer to the problem of freedom? We have said that negative freedom by itself makes the individual an isolated being, whose relationship to the world is distant and distrustful and whose self is weak and constantly threatened. Spontaneous activity is the one way in which man can overcome the terror of aloneness without sacrificing the integrity of his self; for in the spontaneous realization of the self man unites himself anew with the world—with man, nature, and himself. Love is the foremost component of such spontaneity; not love as the dissolution of the self in another person, not love as the possession of another person, but love as spontaneous affirmation of others, as the union of the individual with others on the basis of the preservation of the individual self. The dynamic quality of love lies in this very polarity: that it springs from the need of overcoming separateness, that it leads to oneness—and yet that individuality is not eliminated. Work is the other component; not work as a compulsive activity in order to escape aloneness, not work as a relationship to nature which is partly one of dominating her, partly one of worship of and enslavement by the very products of man's hands, but work as creation in which man becomes one with nature in the act of creation. What holds true of love and work holds true of all spontaneous action, whether it be the realization of sensuous pleasure or participation in the political life of the community. It affirms the individuality of the self and at the same time it unites the self with man and nature. The basic dichotomy that is inherent in freedom—the birth of individuality and the pain of aloneness—is dissolved on a higher plane by man's spontaneous action.

In all spontaneous activity the individual embraces the world. Not only does his individual self remain intact; it becomes stronger and more solidified. *For the self is as strong as it is active.* There is no genuine strength in possession as such, neither of material property nor of mental qualities like emotions or thoughts. There is also no strength in use and manipulation of objects; what we use is not ours simply because we use it. Ours is only that to which we

are genuinely related by our creative activity, be it a person or an inanimate object. Only those qualities that result from our spontaneous activity give strength to the self and thereby form the basis of its integrity. The inability to act spontaneously, to express what one genuinely feels and thinks, and the resulting necessity to present a pseudo self to others and oneself, are the root of the feeling of inferiority and weakness. Whether or not we are aware of it, there is nothing of which we are more ashamed than of not being ourselves, and there is nothing that gives us greater pride and happiness than to think, to feel, and to say what is ours.

This implies that what matters is the activity as such, the process and not the result. In our culture the emphasis is just the reverse. We produce not for a concrete satisfaction but for the abstract purpose of selling our commodity; we feel that we can acquire everything material or immaterial by buying it, and thus things become ours independently of any creative effort of our own in relation to them. In the same way we regard our personal qualities and the result of our efforts as commodities that can be sold for money, prestige, and power. The emphasis thus shifts from the present satisfaction of creative activity to the value of the finished product. Thereby man misses the only satisfaction that can give him real happiness—the experience of the activity of the present moment—and chases after a phantom that leaves him disappointed as soon as he believes he has caught it—the illusory happiness called success.

If the individual realizes his self by spontaneous activity and thus relates himself to the world, he ceases to be an isolated atom; he and the world become part of one structuralized whole; he has his rightful place, and thereby his doubt concerning himself and the meaning of life disappears. This doubt sprang from his separateness and from the thwarting of life; when he can live, neither compulsively nor automatically but spontaneously, the doubt disappears. He is aware of himself as an active and creative individual and recognizes that *there is only one meaning of life: the act of living itself.*

If the individual overcomes the basic doubt concerning himself and his place in life, if he is related to the world by embracing it in the act of spontaneous living, he gains strength as an individual and he gains security. This security, however, differs from the security that characterizes the preindividualist state in the same way in which the new relatedness to the world differs from that of the primary ties. The new security is not rooted in the protection which the individual has from a higher power outside of himself; neither is it a security in which the tragic quality of life is eliminated. The new security is dynamic; it is not based on protection, but on man's spontaneous activity. It is the security acquired each moment by man's spontaneous activity. It is the security that only freedom can give, that needs no illusions because it has eliminated those conditions that necessitate illusions.

Positive freedom as the realization of the self implies the full affirmation of the uniqueness of the individual. Men are born equal but they are also born different. The basis of this difference is the inherited equipment, physiological and mental, with which they start life, to which is added the particular constellation of circumstances and experiences that they meet with. This individual basis of the personality is as little identical with any other as two organisms are ever identical physically. The genuine growth of the self is always a growth on this particular basis; it is an organic growth, the unfolding of a nucleus that is peculiar for this one person and only for him. The development of the automaton, in contrast, is not an organic growth. The growth of the basis of the self is blocked and a pseudo self is superimposed upon this self, which is—as we have seen—essentially the incorporation of extraneous patterns of thinking and feeling. Organic growth is possible only under the condition of supreme respect for the peculiarity of the self of other persons as well as of our own self. This respect for and cultivation of the uniqueness of the self is the most valuable achievement of human culture and it is this very achievement that is in danger today.

The uniqueness of the self in no ways contradicts the principle of equality. The thesis that men are born equal implies that they all share the same fundamental human qualities, that they share the basic fate of human beings, that they all have the same inalienable claim on freedom and happiness. It furthermore means that their relationship is one of solidarity, not one of domination–submission. What the concept of equality does not mean is that all men are alike. Such a concept of equality is derived from the role that the individual plays in his economic activities today. In the relation between the man who buys and the one who sells, the concrete differences of personality are eliminated. In this situation only one thing matters, that the one has something to sell and the other has money to buy it. In economic life one man is not different from another; as real persons they are, and the cultivation of their uniqueness is the essence of individuality.

Positive freedom also implies the principle that there is no higher power than this unique individual self, that man is the center and purpose of his life; that the growth and realization of man's individuality is an end that can never be subordinated to purposes which are supposed to have greater dignity. This interpretation may arouse serious objections. Does it not postulate unbridled egotism? Is it not the negation of the idea of sacrifice for an ideal? Would its acceptance not lead to anarchy? These questions have actually already been answered, partly explicitly, partly implicitly, during our previous discussion. However, they are too important for us not to make another attempt to clarify the answers and to avoid misunderstanding.

To say that man should not be subject to anything higher than himself does not deny the dignity of ideals. On the contrary, it is the strongest affirmation of ideals. It forces us, however, to a critical analysis of what an ideal is. One is generally apt today to assume that an ideal is any aim whose achievement does not imply material gain, anything for which a person is ready to sacrifice egotistical ends. This is a purely psychological—and for that matter relativistic—concept of an ideal. From this subjectivist viewpoint a Fascist, who is driven by the desire to subordinate himself to a higher power and at the same time to overpower other people, has an ideal just as much as the man who fights for human equality and freedom. On this basis the problem of ideals can never be solved.

We must recognize the difference between genuine and fictitious ideals, which is just as fundamental a difference as that between truth and falsehood. All genuine ideals have one thing in common: they express the desire for something which is not yet accomplished but which is desirable for the purposes of the growth and happiness of the individual.* We may not always know what serves this end, we may disagree about the function of this or that ideal in terms of human development, but this is no reason for a relativism which says that we cannot know what furthers life or what blocks it. We are not always sure which food is healthy and which is not, yet we do not conclude that we have no way whatsoever of recognizing poison. In the same way we can know, if we want to, what is poisonous for mental life. We know that poverty, intimidation, isolation, are directed against life; that everything that serves freedom and furthers the courage and strength to be oneself is for life. What is good or bad for man is not a metaphysical question, but an empirical one that can be answered on the basis of an analysis of man's nature and the effect which certain conditions have on him.

But what about "ideals" like those of the Fascists which are definitely directed against

life? How can we understand the fact that men are following these false ideals as fervently as others are following true ideals? The answer to this question is provided by certain psychological considerations. The phenomenon of masochism shows us that men can be drawn to the experiencing of suffering or submission. There is no doubt that suffering, submission, or suicide is the antithesis of positive aims of living. Yet these aims can be subjectively experienced as gratifying and attractive. This attraction to what is harmful in life is the phenomenon which more than any other deserves the name of a pathological perversion. Many psychologists have assumed that the experience of pleasure and the avoidance of pain is the only legitimate principle guiding human action; but dynamic psychology can show that the subjective experience of pleasure is not a sufficient criterion for the value of certain behavior in terms of human happiness. The analysis of masochistic phenomena is a case in point. Such analysis shows that the sensation of pleasure can be the result of a pathological perversion and proves as little about the objective meaning of the experience as the sweet taste of a poison would prove about its function for the organism.** We thus come to define a genuine ideal as any aim which furthers the growth, freedom, and happiness of the self, and to define as fictitious ideals those compulsive and irrational aims which subjectively are attractive experiences (like the drive for submission), but which actually are harmful to life. Once

---

*Cf. Max Otto, *The Human Enterprise* (New York: T. S. Croft, 1940), chaps. 4 and 5.

**The question discussed here leads to a point of great significance which I want at least to mention: that problems of ethics can be clarified by dynamic psychology. Psychologists will only be helpful in this direction when they can see the relevance of moral problems for the understanding of personality. Any psychology, including Freud's, which treats such problems in terms of the pleasure principle, fails to understand one important sector of personality and leaves the field to dogmatic and unempirical doctrines of morality. The analysis of self-love, masochistic sacrifice, and ideals as offered in this book provides illustrations for this field of psychology and ethics that warrant further development.

we accept this definition, it follows that a genuine ideal is not some veiled force superior to the individual, but that it is the articulate expression of utmost affirmation of the self. Any ideal which is in contrast to such affirmation proves by this very fact that it is not an ideal but a pathological aim.

From here we come to another question, that of sacrifice. Does our definition of freedom as nonsubmission to any higher power exclude sacrifices, including the sacrifice of one's life?

This is a particularly important question today, when Fascism proclaims self-sacrifice as the highest virtue and impresses many people with its idealistic character. The answer to this question follows logically from what has been said so far. There are two entirely different types of sacrifices. It is one of the tragic facts of life that the demands of our physical self and the aims of our mental self can conflict; that actually we may have to sacrifice our physical self in order to assert the integrity of our spiritual self. This sacrifice will never lose its tragic quality. Death is never sweet, not even if it is suffered for the highest ideal. It remains unspeakably bitter, and still it can be the utmost assertion of our individuality. Such sacrifice is fundamentally different from the "sacrifice" which Fascism preaches. There, sacrifice is not the highest price man may have to pay to assert his self, but it is an aim in itself. This masochistic sacrifice sees the fulfillment of life in its very negation, in the annihilation of the self. It is only the supreme expression of what Fascism aims at in all its ramifications—the annihilation of the individual self and its utter submission to a higher power. It is the perversion of true sacrifice as much as suicide is the utmost perversion of life. True sacrifice presupposes an uncompromising wish for spiritual integrity. The sacrifice of those who have lost it only covers up their moral bankruptcy.

One last objection is to be met: If individuals are allowed to act freely in the sense of spontaneity, if they acknowledge no higher authority than themselves, will anarchy be the inevitable result? Insofar as the word anarchy stands for heedless egotism and destructiveness, the determining factor depends upon one's understanding of human nature. I can only refer to what has been pointed out in the chapter dealing with mechanisms of escape: that man is neither good nor bad; that life has an inherent tendency to grow, to expand, to express potentialities; that if life is thwarted, if the individual is isolated and overcome by doubt or a feeling of aloneness and powerlessness, then he is driven to destructiveness and craving for power or submission. If human freedom is established as *freedom to*, if man can realize his self fully and uncompromisingly, the fundamental cause for his asocial drives will have disappeared and only a sick and abnormal individual will be dangerous. This freedom has never been realized in the history of mankind, yet it has been an ideal to which mankind has stuck even if it was often expressed in abstruse and irrational forms. There is no reason to wonder why the record of history shows so much cruelty and destructiveness. If there is anything to be surprised at—and encouraged by—I believe it is the fact that the human race, in spite of all that has happened to men, has retained—and actually developed—such qualities of dignity, courage, decency, and kindness as we find them throughout history and and in countless individuals today.

If by anarchy one means that the individual does not acknowledge any kind of authority, the answer is to be found in what has been said about the difference between rational and irrational authority. Rational authority—like a genuine ideal—represents the aims of growth and expansion of the individual. It is, therefore, in principle never in conflict with the individual and his real, and not his pathological, aims.

It has been the thesis of this book that freedom has a twofold meaning for modern man: that he has been freed from traditional authorities and has become an "individual," but that at the same time he has become isolated, powerless, and an instrument of purposes outside of himself, alienated, from himself and others; furthermore, that this state undermines his self, weakens and frightens him, and makes him ready for submission to new kinds of bondage. Positive freedom on the other hand is identical with the full realization of the individual's potentialities, together with his ability to live actively and spontaneously. Freedom has reached a critical point where, driven by the logic of its own dynamism, it threatens to change into its opposite. The future of democracy depends on the realization of the individualism that has been the ideological aim of modern thought since the Renaissance. The cultural and political crisis of our day is not due to the fact that there is too much individualism but that what we believe to be individualism has become an empty shell. The victory of freedom is possible only if democracy develops into a society in which the individual, his growth and happiness, is the aim and purpose of culture, in which life does not need any justification in success or anything else, and in which the individual is not subordinated to or manipulated by any power outside of himself, be it the State or the economic machine; finally, a society in which his conscience and ideals are not the internalization of external demands, but are really *his* and express the aims that result from the peculiarity of his self. These aims could not be fully realized in any previous period of modern history; they had to remain largely ideological aims, because the material basis for the development of genuine individualism was lacking. Capitalism has created this premise. The problem of production is solved—in principle at least—and we can visualize a future of abundance, in which the fight for economic privileges is no longer necessitated by economic scarcity. The problem we are confronted with today is that of the organization of social and economic forces, so that man as a member of organized society—may become the master of these forces and cease to be their slave.

I have stressed the psychological side of freedom, but I have also tried to show that the psychological problem cannot be separated from the material basis of human existence, from the economic, social, and political structure of society. It follows from this premise that the realization of positive freedom and individualism is also bound up with economic and social changes that will permit the individual to become free in terms of the realization of his self. It is not the aim of this book to deal with the economic problems resulting from that premise or to give a picture of economic plans for the future. But I should not like to leave any doubt concerning the direction in which I believe the solution to lie.

In the first place this must be said: We cannot afford to lose any of the fundamental achievements of modern democracy—either the fundamental one of representative government, that is, government elected by the people and responsible to the people, or any of the rights which the Bill of Rights guarantees to every citizen. Nor can we compromise the newer democratic principle that no one shall be allowed to starve, that society is responsible for all its members, that no one shall be frightened into submission and lose his human pride through fear of unemployment and starvation. These basic achievements must not only be preserved; they must be fortified and expanded.

In spite of the fact that this measure of democracy has been realized—though far from completely—it is not enough. Progress for democracy lies in enhancing the actual freedom, initiative, and spontaneity of the individual, not only in certain private and spiritual matters, but above all in the activity fundamental to every man's existence, his work.

What are the general conditions for that? The irrational and planless character of society must be replaced by a planned economy that represents the planned and concerted effort of society as such. Society must master the social problem as rationally as it has mastered nature. One condition for this is the elimination of the secret rule of those who, though few in number, wield great economic power without any responsibility to those whose fate depends on their decisions. We may call this new order by the name of democratic socialism but the name does not matter; all that matters is that we establish a rational economic system serving the purposes of the people. Today the vast majority of the people not only have no control over the whole of the economic machine, but they have little chance to develop genuine initiative and spontaneity at the particular job they are doing. They are "employed," and nothing more is expected from them than that they do what they are told. Only in a planned economy in which the whole nation has rationally mastered the economic and social forces can the individual share responsibility and use creative intelligence in his work. All that matters is that the opportunity for genuine activity be restored to the individual; that the purposes of society and of his own become identical, not ideologically but in reality; and that he apply his effort and reason actively to the work he is doing, as something for which he can feel responsible because it has meaning and purpose in terms of his human ends. We must replace manipulation of men by active and intelligent co-operation, and expand the principle of government of the people, by the people, for the people, from the formal political to the economic sphere.

The question of whether an economic and political system furthers the cause of human freedom cannot be answered in political and economic terms alone. The only criterion for the realization of freedom is whether or not the individual actively participates in determining his life and that of society, and this not only by the formal act of voting but in his daily activity, in his work, and in his relations to others. Modern political democracy, if it restricts itself to the purely political sphere, cannot sufficiently counteract the results of the economic insignificance of the average individual. But purely eco-

nomic concepts like socialization of the means of production are not sufficient either. I am not thinking here so much of the deceitful usage of the word socialism as it has been applied—for reasons of tactical expediency—in National Socialism. I have in mind Russia where socialism has become a deceptive word; for although socialization of the means of production has taken place, actually a powerful bureaucracy manipulates the vast mass of the population; this necessarily prevents the development of freedom and individualism, even if government control may be effective in the economic interest of the majority of the people.

Never have words been more misused in order to conceal the truth than today. Betrayal of allies is called appeasement, military aggression is camouflaged as defense against attack, the conquest of small nations goes by the name of a pact of friendship, and the brutal suppression of the whole population is perpetrated in the name of National Socialism. The words democracy, freedom, and individualism become objects of this abuse too. There is one way to define the real meaning of the difference between democracy and Fascism. Democracy is a system that creates the economic, political, and cultural conditions for the full development of the individual. Fascism is a system that, regardless under which name, makes the individual subordinate to extraneous purposes and weakens the development of genuine individuality.

Obviously, one of the greatest difficulties in the establishment of the conditions for the realization of democracy lies in the contradiction between a planned economy and the active co-operation of each individual. A planned economy of the scope of any big industrial system requires a great deal of centralization and, as a consequence, a bureaucracy to administer this centralized machine. On the other hand, the active control and co-operation by each individual and by the smallest units of the whole system requires a great amount of decentralization. Unless planning from the top is blended with active participation from below, unless the stream of social life continuously flows from below upwards, a planned economy will lead to renewed manipulation of the people. To solve this problem of combining centralization with decentralization is one of the major tasks of society. But it is certainly no less soluble than the technical problems we have already solved and which have brought us an almost complete mastery over nature. It is to be solved, however, only if we clearly recognize the necessity of doing so and if we have faith in the people, in their capacity to take care of their real interests as human beings.

In a way it is again the problem of individual initiative with which we are confronted. Individual initiative was one of the great stimuli both of the economic system and also of personal development under liberal capitalism. But there are two qualifications: it developed only selected qualities of man, his will and rationality, while leaving him otherwise subordinate to economic goals. It was a principle that functioned best in a highly individualized and competitive phase of capitalism which had room for countless independent economic units. Today this space has narrowed down. Only a small number can exercise individual initiative. If we want to realize this principle today and enlarge it so that the whole personality becomes free, it will be possible only on the basis of the rational and concerted effort of a society as a whole, and by an amount of decentralization which can guarantee real, genuine, active co-operation and control by the smallest units of the system.

Only if man masters society and subordinates the economic machine to the purposes of human happiness and only if he actively participates in the social process, can he overcome what now drives him into despair—his aloneness and his feeling of powerlessness. Man does not suffer so much from poverty today as he suffers from the fact that he has become a cog in a large machine, an automaton, that his life has become empty and lost its meaning. The victory over all kinds of authoritarian systems will be possible only if democracy does not retreat but takes the offensive and proceeds to realize what has been its aim in the minds of those who fought for freedom throughout the last centuries. It will triumph over the forces of nihilism only if it can imbue people with a faith that is the strongest the human mind is capable of, the faith in life and in truth, and in freedom as the active and spontaneous realization of the individual self.

Notes

1. Erich Fromm, *Escape from Freedom* (New York: Holt, Rinehart & Winston, 1941), p. 207.
2. Ibid.

Afterword / Opportunity of Freedom

The selections in this part throw a series of spotlights on various aspects of freedom. Socrates' speeches at his trial make clear that freedom of thought and of action depend upon a social context for their definition and preservation. He feels obliged to obey the dictates of God rather than those of men, but he also has great respect, as he makes clear later in the *Crito,* for the laws of his native city-state, Athens (see Part III). Under these laws he has been able to follow freely his self-chosen life of philosophical searcher and interrogator. Nowhere except in Athens, he recognizes, would the life of free inquiry have been so appreciated, respected, and protected. As an exile in a lawless land, one would be more constrained by forces, social and natural, over which one had no control. Better to die under bad laws than to live under no laws at all. Socrates has a typical Greek viewpoint in his deep conviction that man is a social animal and that, because of this fundamental fact, man is the only animal that can attain a meaningful freedom under a government of law. He accepts his sentence and goes to his death not because his sentence is just, but because it is lawful and his acceptance of it right under the circumstances. Death for him was in accord with his inner divine moral law and gave him a way out without breaking manmade, externally imposed laws.

Thoreau's conception of freedom at first seems to be more anarchistic than Socrates'. No laws, no restraints, no external sanctions equal, it seems, freedom. But Thoreau certainly was no advocate of license, which, like most careful thinkers, he would distinguish from freedom. To the contrary, he recognized and condemned very explicitly in *Walden* those who abused their freedom and who polluted their mental and physical environments without caring or feeling responsible. The good man, for Thoreau, would be a man like Socrates or Jesus who not only could be a law unto himself, but at the same time could exemplify the universal moral law which all men should follow. Thoreau sought to obey that higher transcendental law which infused nature and human nature with spiritual significance. When a man has rapport with that law he will not hesitate to ignore or defy the lower human laws which, more often than not, according to Thoreau, fence men in and reality out. "This above all, to thine own (higher) self be true."

Dostoyevsky looked at freedom from the perspective of one who had been reborn to it. As a man who had temporarily lost his freedom in punishment by state authority for activities considered subversive, Dostoyevsky appreciated fully the extent to which external sanctions or enforcing agencies could impinge upon and transform the values of the persons confronting them. As a creative genius, he highly valued freedom of art, thought, and action. Going into prison a radical, Dostoyevsky came out a conservative with a renewed sense of loyalty to the Czar as well as a staunch faith in the orthodox religion of the state. This knowledge makes the reading of the "Legend of the Grand Inquisitor" a more complex and controversial experience. Is the author on the side of Christ or the Grand Inquisitor? Does he favor freedom or authority? Are the alternatives this simple? What message about the two is Dostoyevsky trying to convey? Is he perhaps trying to make us aware not only of the appeal of freedom but also of the less apparent appeal of authority? Authority can assuage guilt; it can impose upon life a pattern and thus a meaning; it can arouse a sense of awe in human beings and silence dissent by force. Through its ability to accumulate and hoard power, it can develop ways of controlling human beings which eventually can make them love the calamity of tyranny and loathe the opportunity of freedom. Yet Dostoyevsky the Christian identifies Christ as the liberator of man and as the champion of freedom. Man becomes genuinely free, he may be suggesting, only by a subservient and harmonious relationship to Christ.

As socialists and naturalistic humanists, Mill and Fromm founded their conceptions of freedom solely on human relationships within a natural rather than supernatural sphere. Like the Chinese sage, Confucius, Mill stresses the importance of respecting the rights of others. A man is free to do what he wills only insofar as his actions do not interfere with another man's freedom to do what he wills. The domain of his freedom stops where another man's domain begins. Ideally, legislation has as one of its chief goals the guarantee and protection of freedom under law. Thus it seems natural for Mill the utilitarian, like his predecessor and mentor Jeremy Bentham, to devote much of his time and effort to political theory and social reform. Although Fromm is primarily a psychologist, whose analysis of problems relating to freedom grew out of his interest and concern for understanding human behavior and treating behavioral disorders, he has made clear his commitment to the reconstruction of social institutions and the re-forming of human nature. A utopian planner, Fromm envisages radical but peaceful evolutionary changes in society that can be brought about by cooperative human efforts. He heralds a new era of freedom which can issue from what he calls a "revolution of hope."

Related Reading

(Works marked * are available in paperbound editions.)

Adler, Mortimer J. *The Idea of Freedom: A Dialectical Examination of the Conceptions of Freedom.* 2 vols. Garden City: 1958, 1961.

Anschutz, R. P. *The Philosophy of John Stuart Mill.* Oxford: Clarendon Press, 1953.

*Apter, David E. and James Joll. *Anarchism Today.* New York: Doubleday, 1972.

Barth, Alan. *The Price of Liberty.* New York: Viking, 1961.

Bury, John. *A History of Freedom of Thought.* New York: Oxford University Press, 1913.

Cohen, Morris R. *The Faith of a Liberal.* New York: Holt, 1946.

Dewey, John. *Freedom and Culture.* New York: Putnam, 1939.

Ebenstein, William. *Today's Isms,* 3d ed. Englewood Cliffs, N. J.: Prentice Hall, 1961.

Edman, Irwin. *Foundations of Freedom: The Growth of the Democratic Idea.* New York: Reynal and Hitchcock, 1941.

*Fromm, Erich. *The Sane Society.* New York: Fawcett Publications, 1955.

*——. *The Revolution of Hope: Toward a Humanized Technology.* New York: Bantam, 1968.

Harris, Robert T. *Social Ethics.* New York: Lippincott, 1962.

*Highet, Gilbert. *Man's Unconquerable Mind.* New York: Columbia University Press, 1960.

Hook, Sidney. *Political Power and Personal Freedom.* New York: Criterion, 1959.

——. *The Paradoxes of Freedom.* Berkeley and Los Angeles: University of California Press, 1964.

*Horowitz, Irving L. *The Anarchists.* New York: Dell, 1964.

*Kirk, Russell. *The Conservative Mind from Burke to Santayana.* Chicago: Regnery, 1953.

*Kostelanetz, Richard, ed. *Beyond Left and Right: Radical Thought for Our Times.* New York: Morrow, 1968.

*Meiklejohn, Alexander. *Political Freedom.* New York: Galaxy Books, 1965.

Muller, Herbert J. *Issues of Freedom.* New York, Harper, 1960.

*Murray, James G. *Henry David Thoreau.* New York: Washington Square Press, 1968.

*Nobile, Philip. *The Con III Controversy: The Critics Look at the Greening of America.* New York: Pocket Books, 1971.

*Paul, Sherman. *Thoreau, a Collection of Critical Essays.* Englewood Cliffs, N. J.: Prentice-Hall, 1962.

*Rand, Ayn. *Capitalism: The Unknown Ideal.* New York: Signet, 1967.

*Reich, Charles. *The Greening of America*. New York: Random House, 1970.

*Robinson, Paul A. *The Freudian Left: Wilhelm Reich, Geza Roheim, Herbert Marcuse*. New York: Harper, 1969.

 Skinner, B. F. *Beyond Freedom and Dignity*. New York: Alfred A. Knopf, 1971.

*Wagar, W. Warren. *The City of Man*. Baltimore: Penguin Books, 1963.

*Weldon, T. D. *The Vocabulary of Politics*. Baltimore: Penguin Books, 1953.

*Wellek, René. *Dostoyevsky, a Collection of Critical Essays*. Englewood Cliffs, N. J.: Prentice-Hall, 1962.

PART FOUR

Confrontation with Moral Crisis:
Commitment to the Good

All good and evil consists in sensation.

Epicurus

Evil is the axis of the universe.

Marquis de Sade

A culture which permits science to
destroy traditional values but which
distrusts its power to create new ones is
destroying itself.

John Dewey

There is no such thing as perpetual tranquillity of mind,
while we live here.

Thomas Hobbes

Power is the object of man's pursuit.

C. A. Helvetius

The peace we seek so eagerly has been
here all the times.

D. T. Suzuki

The mental situation today compels man, compels every
individual, to fight wittingly on behalf of his true essence.

Karl Jaspers

Is not man a miserable creature? Scarcely is it in his
power . . . to enjoy a single and entire pleasure, yet he is at
pains, by reasoning about it, to curtail it.

Michel de Montaigne

How could anything so good be bad?

Old Vaudeville Song

Question of ultimate ends are not
amenable to direct proof.

John Stuart Mill

Life is occupied both in perpetuating itself and in
surpassing itself; if all it does is maintain itself, then living
is only not dying.

Simone de Beauvoir

The Good is simply what God wills and
that we should do.

Emil Brunner

The value of morality is for the first time
called into question.

Friedrich Nietzsche

Introduction / Searching for the Good Life

In its broadest sense, *life style* refers to a person's way of existing. It includes not only the externals of dress, length of hair, and language, but also basic attitudes toward sex, the family, community, livelihood, and artistic taste. The adoption of a new life style may grow out of disillusion and disaffection with the prevalent pattern of a bourgeois, consumer society, or it may arise out of a deep religious conversion as an attempt to revitalize an older ideal of life. In any case, a life style involves the conscious or unconscious acceptance of an ideal of life.

The search for new alternatives is to be found at the institutional as well as the personal level. Our change-oriented society has a powerful influence on the family as a unit and center of value. The mobility of the population and changing social relationships in modern society have profoundly affected the traditional role of parents and the authoritarian function they often assumed. The recent increase in experimental communes expresses the need to find alternatives to the values and social structure of traditional familial-social relationships.

Changing social patterns in a technological society have also affected the value put upon work as an essential part of the good life. The value and goals of the work-oriented industrial society were economic success, personal independence, and self-reliance. The increase of goods and services in an affluent society has made leisure more available to more people. Should this trend continue, serious questions arise about the quality of life. Will this leisure time be used for education or the re-creation of the individual? Or will we become a society in which people spend their time staring blankly at television programs produced expressly to give them bland pleasure and docility?

The question of what ought to be the aim of human life and society is crucial today for other reasons. The accelerating productive capacities of mankind portend the exhaustion of the earth's energy resources and ecological disaster. The population explosion confronts us with the possibility of an earth crammed with people fighting for even the barest necessities of life. A recognition of these possibilities has affirmed values long taken for granted: privacy, quiet, clean air, and a decent environment. In modern times, the question of the good life often takes the form of a question about the quality of life, now and in the future.

Today many diverse moral ideals vie for our attention like products in a supermarket. Each seems to offer an ideal of the good, whether it is defined as happiness, pleasure, power, love, self-realization, community, holiness, money, or social service. Partly because of the multiplicity of claims, we tend to be sceptical, and perhaps somewhat cynical, regarding the absolute validity of any choice. Discussions of whether there is a *summum bonum,* a highest good which can be claimed to be the ultimate aim of human life, are apt to be entered into with a great deal of scepticism. We are confronted with the cultural variability of moral values: what is considered to be good or bad seems reducible to that which is approved or disapproved in a society. In addition, philosophers have suggested recently that moral statements in which occur such words as "good," "bad," "right," or "wrong" merely express favorable or unfavorable attitudes on the part of the speaker. Scepticism regarding the view that there is a valid way to settle disagreements about the good seems characteristic of our time.

Perhaps the scepticism is justified. We often debate the alternatives without any clear idea of how we would go about justifying our value judgments or, indeed, without any clear grasp of the meaning of such key notions as good, bad, right, or wrong. Yet rational deliberation also seems required. Many of our moral beliefs and ideals are extremely vague and often incompatible with other values we hold. To form our attitudes and guide our actions by such a bewildering jumble of beliefs is often tantamount to not being guided at all. An unwillingness to choose a life style can be a form of self-deception, a way of hiding behind the momentary security of our prejudices or the comfort of custom and tradition. Perhaps the Socratic creed is correct after all: the examined life is best. We should make a critical assessment of some of the major theories about the good. We should also consider rationally the consequences of our commitments and try to relate theory and practice consistently.

For the purpose of analysis, philosophers usually separate the question of the rightness or wrongness of actions from the question of what are desirable goals for our actions. However, the two questions are often closely related. Decisions regarding the rightness or wrongness of an action often depend upon what we consider morally good, or what values are worth pursuing. In the first selection that follows, Socrates in the *Crito* confronts a moral situation in which his ideal of the examined life, indeed his life style, is once again on trial (see the *Apology* in Part I). Socrates considered loyalty to the laws of the city-state a good, and this value played a part in his decision to act as he did. In the second selection, a later Greek philosopher, Epicurus, provides us with another view of the good life: one which is filled with prudent pleasures and the absence of pain. Like the Buddhists, Epicurus believed that man can be liberated from suffering and fear of death, although his "prudence" falls far short of their asceticism.

Indirectly, the next three selections also provide us with a concept of the good life. However, they do so within the context of a severe critique of traditional moral ideals and approaches to the good. Writing in the nineteenth century, Friedrich Nietzsche confronts what he considers to be a breakdown in the traditional justification for good and evil. He asks us to inquire into the question of the good in a radically new way and to view moralities as derived from a basic creative energy in man. He proposes a morality that affirms and liberates this power and allows man to give himself new goals and directions.

In our century, the American philosopher John Dewey asks for a new approach to the good, to be patterned after the attitudes and methods found successful in the natural sciences. The central focus should not be the definition of the good as some fixed absolute, but the adoption of a procedure for intelligent deliberation in specific moral situations.

According to Karl Jaspers, a recent German philosopher, man constantly decides what and who he is through his moral choices; commitments to certain values are the essential means of his freedom and self-creation. Jaspers stresses the importance of personal commitment in a technological society that increasingly encroaches upon it. Although man often evades and shirks his responsibility to choose, he can never discover a sense of his authentic existence without it. The author gives examples of conscientious men who acted from genuine commitment to the good, not out of inclination or concern with practical consequences. He believes the authentic self requires a sense of community through love, which can overcome the alienation of man from man. Thus he, like the other thinkers in this part, suggests new alternatives for the moral crisis faced by man.

10 / Conflict of Moral Values
Socrates

Plato's *Apology* highlighted Socrates' conviction that we should examine our beliefs critically. "For I am and always have been one of those natures who must be guided by reason," Socrates declares in the *Crito*. Socrates was committed to acting wisely; he voluntarily suffered death rather than do what he reasoned to be wrong. Plato wrote the *Crito* as part of the continuing story of the martyrdom of his beloved teacher, Socrates.

As Plato presents the story, Socrates was concerned mainly with problems of human values and conduct. Plato's dialogues, most of which use Socrates as the main character, explore these problems. They reveal philosophy as the search for enlightenment regarding the fundamental purpose of human existence. Separately, each dialogue is a search for definitions of such notions as justice, piety, and courage. Together, the dialogues are Plato's way of leading us to find our way to philosophy, to love wisdom.

Socrates remained convinced that once the debris of vague and unquestioned moral concepts was cleared away, men could discover the goods that are worth seeking and the rules that ought to govern human action. Knowledge is the necessary prerequisite to right living and conduct, because it enables a person to discern between what has value and what has not. Human virtue or excellence comes not by chance or by blindly following the opinions of others, but by knowing the principles that regulate and control the appetites and passions of men. The function of reason and philosophic dialogue is to seek those standards that will hold up against the shifting beliefs and scepticism of man.

The example of the life of Socrates indicates that merely declaring the examined life as an ideal is not enough; the test is in pursuing the ideal. Many of our most important beliefs are highly personal convictions. To be willing to clarify, criticize, and modify these is to be willing to risk radical change in outlook and direction. It may also involve incurring the ridicule of the society in which we live. Philosophizing in the Socratic sense is a task that takes a great deal of intellectual discipline, uncompromising honesty, and courage. Socrates lived in an age when it was dangerous to be a philosopher. Despite this, he was committed to living such a life.

The ethical thrust of the questions of Socrates and Plato was relevant for the historical period in which they lived. During the last thirty years of his life, Socrates witnessed the disastrous and lengthy war (431–404 B.C.) between Athens and a coalition of Greek states headed by Sparta. The power of Athens was being sapped from within and without by this costly and divisive war. Athens surrendered to Sparta and, following a brief period of rapid political changes, democracy was restored to Athens. Socrates, who remained relatively independent of these political changes, had been especially critical of the follies of Athenian democracy. In 399 B.C., trumped-up charges of corrupting the young and teaching false religion were brought against him. To those who had the most to lose under the newly restored democracy, Socrates' presence in Athens was unsettling. He was a troublemaker, a subverter of the status quo, or, at the very least, a witty but dangerous buffoon.

The *Crito*, which depicts the scene in the jail where Socrates is awaiting the day of his execution, is given here complete. But a full vindication of the death of Socrates cannot be had unless many other dialogues of Plato are read and related to one another. Especially, this includes the *Apology,* which presents Socrates' defense of himself at his trial, and the *Phaedo,* which contains an extended discussion between Socrates and his friends concerning the nature of the philosopher, the soul, and the possibility of immortality. This latter dialogue ends with a moving description of the last few minutes in the life of Socrates. For Plato, the death of Socrates represented the culmination of a life of philosophical commitment to the good.

Crito

PERSONS OF THE DIALOGUE: *Socrates, Crito*
SCENE: *The Prison of Socrates*

SOCRATES Why have you come at this hour, Crito? It must be quite early?

CRITO Yes, certainly.

SOCRATES What is the exact time?

CRITO The dawn is breaking.

SOCRATES I wonder that the keeper of the prison would let you in.

CRITO He knows me, because I often come, Socrates; moreover, I have done him a kindness.

SOCRATES And are you only just arrived?

CRITO No, I came some time ago.

SOCRATES Then why did you sit and say nothing, instead of awakening me?

CRITO I should not have liked myself, Socrates, to be in such great trouble and unrest as you are—indeed I should not; I have been watching with amazement your peaceful slumbers; and for that reason I did not awake you, because I wished to minimize the pain. I have always thought you to be of a happy disposition; but never did I see anything like the easy, tranquil manner in which you bear this calamity.

SOCRATES Why, Crito, when a man has reached my age he ought not to be repining at the approach of death.

CRITO And yet other old men find themselves in similar misfortunes, and age does not prevent them from repining.

SOCRATES That is true. But you have not told me why you come at this early hour.

CRITO I come to bring you a message which is sad and painful; not, as I believe, to yourself, but to all of us who are your friends, and saddest of all to me.

SOCRATES What? Has the ship come from Delos, on the arrival of which I am to die?

CRITO No, the ship has not actually arrived, but she will probably be here today, as persons who have come from Sunium tell me that they left her there; and therefore tomorrow, Socrates, will be the last day of your life.

SOCRATES Very well, Crito; if such is the will of God, I am willing; but my belief is that there will be a delay of a day.

CRITO Why do you think so?

SOCRATES I will tell you. I am to die on the day after the arrival of the ship.

CRITO Yes; that is what the authorities say.

SOCRATES But I do not think that the ship will be here until tomorrow; this I infer from a vision which I had last night, or rather only just now, when you fortunately allowed me to sleep.

CRITO And what was the nature of the vision?

SOCRATES There appeared to me the likeness of a woman, fair and comely, clothed in bright raiment, who called to me and said: O Socrates,

"The third day hence to fertile Phthia shalt thou go."[1]

From Plato, "Crito" in *The Dialogues of Plato,* trans. Benjamin Jowett, 3d ed. (New York: Oxford University Press, 1892).

CRITO What a singular dream, Socrates!

SOCRATES There can be no doubt about the meaning, Crito, I think.

CRITO Yes; the meaning is only too clear. But, oh! my beloved Socrates, let me entreat you once more to take my advice and escape. For if you die I shall not only lose a friend who can never be replaced, but there is another evil: people who do not know you and me will believe that I might have saved you if I had been willing to give money, but that I did not care. Now, can there be a worse disgrace than this—that I should be thought to value money more than the life of a friend? For the many will not be persuaded that I wanted you to escape, and that you refused.

SOCRATES But why, my dear Crito, should we care about the opinion of the many? Good men, and they are the only persons who are worth considering, will think of these things truly as they occurred.

CRITO But you see, Socrates, that the opinion of the many must be regarded, for what is now happening shows that they can do the greatest evil to any one who has lost their good opinion.

SOCRATES I only wish it were so, Crito; and that the many could do the greatest evil; for then they would also be able to do the greatest good—and what a fine thing this would be! But in reality they can do neither; for they cannot make a man either wise or foolish; and whatever they do is the result of chance.

CRITO Well, I will not dispute with you; but please to tell me, Socrates, whether you are not acting out of regard to me and your other friends: are you not afraid that if you escape from prison we may get into trouble with the informers for having stolen you away, and lose either the whole or a great part of our property; or that even a worse evil may happen to us? Now, if you fear on our account, be at ease; for in order to save you, we ought surely to run this, or even a greater risk; be persuaded, then, and do as I say.

SOCRATES Yes, Crito, that is one fear which you mention, but by no means the only one.

CRITO Fear not—there are persons who are willing to get you out of prison at no great cost; and as for the informers, they are far from being exorbitant in their demands—a little money will satisfy them. My means, which are certainly ample, are at your service, and if you have a scruple about spending all mine, here are strangers who will give you the use of theirs; and one of them, Simmias the Theban, has brought a large sum of money for this very purpose; and Cebes and many others are prepared to spend their money in helping you to escape. I say, therefore, do not hesitate on our account, and do not say, as you did in the court, that you will have a difficulty in knowing what to do with yourself anywhere else. For men will love you in other places to which you may go, and not in Athens only; there are friends of mine in Thessaly, if you like to go to them, who will value and protect you, and no Thessalian will give you any trouble. Nor can I think that you are at all justified, Socrates, in betraying your own life when you might be saved; in acting thus you are playing into the hands of your enemies, who are hurrying on your destruction. And further I should say that you are deserting your own children; for you might bring them up and educate them; instead of which you go away and leave them, and they will have to take their chance; and if they do not meet with the usual fate of orphans, there will be small thanks to you. No man should bring children into the world who is unwilling to persevere to the end in their nurture and education. But you appear to be choosing the easier part, not the better and manlier, which would have been more becoming in one who professes to care for virtue in all his actions, like yourself. And, indeed, I am ashamed not only of you, but of us who are your friends, when I reflect that the whole business will be attributed entirely to our want of courage. The trial need never have come on, or might have been managed differently; and this last act, or crowning folly, will seem to have occurred through our negligence and cowardice, who might have saved you, if we had been good for anything; and you might have saved yourself, for there was no difficulty at all. See now, Socrates, how sad and discreditable are the consequences, both to us and you. Make up your mind, then, or rather have your mind already made up, for the time of deliberation is over, and there is only one thing to be done, which must be done this very night, and if we delay at all will be no longer practicable or possible; I beseech you therefore, Socrates, be persuaded by me, and do as I say.

SOCRATES Dear Crito, your zeal is invaluable, if a right one; but if wrong, the greater the zeal the greater the danger; and therefore we ought to consider whether I shall or shall not do as you say. For I am and always have been one of those natures who must be guided by reason, whatever the reason may be which upon reflection appears to me to be the best; and now that this chance has befallen me, I cannot repudiate my own words: the principles which I have hitherto honoured and revered I still honour, and unless we can at once find other and better principles, I am certain not to agree with you; no, not even if the power of the multitude could inflict many more imprisonments, confiscations, deaths, frightening us like children with hobgoblin terrors. What will be the fairest way of considering the question? Shall I return to your old argument about the opinions of men?—we were saying that some of them are to be regarded, and others not. Now, were we right in maintaining this before I was condemned? And has the argument which was once good now proved to be talk for the sake of talking—mere childish nonsense? That is what I want to consider with your help, Crito:—whether, under my present circumstances, the argument appears to be in any way different or not; and is to be allowed by me or disallowed. That argument, which, as I believe, is maintained by many persons of authority, was to the effect, as I was saying, that the opinions of some men are to be regarded, and of other men not to be regarded. Now you, Crito, are not going to die tomorrow—at least, there is no human probability of this—and therefore you are disinterested and not liable to be deceived by the circumstances in which you are placed. Tell me, then, whether I am right in saying that some opinions, and the opinions of some men only, are to be valued, and that other opinions, and the opinions of other men, are not to be valued.

I ask you whether I was right in maintaining this?

CRITO   Certainly.

SOCRATES   The good are to be regarded, and not the bad?

CRITO   Yes.

SOCRATES   And the opinions of the wise are good, and the opinions of the unwise are evil?

CRITO   Certainly.

SOCRATES   And what was said about another matter? Is the pupil who devotes himself to the practice of gymnastic supposed to attend to the praise and blame and opinion of every man, or of one man only—his physician or trainer, whoever he may be?

CRITO   Of one man only.

SOCRATES   And he ought to fear the censure and welcome the praise of that one only, and not of the many?

CRITO   Clearly so.

SOCRATES   And he ought to act and train, and eat and drink in the way which seems good to his single master who has understanding, rather than according to the opinion of all other men put together?

CRITO   True.

SOCRATES   And if he disobeys and disregards the opinion and approval of the one, and regards the opinion of the many who have no understanding, will he not suffer evil?

CRITO   Certainly he will.

SOCRATES   And what will the evil be, whither tending and what affecting, in the disobedient person?

CRITO   Clearly, affecting the body; that is what is destroyed by the evil.

SOCRATES   Very good; and is not this true, Crito, of other things which we need not separately enumerate? In questions of just and unjust, fair and foul, good and evil, which are the subjects of our present consultation, ought we to follow the opinion of the many and to fear them; or the opinion of the one man who has understanding? ought we not to fear and reverence him more than all the rest of the world: and if we desert him shall we not destroy and injure that principle in us which may be assumed to be improved by justice and deteriorated by injustice;—there is such a principle?

CRITO   Certainly there is, Socrates.

SOCRATES   Take a parallel instance:—if, acting under the advice of those who have no understanding, we destroy that which is improved by health and is deteriorated by disease, would life be worth having? And that which has been destroyed is—the body?

CRITO   Yes.

SOCRATES   Could we live, having an evil and corrupted body?

CRITO   Certainly not.

SOCRATES   And will life be worth having, if that higher part of man be destroyed, which is improved by justice and depraved by injustice? Do we suppose that principle, whatever it may be in man, which has to do with justice and injustice, to be inferior to the body?

CRITO   Certainly not.

SOCRATES   More honourable than the body?

CRITO   Far more.

SOCRATES   Then, my friend, we must not regard what the many say of us: but what he, the one man who has understanding of just and unjust, will say, and what the truth will say. And therefore you begin in error when you advise that we should regard the opinion of the many about just and unjust, good and evil, honourable and dishonourable.—"Well," some one will say, "But the many can kill us."

CRITO   Yes, Socrates; that will clearly be the answer.

SOCRATES   And it is true: but still I find with surprise that the old argument is unshaken as ever. And I should like to know whether I may say the same of another proposition—that not life, but a good life, is to be chiefly valued?

CRITO   Yes, that also remains unshaken.

SOCRATES   And a good life is equivalent to a just and honourable one—that holds also?

CRITO   Yes, it does.

SOCRATES   From these premises I proceed to argue the question whether I ought or ought not to try to escape without the consent of the Athenians: and if I am clearly right in escaping, then I will make the attempt; but if not, I will abstain. The other considerations which you mention, of money and loss of character and the duty of educating one's children, are, I fear, only the doctrines of the multitude, who would be as ready to restore people to life, if they were able, as they are to put them to death—and with as little reason. But now, since the argument has thus far prevailed, the only question which remains to be considered is, whether we shall do rightly either in escaping or in suffering others to aid in our escape and paying them in money and thanks, or whether in reality we shall not do rightly; and if the latter, then death or any other calamity which may ensue on my remaining here must not be allowed to enter into the calculation.

CRITO   I think that you are right Socrates; how then shall we proceed?

SOCRATES   Let us consider the matter together, and do you either refute me if you can, and I will be convinced; or else cease, my dear friend, from repeating to me that I ought to escape against the wishes of the Athenians: for I highly value your attempts to persuade me to do so, but I may not be persuaded against my own better judgment. And now please to consider my first position, and try how you can best answer me.

CRITO   I will.

SOCRATES   Are we to say that we are never intentionally to do wrong, or that in one way we ought and in another way we ought not to do wrong, or is doing wrong always evil and dishonourable, as I was just now saying, and as has been already acknowledged by us? Are all our former admissions which were made within a few days to be thrown away? And have we, at our age, been earnestly discoursing with one another all our life long only to discover that we are no better than children? Or, in spite of the opinion of the many, and in spite of consequences whether better or worse, shall we insist on the truth of what was then said, that injustice is always an evil and dishonour to him who acts unjustly? Shall we say so or not?

CRITO   Yes.

SOCRATES   Then we must do no wrong?

CRITO   Certainly not.

SOCRATES   Nor when injured injure in return, as the many imagine; for we must injure no one at all?

CRITO   Clearly not.

SOCRATES   Again, Crito, may we do evil?

CRITO   Surely, not, Socrates.

SOCRATES   And what of doing evil in return for evil, which is the morality of the many—is that just or not?

CRITO   Not just.

SOCRATES   For doing evil to another is the same as injuring him?

CRITO   Very true.

SOCRATES   Then we ought not to retaliate or

render evil for evil to any one, whatever evil we may have suffered from him. But I would have you consider, Crito, whether you really mean what you are saying. For this opinion has never been held, and never will be held, by any considerable number of persons; and those who are agreed and those who are not agreed upon this point have no common ground, and can only despise one another when they see how widely they differ. Tell me, then, whether you agree with and assent to my first principle, that neither injury nor retaliation nor warding off evil by evil is ever right. And shall that be the premise of our argument? Or do you decline and dissent from this? For so I have ever thought, and continue to think; but, if you are of another opinion, let me hear what you have to say. If, however, you remain of the same mind as formerly, I will proceed to the next step.

CRITO   You may proceed, for I have not changed my mind.

SOCRATES   Then I will go on to the next point, which may be put in the form of a question:—Ought a man to do what he admits to be right, or ought he to betray the right?

CRITO   He ought to do what he thinks is right.

SOCRATES   But if this is true, what is the application? In leaving the prison against the will of the Athenians, do I wrong any? or rather do I not wrong those whom I ought least to wrong? Do I not desert the principles which were acknowledged by us to be just—what do you say?

CRITO   I cannot tell, Socrates; for I do not know.

SOCRATES   Then consider the matter in this way:—Imagine that I am about to play truant (you may call the proceeding by any name which you like), and the laws and the government come and interrogate me: "Tell us, Socrates," they say; "what are you about? are you not going by an act of yours to overturn us—the laws, and the whole state, as far as in you lies? Do you imagine that a state can subsist and not be overthrown, in which the decisions of law have no power, but are set aside and trampled upon by individuals?" What will be our answer, Crito, to these and the like words? Any one, and especially a rhetorician, will have a good deal to say on behalf of the law which requires a sentence to be carried out. He will argue that this law should not be set aside; and shall we reply, "Yes; but the state has injured us and given an unjust sentence." Suppose I say that?

CRITO   Very good, Socrates.

SOCRATES   "And was that our agreement with you?" the law would answer; "or were you to abide by the sentence of the state?" And if I were to express my astonishment at their words, the law would probably add: "Answer, Socrates, instead of opening your eyes—you are in the habit of asking and answering questions. Tell us,—What complaint have you to make against us which justifies you in attempting to destroy us and the state? In the first place did we not bring you into existence? Your father married your mother by our aid and begat you. Say whether you have any objection to urge against those of us who regulate marriage?" None, I should reply. "Or against those of us who after birth regulate the nurture and education of children, in which you also were trained? Were not the laws, which have the charge of education, right in commanding your father to train you in music and gymnastic?" Right, I should reply. "Well, then, since you were brought into the world and nurtured and educated by us, can you deny in the first place that you are our child and slave, as your fathers were before you? And if this is true, you are not on equal terms with us; nor can you think that you have a right to do to us what we are doing to you. Would you have any right to strike or revile or do any other evil to your father or your master, if you had one, because you have been struck or reviled by him, or received some other evil at his hands?—you would not say this? And because we think right to destroy you, do you think that you have any right to destroy us in return, and your country as far as in you lies? Will you, O professor of true virtue, pretend that you are justified in this? Has a philosopher like you failed to discover that our country is more to be valued and higher and holier far than mother or father or any ancestor, and more to be regarded in the eyes of the gods and of men of understanding? also to be soothed, and gently and reverently entreated when angry, even more than a father, and either to be persuaded, or if not persuaded, to be obeyed? And when we are punished by her, whether with imprisonment or stripes, the punishment is to be endured in silence; and if she lead us to wounds or death in battle, thither we follow as is right; neither may any one yield or retreat or leave his rank, but whether in battle or in a court of law, or in any other place, he must do what his city and his country order him; or he must change their view of what is just: and if he may do no violence to his father or mother, much less may he do violence to his country." What answer shall we make to this, Crito? Do the laws speak truly, or do they not?

CRITO I think that they do.

SOCRATES Then the laws will say: "Consider, Socrates, if we are speaking truly that in your present attempt you are going to do us an injury. For, having brought you into the world, and nurtured and educated you, and given you and every other citizen a share in every good which we had to give, we further proclaim to any Athenian by the liberty which we allow him, that if he does not like us when he has become of age and has seen the ways of the city, and made our acquaintance, he may go where he pleases and take his goods with him. None of us laws will forbid him or interfere with him. Any one who does not like us and the city, and who wants to emigrate to a colony or to any other city, may go where he likes, retaining his property. But he who has experience of the manner in which we order justice and administer the State, and still remains, has entered into an implied contract that he will do as we command him. And he who disobeys us is, as we maintain, thrice wrong; first, because in disobeying us he is disobeying his parents; secondly, because we are the authors of his education; thirdly, because he has made an agreement with us that he will duly obey our commands; and he neither obeys them nor convinces us that our commands are unjust; and we do not rudely impose them, but give him the alternative of obeying or convincing us;—that is what we offer, and he does neither.

"These are the sort of accusations to which, as we were saying, you, Socrates, will be exposed if you accomplish your intentions; you, above all other Athenians." Suppose now I ask, why I rather than anybody else? they will justly retort upon me that I above all other men have acknowledged the agreement. "There is clear proof," they will say, "Socrates, that we and the city were not displeasing to you. Of all Athenians you have been the most constant resident in the city, which, as you never leave, you may be supposed to love. For you never went out of the city either to see the games, except once when you went to the Isthmus, or to any other place unless when you were on military service; nor did you travel as other men do. Nor had you any curiosity to know other States or their laws: your affections did not go beyond us and our State; we were your special favourites, and you acquiesced in our government of you; and here in this city you begat your children, which is a proof of your satisfaction. Moreover, you might in the course of the trial, if you had liked, have fixed the penalty at banishment; the State which refuses to let you go now would have let you go then. But you pretended that you preferred death to exile, and that you were not unwilling to die. And now you have forgotten these fine sentiments, and pay no respect to us, the laws, of whom you are the destroyer; and are doing what only a miserable slave would do, running away and turning your back upon the compacts and agreements which you made as a citizen. And, first of all, answer this very question: Are we right in saying that you agreed to be governed according to us in deed, and now in word only? Is that true or not?" How shall we answer, Crito? Must we not assent?

CRITO We cannot help it, Socrates.

SOCRATES Then will they not say: "You, Socrates, are breaking the covenants and agreements which you made with us at your leisure, not in any haste or under any compulsion or deception, but after you have had seventy years to think of them, during which time you were at liberty to leave the city, if we were not to your mind, or if our covenants appeared to you to be unfair. You had your choice, and might have gone either to Lacedaemon or Crete, both which States are often praised by you for their good government, or to some other Hellenic or foreign State. Whereas you, above all other Athenians, seemed to be so fond of the State, or, in other words, of us, her laws (and who would care about a State which has no laws?), that you never stirred out of her; the halt, the blind, the maimed were not more stationary in her than you were. And now you run away and forsake your agreements. Not so, Socrates, if you will take our advice; do not make yourself ridiculous by escaping out of the city.

"For just consider, if you transgress and err in this sort of way, what good will you do either to yourself or to your friends? That your friends will be driven into exile and deprived of citizenship, or will lose their property, is tolerably certain; and you yourself, if you fly to one of the neighboring cities, as, for example, Thebes or Megara, both of which are well governed, will come to them as an enemy, Socrates, and their government will be against you, and all patriotic citizens will cast an evil eye upon you as a subverter of the laws, and you will confirm in the minds of the judges the justice of their own condemnation of you. For he who is a corrupter of the laws is more than likely to be a corrupter of the young and foolish portion of mankind. Will you then flee from well-ordered cities and virtuous men? and is existence worth having on these terms? Or will you go to them without shame, and talk to them, Socrates? And what will you say to them? What you say here about virtue and justice and institutions and laws being the best things among men? Would that be decent of you? Surely not. But if you go away from well-governed States to Crito's friends in Thessaly, where there is great disorder and licence, they will be charmed to hear the tale of your escape from prison, set off with ludicrous particulars of the manner in which you were wrapped in a goatskin or some other disguise, and metamorphosed as the manner is of runaways; but will there be no one to remind you that in your old age you were not ashamed to violate the most sacred laws from a miserable desire of a little more life? Perhaps not, if you keep them in a good temper; but if they are out of temper you will hear many degrading things; you will live, but how?—as the flatterer of all men, and the servant of all men; and doing what?—eating and drinking in Thes-

saly, having gone abroad in order that you may get a dinner. And where will be your fine sentiments about justice and virtue? Say that you wish to live for the sake of your children—you want to bring them up and educate them—will you take them into Thessaly and deprive them of Athenian citizenship? Is this the benefit which you will confer upon them? Or are you under the impression that they will be better cared for and educated here if you are still alive, although absent from them; for your friends will take care of them? Do you fancy that if you are an inhabitant of Thessaly they will take care of them, and if you are an inhabitant of the other world that they will not take care of them? Nay; but if they who call themselves friends are good for anything, they will—to be sure they will.

"Listen, then, Socrates, to us who have brought you up. Think not of life and children first, and of justice afterwards, but of justice first, that you may be justified before the princes of the world below. For neither will you nor any that belong to you be happier or holier or juster in this life, or happier in another, if you do as Crito bids. Now you depart in innocence, a sufferer and not a doer of evil; a victim, not of the laws but of men. But if you go forth, returning evil for evil; and injury for injury, breaking the covenants and agreements which you have made with us, and wronging those whom you ought least of all to wrong, that is to say, yourself, your friends, your country, and us, we shall be angry with you while you live, and our brethren, the laws in the world below, will receive you as an enemy; for they will know that you have done your best to destroy us. Listen, then, to us and not to Crito."

This, dear Crito, is the voice which I seem to hear murmuring in my ears, like the sound of the flute in the ears of the mystic; that voice, I say, is humming in my ears, and prevents me from hearing any other. And I know that anything more which you may say will be vain. Yet speak, if you have anything to say.

CRITO I have nothing to say, Socrates.

SOCRATES Leave me, then, Crito, to fulfil the will of God, and to follow whither he leads.

Note

1. Homer, Il. ix. 363.

The Life of Pleasure
Epicurus

Epicurus (341–270 B.C.) represents a type of ethical philosophy called hedonism. (*Hedone* was the Greek word for pleasure.) Epicurus held that pleasure was the only intrinsic good and our own long-run pleasure the criterion for deciding our actions and course of life.

Epicurus came to Athens in 306 B.C. to establish his garden, which became the center of his philosophical teaching and a retreat for his followers. Like Socrates, he considered ethical questions and self-knowledge (especially knowledge of human desires) the focal point for philosophical inquiry. Knowledge is virtue, but virtue itself is good only insofar as its practice produces a life free from bodily pain and a troubled soul. Wisdom, for Epicurus, was essentially prudence—a judicious, intelligent, and temperate consideration of our choices and the consequences of our choices regarding the pleasure and pain they will yield. Epicurus emphasized the pleasures of intellectual pursuits; a state of imperturbability of mind, serenity, and freedom from pain was his moral ideal. This he called *ataraxia*.

The teachings of Epicurus are not to be identified with the popular connotations of the term "epicure." Restaurants using this name perhaps should serve only bread, cheese, and water if they want to be consistent with his doctrines. Epicurus favored the simple life, not the habits of a gourmet or of a person who believes that the immediate gratification of the most intense sensual desires is the aim in life.

The hedonism of Epicurus should be clarified in another respect. He is a *psychological* hedonist insofar as he believes that man is so constituted as to seek to pursue his own pleasure. The fundamental motive of man's actions is the desire to attain pleasure and to avoid pain. Jeremy Bentham stated this view very clearly in the eighteenth century.

Nature has placed mankind under the governance of two sovereign masters, *pain* and *pleasure*. It is for them alone to point out what we ought to do, as well as to determine what we shall do. On the one hand the standard of right and wrong, on the other the chain of causes and effects, are fastened to their throne. They govern us in all we do, in all we say, in all we think: every effort to throw off our subjection, will serve but to demonstrate and confirm it. In words a man may pretend to abjure their empire; but in reality he will remain subject to it all the while.[1]

Epicurus is also an *ethical* hedonist in that he believes that man ought to attempt to achieve the maximum pleasure over his lifetime. The former view states that by his psychological make-up, man does seek pleasure and the avoidance of pain; the latter view holds that man, by knowledge, can and ought to seek the correct pleasures. The criteria of any action ought to be the pleasure it makes possible for the person.

Epicurus was highly critical of the shortsighted way pleasure was sought and the ignorance of people regarding their own good. Out of ignorance, we create many of our own unlimited and unrealistic desires, and then we torture ourselves because we cannot obtain satisfaction. The most pervasive pain and suffering of mankind arises because of ignorant craving and the frustration that ensues.

Nothing is sufficient for him to whom what is sufficient seems little.[2]

It is not the stomach which is insatiable, as is generally said, but the false opinion that the stomach needs an unlimited amount to fill it.[3]

Ignorance also brings about unnecessary anxieties and fears. The fear of death and the fear of divine retribution, the two fears which seemed to trouble his contemporaries most, are dispelled by knowledge. Lucretius, a Roman Epicurean who lived during the first half of the first century before Christ, makes this point in his long philosophical poem *On Nature* (*De Rerum Natura*).

Why do you doubt that the power over men's fears and cares lies altogether in philosophy, especially since our whole life is a struggle in the dark? Like children in the blinding darkness, who tremble and fear everything, so at times we, although in the light, fear things no more worthy of being feared than the phantoms at which children in the dark shudder, imagining they are upon them. This terror, this darkness of the soul, must be dispelled neither by the rays of the sun nor by the bright weapons of the day but by an understanding of the outer form and the inner law of Nature.[4]

An understanding of the laws of nature, which is obtained by a study of philosophy, is thus the necessary condition of a serene life. Believing in myths and stories increases man's fears and anxieties. By "understanding the laws of nature," both Epicurus and Lucretius meant comprehending and appreciating the truth of the theory of nature and the universe as expounded by Democritus (fifth century B.C.). According to this theory, the universe is made up of an infinite number of uncreated atoms. These differ in shape and size and, in their mechanical motion in infinite space, constitute man and all other objects perceived by our senses. To understand that the universe is so constituted is to see that the gods are not purposive agents and that they do not interfere with the actions of men for good or for evil. The fear that the gods will punish you, or the hope that they will reward you, are popular beliefs but are wholly unfounded. So is the fear of death, for there is no immortal soul that survives the death of the body. Man is comprised of atoms in motion in space, nothing more. As Democritus put it:

We are born once and cannot be born twice, but for all time must be no more. But you, who are not master of tomorrow, postpone your happiness: life is wasted in procrastination and each one of us dies without allowing himself leisure.[5]

The philosophy of Epicurus is summed up in the following letter he wrote to one of his disciples.

Letter to Menoeceus

Let no one when young delay to study philosophy, nor when he is old grow weary of his study. For no one can come too early or too late to secure the health of his soul. And the man who says that the age for philosophy has either not yet come or has gone by is like the man who says that the age for happiness is not yet come to him, or has passed away. Wherefore both when young and old a man must study philosophy, that as he grows old he may be young in blessings through the grateful recollection of what has been, and that in youth he may be old as well, since he will know no fear of what is to come. We must then meditate on the things that make our happiness, seeing that when that is with us we have all, but when it is absent we do all to win it.

The things which I used unceasingly to commend to you, these do and practise, considering them to be the first principles of the good life. First of all believe that god is a being immortal and blessed, even as the common idea of a god is engraved on men's minds, and do not assign to him anything alien to his immortality or ill-suited to his blessedness: but believe about him everything that can uphold his blessedness and immortality. For gods there are, since the knowledge of them is by clear vision. But they

Reprinted by permission from Whitney J. Oates, ed. *The Stoic and Epicurean Philosophers* (New York: Modern Library, Random House, 1940), pp. 30–33. Originally printed in *Epicurus, The Extant Remains,* trans. Cyril Bailey, copyright © 1926 by The Clarendon Press. By permission of the Clarendon Press.

are not such as the many believe them to be: for indeed they do not consistently represent them as they believe them to be. And the impious man is not he who denies the gods of the many, but he who attaches to the gods the beliefs of the many. For the statements of the many about the gods are not conceptions derived from sensation, but false suppositions, according to which the greatest misfortunes befall the wicked and the greatest blessings the good by the gift of the gods. For men being accustomed always to their own virtues welcome those like themselves, but regard all that is not of their nature as alien.

Become accustomed to the belief that death is nothing to us. For all good and evil consists in sensation, but death is deprivation of sensation. And therefore a right understanding that death is nothing to us makes the mortality of life enjoyable, not because it adds to it an infinite span of time, but because it takes away the craving for immortality. For there is nothing terrible in life for the man who has truly comprehended that there is nothing terrible in not living. So that the man speaks but idly who says that he fears death not because it will be painful when it comes, but because it is painful in anticipation. For that which gives no trouble when it comes, is but an empty pain in anticipation. So death, the most terrifying of ills, is nothing to us, since so long as we exist death is not with us; but when death comes, then we do not exist. It does not then concern either the living or the dead, since for the former it is not, and the latter are no more.

But the many at one moment shun death as

the greatest of evils, at another yearn for it as a respite from the evils in life. But the wise man neither seeks to escape life nor fears the cessation of life, for neither does life offend him nor does the absence of life seem to be any evil. And just as with food he does not seek simply the larger share and nothing else, but rather the most pleasant, so he seeks to enjoy not the longest period of time, but the most pleasant.

And he who counsels the young man to live well, but the old man to make a good end, is foolish, not merely because of the desirability of life, but also because it is the same training which teaches to live well and to die well. Yet much worse still is the man who says it is good not to be born, but

once born make haste to pass the gates of
Death.   [Theognis, 427]

For if he says this from conviction why does he not pass away out of life? For it is open to him to do so, if he had firmly made up his mind to this. But if he speaks in jest, his words are idle among men who cannot receive them.

We must then bear in mind that the future is neither ours, nor yet wholly not ours, so that we may not altogether expect it as sure to come, nor abandon hope of it, as if it will certainly not come.

We must consider that of desires some are natural, others vain, and of the natural some are necessary and others merely natural; and of the necessary some are necessary for happiness, others for the repose of the body, and others for very life. The right understanding of these facts enables us to refer all choice and avoidance to the health of the body and the soul's freedom from disturbance, since this is the aim of the life of blessedness. For it is to obtain this end that we always act, namely, to avoid pain and fear. And when this is once secured for us, all the tempest of the soul is dispersed, since the living creature has not to wander as though in search of something that is missing, and to look

for some other thing by which he can fulfill the good of the soul and the good of the body. For it is then that we have need of pleasure, when we feel pain owing to the absence of pleasure; but when we do not feel pain, we no longer need pleasure. And for this cause we call pleasure the beginning and end of the blessed life. For we recognize pleasure as the first good innate in us, and from pleasure we begin every act of choice and avoidance, and to pleasure we return again, using the feeling as the standard by which we judge every good.

And since pleasure is the first good and natural to us, for this very reason we do not choose every pleasure, but sometimes we pass over many pleasures, when greater discomfort accrues to us as the result of them: and similarly we think many pains better than pleasures, since a greater pleasure comes to us when we have endured pains for a long time. Every pleasure then because of its natural kinship to us is good, yet not every pleasure is to be chosen: even as every pain also is an evil, yet not all are always of a nature to be avoided. Yet by a scale of comparison and by the consideration of advantages and disadvantages we must form our judgment on all these matters. For the good on certain occasions we treat as bad, and conversely the bad as good.

And again independence of desire we think a great good—not that we may at all times enjoy but a few things, but that, if we do not possess many, we may enjoy the few in the genuine persuasion that those have the sweetest pleasure in luxury who least need it, and that all that is natural is easy to be obtained, but that which is superfluous is hard. And so plain savours bring us a pleasure equal to a luxurious diet, when all the pain due to want is removed; and bread and water produce the highest pleasure, when one who needs them puts them to his lips. To grow accustomed therefore to simple and not luxurious diet gives us health to the full, and makes a man alert for the needful employments of life, and when after long intervals we approach luxuries, disposes us better towards them, and fits us to be fearless of fortune.

When, therefore, we maintain that pleasure is the end, we do not mean the pleasures of profligates and those that consist in sensuality, as is supposed by some who are either ignorant or disagree with us or do not understand, but freedom from pain in the body and from trouble in the mind. For it is not continuous drinkings and revellings, nor the satisfaction of lusts, nor the enjoyment of fish and other luxuries of the wealthy table, which produce a pleasant life, but sober reasoning, searching out the motives for all choice and avoidance, and banishing mere opinions, to which are due the greatest disturbance of the spirit.

Of all this the beginning and the greatest good is prudence. Wherefore prudence is a more precious thing even than philosophy: for from prudence are sprung all the other virtues, and it teaches us that it is not possible to live pleasantly without living prudently and honourably and justly, nor, again, to live a life of prudence, honour, and justice without living pleasantly. For the virtues are by nature bound up with the pleasant life, and the pleasant life is inseparable from them. For indeed who, think you, is a better man than he who holds reverent opinions concerning the gods, and is at all times free from fear of death, and has reasoned out the end ordained by nature? He understands that the limit of good things is easy to fulfill and easy to attain, whereas the course of ills is either short in time or slight in pain: he laughs at destiny, whom some have introduced as the mistress of all things. He thinks that with us lies the chief power in determining events, some of which happen by necessity and some by chance, and some are within our control; for while necessity cannot be called to account, he sees that chance is inconstant, but that which is in our control is subject to no master, and to it are naturally attached praise and blame. For, indeed, it were better to follow the myths about the gods than to become a slave to the destiny of the natural philosophers: for the former suggests a hope of placating the gods by worship, whereas the latter involves a necessity which knows no placation. As to chance, he does not regard it as a god as most men do (for in a god's acts there is no disorder), nor as an uncertain cause of all things: for he does not believe that good and evil are given by chance to man for the framing of a blessed life, but that opportunities for great good and great evil are afforded by it. He therefore thinks it better to be unfortunate in reasonable action than to prosper in unreason. For it is better in a man's actions that what is well chosen should fail, rather than that what is ill chosen should be successful owing to chance.

Meditate therefore on these things and things akin to them night and day by yourself, and with a companion like to yourself, and never shall you be disturbed waking or asleep, but you shall live like a god among men. For a man who lives among immortal blessings is not like to a mortal being.

Notes

1. Jeremy Bentham, *An Introduction to the Principles of Morals and Legislation* (New York: Hafner Publishing Co., Inc., 1948), pp. 1-2.
2. Epicurus in Whitney J. Oates, ed. *The Stoic and Epicurean Philosophers* (New York: The Modern Library, Random House, Inc., 1940), p. 44.
3. Ibid., p. 43.
4. Lucretius, *On Nature,* trans. R. M. Geer (New York: The Bobbs-Merrill Co., Inc., 1965), p. 42.
5. Democritus in Oates, *op cit.,* p. 40.

Historically, most people have believed that the ultimate authority in questions concerning morality and the good life has been God. This vertical reference to a spiritual and moral power higher than man is the common factor in most religions and religious philosophies, although the names and conceptions of this ultimate source have varied: Brahma for the Hindu, Tao for the Taoist, Allah for the Muslim, and God for the Christian and Jew. The continuance of this influence is attested to by the fact that many people who give little credence to any one set of religious doctrines believe that religious faith is indispensable for any valid moral code. We still hear the statement that "without the belief in God, anything goes" (see Dostoyevsky in Part III and Niebuhr in Part VI).

For Nietzsche, God, the prime source and sanction for what was considered of highest worth, was "dead." Thus the traditional justification for the old moral ideals and codes had collapsed; concepts of good and evil were based upon a set of illusions in which man could no longer believe. Nietzsche believed that man must re-examine his values in order to understand his position in the scheme of things. He is calling for a revolution not only in what man prizes and esteems, but in his conception of himself as a creature in a world devoid of any supernatural meaning.

In 1887, Nietzsche's *Toward a Genealogy of Morals* advanced the view that morals are not handed down or commanded by any god or transcendental source. His studies in philology led him to the thesis that morals have natural sources. They perform mainly social functions. They differ because they answer changing needs, desires, and circumstances of different types of societies. Nietzsche believed that man should begin to research the history of morals. He envisioned the research as a cooperative, interdisciplinary study of different types of moralities, and of the evolution of moralities in relation to the psychological, social, and cultural conditions in which they arise and of which they are expressions.

Philosophers had paid too little attention to the data to be found in a close study of moral feelings, habits, and traditions of groups and societies in history. Philosophers had also been insufficiently aware of the prevailing values of their own age. Their work had all too often been a form of uncon-scious special pleading because they had underestimated the grip of the ways of thinking and valuing of their own times. Although moral philosophers had hidden behind the veil of objectivity and reason, their ethical theories merely fixed and systematized the then-prevailing set of values. They began their work as critics of the moral values of their own day; they ended up apologizing for that scale of values. Nietzsche would have us compare many moralities as they have revealed themselves in history and question the func-tion and worth of these values.

Nietzsche conceived that the "will to power" is the primal life force ex-pressed through nature in organic evolution and in the growth struggle of plant, animal, and child. It is the basic source from which all of life's drives, functions, and activities have evolved. For example, Nietzsche saw the sex drive as the expression of a more basic impulse for power and dominance. Pleasure accompanies the sexual act, but it is not the main object. The soldier's lust for combat, even at the risk of losing his life, is another expres-sion of the will to power. The student's desire to master a problem or topic is an example at a different level. "Surpassing" and "going beyond" are terms that convey the active nature of the will to power. In his best known work, *Thus Spake Zarathustra,* Nietzsche wrote:

And this secret spoke Life herself unto me. "Behold," said she, "I am that *which must ever surpass itself.*"

To be sure, ye call it will to procreation, or impulse towards a goal, towards the higher, remoter, more manifold: but all that is one and the same secret.

Rather would I succumb than disown this one thing; and verily, where there is succumbing and leaf-falling, lo, there doth Life sacrifice itself — for power!

Nietzsche found exemplifications of the will to power in art, religion, sci-ence, human relations, and morality. Moral codes and the philosophies that attempt to justify them are expressions and symptoms of the will to power. Human existence is permeated by values and valuing, and moralities are expressions of organic energies. How an individual or a culture selectively accepts, reiterates, rejects, or creates values determines what that man or culture is. Nietzsche advocates not a morality of denial, but a morality that will bring man's creative energies to their greatest expression.

The whisper of controversy about Friedrich Nietzsche and his writings began prior to his death in 1900. Nietzsche was unaware of most of the reaction; a mental illness had overtaken him ten years earlier. This contro-versy has increased: Nietzsche is pronounced a saint and genius by some, a satan and madman by others. The myths about Nietzsche are many and cannot be dispelled short of a full reading of all his works and a careful study of his meaning, which is what he would have wanted.

A Morality Beyond Good and Evil

. . . All the philosophers, with a pedantic and ridiculous seriousness, demanded of themselves something very much higher, more pretentious, and ceremonious, when they concerned themselves with morality as a science: they wanted to *give a basis* to morality—and every philosopher hitherto has believed that he has given it a basis; morality itself, however, has been regarded as something "given." . . . It was precisely owing to moral philosophers knowing the moral facts imperfectly, in an arbitrary epitome, or an accidental abridgement—perhaps as the morality of their environment, their position, their church, their *Zeitgeist*, their climate and zone—it was precisely because they were badly instructed with regard to nations, eras, and past ages, and were by no means eager to know about these matters, that they did not even come in sight of the real problems of morals—problems which only disclose themselves by a comparison of *many* kinds of morality. In every "Science of Morals" hitherto, strange as it may sound, the problem of morality itself has been *omitted;* there has been no suspicion that there was anything problematic there! That which philosophers called "giving a basis to morality," and endeavoured to realise, has, when seen in a right light, proved merely a learned form of good *faith* in prevailing morality, a new means of its *expression,* consequently

From *The Complete Works of Friedrich Nietzsche,* ed. Oscar Levy (Edinburgh: T. N. Foulis, 1909–11), vol. XII (*Beyond Good and Evil*) and vol. XIII (*The Genealogy of Morals*).

just a matter-of-fact within the sphere of a definite morality, yea, in its ultimate motive, a sort of denial that it is *lawful* for this morality to be called in question—and in any case the reverse of the testing, analysing, doubting, and vivisecting of this very faith. . . .[1]

. . . He, however, who . . . learns how to put questions, will experience what I experienced:—a new and immense vista unfolds itself before him, a sense of potentiality seizes him like a vertigo, every species of doubt, mistrust, and fear springs up, the belief in morality, nay, in all morality, totters,—finally a new demand voices itself. Let us speak out this *new demand:* we need a *critique* of moral values, *the value of these values* is for the first time to be called into question—and for this purpose a knowledge is necessary of the conditions and circumstances out of which these values grew, and under which they experienced their evolution and their distortion (morality as a result, as a symptom, as a mask, as Tartuffism, as disease, as a misunderstanding; but also morality as a cause, as a remedy, as a stimulant, as a fetter, as a drug), especially as such a knowledge has never existed up to the present time nor is even now generally desired. The value of these "values" was taken for granted as an indisputable fact, which was beyond all question. . . .[2]

Now the first argument that comes ready to my hand is that the real homestead of the concept "good" is sought and located in the wrong place: the judgment "good" did *not* originate among those to whom goodness was shown. Much rather has it been the good themselves, that is, the aristocratic, the powerful, the high-stationed, the high-minded, who have felt that they themselves were good, and that their actions were good, that is to say of the first order, in contradistinction to all the low, the low-minded, the vulgar, and the plebeian. It was out of this pathos of distance that they first arrogated the right to create values for their own profit, and to coin the names of such values. . . . The pathos of nobility and distance, as I have said, the chronic and despotic *esprit de corps* and fundamental instinct of a higher dominant race coming into association with a meaner race, an "under race," this is the origin of the antithesis of good and bad. . . .[3]

The guide-post which first put me on the *right* track was this question—what is the true etymological significance of the various symbols for the idea "good" which have been coined in the various languages? I then found that they all led back to *the same evolution of the same idea* —that everywhere "aristocrat," "noble" (in the social sense) is the root idea, out of which have necessarily developed "good" in the sense of "with aristocratic soul," "noble," in the sense of "with a soul of high calibre," "with a privileged soul"—a development which invariably runs parallel with that other evolution by which "vulgar," "plebeian," "low," are made to change finally into "bad.". . .[4]

In a tour through the many finer and coarser moralities which have hitherto prevailed or still prevail on the earth, I found certain traits recurring regularly together, and connected with one another, until finally two primary types revealed themselves to me, and a radical distinction was brought to light. There is *master-morality* and *slave-morality;*—I would at once add, however, that in all higher and mixed civilisations, there are also attempts at the reconciliation of the two moralities; but one finds still oftener the confusion and mutual misunderstanding of them, indeed, sometimes their close juxtaposition—even in the same man, within one soul. The distinctions of moral values have either originated in a ruling caste, pleasantly conscious of being different from the ruled—or among the ruled class, the slaves and dependents of all sorts. In the first case, when it is the rulers who determine the conception "good," it is the exalted, proud disposition which is regarded as the distinguishing feature, and that which determines the order of rank. The noble type of man separates from himself the beings in whom the opposite of this exalted, proud disposition displays itself: he despises them. Let it at once be noted that in this first kind of morality the antithesis "good" and "bad" means practically the same as "noble" and "despicable";—the antithesis "good" and "*evil*" is of a different origin. The cowardly, the timid, the insignificant, and those thinking merely of narrow utility are despised; moreover, also, the distrustful, with their constrained glances, the self-abasing, the dog-like kind of men who let themselves be abused, the mendicant flatterers, and above all the liars:—it is a fundamental belief of all aristocrats that the common people are untruthful. "We truthful ones"—the nobility in ancient Greece called themselves. It is obvious that everywhere the designations of moral value were at first applied to *men,* and were only derivatively and at a later period applied to *actions;* it is a gross mistake, therefore, when historians of morals start questions like, "Why have sympathetic actions been praised?" The noble type of man regards *himself* as a determiner of values; he does not require to be approved of; he passes the judgment: "What is injurious to me is injurious in itself"; he knows that it is he himself only who confers honour on things; he is a *creator of values*. He honours whatever he recognises in himself: such morality is self-glorification. In the foreground there is the feeling of plentitude, of power, which seeks to overflow, the happiness of high tension, the consciousness of a wealth which would fain give and bestow: —the noble man also helps the unfortunate, but not—or scarcely—out of pity, but rather from an impulse generated by the super-abundance of power. The noble man honours in himself the powerful one, him also who has power over himself, who knows how to speak and how to keep silence, who takes pleasure in subjecting himself to severity and hardness, and has reverence for all that is severe and hard. "Wotan placed a hard heart in my breast," says an old Scandinavian Saga: it is thus rightly expressed from the soul of a proud Viking. Such a type of man is even proud of *not* being made for sympathy; the hero of the Saga therefore adds warningly: "He who has not a hard heart when young, will never have one." The noble and brave who think thus are the furthest removed from the morality which sees precisely in sympathy, or in acting for the good of others, or in *désintéressement,* the characteristic of the moral; faith in oneself, pride in oneself, a radical enmity and irony towards "selflessness," belong as definitely to noble morality, as do a careless scorn and precaution in presence of sympathy and the "warm heart."—It is the powerful who *know* how to honour, it is their art, their domain for invention. The profound reverence for age and for tradition—all law rests on this double reverence,—the belief and prejudice in favour of ancestors and unfavourable to newcomers, is typical in the morality of the powerful; and if, reversely, men of "modern ideas" believe almost instinctively in "progress" and the "future," and are more and more lacking in respect for old age, the ignoble origin of these "ideas" has complacently betrayed itself thereby. A morality of the ruling class, however, is more especially foreign and irritating to present-day taste in the sternness of its principle that one has duties only to one's equals; that one may act towards beings of a lower rank, towards all that is foreign, just as seems good to one, or "as the heart desires," and in any case "beyond good and evil": it is here that sympathy and similar sentiments can have a place. . . . It is otherwise with the second type of morality, *slave-morality.* Supposing that the abused, the oppressed, the suffering, the unemancipated, the weary, and those uncertain of themselves, should moralise, what will be the common element in their moral estimates? Probably a pessimistic suspicion with regard to the entire situation of man will find expression, perhaps a condemnation of man, together with his situation. The slave has an unfavourable eye for the virtues of the powerful; he has a scepticism and distrust, a *refinement* of distrust of everything "good" that is there honoured—he would fain persuade himself that the very happiness there is not genuine. On the other hand, *those* qualities which serve to alleviate the existence of sufferers are brought into prominence and flooded with light; it is here that sympathy, the kind, helping hand, the warm heart, patience, diligence, humility, and friendliness attain to honour; for here these are the most useful qualities, and almost the only means of supporting the burden of existence. Slave-morality is essentially the morality of utility. Here is the seat of the origin of the famous antithesis "good" and "evil":—power and dangerousness are assumed to reside in the evil, a certain dreadfulness, subtlety, and strength, which do not admit of being despised. According to slave-morality, therefore, the "evil" man arouses fear; according to master-morality, it is precisely the "good" man who arouses fear and seeks to arouse it, while the bad man is regarded as the despicable being. . . .[5]

The revolt of the slaves in morals begins in the very principle of *resentment* becoming creative and giving birth to values—a resentment experienced by creatures who, deprived as they are of the proper outlet of action, are forced to find their compensation in an imaginary revenge. While every aristocratic morality springs from a triumphant affirmation of its own demands, the slave morality says "no" from the very outset to what is "outside itself," "different from itself," and "not itself": and this "no" is its creative deed. This volte-face of the valuing standpoint—this *inevitable* gravitation to the objective instead of back to the subjective—is typical of "resentment": the slave-morality requires as the condition of its existence an external and objective world, to employ physiological terminology, it requires objective stimuli to be capable of action at all—its action is fundamentally a reaction. The contrary is the case when we come to the aristocrat's system of values: it acts and grows spontaneously, it merely seeks its antithesis in order to pronounce a more grateful and exultant "yes" to its own self;—its negative conception, "low," "vulgar," "bad," is merely a pale late-born foil in comparison with its positive and fundamental conception (saturated as it is with life and passion), of "we aristocrats, we good ones, we beautiful ones, we happy ones. . . ."

. . . The "well-born" simply *felt* themselves the "happy"; they did not have to manufacture their happiness artificially through looking at their enemies, or in cases to talk and *lie themselves into* happiness (as is the custom with all resentful men); and similarly, complete men as they were, exuberant with strength, and consequently *necessarily* energetic, they were too wise to dissociate happiness from action—activity becomes in their minds necessarily counted as happiness . . .—all in sharp contrast to the "happiness" of the weak and the oppressed, with their festering venom and malignity, among whom happiness appears essentially as a narcotic, a deadening, a quietude, a peace, a "Sabbath," an enervation of the mind and relaxation of the limbs,—in short, a purely *passive* phenomenon. While the aristocratic man lived in confidence and openness with himself, . . . the resentful man, on the other hand, is neither sincere nor

naïf, nor honest and candid with himself. His soul *squints;* his mind loves hidden crannies, tortuous paths and backdoors, everything secret appeals to him as *his* world, *his* safety, *his* balm; he is past master in silence, in not forgetting, in waiting, in provisional self-depreciation and self-abasement. A race of such *resentful* men will of necessity eventually prove more *prudent* than any aristocratic race, it will honour prudence on quite a distinct scale, as, in fact, a paramount condition of existence. . . . When the resentment of the aristocratic man manifests itself, it fulfills and exhausts itself in an immediate reaction, and consequently instills no *venom:* on the other hand, it never manifests itself at all in countless instances, when in the case of the feeble and weak it would be inevitable. . . .

. . . These two words "bad" and "evil," how great a difference do they mark, in spite of the fact that they have an identical contrary in the idea "good." But the idea "good" is *not* the same: much rather let the question be asked, "Who is really evil according to the meaning of the morality of resentment?" In all sternness let it be answered thus:—*just* the good man of the other morality, just the aristocrat, the powerful one, the one who rules, but who is distorted by the venomous eye of resentfulness, into a new colour, a new signification, a new appearance. . . . Granted the truth of the theory now believed to be true, that the very *essence of all civilisation* is to *train* out of man, the beast of prey, a tame and civilised animal, a domesticated animal, it follows indubitably that we must regard as the real *tools of civilisation* all those instincts of reaction and resentment, by the help of which the artistocratic races, together with their ideals, were finally degraded and overpowered. . . .

. . . In the dwarfing and levelling of the European man lurks *our* greatest peril, for it is this outlook which fatigues—we see today nothing which wishes to be greater, we surmise that the process is always still backwards, still backwards towards something more attenuated, more inoffensive, more cunning, more comfortable, more mediocre, more indifferent, more Chinese, more Christian—man, there is no doubt about it, grows always "better"—the destiny of Europe lies even in this—that in losing the fear of man, we have also lost the hope in man, yes, the will to be man. The sight of man now fatigues.—What is present-day Nihilism if it is not *that*?—We are tired of *man*. . . .[6]

. . . To *reverse* all estimates of value—*that* is what they had to do! And to shatter the strong, to spoil great hopes, to cast suspicion on the delight in beauty, to break down everything autonomous, manly, conquering, and imperious—all instincts which are natural to the highest and most successful type of "man"—into uncertainty, distress of conscience, and self-destruction; forsooth, to invert all love of the earthly and of supremacy over the earth, into hatred of the earth and earthly things—*that* is the task the Church imposed on itself, and was obliged to impose, until, according to its standard of value, "unworldliness," "unsenuousness," and "higher man" fused into one sentiment. If one could observe the strangely painful, equally coarse and refined comedy of European Christianity with the derisive and impartial eye of an Epicurean god, I should think one would never cease marvelling and laughing; does it not actually seem that some single will has ruled over Europe for eighteen centuries in order to make a *sublime abortion* of man? He, however, who, with opposite requirements (no longer Epicurean) and with some divine hammer in his hand, could approach this almost voluntary degeneration and stunting of mankind, as exemplified in the European Christian (Pascal, for instance), would he not have to cry aloud with rage, pity, and horror: "Oh, you bunglers, presumptuous pitiful bunglers, what have you done! Was that a work for your hands? How you have hacked and botched my finest stone! What have *you* presumed to do!"—I should say that Christianity has hitherto been the most portentous of presumptions. Men, not great enough, nor hard enough, to be entitled as artists to take part in fashioning *man*; men, not sufficiently strong and far-sighted to *allow,* with sublime self-constraint, the obvious law of the thousandfold failures and perishings to prevail; men, not sufficiently noble to see the radically different grades of rank and intervals of rank that separate man from man:—*such* men, with their "equality before God," have hitherto swayed the destiny of Europe; until at last a dwarfed, almost ludicrous species has been produced, a gregarious animal, something obliging, sickly, mediocre, the European of the present day. . . .[7]

. . . I regard the bad conscience as the serious illness which man was bound to contract under the stress of the most radical change which he has ever experienced—that change when he found himself finally imprisoned within the pale of society and of peace.

Just like the plight of the water-animals, when they were compelled either to become land-animals or to perish, so was the plight of these half-animals, perfectly adapted as they were to the savage life of war, prowling, and adventure—suddenly all their instincts were rendered worthless and "switched off." Henceforward they had to walk on their feet—"carry themselves," whereas heretofore they had been carried by the water: a terrible heaviness oppressed them. They found themselves clumsy in obeying the simplest directions, confronted with this new and unknown world they had no longer their old guides—the regulative instincts that had led them unconsciously to safety—they were reduced, were those unhappy creatures, to thinking, inferring, calculating, putting together causes and results, reduced to that poorest and most erratic organ of theirs, their "consciousness." I do not believe there was ever in the world such a feeling of misery, such a leaden discomfort—further, those old instincts had not immediately ceased their demands! Only it was difficult and rarely possible to gratify them: speaking broadly, they were compelled to satisfy themselves by new and, as it were, hole-and-corner methods. All instincts which do not find a vent without, *turn inwards*—this is what I mean by the growing "internalisation" of man: consequently we have the first growth in man, of what subsequently was called his soul. The whole inner world, originally as thin as if it had been stretched between two layers of skin, burst apart and expanded proportionately, and obtained depth, breadth, and height, when man's external outlet became *obstructed*. These terrible bulwarks, with which the social organisation protected itself against the old instincts of freedom (punishments belong pre-eminently to these bulwarks), brought it about that all those instincts of wild, free, prowling man became turned backwards *against man himself*. Enmity, cruelty, the delight in persecution, in surprises, change, destruction—the turning all these instincts against their own possessors: this is the origin of the "bad conscience." It was man, who, lacking external enemies and obstacles, and imprisoned as he was in the oppressive narrowness and monotony of custom, in his own impatience lacerated, persecuted, gnawed, frightened, and ill-treated himself; it was this animal in the hands of the tamer, which beat itself against the bars of its cage; it was this being who, pining and yearning for that desert home of which it had been deprived, was compelled to create out of its own self, an adventure, a torture-chamber, a hazardous and perilous desert —it was this fool, this homesick and desperate prisoner—who invented the "bad conscience." But thereby he introduced that most grave and sinister illness, from which mankind has not yet recovered, the suffering of man from the disease called man, as the result of a violent breaking from his animal past, the result, as it were, of a spasmodic plunge into a new environment and new conditions of existence, the result of a declaration of war against the old instincts, which up to that time had been the staple of

his power, his joy, his formidableness. Let us immediately add that this fact of an animal ego turning against itself, taking part against itself, produced in the world so novel, profound, unheard-of, problematic, inconsistent and *pregnant* a phenomenon, that the aspect of the world was radically altered thereby. . . .[8]

. . . That will for self-torture, that inverted cruelty of the animal man, who, turned subjective and scared into introspection (encaged as he was in "the State," as part of his taming process), invented the bad conscience so as to hurt himself, after the *natural* outlet for this will to hurt, became blocked—in other words, this man of the bad conscience exploited the religious hypothesis so as to carry his martyrdom to the ghastliest pitch of agonised intensity. Owing something to *God*: this thought becomes his instrument of torture. He apprehends in God the most extreme antitheses that he can find to his own characteristic and ineradicable animal instincts, he himself gives a new interpretation to these animal instincts as being against what he "owes" to God (as enmity, rebellion, and revolt against the "Lord," the "Father," the "Sire," the "Beginning of the world"), he places himself between the horns of the dilemma, "God" and "Devil." Every negation which he is inclined to utter to himself, to the nature, naturalness, and reality of his being, he whips into an ejaculation of "yes," uttering it as something existing, living, efficient, as being God, as the holiness of God, the judgment of God, as the hangmanship of God, as transcendence, as eternity, as unending torment, as hell, as infinity of punishment and guilt. This is a kind of madness of the will in the sphere of psychological cruelty which is absolutely unparalleled:—man's *will* to find himself guilty and blameworthy to the point of inexpiability, his *will* to think of himself as punished, without the punishment ever being able to balance the guilt, his *will* to infect and to poison the fundamental basis of the universe with the problem of punishment and guilt, in order to cut off once and for all any escape out of this labyrinth of "fixed ideas," his will for rearing an ideal—that of the "holy God"—face to face with which he can have tangible proof of his own unworthiness. Alas for this mad melancholy beast man! . . . In man there is so much that is ghastly—too long has the world been a mad-house.[9]

Notes

1. Friedrich Nietzsche, *Beyond Good and Evil*, trans. Helen Zimmern in *The Complete Works of Friedrich Nietzsche*, vol. XII, ed. Oscar Levy (London: T. N. Foulis, 1911), pp. 103–105.

2. Friedrich Nietzsche, *The Genealogy of Morals*, trans. Horace B. Samuel in *The Complete Works of Friedrich Nietzsche*, vol. XIII, ed. Oscar Levy (Edinburgh: T. N. Foulis, 1911), p. 9.

3. Ibid., pp. 19–20.

4. Ibid., pp. 22–23.

5. Nietzsche, *Beyond Good and Evil*, pp. 227–231 (with omissions).

6. Nietzsche, *Genealogy of Morals*, pp. 34–44 (with omissions).

7. Nietzsche, *Beyond Good and Evil*, pp. 83–84.

8. Nietzsche, *Genealogy of Morals*, pp. 99–102.

9. Ibid., pp. 112–113.

13 / Dynamic Morality
Dewey

Early in his career, the American philosopher John Dewey (1859–1952) recognized the necessity for an overall reconstruction of social and educational institutions. In his later writings he stressed the urgency of the crisis and the need for its intelligent resolution. Traditional mores and theories about the standards and principles by which man judges life and makes his moral decisions were in trouble. The root of the crisis was the incompatibility of traditional values and ideals with the changed circumstances of man's existence brought about by the scientific and industrial revolutions. Dewey suggested that an approach to morality be patterned after scientific attitudes and methods but directing inquiry into human and essentially moral problems. This would begin to heal the breach between man's outmoded beliefs about values and his largely unguided contemporary experience.

Dewey believed that a major obstacle to the needed reconstruction was traditional philosophy and the way in which it presented moral problems and their solutions. One of his major criticisms of traditional philosophers was that they had been too enamored with the search for fixed truths. They believed that only the immutable truth could be the proper object of human knowledge. Many ancient philosophers believed that the world presented to us by sense perception and ordinary experience cannot yield certain knowledge. The world as grasped by theoretical understanding, as contrasted with the world of opinion and practice, became the aim of the philosopher.

This spectator view of knowledge carried with it a distinction between knowing, as a pure intellectual activity, and doing. This was generalized into a separation of the theoretical and the practical and it depreciated doing, making, and action. It did not see human thought as a purposive and reflective activity by which man relates to and changes his environment. Instead of emphasizing the practical and experimental and ameliorating the hazards and precariousness of human existence, it emphasized changing the inner soul and focused upon an ideal, much more perfect world. This emphasis had given man consolation and some good literature, but it had diverted him from his real task.

Dewey was against this approach to morality. Reason is not a searchlight by which, if we focus correctly, the eternal verities will be grasped. Thinking is a human instrument for man's interaction with his physical and social environment. Human values and moral problems come into play when some practical choice is made involving human conduct, desires, and satisfactions. Human aims are not to be taken as fixed ends in advance of inquiry into, and intelligent deliberation about, concrete moral situations. Nor are the ends of human action separable from the means for carrying them out. Dewey believed that we ought to assess the various roads to human improvement rather than argue about the validity of this or that description of the final destination. The value of science is not any one conclusion or theory but its adoption of an open-ended procedure and method; the important thing in morals is not a conclusion or definition about the good, but the adoption of a procedure for intelligent deliberation. The good life is one in which man avoids making moral choices by instinct or habit and is intelligently guided by changing needs and circumstances.

Since the Renaissance and the rise of science, the traditional view of moral values as belonging to a higher and more spiritual realm had been on the defensive. The new science seemed to have stripped the world of the qualities that made it beautiful and good and had ruled out everything but a world composed of particles acting according to mechanical laws. There was no place for value in a world of fact.

Dewey's reaction to this was not to lament the loneliness of man in a meaningless universe nor to portray him as heroically asserting values despite their ultimate meaninglessness. Rather he denied this picture of both science and human morality; he denied the separation of man and nature. He tried to reconcile the two by looking for one method that would deal with both factors in man's existence. Since values are a part of human experience, man should use his intelligence to judge the conditions and results of human satisfactions and, accordingly, his future desires, affections, and enjoyments.

That the structure of man's society, his habits, living conditions, and daily life have been radically transformed by the scientific and technological revolutions is even more obvious to us than it was to Dewey. Man's behavior and the context of his moral decisions have been profoundly influenced and altered by, for example, such recent developments in medicine as birth control methods, new ways of prolonging life, and organ transplants. These developments affect the way in which man lives (and dies) in his environment. Despite all of these outward changes, man's institutions and his concepts of himself and the good remain relatively the same. Thus there is a cultural and moral lag between man's inner thoughts and the conditions of his outward behavior. The scientific attitude should be used to create new attitudes and beliefs about morals rather than to remain largely subordinate to the instincts of man or the inertia of his institutions.

Reconstruction in Moral Conceptions

Morals is not a catalogue of acts nor a set of rules to be applied like drugstore prescriptions or cook-book recipes. The need in morals is for specific methods of inquiry and of contrivance: Methods of inquiry to locate difficulties and evils; methods of contrivance to form plans to be used as working hypotheses in dealing with them. And the pragmatic import of the logic of individualized situations, each having its own irreplaceable good and principle, is to transfer the attention of theory from preoccupation with general conceptions to the problem of developing effective methods of inquiry.

Two ethical consequences of great moment should be remarked. The belief in fixed values has bred a division of ends into intrinsic and instrumental, of those that are really worth while in themselves and those that are of importance only as means to intrinsic goods. Indeed, it is often thought to be the very beginning of wisdom, of moral discrimination, to make this distinction. Dialectically, the distinction is interesting and seems harmless. But carried into practice it has an import that is tragic. Historically, it has been the source and justification of a hard and fast difference between ideal goods on one side and material goods on the other. At present those who would be liberal

conceive intrinsic goods as esthetic in nature rather than as exclusively religious or as intellectually contemplative. But the effect is the same. So-called intrinsic goods, whether religious or esthetic, are divorced from those interests of daily life which because of their constancy and urgency form the preoccupation of the great mass. Aristotle used this distinction to declare that slaves and the working class though they are necessary *for* the state—the commonweal—are not constituents *of* it. That which is regarded as *merely* instrumental must approach drudgery; it cannot command either intellectual, artistic or moral attention and respect. Anything becomes *unworthy* whenever it is thought of as intrinsically lacking worth. So men of "ideal" interests have chosen for the most part the way of neglect and escape. The urgency and pressure of "lower" ends have been covered up by polite conventions. Or, they have been relegated to a baser class of mortals in order that the few might be free to attend to the goods that are really or intrinsically worth while. This withdrawal, in the name of higher ends, has left, for mankind at large and especially for energetic "practical" people the lower activities in complete command.

No one can possibly estimate how much of the obnoxious materialism and brutality of our economic life is due to the fact that economic ends have been regarded as *merely* instrumental. When they are recognized to be as intrinsic and final in their place as any others, then it will be seen that they are capable of

From John Dewey, *Reconstruction in Philosophy*. Original edition, copyright 1920 by Henry Holt and Co. Enlarged edition, copyright 1948 by Beacon Press. Reprinted by permission of Beacon Press.

idealization, and that if life is to be worth while, they must acquire ideal and intrinsic value. Esthetic, religious and other "ideal" ends are now thin and meagre or else idle and luxurious because of the separation from "instrumental" or economic ends. Only in connection with the latter can they be woven into the texture of daily life and made substantial and pervasive. The vanity and irresponsibility of values that are merely final and not also in turn means to the enrichment of other occupations of life ought to be obvious. But now the doctrine of "higher" ends gives aid, comfort and support to every socially isolated and socially irresponsible scholar, specialist, esthete and religionist. It protects the vanity and irresponsibility of his calling from observation by others and by himself. The moral deficiency of the calling is transformed into a cause of admiration and gratulation.

The other generic change lies in doing away once for all with the traditional distinction between moral goods, like the virtues, and natural goods like health, economic security, art, science and the like. The point of view under discussion is not the only one which has deplored this rigid distinction and endeavored to abolish it. Some schools have even gone so far as to regard moral excellencies, qualities of character as of value only because they promote natural goods. But the experimental logic when carried into morals makes every quality that is judged to be good according as it contributes to amelioration of existing ills. And in so doing, it enforces the moral meaning of natural science. When all is said and done in criticism of present social deficiencies, one may well wonder whether the root difficulty does not lie in the separation of natural and moral science. When physics, chemistry, biology, medicine, contribute to the detection of concrete human woes and to the development of plans for remedying them and relieving the human estate, they become moral; they become part of the apparatus of moral inquiry or science. The latter then loses its peculiar flavor of the didactic and pedantic;

its ultra-moralistic and hortatory tone. It loses its thinness and shrillness as well as its vagueness. It gains agencies that are efficacious. But the gain is not confined to the side of moral science. Natural science loses its divorce from humanity; it becomes itself humanistic in quality. It is something to be pursued not in a technical and specialized way for what is called truth for its own sake, but with the sense of its social bearing, its intellectual indispensableness. It is technical only in the sense that it provides the technique of social and moral engineering.

When the consciousness of science is fully impregnated with the consciousness of human value, the greatest dualism which now weighs humanity down, the split between the material, the mechanical, the scientific and the moral and ideal will be destroyed. Human forces that now waver because of this division will be unified and reinforced. As long as ends are not thought of as individualized according to specific needs and opportunities, the mind will be content with abstractions, and the adequate stimulus to the moral or social use of natural science and historical data will be lacking. But when attention is concentrated upon the diversified concretes, recourse to all intellectual materials needed to clear up the special cases will be imperative. At the same time that morals are made to focus in intelligence, things intellectual are moralized. The vexatious and wasteful conflict between naturalism and humanism is terminated.

These general considerations may be amplified. First: Inquiry, discovery take the same place in morals that they have come to occupy in sciences of nature. Validation, demonstration become experimental, a matter of consequences. Reason, always an honorific term in ethics, becomes actualized in the methods by which the needs and conditions, the obstacles and resources, of situations are scrutinized in detail, and intelligent plans of improvement are worked out. Remote and abstract generalities promote jumping at conclusions, "anticipations of nature." Bad consequences are then deplored as due to natural perversity and untoward fate. But shifting the issue to analysis of a specific situation makes inquiry obligatory and alert observation of consequences imperative. No past decision nor old principle can ever be wholly relied upon to justify a course of action. No amount of pains taken in forming a purpose in a definite case is final; the consequences of its adoption must be carefully noted, and a purpose held only as a working hypothesis until results confirm its rightness. Mistakes are no longer either mere unavoidable accidents to be mourned or moral sins to be expiated and forgiven. They are lessons in wrong methods of using intelligence and instructions as to a better course in the future. They are indications of the need of revision, development, readjustment. Ends grow, standards of judgment are improved. Man is under just as much obligation to develop his most advanced standards and ideals as to use conscientiously those which he already possesses. Moral life is protected from falling into formalism and rigid repetition. It is rendered flexible, vital, growing.

In the second place, every case where moral action is required becomes of equal moral importance and urgency with every other. If the need and deficiencies of a specific situation indicate improvement of health as the end and good, then for that situation health is the ultimate and supreme good. It is no means to something else. It is a final and intrinsic value. The same thing is true of improvement of economic status, of making a living, of attending to business and family demands—all of the things which under the sanction of fixed ends have been rendered of secondary and merely instrumental value, and so relatively base and unimportant. Anything that in a given situation is an end and good at all is of equal worth, rank and dignity with every other good of any other situation, and deserves the same intelligent attention.

We note thirdly the effect in destroying the roots of Phariseeism. We are so accustomed to

thinking of this as deliberate hypocrisy that we overlook its intellectual premises. The conception which looks for the end of action within the circumstances of the actual situation will not have the same measure of judgment for all cases. When one factor of the situation is a person of trained mind and large resources, more will be expected than with a person of backward mind and uncultured experience. The absurdity of applying the same standard of moral judgment to savage peoples that is used with civilized will be apparent. No individual or group will be judged by whether they come up to or fall short of some fixed result, but by the direction in which they are moving. The bad man is the man who no matter how good he *has* been is beginning to deteriorate, to grow less good. The good man is the man who no matter how morally unworthy he *has* been is moving to become better. Such a conception makes one severe in judging himself and humane in judging others. It excludes that arrogance which always accompanies judgment based on degree of approximation to fixed ends.

In the fourth place, the process of growth, of improvement and progress, rather than the static outcome and result, becomes the significant thing. Not health as an end fixed once and for all, but the needed improvement in health—a continual process—is the end and good. The end is no longer a terminus or limit to be reached. It is the active process of transforming the existent situation. Not perfection as a final goal, but the ever-enduring process of perfecting, maturing, refining is the aim in living. Honesty, industry, temperance, justice, like health, wealth and learning, are not goods to be possessed as they would be if they expressed fixed ends to be attained. They are directions of change in the quality of experience. Growth itself is the only moral "end."

Although the bearing of this idea upon the problem of evil and the controversy between optimism and pessimism is too vast to be here discussed, it may be worth while to touch upon it superficially. The problem of evil ceases to be a theological and metaphysical one, and is perceived to be the practical problem of reducing, alleviating, as far as may be removing, the evils of life. Philosophy is no longer under obligation to find ingenious methods for proving that evils are only apparent, not real, or to elaborate schemes for explaining them away or, worse yet, for justifying them. It assumes another obligation:—That of contributing in however humble a way to methods that will assist us in discovering the causes of humanity's ills. Pessimism is a paralyzing doctrine. In declaring that the world is evil wholesale, it makes futile all efforts to discover the remediable causes of specific evils and thereby destroys at the root every attempt to make the world better and happier. Wholesale optimism, which has been the consequence of the attempt to explain evil away, is, however, equally an incubus.

After all, the optimism that says that the world is already the best possible of all worlds might be regarded as the most cynical of pessimisms. If this is the best possible, what would a world which was fundamentally bad be like? Meliorism is the belief that the specific conditions which exist at one moment, be they comparatively bad or comparatively good, in any event may be bettered. It encourages intelligence to study the positive means of good and the obstructions to their realization, and to put forth endeavor for the improvement of conditions. It arouses confidence and a reasonable hopefulness as optimism does not. For the latter in declaring that good is already realized in ultimate reality tends to make us gloss over the evils that concretely exist. It becomes too readily the creed of those who live at ease, in comfort, of those who have been successful in obtaining this world's rewards. Too readily optimism makes the men who hold it callous and blind to the sufferings of the less fortunate, or ready to find the cause of troubles of others in their personal viciousness. It thus co-operates with pessimism, in spite of the extreme nominal differences between the two, in benumbing sympathetic insight and intelligent effort in reform. It beckons men away from the world of relativity and change into the calm of the absolute and eternal.

The import of many of these changes in moral attitude focusses in the idea of happiness. Happiness has often been made the object of the moralists' contempt. Yet the most ascetic moralist has usually restored the idea of happiness under some other name, such as bliss. Goodness without happiness; valor and virtue without satisfaction, ends without conscious enjoyment— these things are as intolerable practically as they are self-contradictory in conception. Happiness is not, however, a bare possession; it is not a fixed attainment. Such a happiness is either the unworthy selfishness which moralists have so bitterly condemned, or it is, even if labelled bliss, an insipid tedium, a millennium of ease in relief from all struggle and labor. It could satisfy only the most delicate of molly-coddles. Happiness is found only in success; but success means succeeding, getting forward, moving in advance. It is an active process, not a passive outcome. Accordingly it includes the overcoming of obstacles, the elimination of sources of defect and ill. Esthetic sensitiveness and enjoyment are a large constituent in any worthy happiness. But the esthetic appreciation which is totally separated from renewal of spirit, from re-creation of mind and purification of emotion is a weak and sickly thing, destined to speedy death from starvation. That the renewal and re-creation come unconsciously not by set intention but makes them the more genuine. . . .

If a few words are added upon the topic of education, it is only for the sake of suggesting that the educative process is all one with the moral process, since the latter is a continuous passage of experience from worse to better. Education has been traditionally thought of as preparation: as learning, acquiring certain things because they will later be useful. The end is remote, and education is getting ready, is a preliminary to something more important to happen later on. Childhood is only a preparation for adult life, and adult life for another life. Always the future, not the present, has been the significant thing in education: Acquisition of knowledge and skill for future use and enjoyment; formation of habits required later in life in business, good citizenship and pursuit of science. Education is thought of also as something needed by some human beings merely because of their dependence upon others. We are born ignorant, unversed, unskilled, immature, and consequently in a state of social dependence. Instruction, training, moral discipline are processes by which the mature, the adult, gradually raise the helpless to the point where they can look out for themselves. The business of childhood is to grow into the independence of adulthood by means of the guidance of those who have already attained it. Thus the process of education as the main business of life ends when the young have arrived at emancipation from social dependence.

These two ideas, generally assumed but rarely explicitly reasoned out, contravene the conception that growing, or the continuous reconstruction of experience, is the only end. If at whatever period we choose to take a person, he is still in process of growth, then education is not, save as a by-product, a preparation for something coming later. Getting from the present the degree and kind of growth there is in it is education. This is a constant function, independent of age. The best thing that can be said about any special process of education, like that of the formal school period, is that it renders its subject capable of further education: more sensitive to conditions of growth and more able to take advantage of them. Acquisition of skill, possession of knowledge, attainment of culture are not ends: they are marks of growth and means to its continuing.

The contrast usually assumed between the period of education as one of social dependence and of maturity as one of social independence does harm. We repeat over and over that man is a social animal, and then confine the significance of this statement to the sphere in which sociality usually seems least evident, politics. The heart of the sociality of man is in education. The idea of education as preparation and of adulthood as a fixed limit of growth are two sides of the same obnoxious untruth. If the moral business of the adult as well as the young is a growing and developing experience, then the instruction that comes from social dependencies and interdependencies are as important for the adult as for the child. Moral independence for the adult means arrest of growth, isolation means induration. We exaggerate the intellectual dependence of childhood so that children are too much kept in leading strings, and then we exaggerate the independence of adult life from intimacy of contacts and communication with others. When the identity of the moral process with the processes of specific growth is realized, the more conscious and formal education of childhood will be seen to be the most economical and efficient means of social advance and reorganization, and it will also be evident that the test of all the institutions of adult life is their effect in furthering continued education. Government, business, art, religion, all social institutions have a meaning, a purpose. That purpose is to set free and to develop the capacities of human individuals without respect to race, sex, class or economic status. And this is all one with saying that the test of their value is the extent to which they educate every individual into the full stature of his possibility. Democracy has many meanings, but if it has a moral meaning, it is found in resolving that the supreme test of all political institutions and industrial arrangements shall be the contribution they make to the all-around growth of every member of society.

14 / The Courage to Choose
Jaspers

The life of Socrates in ancient Athens has been the traditional model of what it means to philosophize. Divergent philosophical traditions have claimed him as inspiration. Much of contemporary Anglo-American philosophy is interested in the language and meaning of ethical terms and sentences and stresses conceptual and methodological clarity as the primary value of philosophy. This emphasis has been traced to Socrates' arguments against the tyranny of conventional opinions and conceptions. Plato's dialogues and many of Aristotle's treatises begin with the analysis of language and the question of meaning.

The existentialists focus upon another dimension of Socrates—a personal, human dimension which was at the center of Plato's fascination with the man. In the *Phaedo* and the *Symposium,* Plato presents moving descriptions of Socrates: his commitment to self-knowledge, his long periods of meditation, his conviction of his special calling, and his love of wisdom. As we saw in the *Crito,* the integrity of that commitment was sustained even in the face of death. For Socrates, philosophy was a way of life, an endless effort to work out of the despair, the fear, and the confusion of existence.

The German philosopher, Friedrich Nietzsche, and the Danish theologian, Soren Kierkegaard, are the most important precursors of existentialist attitudes and approaches to philosophy. Most of the themes of modern existentialism have roots in these two nineteenth-century thinkers: criticism of the construction of abstract scientific and philosophical systems in which the concrete experiences of individuals are lost; fear of the submergence of the individual in mass society; and discussion of the emotions and deep feelings aroused by the human condition, such as guilt, bad conscience, dread, despair, and radical loneliness.

Contemporary existentialists are generally critical of those philosophies which, in the interest of following science, attempt to reduce human life to a set of universal and objective properties. For example, they would take issue with Dewey's emphasis upon adopting the scientific ethos of reliable beliefs for the resolution of moral disagreements. Philosophy, they insist, springs from the conditions of human life, which include the fact that science is limited in assessing and resolving the ultimate questions about the meaning and purpose of human existence.

Like Kierkegaard and Nietzsche, today's existentialists stress the human mode of being apart from the mode of being characteristic of an object in nature. Their writings point to the unique characteristics that are a part of the conscious reality or "situation," which is the person. Man is uniquely self-conscious, cares about himself and his values, and exists in a felt time that is quite different from the quantified minutes registered by the clock. His present includes his past and the open possibilities of the future, including the fact of death. Because man is open to the future, he is incomplete, he *exists*, which means he stands outside himself and beyond himself. This self-transcendence is an integral part of what human life means. Man is free to make decisions and to realize that he is responsible for what he becomes.

Another common theme of the existentialists is the spiritual threat that technology and mass society present to the individual. Dewey anticipated this threat and conceived of ways by which man could achieve a more harmonious relationship with nature. Today man lives both mentally and physically within an environment of his own creation. The possibility of genetic control, vast communication networks, and the weapons of war now present the possibility of a complete control of man and a devaluation of his individuality. Science has given us the means to master the world, but man is threatened by the loss of his own self-identity (see Part IV).

The existentialists do not present an ethical system in any traditional sense of that term. While they are generally against even any abstract rules by which we might hope to guide our actions, much of their work does have an ethical thrust. They point out the unique and fragmented situation of modern man, the uncertainties and contradictions of his life, and the dangers to his autonomy. They suggest that we should live "authentically," be conscious of a deeper and wider self, stay "open," and perhaps find the standard of value in our own commitments. Dewey's ethics asks us to modify our natural and social environments in order to increase human satisfactions; the existentialists seem most often to be asking us to realize more fully our self amid increasingly impossible odds. For many, philosophy is this inner process and personal activity by which man focuses upon his own perplexities as he attempts to become more fully himself. The Socratic "examined life" is itself the most significant moral commitment.

Most of the above general themes are treated in the works of the German psychiatrist and philosopher Karl Jaspers, although he has disclaimed the title of existentialist. He discusses, among other topics, the human mode of being, man's situation not only "in the world," but also in his own awareness, concern, and consciousness; the threat to man inherent in the new conditions brought about by science and technology; the ambiguities and cleavages of human life and consciousness; and the need today for what is essentially moral courage.

In the following selection, Jaspers asserts that the individual shows himself in his decisions, especially in times of deep personal crisis. What an individual is does not have the form of an intellectual truth but emerges from the free and rational commitments he makes. For Dewey, an examined life results in a life of more intelligent action. For Jaspers, a reflective life leads to a person's being more fully aware of his existence. I become more fully myself as I develop this inner awareness and bring myself into communication and dialogue with others. For Jaspers, Socrates heeded the command of the unconditional imperative; his decision at the trial and in jail became the substance of the man.

The Unconditional Imperative

In love, in battle, in pursuing lofty tasks, men often act without regard for consequences, unconditionally. When a man acts unconditionally his life is not the ultimate, he subordinates it to something else.

When we obey the unconditional imperative, our empirical existence becomes in a sense the raw material of the idea, of love, of a loyalty. It is encompassed in an eternal aim, it is as it were consumed, and it is not allowed drift at random in the stream of life. Only at the limit, in extreme situations, can the call of the unconditional lead to loss of life, to acceptance of inevitable death, while in bondage to the conditional we wish first, last, and at any price to preserve our physical existence.

Men have, for example, risked their lives in a common struggle for a common life in the world. Solidarity was then the ultimate condition.

Originally such communities were built upon trust but later they came to be based on the inspiring command of an authority in which men believed, so that faith in this authority became a source of the absolute. This faith freed men from uncertainty, spared them the need to inquire for themselves. However, the unconditional in this form was subject to a tacit condition, namely the success of the authority. The believer desired to live through his obedience. If the authority ceased to be successful as

From Karl Jaspers, *The Way to Wisdom,* trans. by Ralph Manheim. New Haven: Yale University Press, 1954, pp. 52–62. Copyright 1954 by Yale University Press. Reprinted by permission.

a power, and men lost their faith in it, a ruinous emptiness arose.

And the only escape from this emptiness is for man himself as an individual to win authentic being as the foundation of his decisions.

This has happened in history when individuals staked their lives through obedience to an absolute imperative: they remained loyal where disloyalty would have destroyed everything, where a life saved through disloyalty would have been poisoned, where a betrayal of absolute being would have made a saved life wretched.

The purest example is perhaps Socrates. Living in the lucidity of his reason, out of the Comprehensive of nonknowledge, he went his way unswervingly, undeterred by the passions of anger, hatred, selfrighteousness; he made no concession, refused to avail himself of the opportunity for flight, and died happy, staking everything on his faith.

Certain martyrs, like Thomas More, have displayed the purest moral energy in their faith. The martyrdom of some others is subject to question. To die for something in order to bear witness to it is to give an aim to one's death, hence to make it impure. Where martyrs have actually been inspired by a longing to die, perhaps in imitation of Christ, by a death urge which not infrequently darkens the soul with symptoms of hysteria, the impurity is still greater.

Rare are the philosophers who, without firm allegiance to a community of faith, standing alone before God, have realized the maxim: To philosophize is to learn how to die. Seneca, for years awaiting his death sentence, overcame the desire to escape dictated by his understanding; in the end he did not betray himself by unworthy actions, and he preserved his composure when Nero demanded his death. Boethius died innocently, sentenced by a barbarian: he died philosophizing in full lucidity, turned toward authentic being. Bruno overcame his doubts and withdrew what concessions he had made, in the high resolve to stand fast for no purpose, even if it meant death at the stake.

Seneca, Boethius, Bruno were men with their weaknesses, their failures, men such as ourselves. They had to conquer themselves. And this is why they can point the way for us. For saints after all are figures who for us can live only in the twilight, or in the unreal light of myth, but cannot stand up under realistic scrutiny. The unconditional acts of which men as men were capable give us true encouragement, while the imaginary provides only empty edification.

We have recalled historical examples of men who knew how to die. Let us now attempt to elucidate the unconditional imperative.

When I ask myself: What shall I do? I arrive at an answer by adducing finite aims and means by which to attain them. I must obtain food and for this work is needed. I must live with men in a community: here I am helped by certain rules of conduct. In every case an aim determines the means appropriate to it.

But my basis for recognizing these aims lies either in some unquestioned practical interest or in utility. Empirical existence, however, is no ultimate end, because the questions remain: What kind of existence? and What for?

Or else the imperative is grounded in an authority which I must obey because someone else has willed it or because "It is written." But such authority remains unquestioned and hence unexamined.

All such imperatives are conditional. For they make me dependent on something outside me, on practical aims or authority. Unconditional imperatives on the other hand have their source in myself. Conditional imperatives confront me as fixed but transient principles, by which I can outwardly sustain myself. Unconditional imperatives come from within me, sustaining me inwardly by that which in myself is not only myself.

The unconditional imperative comes to me as the command of my authentic self to my mere empirical existence. I become aware of myself as of that which I myself am, because it is what I ought to be. This awareness is obscure at the beginning and lucid at the end of my unconditional action. When we become aware of the imperative our questioning ceases in the certainty of being—though in temporal life there is at once a new beginning of questioning, and in a changed situation certainty must forever be gained anew.

This imperative precedes every aim, it is that which determines all aims. Accordingly it is not an object of our will but its source.

The unconditional is a foundation of action and hence not an object of knowledge but an element of faith. In so far as I know the reasons and aims of my action, I am in the finite, I am subject to conditions. Only when I live by something that can no longer be explained by object knowledge do I live by the unconditional.

A few propositions may suggest the meaning of the unconditional imperative.

First: as opposed to passive acceptance of things as they are, the unconditional attitude implies a decision, lucidly taken, out of an unfathomable depth, a decision with which I myself am identical. What does this mean?

It means to partake in the eternal, in being. Accordingly, it implies absolute reliability and loyalty, which derive not from nature but from our decision. The decision is arrived at only through lucidity which is the product of reflection. Expressed in psychological terms, the unconditional attitude does not lie in the momentary state of any man. Even though he may reveal overpowering energy in his momentary activity, it suddenly slackens, he grows forgetful and unreliable. Nor does the unconditional decision reside in the innate character, for the character can be transformed in rebirth. Nor does it reside in what we call in mythological terms a man's demon, for this demon is without loyalty. Overpowering as it may be, no mode of passion, of vital will, of self-assertion, is unconditional in the moment; all are relative and hence perishable.

Thus the unconditional demands an existential decision that has passed through reflection. This means that it does not arise from any natural state but out of freedom, which cannot help being what it is, not because of any natural law but because of its foundation in transcendence.

It is the unconditional which decides the ultimate basis of a man's life, which determines whether it is significant or meaningless. The unconditional is hidden, only in extreme situations does it by silent decision determine a man's road; it is never positively demonstrable, though it always sustains life through existence and can be infinitely elucidated.

Just as trees sink their roots deeply and grow high in the air, so is the fulfilled man rooted in the unconditional; all others are like shrubs which can be pulled up and transplanted, which are interchangeable and in the mass indestructible. But this metaphor is inappropriate, since man arrives at his unconditional foundation not by degrees but by a leap into another dimension.

Second: The unconditional imperative has reality in the man who follows it in faith and awareness.

It cannot be proved, cannot be shown to exist empirically in the world—historical proofs are mere intimations. What we know is always conditional. The unconditional within us has no existence if we apply the yardstick of demonstrable knowledge. A demonstrated unconditional is merely a powerful force, a fanaticism, a frenzy or a madness. If it is asked whether there is any authentic unconditional in the world, the sceptical answer carries universal force of conviction.

For example: it is doubtful whether there is unconditional love, which is rooted in the eternal foundation and does not merely consist in human inclination, passion, habit, and fidelity to a promise. The possibility of authentic communication in loving contest can be denied. That which is demonstrable is by that same token not unconditional.

Third: The unconditional is timeless in time.

The unconditional imperative is not given like empirical existence. It grows within man in time. Only when man conquers himself and goes where his decision unerringly leads him does the unconditional come into its own. Steadfastness of purpose, abstract singlemindedness, mere perseverance in man are not convincing signs that he lives by the unconditional imperative.

In our temporal existence the unconditional attitude is manifested in the experience of extreme situations and in situations when we are in danger of becoming untrue to ourselves.

But the unconditional itself is never entirely temporal. Whenever it may be, it also cuts across time. Regardless of when it is conquered, it is eternal, existing in every new moment through recurrent rebirth from the source. Hence: Where a development in time seems to have given us possession of it, all can still be betrayed in a moment. Conversely, where a man's past seems to be mere factuality, weighing him down under endless contingencies to the point of annihilation, he can nevertheless at any moment begin as it were from the beginning through sudden awareness of the unconditional.

These propositions, it is true, suggest the meaning of the unconditional imperative but do not elucidate its content, which becomes clear only through the antithesis of good and evil.

In heeding the command of the unconditional we effect a choice. A decision becomes the substance of the man. He has chosen what he understands as the good in the decision between good and evil.

Good and evil are differentiated on three levels.

1. We regard as evil the immediate and unrestrained surrender to passions and sensual impulses, to the pleasure and happiness of this world, to empirical existence as such; in short, evil is the life of the man who remains in the sphere of the contingent, who merely lives from day to day like an animal, well or badly, in the unrest of change—a life in which there is no decision.

Good in contradistinction is the life of the man who does not reject the happiness of this world but subordinates it to the morally admissible, seen as the universal law of just action. This morally admissible is the absolute.

2. True evil, as distinguished from mere weakness, which surrenders to the natural bent, consists in what Kant called perversion: I do good only if it does me no harm or does not cost me too much; or stated abstractly: although I will the unconditional embodied in the moral imperative, I follow the law of the good only in so far as it is compatible with undisturbed sensual pleasure; only on this condition, and in no unconditional sense, do I wish to be good. This pseudo-virtue might be called a luxury of fortunate circumstances in which I can afford to be good. In the case of conflict between moral imperative and my vital interest, I may, according to the magnitude of this interest, be secretly capable of any villany. In order to avert my own death, I may obey orders to commit murder. Or I may allow my favoured position which saves me from conflict to blind me to my evil.

It is good, in contradistinction, to lift oneself out of this condition of contingency, wherein the unconditional is subordinated to the requirements of vital happiness, and return to an authentic life in the unconditional. This is a conversion from continuous self-betrayal and impurity of motives to the seriousness of the unconditional.

3. On this level, evil is only the will to evil —the will to destruction as such, the urge to inflict torture, cruelty, annihilation, the nihilistic will to ruin everything that is and has value.

Good, in contradistinction, is the unconditional, which is love and hence the will to reality.

Let us compare these three levels.

On the first level, the relation between good and evil is moral: the question is whether our natural inclinations are governed by a will subservient to moral laws. In Kant's words, duty is opposed to inclination.

On the second level, the relation is ethical: the essential is the authenticity of our motives. The purity of the unconditional is opposed to an impurity which consists in the reversal of the relation of contingency, in which the unconditional is made contingent on practical conditions.

On the third level, the relation becomes metaphysical: here the essential lies in the motives themselves. Love is opposed to hate. Love impels to being, hate to nonbeing. Love grows in bond with transcendence; hate, severed from transcendence, dwindles into the abstract punctuality of the ego. Love works as a quiet building in the world; hate as a loud catastrophe, submerging being in empirical existence and destroying empirical existence itself.

On each level an alternative is revealed, a decision is called for. A man can only want one thing or the other, if he is authentic. He follows inclination or duty, he lives in perversion or in purity of motive, he lives out of hate or out of love. But he can fail to decide. Instead of deciding, we vacillate and stumble through life, combine the one with the other and even accept such a state of things as a necessary contradiction. This indecision is in itself evil. Man awakens only when he distinguishes between good and evil. He becomes himself when he decides which way he is going and acts accordingly.

We must all continuously recapture ourselves from indecision. We are so little capable of fulfilling ourselves in goodness that the very force of the passions that drive us headlong through life is indispensable to the lucidity of duty; when we really love we cannot help hating whatever threatens our love; and it is precisely when we feel certain that our motives are pure that we succumb to the perversion of impurity.

The decision has its special character on each of the three levels. Morally, man seeks to base his decision on thought. Ethically, he rehabilitates himself from perversion through a rebirth of his good will. Metaphysically, he achieves awareness of being given to himself in his ability to love. He chooses the right, his motives become authentic, he lives out of love. Only when the three levels become one is the unconditional realized.

To live out of love seems to include all the rest. True love gives certainty regarding the ethical truth of its acts. St. Augustine says: Love and do what thou wilt. But it is impossible for us men to live solely by love, this force of the highest level, for we fall constantly into errors and misunderstandings. Hence we must not rely blindly in our love at every moment but must elucidate it. And for the same reason we finite beings need the discipline by which we conquer our passions, and because of the impurity of our motives we require distrust of ourselves. When we feel sure of ourselves, that is precisely when we are going astray.

Only the unconditional character of the good fills mere duties with content, purifies our ethical motives, dissolves the destructive will of hatred.

But the foundation of love, in which the unconditional is grounded, is identical with the will to authentic reality. I want what I love to be. And I cannot perceive what authentically is without loving it.

Afterword / Contemporary Vertigo

Nietzsche stated that for those who really begin to question the old ideals, a new vista unfolds: "a sense of potentiality seizes him like a vertigo, every species of doubt, mistrust, and fear springs up, the belief in morality, nay, the belief in all morality, totters" (above, p. 167). This theme of moral uncertainty is often stressed in modern times. For Nietzsche, the loss of a religious basis for values (the "death" of God) is to be replaced by a radical humanism. For Dewey, the disarray of society and the tensions between our traditional values and the new conditions of our outward behavior may be overcome by the humanization of science and the adoption of scientific methods in morality.

Jaspers, although appreciative of science and its method, sees man's moral situation from a different perspective. Existential decisions, made in such extreme situations as guilt, suffering, and death, arise from the changing conditions of life and cannot be solved by scientific reasoning. Jaspers stresses not the consequences of our moral choices, but the conditions and motives of the individual that make authentic moral choice possible. The realization of the unconditional imperative through a free and total commitment to it unifies his life and opens him up to that which goes beyond his finite self.

We can opt for what looks to be an easier salvation. Epicurus defines the good in terms of pleasure and serenity. The tranquility promised by many religions and cults today is an attractive solution to many. Others find more positive and immediate pleasures in the exotic theatre, group sex, and in various pill and liquid forms. We are not only more materially affluent than the ancient Greeks but also have more experiences available to us. Wider, more open experience seems to be an ideal sought after in encounter groups, communes, Woodstock experiences, or a new church.

Nietzsche's work strikes another familiar chord: the current belief that our values and moral ideals are not rationally arrived at but are expressions of man as an essentially nonrational creature. Contrary to the faith of Socrates, virtue and happiness have very little to do with conscious knowledge and the examined life. What we consider good is not a product of rational choice; the expression "good" is merely a sign language of the emotions. Nietzsche first questioned what we now are quite used to questioning: the relevance and potency of reason in our moral choices, our politics, our race relations, and our international relations. The contemporary vertigo is shot through with a profound scepticism regarding the possibility of a rational solution to the moral problems that beset modern man. For Socrates, on the other hand, moral character, moral action, and reason were intimately bound together. The examined life was best.

Besides the ideal of the examined life, the *Crito* suggests the problems that may occur when the individual's right to pursue his ideal of the good conflicts with the authority of the state and the opinions of society. In exercising our rights to life, liberty, and the pursuit of happiness, each of us must confront the problem of reconciling the conflict between these rights, the authority of the state, and the pressures of society. Also, the issue of *conscience* (Socrates' "voice") vs. *the law* has been revived in our time by those conscientious objectors who have refused to participate in what they consider to be unjust wars.

We have not arrived at that final ideal, a satisfactory definition of the good. If Dewey is correct, finding a fixed definition is not so important as realizing value possibilities in experience. Science and technology have confronted us with not only undreamed of possibilities but also some very real, immediate, and momentous choices. Nietzsche's question about "what type of man shall be *bred,* shall be *willed,* for being higher in value" suggests a real option today in light of recent developments in genetic engineering. We may sometimes call ourselves "lords of the earth," yet we often feel vulnerable and helpless to control the accelerating changes we ourselves have brought about. We have stockpiled weapons and glutted ourselves with goods and services. The power of our knowledge and techniques is no longer in question. Our wisdom is. Socrates' question, What course of life is best? is more urgent today than it ever was.

Related Reading

(Works marked * are available in paperbound editions)

*Ayer, A. J. *Language, Truth and Logic.* New York: Dover, 1936.

Barnes, Hazel. *An Existential Ethics.* New York: Alfred Knopf, 1967.

Brandt, Richard B. *Ethical Theory.* Englewood Cliffs, N. J.: Prentice-Hall, 1959.

Danto, Arthur C. *Nietzsche as Philosopher.* New York: Macmillan Co., 1965.

*De Beauvoir, Simone. *The Ethics of Ambiguity.* New York: Citadel, 1964.

*Dewey, John. *The Quest for Certainty.* New York: Minton, Balch & Company, 1929.

*————. *Art as Experience*. New York: Capricorn Books, 1934.

*————. *Individualism Old and New*. New York: Capricorn Books, 1962.

Dewitt, N. W. *Epicurus and his Philosophy*. Minneapolis: University of Minnesota Press, 1954.

*Field, G. C. *Plato and His Contemporaries,* 3d. ed. New York: Barnes & Noble, Inc., 1967.

*Frankena, W. D. *Ethics*. Englewood Cliffs, N. J.: Prentice-Hall, 1963.

*Guthrie, W. K. C. *The Greek Philosophers*. New York: Harper & Row, 1960.

Hill, Thomas H. *Contemporary Ethical Theories*. New York: Macmillan, 1959.

Hook, Sidney. *John Dewey: An Intellectual Portrait*. New York: Day, 1939.

Hospers, John. *Human Conduct: An Introduction to the Problem of Ethics*. New York: Harcourt, Brace and World, Inc., 1961 (especially chapters 2, 3, and 4).

Jaspers, Karl. *The Perennial Scope of Philosophy,* trans. R. Manheim. New York: Philosophical Library, 1949.

————. *Reason and Anti-Reason in Our Time,* trans. S. Goodman. New Haven: Yale University Press, 1952.

*————. *Man in the Modern Age,* trans. Eden and Cedar Paul. Garden City, N. Y.: Anchor Books, Doubleday & Co., 1957.

Kaufman, Walter, ed. and trans. *The Portable Nietzsche*. New York: Viking Press, 1954.

————. *Nietzsche: Philosopher, Psychologist, Antichrist*. New York: Meridian Books, 1956.

————, ed. and trans. *Basic Writings of Nietzsche*. New York: Modern Library, 1968.

Kerner, George C. *The Revolution in Ethical Theory*. New York: Oxford, 1966.

Kurtz, Paul, ed. *Moral Problems in Contemporary Society: Essays in Ethics*. Englewood Cliffs, N. J.: Prentice-Hall, 1969.

*Lucretius. *On Nature,* trans. R. M. Geer. New York: Bobbs-Merrill Co., 1965.

*Moore, G. E. *Principia Ethics*. Cambridge: Cambridge University Press, 1903 (chapter 3).

Morgan, George A. *What Nietzsche Means*. New York: Harper & Row, 1941.

*Mumford, Lewis. *The Conduct of Life*. New York: Harcourt Brace, 1951.

*Rorty, Amelie. *Pragmatic Philosophy*. New York: Doubleday & Co., 1966.

*Taylor, A. E. *Plato: The Man and His Work*. New York: Meridian Books, 1957.

*Taylor, Richard. *Good and Evil: A New Direction*. New York: Macmillan Co., 1970.

*Vlastos, Gregory, ed. *The Philosophy of Socrates: A Collection of Critical Essays*. New York: Doubleday & Co., 1971.

*Warmington, E. H. and P. G. Rouse. *Great Dialogues of Plato* (trans. Rouse). New York: The New American Library, 1956.

PART FIVE

Confrontation with Man: Commitment to His Transformation

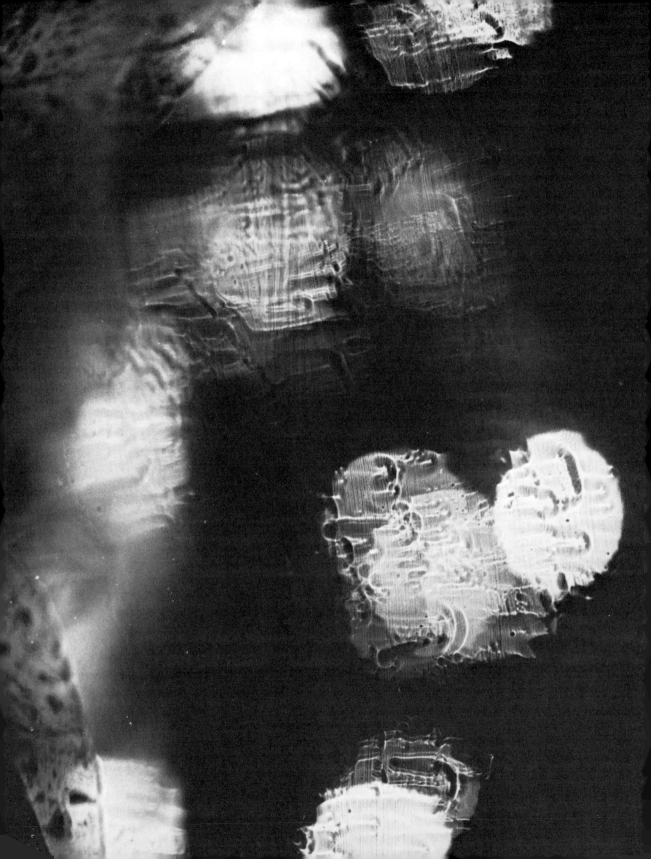

At the deepest level of human existence Man as we have
known him is on the verge of becoming something else.
                                        Victor Ferkiss

Man is a rational animal.
                                        Aristotle

Man is the dwarf of himself.
                        Ralph Waldo Emerson

We are our choices. Man is freedom.
                        Jean-Paul Sartre

Man is the product of causes which had no provision of
the end they were achieving.
                                        Bertrand Russell

With all these exalted powers — Man still bears in his
bodily frame the indelible stamp of his lowly origin.
                                        Charles Darwin

We are tired of man. Man, he suffers from
the disease called Man.
                        Friedrich Nietzsche

Man is *res cogitans* — a thinking
substance.
                                        René Descartes

Man is always something more than he
knows of himself.
                                        Karl Jaspers

Things are in the saddle, and ride
mankind.
                        Ralph Waldo Emerson

The man of the future could be glimpsed in
the attitude of our fighter.
                                        Che Guevara

The union of mathematician with the past, fervor with
measure, passion with correctness, this surely is the
ideal.
                                        William James

We are hollow men. We are stuffed men.
                                        T. S. Eliot

The soul of man is the lamp of God.
                        Hebrew Proverb

As individuals express their life, so they are.
                                        Karl Marx

Introduction / Man the Problem

A sigh of resignation usually accompanies the remark, You can't change human nature. But is the statement true? And what is "human nature"? Man is an animal who anticipates the future and confronts doubt, authority, moral choice, religious and aesthetic experience. He is an animal who commits himself to belief, freedom, the good, faith, and artistic creation. He is also puzzled by questions about his own nature and the many conflicting definitions and images of human nature found in anthropology, literature, and philosophy.

The variety in answers to the question of human nature makes it difficult to be objective. Since the questioner is a member of the class to which the question is directed, and the question is about us, are our answers liable to be in terms of our own personal characteristics? Is our image of man going to be, in each case, glaringly close to a self-image?

While there are disagreements as to the correct definition, for some the question itself, What is man?, is too general and confused. It needs to be broken down into questions whose meaning and verification are clearer and more definite. Many contemporary Anglo-American philosophers have suspended the general question and replaced it with more specific questions concerning the meaning of terms, such as *mind, consciousness,* and *self,* the distinction between computer operations and human thinking, and the criteria for determining personal identity.

Other philosophers are critical of the question, not because of its generality and vagueness, but because of its implicit assumptions. To ask, What is man? is to make man into an object and to presume that we are to inquire into the nature of man in the same way in which we inquire into the nature of a mosquito or a chair. The question might perhaps be changed to, Who is man? or some other rephrasing, so as not to predetermine the kind of answer. If the essence of man is that he is not an object that can be studied by one of the sciences, we need other methods for dealing with the unique, lived experience of man. If man is basically a subject in a world of objects, his essence is not reducible to the abstractions of any science developed thus far to deal with objects.

The question of the nature of man is being asked today with renewed vigor, partially because man's image of himself is a broken image. Just as our concept of life is being challenged by the study of viruses and the possibility of creating life out of a test tube, so our traditional concepts of man are being contested by behavioral psychology, cybernetics, and recent developments in biology. The possibility of our fully understanding and controlling the genetic code raises questions as to the direction man will go when he has full control of his own evolution. The creation of androids and the possible discovery of other forms of life in interplanetary travel raise interesting questions about what we consider human. The very pace of scientific, technological, social, and political change requires adjustments. Perhaps "broken image" expresses a too hasty and exaggerated judgment of the impact of the above changes on our image of ourselves; we are still in the process of adjustment. But compared to other ages, our self-image is severely incomplete and disorganized.

This was not always so. The ancient Greek philosophers tended to view the human person as a definite kind of being, an individual being who possessed a rational and social nature. The species of man was fixed eternally. Aristotle expressed this viewpoint with great assurance in his *Nicomachean Ethics*. Man is a rational animal. In the Medieval period, the assurance that man had a definite essence was also pervasive. The human person was a child of God, and the individual soul was directed toward eternal salvation, reconciling his life on earth with his God-given nature. For the greater part of recorded history, man's view of himself was that he had a nature. What man essentially was was not in doubt.

This essentialist theory of human nature is represented in the first selection that follows. Descartes asks the question, "But what, then, am I?" and answers quickly, "A thinking thing," a soul substance which has thought as its essential property. Descartes' new method (see Part Two) is used to defend not only the belief in God, but the certainty of the existence of the soul. He thinks he is justified in drawing sharp distinctions between the essence of man (as soul) and the body, man (as soul) and machine, free will and the mechanical operation of nature. By contrast, an English contemporary of Descartes, Thomas Hobbes, although disagreeing with much of Descartes' philosophy, shared his essentialist approach to the nature of man. But for Hobbes, man is a complex physiological system. Human persons are the sum total of bodily conditions and their effects. Man's behavior exhibits the kind of pattern and lawfulness Galileo found operating the physical world.

In the second selection that follows, the Spanish philosopher Ortega y Gasset challenges this essentialist view. Because of the uniqueness of man's consciousness of being in the world, Ortega denies that man is definable in the sense that there are discoverable sets of properties that designate his nature once and for all. Human life is "radical solitude" and not a system of forces or behavior patterns, although he stresses the importance of circumstances in affecting human behavior.

In the third selection, the Marxist philosopher Herbert Marcuse warns us that technology is providing the means for a new form of totalitarianism. Unless radical social and ideological changes are made, this can lead to a total repression of man's higher potentialities and to a one-dimensional man.

Finally, in the last selection, the psychologist B. F. Skinner is more optimistic than Marcuse about human prospects. He envisages a science of human behavior that will make possible the control of the total human environment and thus the transformation of man. Skinner's viewpoint supports one of the themes of this part: that our conception of human nature is intimately bound up with our attitudes toward social change and the resolution of the problems of man.

15 / Essential Man
Descartes

Part One of this book included a selection on René Descartes' methodology. At a time when the authority of the Roman Catholic Church, scholastic traditions, and doctrines were being questioned, Descartes sought to put man's beliefs on a firmer footing. He felt that philosophy should be based upon the kind of certainty that is characteristic of mathematics and geometry. His method began with recognizing his own existence as soul or mind. Descartes also wanted to find a place for man's spiritual soul within the changing picture of nature that was being born out of Galilean mechanics, to which his own work in mathematics, his theory of light, and his vortex theory of the physical universe were contributing.

For Aristotle and St. Thomas Aquinas, nature exhibited a hierarchical order of values in which everything realized its own appropriate "nature"— its final cause or end. The new physics, which described nature as a system of efficient causes analyzable into quantitative units, was beginning to have great success. The law of inertial motion sees nature as made up of bodies in a perpetual state of motion or of rest. The notion of purpose is not needed to explain its activity. The concepts of final cause, potentiality, and actuality were appropriate for the old views of nature. The new view of nature seemed expressible in the precise language of mathematics. The new nature seemed despiritualized. To Descartes, nature was matter, with its principal attribute of extension in length, breadth, and depth, and so it was governed by the universal laws of matter in motion.

Of course, nature included man's body. Descartes felt that the operation of man's body was explainable in terms of mechanical-physiological principles. In fact, William Harvey (1578–1657), had already suggested such an explanation. Man's body is a vast network of canals, the heart is the pump, and the actions of the body are, for the most part, automatic. Animals, because they lack souls in Descartes' view, operate like automata. "It is Nature which acts in them according to the dispositions of their organs: thus it is seen that a clock composed only of wheels and weights, can number the hours and measure the time more exactly than we with all our skill."

But what of the soul? The soul or mind is not, according to Descartes, a belief that we feign in order to explain the unity of experience. It is not something we infer from our conscious states, but something of which each of us is immediately certain. Descartes is convinced that "I am immediately and with certainty aware of my consciousness and of myself as a thing which is conscious—a mental substance." This mental substance has equal status with matter in the cosmic scheme of things. God created material substance with its perpetual motion and predictable order. He also created soul, an independent, unique mental or spiritual substance. (This "equal but separate" view of matter and spirit is sometimes called the "Cartesian compromise.") Descartes' arguments for this view begin with the argument for the existence of mind or soul, a "thing which thinks," move to proofs for the existence of God and His goodness, and then to proofs and evidence for the existence of the external world of material substance.

It would be difficult to overestimate the influence of Descartes' analysis of body and soul. His assumptions, arguments, and insights into problems in this area are often the framework upon which contemporary discussions are based.[1] Stimulated by Descartes' efforts, philosophers have debated such questions as these: Is the existence of the soul something of which we are immediately certain? If it is not, then on what basis is its existence a legitimate inference? And even if I am aware of my own conscious states, of *my* existence as a thinking thing, how can I ever know that *you* as a conscious being also exist? Am I not shut up within myself alone, aware of only my own private experiences? These problems of the existence of a self, of other persons, and of the basis of communication between or among minds are yet to be settled.

Questions have also arisen from Descartes' radical division of reality into mental phenomena, comprising nonextended, indivisible thinking substances, and physical phenomena, comprising extended, divisible material substances. Since these are, according to Descartes, completely distinct and unique, how does interaction ever take place between them? Most philosophers concur on the failure of Descartes' hypothesis that a tiny pineal gland in the inward part of the brain is the locus of the interaction. But psychosomatic interaction does seem to take place. The condition of my body, say through drugs, does seem to affect my mind. The condition of my mental states in extreme anxiety, for example, does seem to affect my body: my hands sweat and my stomach is upset. What is the nature of this interaction?

The selections that follow outline Descartes' concept of man and formulate some of these important issues regarding human nature.

Note

1. For an excellent example of the modern interest in Descartes, see Willis Doney, ed. *Descartes: A Collection of Critical Essays* (New York: Doubleday and Co., Inc., 1967).

Body and Mind

We cannot doubt of our existence while we doubt, and . . . this is the first knowledge we acquire when we philosophize in order.

While we thus reject all of which we can entertain the smallest doubt, and even imagine that it is false, we easily indeed suppose that there is neither God, nor sky, nor bodies, and that we ourselves even have neither hands nor feet, nor, finally, a body; but we cannot in the same way suppose that we are not while we doubt of the truth of these things; for there is a repugnance in conceiving that what thinks does not exist at the very time when it thinks. Accordingly, the knowledge, I THINK, THEREFORE I AM, is the first and most certain that occurs to one who philosophizes orderly.

. . . We hence discover the distinction between the mind and the body, or between a thinking and corporeal thing.

And this is the best mode of discovering the nature of the mind, and its distinctness from the body: for examining what we are, while supposing, as we now do, that there is nothing really existing apart from our thought, we clearly perceive that neither extension, nor figure, nor local motion, nor anything similar that can be attributed to body, pertains to our nature, and nothing save thought alone; and, consequently, that the notion we have of our mind precedes that of any corporeal thing, and is more certain, seeing we still doubt whether there

From *The Method, Meditations and Philosophy of Descartes,* trans. John Veitch (New York: Tudor Publishing Co., 1901), pp. 188–316 (with omissions).

is any body in existence, while we already perceive that we think.

. . . What thought (*cogitatio*) is:

By the word thought, I understand all that which so takes place in us that we of ourselves are immediately conscious of it; and, accordingly, not only to understand (*intelligere, entendre*), to will (*velle*), to imagine (*imaginari*), but even to perceive (*sentire, sentir*), are here the same as to think (*cogitare, penser*). For if I say, I see, or, I walk, therefore I am; and if I understand by vision or walking the act of my eyes or of my limbs, which is the work of the body, the conclusion is not absolutely certain, because, as is often the case in dreams, I may think that I see or walk, although I do not open my eyes or move from my place, and even, perhaps, although I have no body: but, if I mean the sensation itself, or consciousness of seeing or walking, the knowledge is manifestly certain, because it is then referred to the mind, which alone perceives or is conscious that it sees or walks. . . .

But what, then, am I? A thinking thing, it has been said. But what is a thinking thing? It is a thing that doubts, understands, [conceives], affirms, denies, wills, refuses, that imagines also, and perceives. Assuredly it is not little, if all these properties belong to my nature. But why should they not belong to it? Am I not that very being who now doubts of almost everything; who, for all that, understands and conceives certain things; who affirms one alone as true, and denies the others; who desires to know more of them, and does not wish to be deceived; who imagines many things, sometimes even despite his will; and is likewise percipient of many, as if through the medium of the senses. Is there nothing of all this as true as that I am, even although I should be always dreaming, and although he who gave me being employed all his ingenuity to deceive me? Is there also any one of these attributes that can be properly distinguished from my thought, or that can be said to be separate from myself? For it is of itself so evident that it is I who doubt, I who understand, and I who desire, that it is here unnecessary to add anything by way of rendering it more clear. And I am as certainly the same being who imagines; for, although it may be (as I before supposed) that nothing I imagine is true, still the power of imagination does not cease really to exist in me and to form part of my thought. In fine, I am the same being who perceives, that is, who apprehends certain objects as by the organs of sense, since, in truth, I see light, hear a noise, and feel heat. But it will be said that these presentations are false, and that I am dreaming. Let it be so. At all events it is certain that I seem to see light, hear a noise, and feel heat; this cannot be false, and this is what in me is properly called perceiving, which is nothing else than thinking. From this I begin to know what I am with somewhat greater clearness and distinctness than heretofore. . . .

And, . . . because I know that all which I clearly and distinctly conceive can be produced by God exactly as I conceive it, it is sufficient that I am able clearly and distinctly to conceive one thing apart from another, in order to be certain that the one is different from the other, seeing they may at least be made to exist separately, by the omnipotence of God; and it matters not by what power this separation is made, in order to be compelled to judge them different; and, therefore, merely because I know with certitude that I exist, and because, in the meantime, I do not observe that aught necessarily belongs

to my nature or essence beyond my being a thinking thing, I rightly conclude that my essence consists only in my being a thinking thing, [or a substance whose whole essence or nature is merely thinking]. And although I may, or rather, as I will shortly say, although I certainly do possess a body with which I am very closely conjoined; nevertheless, because, on the one hand, I have a clear and distinct idea of myself, in as far as I am only a thinking and unextended thing, and as, on the other hand, I possess a distinct idea of body, in as far as it is only an extended and unthinking thing, it is certain that I, [that is, my mind, by which I am what I am], is entirely and truly distinct from my body, and may exist without it. . . .

To commence this examination accordingly, I here remark, in the first place, that there is a vast difference between mind and body, in respect that body, from its nature, is always divisible, and that mind is entirely indivisible. For in truth, when I consider the mind, that is, when I consider myself in so far only as I am a thinking thing, I can distinguish in myself no parts, but I very clearly discern that I am somewhat absolutely one and entire; and although the whole mind seems to be united to the whole body, yet, when a foot, an arm, or any other part is cut off, I am conscious that nothing has been taken from my mind; nor can the faculties of willing, perceiving, conceiving, etc., properly be called its parts, for it is the same mind that is exercised [all entire] in willing, in perceiving, and in conceiving, etc. But quite the opposite holds in corporeal or extended things; for I cannot imagine any one of them [how small soever it may be], which I cannot easily sunder in thought, and which, therefore, I do not know to be divisible. This would be sufficient to teach me that the mind or soul of man is entirely different from the body, if I had not already been apprised of it on other grounds.

I remark, in the next place, that the mind does not immediately receive the impression from all the parts of the body, but only from the brain, or perhaps even from one small part of it, viz., that in which the common sense (*sensus communis*) is said to be, which as often as it is affected in the same way, gives rise to the same perception in the mind, although meanwhile the other parts of the body may be diversely disposed, as is proved by innumerable experiments, which it is unnecessary here to enumerate.

I remark, besides, that the nature of body is such that none of its parts can be moved by another part a little removed from the other, which cannot likewise be moved in the same way by any one of the parts that lie between those two, although the most remote part does not act at all. As, for example, in the cord A, B, C, D, [which is in tension], if its last part D, be pulled, the first part A, will not be moved in a different way than it would be were one of the intermediate parts B or C to be pulled, and the last part D meanwhile to remain fixed. And in the same way, when I feel pain in the foot, the science of physics teaches me that this sensation is experienced by means of the nerves dispersed over the foot, which, extending like cords from it to the brain, when they are contracted in the foot, contract at the same time the inmost parts of the brain in which they have their origin, and excite in these parts a certain motion appointed by nature to cause in the mind a sensation of pain, as if existing in the foot: but as these nerves must pass through the tibia, the leg, the loins, the back, and neck, in order to reach the brain, it may happen that although their extremities in the foot are not affected, but only certain of their parts that pass through the loins or neck, the same movements, nevertheless, are excited in the brain by this motion as would have been caused there by a hurt received in the foot, and hence the mind will necessarily feel pain in the foot, just as if it had been hurt; and the same is true of all the other perceptions of our senses.

I remark, finally, that as each of the movements that are made in the part of the brain by which the mind is immediately affected, impresses it with but a single sensation, the most likely supposition in the circumstances is, that this movement causes the mind to experience, among all the sensations which it is capable of impressing upon it, that one which is the best fitted, and generally the most useful for the preservation of the human body when it is in full health. But experience shows us that all the perceptions which nature has given us are of such a kind as I have mentioned; and accordingly, there is nothing found in them that does not manifest the power and goodness of God. Thus, for example, when the nerves of the foot are violently or more than usually shaken, the motion passing through the medulla of the spine to the innermost parts of the brain affords a sign to the mind on which it experiences a sensation, viz., of pain, as if it were in the foot, by which the mind is admonished and excited to do its utmost to remove the cause of it as dangerous and hurtful to the foot. It is true that God could have so constituted the nature of man as that the same motion in the brain would have informed the mind of something altogether different: the motion might, for example, have been the occasion on which the mind became conscious of itself, in so far as it is in the brain, or in so far as it is in some place intermediate between the foot and the brain, or, finally, the occasion on which it perceived some other object quite different, whatever that might be; but nothing of all this would have so well contributed to the preservation of the body as that which the mind actually feels. In the same way, when we stand in need of drink, there arises from this want a certain parchedness in the throat that moves its nerves, and by means of them the internal parts of the brain; and this movement affects the mind with the sensation of thirst, because there is nothing on that occasion which is more useful for us than to be made aware that we have need of drink for the preservation of our health; and so in other instances. . . .

. . . Nor will this appear at all strange to those who are acquainted with the variety of movements performed by the different automata, or moving machines fabricated by human industry, and that with help of but few pieces compared with the great multitude of bones, muscles, nerves, arteries, veins, and other parts that are found in the body of each animal. Such persons will look upon this body as a machine made by the hands of God, which is incomparably better arranged, and adequate to movements more admirable than is any machine of human invention. And here I specially stayed to show that, were there such machines exactly resembling in organs and outward form an ape or any other irrational animal, we could have no means of knowing that they were in any respect of a different nature from these animals; but if there were machines bearing the image of our bodies, and capable of imitating our actions as far as it is morally possible, there would still remain two most certain tests whereby to know that they were not therefore really men. Of these the first is that they could never use words or other signs arranged in such a manner as is competent to us in order to declare our thoughts to others: for we may easily conceive a machine to be so constructed that it emits vocables, and even that it emits some correspondent to the action upon it of external objects which cause a change in its organs; for example, if touched in a particular place it may demand what we wish to say to it; if in another, it may cry out that it is hurt, and such like; but not that it should arrange them variously so as appositely to reply to what is said in its presence, as men of the lowest grade of intellect can do. The second test is, that although such machines might execute many things with equal or perhaps greater perfection than any of us, they would, without doubt, fail in certain others

from which it could be discovered that they did not act from knowledge, but solely from the disposition of their organs: for while Reason is an universal instrument that is alike available on every occasion, these organs, on the contrary, need a particular arrangement for each particular action; whence it must be morally impossible that there should exist in any machine a diversity of organs sufficient to enable it to act in all the occurrences of life, in the way in which our reason enables us to act. Again, by means of these two tests we may likewise know the difference between men and brutes. For it is highly deserving of remark, that there are no men so dull and stupid, not even idiots, as to be incapable of joining together different words, and thereby constructing a declaration by which to make their thoughts understood; and that on the other hand, there is no other animal, however perfect or happily circumstanced which can do the like. Nor does this inability arise from want of organs: for we observe that magpies and parrots can utter words like ourselves, and are yet unable to speak as we do, that is, so as to show that they understand what they say; in place of which men born deaf and dumb, and thus not less, but rather more than the brutes, destitute of the organs which others use in speaking, are in the habit of spontaneously inventing certain signs by which they discover their thoughts to those who, being usually in their company, have leisure to learn their language. And this proves not only that the brutes have less Reason than man, but that they have none at all: for we see that very little is required to enable a person to speak; and since a certain inequality of capacity is observable among animals of the same species, as well as among men, and since some are more capable of being instructed than others, it is incredible that the most perfect ape or parrot of its species, should not in this be equal to the most stupid infant of its kind, or at least to one that was crack-brained, unless the soul of brutes were of a nature wholly different from ours. And we ought not to confound speech with the natural movements which indicate the passions, and can be imitated by machines as well as manifested by animals; nor must it be thought with certain of the ancients, that the brutes speak, although we do not understand their language. For if such were the case, since they are endowed with many organs analogous to ours, they could as easily communicate their thoughts to us as to their fellows. It is also very worthy of remark, that, though there are many animals which manifest more industry than we in certain of their actions, the same animals are yet observed to show none at all in many others: so that the circumstances that they do better than we does not prove that they are endowed with mind, for it would thence follow that they possessed greater Reason than any of us, and could surpass us in all things; on the contrary, it rather proves that they are destitute of Reason, and that it is Nature which acts in them according to the disposition of their organs: thus it is seen, that a clock composed only of wheels and weights, can number the hours and measure time more exactly than we with all our skill.

I had after this described the Reasonable Soul, and shown that it could by no means be educed from the power of matter, as the other things of which I had spoken, but that it must be expressly created; and that it is not sufficient that it be lodged in the human body exactly like a pilot in a ship, unless perhaps to move its members, but that it is necessary for it to be joined and united more closely to the body, in order to have sensations and appetites similar to ours, and thus constitute a real man. I here entered, in conclusion upon the subject of the soul at considerable length, because it is of the greatest moment: for after the error of those who deny the existence of God, an error which I think I have already sufficiently refuted, there is none that is more powerful in leading feeble minds astray from the straight path of virtue than the supposition that the soul of the brutes is of the same nature with our own; and consequently that after this life we have nothing to hope for or fear, more than flies and ants; in place of which, when we know how far they differ we much better comprehend the reasons which establish that the soul is of a nature wholly independent of the body, and that consequently it is not liable to die with the latter; and, finally, because no other causes are observed capable of destroying it, we are naturally led thence to judge that it is immortal. . . .

. . . There are only two modes of thinking in us, viz, the perception of the understanding and the action of the will.

For all the modes of thinking of which we are conscious may be referred to two general classes, the one of which is the perception or operation of the understanding, and the other the volition or operation of the will. Thus, to perceive by the senses (*sentire*), to imagine and to conceive things purely intelligble, are only different modes of perceiving (*percipiendi*); but to desire, to be averse from, to affirm, to deny, to doubt, are different modes of willing. . . .

. . . The chief perfection of man is his being able to act freely or by will, and . . . it is this which renders him worthy of praise or blame.

That the will should be the more extensive is in harmony with its nature; and it is a high perfection in man to be able to act by means of it, that is, freely; and thus in a peculiar way to be the master of his own actions, and merit praise or blame. For self-acting machines are not commended because they perform with exactness all the movements for which they were adapted, seeing their motions are carried on necessarily; but the maker of them is praised on account of the exactness with which they were framed, because he did not act of necessity, but freely; and, on the same principle, we must attribute to ourselves something more on this account, that when we embrace truth, we do so not of necessity, but freely. . . .

. . . The liberty of our will is self-evident.

Finally, it is so manifest that we possess a free will, capable of giving or withholding its assent, that this truth must be reckoned among the first and most common notions which are born with us. This, indeed, has already very clearly appeared, for when essaying to doubt of all things, we went so far as to suppose that even he who created us employed his limitless power in deceiving us in every way, we were conscious nevertheless of being free to abstain from believing what was not in every respect certain and undoubted. But that of which we are unable to doubt at such a time is as self-evident and clear as any thing we can ever know.

. . . It is likewise certain that God has fore-ordained all things.

But because what we have already discovered of God, gives us the assurance that his power is so immense that we would sin in thinking ourselves capable of ever doing anything which he had not ordained beforehand, we should soon be embarrassed in great difficulties if we undertook to harmonize the pre-ordination of God with the freedom of our will, and endeavored to comprehend both truths at once.

. . . How the freedom of our will may be reconciled with the Divine pre-ordination:

But, in place of this, we will be free from these embarrassments if we recollect that our mind is limited, while the power of God, by which he not only knew from all eternity what is or can be, but also willed and pre-ordained it, is infinite. It thus happens that we possess sufficient intelligence to know clearly and distinctly that this power is in God, but not enough to comprehend how he leaves the free actions of men indeterminate; and, on the other hand, we have such consciousness of the liberty and indifference which exists in ourselves, that there is nothing we more clearly or perfectly comprehend: [so that the omnipotence of God ought not to keep us from believing it]. For it would be absurd to doubt of that of which we are fully conscious, and which we experience as existing in ourselves, because we do not comprehend another matter which, from its very nature, we know to be incomprehensible. . . .

16 / Existential Man
Ortega y Gasset

Thomas Hobbes conceived of man as the sum total of his physiological conditions. This perspective led him to a radically different view of man than that of René Descartes who stressed the human psyche, an immaterial thinking substance quite different from the corporeal extended substance with which it somehow interacts.

The approach of contemporary existentialists to the question of the nature of man can be seen vis-à-vis Descartes' discussion of the soul. While they generally consider Descartes one of the most important historical figures in philosophy, as his philosophy begins with man and his consciouness, they do not consider his analysis to be intensive enough. His interest in man's experience tended to be limited by the fact that the *cogito* was an initial premise in a long argument and proof for the existence of God and the external world.

For Descartes, man is primarily a knower, a thinking thing analogous to matter as an extended thing. For the existentialist, man's mode of being is radically distinct from the mode of being of an object in the world. Human existence is unique. Descartes' search for certainty and his infatuation with the virtues of clearness and distinctness also hindered his description of man. In one sense, existentialists deny Descartes' belief that the soul or the mind is more easily known than the body. Human consciouness, as lived experience, has a rich structure of its own that cannot be dealt with within the Cartesian methodology or even by the methods of the empirical sciences.

The term "existential" has acquired a tone and mood that refers to human life as it is lived at its limits—the experience of personal fragmentation, dread, alienation, and forlornness. These human experiences are well illustrated by Dostoyevsky's portraits of Ivan and of Roskolnikov and by some of the characters in the writings of Camus and Kafka. Many feel that such experiences are a pervasive cultural phenomenon in our times. These experiences have been largely ignored by traditional psychology and sociology because they did not seem to lend themselves to objective scientific study. What man *is,* in the fullest sense, and what man can become are today, however, questions that have reached crisis proportions. Modern man, stressing objectivity and scientific rationality, has appeared to have forgotten that there are such questions to be asked. He has been so concerned with the image of himself as a system of forces, functions, or behavioral patterns that he has lost his sense of a soul.

Although he did not call himself an existentialist, the Spanish writer Ortega y Gasset's philosophy has much in common with existentialism.[1] Ortega focuses his attention on life or human existence in its widest, deepest, and most concrete sense. He rejects all attempts to interpret life or existence according to a rational abstract system of philosophy and replaces the concept of pure reason with that of "vital reason." Man does not live in order to think, but he thinks in order to live. Philosophy becomes, in Ortega's view, not only a love of wisdom, but a "general science of love" that binds man's being in many relationships to the entire sweep of human experience.

Also, like the existentialists, Ortega rejects ready-made moral codes and religious dogmas. If morality and religion are to have meaning to individuals, they must grow out of each individual's own circumstances, struggles, and decisions, and spring from his solitariness as well as from his efforts to relate to other persons and to the world. Action, choice, and decision give crucial significance to human existence, which otherwise would be meaningless. There is no escape from the necessity of choosing, deciding, and thus creating oneself through action. For Ortega, as for Sartre, to not decide is still a choice.

Another point which Ortega has in common with the existentialists is his criticism of "mass man" and of the kind of thinking that leads to the collectivization, depersonalization, and regimentation of modern life. Like Nietzsche, he considers the crowd to be "untruth," and abhors slavelike mentality. The most striking and disheartening feature of our time, according to Ortega, is "the revolt of the masses." Because of a powerful historical drift, the complex currents of which he analyzes in his famous work *The Revolt of the Masses*,[2] Ortega thinks that modern life is fast being overwhelmed by mediocrity and barbarism. Having lost its sense of leadership and therefore its sense of direction, the West is drifting toward decadence. Violence is increasing, life is becoming more frivolous and meaningless, and the power of bureaucratic and autocratic states grows more absolute. Even genuine revolutions are no longer possible since the masses have already co-opted power and thus can enforce their will through the machinery of the state. The creative minority, who have won their way to superior achievement through active struggle and self-discipline, could perhaps lead the masses out of the labyrinth into which they have wandered, but probably not until the revolt has run its course or has ended catastrophically.

Unlike most existentialists, however, Ortega does not deal in depth with boundary situations, such as death, guilt, and suffering, or with existential emotions, such as anguish, despair, and forlornness. He does stress the importance of struggle. "All life is the struggle, the effort to be itself,"[3] he writes—and he recognizes that this struggle usually develops out of an individual's painful effort to discover a meaning and purpose for his life. We are forced to be free, he points out. "Life is a permanent crossroads and constant perplexity."[4] But Ortega does not agonize over man's existential predicament, and one finds little of Kierkegaard's emphasis upon anguish or of Sartre's forlornness in his work. Instead, he usually emphasizes the brighter, more hopeful possibilities that can come about if a man has the determination to make of himself a project to be created through his own efforts. "Man's destiny," he believes, "is primarily action."[5] Here he is in perfect accord with Jean-Paul Sartre and Simone de Beauvoir. Man is his own creator, and his actions must be the instruments through which he makes himself according to his own projected changes. He can become what he commits himself to becoming.

The importance of perspective in defining truth, the appreciation of circumstances in delimiting action, and the influence of the past and the future upon man's conception of himself also play important parts in the human drama as Ortega views it. The following essay from Ortega's *Man and People* (1957) stands as a clear and succinct statement of his "philosophical anthropology."

Personal Life

Once again, man has lost himself. For this is nothing new, nothing accidental. Man has been lost many times throughout the course of his history. Indeed it is of the essence of man, in contradistinction to all other beings, that he can lose himself, lose himself in the jungle of his existence, within himself, and thanks to this sensation of being lost can react by setting energetically to work to find himself again. His ability to feel lost and his discomfort at feeling lost are his tragic destiny and his illustrious privilege.

Let us set out, then, to discover, in unimpeachable and unmistakable form, facts of such a characteristic complexion that no other denomination than that of "social phenomena" in the strict sense will seem to us to fit them. There is only one way to accomplish this most rigorous and decisive operation of finding that a type of facts is a reality or phenomenon that is definitely and determinedly different beyond any possible doubt or error, and hence is irreducible to any other type of facts. We must go back to an order of ultimate reality, to an order or area of reality which because it is *radical* (that is, of the root) admits of no other reality beneath it, or rather, on which all others must necessarily appear because it is the basic reality.

This radical reality, on the strict contemplation of which we must finally found and assure

Reprinted from *Man and People* by José Ortega y Gasset. Translated from the Spanish by Willard R. Trask. © 1957 by W. W. Norton & Company, Inc. By permission of W. W. Norton & Company, Inc.

all our knowledge of anything, is our life, human life.

Whenever and wherever I speak of "human life," unless I make a special exception, you must avoid thinking of somebody else's life; each one of you should refer it to your own life and try to make that present to you. Human life as radical reality is only the life of each person, is only *my life*. In deference to idiom, I shall sometimes call it "our life," but you must always understand that by this expression I refer to the life of each individual and not to the life of other people nor to a supposed plural and common life. What we call "other people's lives"— the life of one's friend, of one's sweetheart—is something that appears in the scenario that is *my* life, the life of each, and hence supposes that life. The life of another, even of one nearest and dearest, is for me mere spectacle, like the tree or the cliff or the wandering cloud. I see it, but I *am* not it, that is, I do not live it. If the other has a toothache, his face, the shape taken by his contracted muscles, are patent to me, I see the spectacle of someone suffering pain, but his toothache does not pain me, and what I have of it in no way resembles what I have when my own teeth ache. Strictly, my neighbor's toothache is in the last analysis a supposition, hypothesis, or presumption of my own, it is a presumed pain. My pain, on the contrary, is unquestionable. Properly speaking, we can never be sure that the friend who presents himself to us as suffering from toothache is really suffering from toothache. All that is patent to us of his pain is certain external signs, which are not pain but muscular contraction, wandering gaze, the hand to the cheek—that gesture which is so incongruous with what provokes it, for it looks exactly as if the toothache were a bird and we were putting our hand over it to keep it from flying away. Another's pain is not radical reality, but reality in a sense that is already secondary, derivative, and dubious. What we have of his pain with radical reality is only its aspect, its appearance, the spectacle of it, its signs. This is all of it that is actually patent and unquestionable to us. But the relation between a sign and the thing signified, between an appearance and that which appears in it or simulates it, between an aspect and the thing manifest or "aspected" in it, is always finally questionable and ambiguous. There are those who to gain some private end feign the entire *mise en scène* of a toothache to perfection without suffering it. But we shall see that, on the contrary, our own individual life does not tolerate fictions, because when we feign something to ourselves we of course know that we are feigning. And so our intimate fiction never succeeds in fully establishing itself, for being at bottom aware that it is not genuine, we do not succeed in completely deceiving ourselves, we see through the fraud. This inexorable genuineness of our life, the life, I repeat, of each one of us, this genuineness that is evident, indubitable, unquestionable to itself, is my first reason for calling our life "radical reality."

But there is a second reason. Calling it "radical reality" does not mean that it is the only reality, nor even the highest, worthiest or most sublime, nor yet the supreme reality, but simply that it is the root of all other realities, in the sense that they—any of them—in order to be reality to us must in some way make themselves present, or at least announce themselves, within the shaken confines of our own life. Hence this radical reality—my life—is so little "egoistic," so far from "solipsistic," that in essence it is the open area, the waiting stage, on which any other reality may manifest itself and celebrate its Pentecost. God himself, to be God to us, must somehow or other proclaim his existence to us, and that is why he thunders on Sinai, lashes the money-changers in the temple court, and sails on the three-masted frigate of Golgotha.

It follows that no knowledge of anything is sufficient—that is, sufficiently profound or radical—if it does not begin by searching the sphere that is our life to discover and define where and how that thing makes its appearance in it, looms, springs up, arises, in short exists in it. For this is the proper meaning of the word *exist*—a word that originally, I take it, had strong connotations of struggle and belligerence, for it designates the vital situation in which suddenly, as though sprung from the ground, an enemy appears among us, shows himself or makes himself apparent, energetically blocking our way, that is, resisting us and at the same time affirming himself, making himself firm, before us and against us. Existing includes resisting; so it includes the fact that anything that has existence will affirm itself if we try to suppress it, annihilate it, or consider it unreal. Hence, whatever has existence or arises before us is reality, since reality is everything that, like it or not, we have to reckon with, because, like it or not, *it is there,* it ex-ists, re-sists. A terminological wrongheadedness that verges on the intolerable has for the past few years seen fit to use the words "exist" and "existence" in an abstruse and unverifiable sense precisely the opposite of that which the age-old word bears and expresses in itself.

Today some writers attempt to make the term designate man's mode of being. But man who is always "I"—the I that each of us is—is the only being that does not exist, but *lives* or is alive. Precisely all the other things that are not man, not "I," are the things that *exist,* because they appear, arise, spring up, resist me, assert themselves in the ambit that is my life. Be this said in passing and in all haste.

Now, innumerable attributes can be posited

of this strange and dramatic radical reality, our life. But I shall now single out only the most indispensable one for our theme.

And it is that life is not something that we have bestowed on ourselves; rather, we find it precisely when we find ourselves. Suddenly and without knowing how or why, without any previous forewarning of it, man sees and finds that he is obliged to have his being in an unpremeditated, unforeseen ambit, in a conjunction of completely definite circumstances. Perhaps it will not be irrelevant to point out that this observation—which is the basis of my philosophical thought—was made, just as I have now made it, in my first book, published in 1914. Provisionally and to make it easier to understand, let us call this unpremeditated and unforeseen ambit, this most definite circumstance in which we always find ourselves in our living—let us call it "world." Now, this world, in which in living I am obliged to be, allows me a choice. *Within it* I may choose to be in one place or another. But it is granted to no one to choose the world in which he lives; it is always this one, this present world. We cannot choose the century or the day or the date when we are to live, nor the universe in which we are to move. To live or to be alive or, what is the same thing, to be a man, does not admit of any preparations or preliminary experiments. Life is fired at us point-blank. I have said it before: where and when we are born, or happen to find ourselves after we are born, there and then, like it or not, we must sink or swim. At this moment, every one of you finds himself submerged in an ambient that is an interval in which he must willy-nilly come to terms with that abstruse element, a lecture in philosophy, with something of which he does not know whether it interests him or not, whether he understands it or not, which is portentously devouring an hour of his life—an irreplaceable hour, for the hours of his life are numbered. This is his circumstance, his here and his now. What will he do? For something he *must* do;

either listen to me, or, on the contrary, dismiss me and attend to his own meditations, think of his business or his clients, remember his sweetheart. What will he do? Get up and go, or remain, accepting the fate of spending this hour of his life, which might have been so delightful, in the slaughterhouse of lost hours?

Because, I repeat, there is no escape: we have something to do or have to be doing something *always;* for this life that is given us is not given us ready-made, but instead every one of us has to make it for himself, each his own. This life that is given us is given us empty, and man has to keep filling it for himself, occupying it. Such is our occupation. This is not the case with the stone, the plant, the animal. Their being is given them predetermined and decreed. The stone, when it begins to be, is given not only its existence; its behavior is also determined for it beforehand—namely, to be heavy, to gravitate toward the earth's center. Similarly the animal is given its behavioral repertory, directed by its instincts without any intervention on its part. But man is given the necessity of having always to do something upon pain of succumbing; yet what he has to do is not present to him from the outset and once and for all. Because the strangest and most confounding thing about this circumstance or world in which we have to live is the fact that within its inexorable circle or horizon it always presents us with a variety of possibilities for action, a variety in the face of which we are obliged to choose and hence to exercise our freedom. The circumstance, I repeat—the here and now in which we are inexorably inscribed and imprisoned—does not at every moment impose on us a single act or activity but various possible acts or activities, and cruelly leaves us to our own initiative and inspiration, hence to our own responsibility. In a little while, when you go out into the street, you will have to decide what direction, what route, you will take. And if this happens to you on such a commonplace occasion, much more happens at those solemn decisive moments of life in which the choice to be made is nothing less, for example, than a profession, a career—and career means road and direction. Among the few personal notes that Descartes left at his death there is one, dating from his youth, in which he copied an old line of Ausonius, which in turn reproduces an ancient Pythagorean saying and which runs: *Quod vitae sectabor iter?* "What way, what road shall I choose for my life?" But life is nothing except man's being; so that here we have the most extraordinary, extravagant, dramatic, and paradoxical thing about the human condition—namely, that man is the only reality that does not simply consist in being but must choose its own being. For if we analyze the commonplace thing that is going to occur in a little while —the fact that each of us will have to choose and decide the direction of the street he is going to take—you will see that the choice of such a seemingly simple act will be made only with the intervention of the entire choice that you have already made, the choice that at this moment, as you sit here, you carry secretly in your inmost selves, in your most hidden depths: the choice of a type of humanity, of a way of being man, that you seek to realize in your living.

In order not to lose our bearings, let us summarize what has been said so far: Life in the sense of human life, hence in the biographical not the biological sense—if biology is taken to mean the psychosomatic—life is the fact that someone whom we call man, as we could and perhaps should call him X (you will soon see why), finds himself having to be in the circumstance or world. But our being as "being in the circumstance" is not still and simply passive. To be, that is, to continue being, it has always to be doing something, but what it has to do is not imposed on it or predetermined for it; it has to choose and decide for itself, untransferably, for itself and before itself, upon its own sole responsibility. Nobody can take its place in deciding what it is going to do, for even submitting to another's will has to be its own decision.

This obligation to choose, and hence willy-nilly to be free, to be on its own account and at its own risk, proceeds from the fact that the circumstance is never one-sided, it always has several, often many sides. In other words, it invites us to different possibilities of acting, of being. So we spend our lives saying to ourselves: "on the one hand," I would do, think, feel, want, decide *this,* but "on the other hand" . . . Life is many-sided. Every moment and every place opens different roads to us. As the ancient Indian book says: "Wherever a man sets his foot, he treads a hundred paths." So life is a permanent crossroads, a constant perplexity. This is why I am always saying that to my mind the best title for a book of philosophy is the one borne by a book of Maimonides': *More Nebuchim*—"Guide for the Perplexed."

When we want to describe a situation of the utmost extremity in our life, where circumstances appear to offer us no way out and hence no choice, we Spaniards say that we are "between the sword and the wall." Death is certain, there is no escaping it! Could there be less choice? Yet it is clear that the expression invites us to choose *between* the wall *and* the sword. Terrifying and proud privilege that man at times enjoys and suffers under—choosing the pattern of his own death: death of a coward or death of a hero, an ugly or a beautiful death!

Escape is possible from every circumstance, even the most extreme. What there is no escaping is having to do something and above all having to do what in the last analysis is the most difficult and painful of things—choosing, preferring. How many times have we not told ourselves that we should prefer not to prefer? From which it follows that what is given me when life is given me is simply "things to do." Life, as we all know only too well, "takes a lot of doing." And the most important thing is to make sure that what we choose to do in each case is not *just anything,* but the thing that has to be done—done here and now—that it is our true vocation, our genuine "thing to do."

Among all the characteristics of radical reality or life which I have mentioned, and which are a very small part of those that would have to be described to give any adequate idea of it, the one that I now want to emphasize is the one expressed in a great platitude: namely, that life is untransferable and that each man has to live his own; that no one can take over his task of living for him; that the toothache he suffers from has to hurt him and he cannot transfer even a fraction of the pain from it to anyone else; that he can delegate no one to choose and decide for him what he will do, what he will be; that no one can replace him or surrogate for him in feeling and wanting; that, finally, he cannot make his neighbor think for him the thoughts that he has to think in order to orient himself in the world (in the world of things and in the world of men) and thus find his right line of conduct—hence, that he must be convinced or not convinced, must see truths and see through nonsense, on his own account, without any possible substitute, deputy, or proxy.

I can repeat mechanically that two and two make four, without knowing what I am saying, simply because I have heard it countless times; but really to think it on my own account—that is, to acquire the clear certainty that "two and two veritably make four and not three or five"— *that* I have to do for myself, by myself, I alone— or, what is the same thing, I in my solitude. And as the same is true of my decisions, volitions, feelings, it follows that since human life in the strict sense is untransferable, it is essentially *solitude, radical solitude.*

But let there be no misunderstanding here. In no sense would I suggest that I am the only thing that exists. In the first place, you will have noticed that, even though "life" in the proper and original sense is that of each one of us, hence *my* life, I have used that possessive pronoun as little as possible, just as I have scarcely used the personal pronoun "I." If I have done so occasionally, it has been merely to make it easier for you to get a preliminary view of what this strange radical reality human life is. I have preferred using the terms "man," "the living being," or "each one of us." In another lecture you will see the reason for this reservation. But actually, and after a few detours that we shall make, what we are dealing with is clearly life, *my* life and *myself.* This man—this self, this "I" —is finally in radical solitude; but—I repeat— this does not mean that he alone is, that he is the sole reality, or at least the radical reality. What I have thus termed is not only I, nor is it man—it is life, man's life. Now, this includes an enormous number of things. European thought has traveled beyond the philosophical idealism that was dominant from the year 1640, in which Descartes proclaimed it—the philosophical idealism for which there is no reality except the ideas of my "I," of an "I," of my *moi-même,* of which Descartes said, *"moi qui ne suis qu'une chose qui pense."* For this philosophical idealism, things, the world, my body itself, would be only ideas of things, imagination of a world, fantasy of my body. Only the mind would exist and everything else would be a tenacious and exuberant dream, an infinite phantasmagoria secreted by my mind. Life would thus be the easiest thing imaginable. To live would be for me to exist within myself, floating on the sea of my own ideas, without having a need to reckon with anything but my own ideas. This is what has been called idealism. I should encounter nothing. I should not have to be in the world, the world would be in me, like an endless reel of film unwinding within me. Nothing would disturb me. I should be like God who floats, alone and unique, on himself, with no shipwreck possible because he is at once the swimmer and the sea in which he swims. If there were two Gods, they would confront each other. This conception of the real has been superseded by my generation and, within my generation, very concretely and vigorously by myself.

No, life is not my mind, my ideas, being all that exists; it is the very contrary. From the time of Descartes Western man had been left without a world. But *to live* means having to be outside of myself, in the absolute "outside" that is the circumstance or world; it is having, like it or not, constantly and incessantly to face and clash with whatever makes up that world: minerals, plants, animals, other men. There is no getting out of it. I have to tackle all that. Willy-nilly I have to come to some kind of terms with all that. But this—finding myself amid all that and having to come or fail to come to terms with all that—this finally happens to me alone and I have to do it alone without any possibility that *on the decisive plane*—note that I say "on the decisive plane"—anyone can lend me a hand.

This means that we are a long way from Descartes, from Kant, and their Romantic successors—Schelling, Hegel, from what Carlyle called "transcendental moonshine." But, needless to say, we are even farther from Aristotle.

We are, then, far from Descartes, from Kant. We are even farther from Aristotle and St. Thomas. Is it perhaps our duty and our destiny —not only those of us who are philosophers but all of us—to keep going farther and still farther? I shall not answer that question now. I shall not even tell you from *what* we must, willy-nilly, get farther and farther. Let that large question mark stand here, for everyone to do as he pleases with—use it as a lasso to catch the future, or just hang himself with it.

The radical solitude of human life, the being of man, does not, then, consist in there really being nothing except himself. Quite the contrary—there is nothing less than the universe, with all that it contains. There is, then, an infinity of things but—there it is!—amid them Man in his radical reality is alone—alone *with* them. And since among these things there are other human beings, he is *alone with* them too. If but one unique being existed, it could not properly be said to be alone. Uniqueness has nothing to do with solitude. If we were reflecting on the Portuguese "*saudade*"—*saudade,* of course, is the Galician-Portuguese form of "*solitudinem*," "solitude"—we should say more about

solitude and we should see that solitude is always *solitude from* someone; that is, it is a being left *alone* and a lacking. And this is so true that the word by which the Greeks expressed "mine" and "solitary"—*monos*—comes from *mone*, which means "to remain"—understanding "to *remain without*"—without others. Whether because they have died, whether because they have gone away, in any case because they have left us—have left us . . . alone. Or alternatively, because we leave them, flee from them and go to the desert and into retirement to lead the life of *mone*. Whence *monachos, monastery,* and *monk*. And in Latin *solus,* as Meillet (whose extreme strictness in phonetics and whose lack of talent in semantics obliges me to weigh my spontaneous etymological findings against his observations) is inclined to think—*solus* comes from *sed-lus,* that is from the one who remains sitting when the rest have gone away. Our Lady of Solitude is the Virgin who remains *solitary* of Jesus, who has been killed; and the sermon preached in Holy Week and called the "Sermon on Solitude" meditates on the most sorrowful of Christ's words: *Eli, eli—lamma sabachthani—* "My God, my God, why hast thou forsaken me? Why hast thou left me solitary of thee?" This is the expression that most profoundly declares God's will to become man—to accept what is most radically human in man, his radical solitude.

And this is the moment to mention Leibniz. I need not say that I shall not spend even a moment expounding his doctrine. I shall confine myself to remarking for those who know Leibniz well that the best translation of his most important term—*monad*—is not unit nor yet unicity. Monads have no windows. They are shut up in themselves—this is idealism. But in its ultimate sense, Leibniz's conception of the monad would be best expressed by calling the monads "solitudes." In Homer too a centurion thrusts a lance into Aphrodite's body, and the delicious blood of Olympian woman gushes out, and she goes running to her father Zeus, whimpering like any pampered girl. No, no—Christ was man above all and before all because God left him alone, solitary—*sabachthani*.

In proportion as we take possession of life and come to know it, we observe that when we came to it, everyone else had gone away and that we have to live our radical living . . . alone, and that only in our solitude are we our truth.

From this substrate of radical solitude that is irremediably our life, we constantly emerge with a no less radical longing for companionship. Could we but find one whose life would wholly fuse with, would interpenetrate ours! We make all sorts of attempts to attain this. One of them is friendship. But the greatest of them all is what we call love. Genuine love is nothing but the attempt to exchange two solitudes.

Belonging to and forming an essential part of the solitude that we are, are all the things and beings in the universe which are there about us, forming our environment, articulating our circumstance; but which never fuse with the "each" that one is, which on the contrary are always *the other,* the absolutely other—a strange and always more or less disturbing, negative, and hostile and at best unconcurring element, which for that reason we are aware of as what is alien to and outside [*fuera*] of us, as foreign [*forastero*]—because it oppresses, compresses, and represses us: the world.

We see, then, that in the face of any idealistic and solipsistic philosophy, our life poses these two terms with identical value as reality: the somebody, the X, the Man who lives; and the world, environment, or circumstance in which, like it or not, he has to live.

It is in this world, environment, or circumstance that we must look for a reality that in all strictness, in contradistinction to all others, we can and should call "social."

Man, then, finding himself alive, finds himself having to come to terms with what we have called environment, circumstance, or world. Whether these three words will gradually take on separate meanings for us is something that does not concern us now. At this moment, they mean the same thing to us, namely the foreign, alien element "outside of himself," in which man has to work at being. That world is a great thing, an immense thing, with shadowy frontiers and full to bursting with smaller things, with what we call "things" and commonly distinguish in a broad and rough classification, saying that in the world there are minerals, plants, animals, and men. What these things are is the concern of the various sciences—for example, biology treats of plants and animals. But biology, like any other science, is a particular activity with which certain men concern themselves *in* their lives, that is, after they are already living. Biology and any other science, then, supposes that before its operations begin all these things are already within our view, exist for us. And this fact that things *are* for us, originally and primarily in our human life, before we are physicists, mineralogists, biologists, and so on, represents what these things are in their radical reality. What the sciences afterwards tell us about them may be as plausible, as convincing, as true as you please, but it remains clear that they have drawn all of it, by complicated intellectual methods, from what in the beginning, primordially and with no further ado, things were to us in our living. The Earth may be a planet in a certain solar system belonging to a certain galaxy or nebula, and may be made of atoms, each one of which in its turn contains a multiplicity of things, of quasi-things or guess-what things called electrons, protons, mesons, neutrons, and so on. But none of this knowledge would exist if the earth did not exist before it as a component of our life, as something with which we have to come to terms and hence something that is of import to us, matters to us— that matters to us because it confronts us with certain difficulties and provides us with certain facilities. This means that on this pre-existent and radical plane from which the sciences set out and which they assume, the Earth is none of these things that physics and astronomy tell us it is, but is what firmly holds me up, is terra firma, in contradistinction to the sea, in which I sink (the word *terra,* according to Bréal, comes from *tersa,* "dry"), it is what I sometimes have laboriously to climb, because it inclines upward, sometimes easily descend because it inclines downward, it is what parts and separates me from the woman I love or forces me to live close to someone whom I loathe, it is what makes some things far from me and others near me, some *here* and others *there* and others *yonder,* and so on and so on. These and many similar attributes are the genuine reality of the earth, just as it appears to me in the radical ambit of my life. Please observe that all these attributes— supporting me, making me go up or down hill, making me tire myself in crossing it to where what I need happens to be, separating me from those I love, and so on—all refer to me; so that the Earth in its primordial appearance consists entirely in utilitarian references in respect to me. You will find the same if you take any other example—tree, animal, ocean, river. If we leave out of consideration what they are in reference to us, I mean, their *being for* some use of ours—as means, instruments or, vice versa, as impediments and difficulties for our ends—they are left being nothing. Or, to put it differently: everything that composes, fills, and makes up the world in which man finds himself at birth possesses no independent condition *of itself,* possesses no being of its own, *is nothing in itself*—but is simply something *for* or *something against* our ends. We ought not to have called them "things," then, in view of the meaning, that the word bears for us today. A "thing" means something that has its own being, independently of me, independently of what it *is for* man. If this is the case with everything in the circumstance or world, it means that the world in its radical reality is a body of somethings with which I, man, can or must do this or that—that it is a body of means and impediments, facilities and difficulties which, in order to live in any real sense, I encounter. Things are not originally "things," but something that I try to use or avoid in order to live and to live as well as possible; are, therefore, that with which I occupy myself and by which I am occupied, with which I act and operate, with which I succeed or fail to do what I want to do; in short, they are concerns to which I am constantly attending. And since "to do" and "to occupy oneself," "to have concerns" is expressed in Greek by "practice," *praxis*— things are radically *pragmata* and my relation to them is *pragmatic.* Unfortunately, at least so far as I am aware, our language does not have a word that adequately expresses what the word *pragma* does. We can only say that a thing, as *pragma,* is not something that exists by itself and has nothing to do with me. In the world or circumstance of each one of us there is nothing that has nothing to do with us and in turn we have to do with whatever forms part of this same circumstance or world. This is composed exclusively of references to me, and I am remanded to whatever it contains, I depend on it, for better or for worse; everything is favorable or adverse to me, caress or friction, flattery or injury, service or harm. A thing as *pragma,* then, is something that I manipulate for a particular end, that I deal with or avoid, that I must count upon or discount; it is an instrument or an impediment *for:* a task, a chattel, a gadget, a deficiency, a failure, an obstacle; in short, it is a concern to be attended to, something that to a greater or less degree is of import for me, that I lack, that I have too much of, hence an *importance.* I hope, now that I have accumulated all these various expressions, that the difference will begin to be clear if you contrast in your minds the idea of a world of things and the idea of a world of concerns or importances. In a world of things we play no part: it and everything in it is *of itself.* But in a world of concerns or importances, everything consists solely in its reference to us, everything plays a part in us, that is, everything is of import to us and *is* only to the extent to which and in the way in which it concerns, is of import to, and affects us.

Such is the radical truth concerning what the world is—because it expresses the world's "consistency" or that in which it originally consists as element in which we have to live our life. Everything else that the sciences tell us about this world is and was at best a secondary, derivative, hypothetical, and questionable truth—for the simple reason, I repeat, that we begin to practice science after we are already living in the world and hence when for us the world is already this that it is. Science is only one of the countless activities, actions, operations that man *practices** in his life.

Man *practices* science as he *practices* patience, as he *attends to* his affairs [*hacienda*], as he *practices* poetry, politics, business, *makes* journeys, *makes* love, *makes believe, marks* time, and above all, man *conjures up* illusions.

All these locutions represent the most ordinary, familiar, colloquial kind of speech. Yet now we see that they are technical terms in a theory of human life. To the shame of philosophers it must be said that they have never seen the radical phenomenon that is our life. They

* [This and all the italicized verbs in the following passage are expressed in Spanish by the verb *hacer*, "to do, to make." They thus echo and carry on the idea that "we have something to *do* or have to be *doing* something *always;* for this life that is given us is not given us ready-made, but instead every one of us has to *make* it for himself, each his own" (p. 212, above).—*Translator.*]

have always turned their backs on it, and it has been the poets and novelists, but above all the "ordinary man," who has been aware of it with its modes and situations. Hence this series of terms represents a series of titles announcing great philosophical themes on which much would need to be said. Think of the profound problem expressed in the locution "mark time" [*hacer tiempo*]—nothing less than waiting, expectation, and hope. What is hope in man? Can man live without it? Some years ago Paul Morand sent me a copy of his biography of Maupassant, with a dedication that read: "I send you this life of a man 'qui n'espérait pas,' who did not hope." Was Morand right? Can there be such a thing—literally and formally—as human living that is not hoping? Is not the primary and most essential function of life expectation, and its most visceral organ hope? As you see, the subject is immense.

And what of that other mode of life in which man *makes believe, pretends*—is it any less interesting? What is this strange, ungenuine *doing* to which man sometimes devotes himself precisely for the purpose of really *not doing* even what he is *doing*—the writer who is not a writer but who *pretends* he is a writer, the woman who is scarcely feminine but who *pretends* she is a woman, *pretends* to smile, *pretends* disdain, *pretends* desire, *pretends* love, incapable of really *doing* any of these things?

Notes

1. See Janet W. Diaz, *The Major Themes of Existentialism in the Work of José Ortega y Gasset* (Chapel Hill, N.C.: University of North Carolina Press, 1970).

2. José Ortega y Gasset, *The Revolt of the Masses* (New York: W. W. Norton, 1932).

3. Ibid., p. 99.

4. José Ortega y Gasset, *Man and People* (New York: W. W. Norton, 1957), p. 58.

5. Ibid., p. 23.

17 / One-Dimensional Man
Marcuse

Karl Marx believed that man's labor should be the means by which he realizes and expresses his life; instead it is the source of his bonds and alienation. The industrial society and the capitalist system of production assure the worker's disaffection from the system. They also prevent his self-realization. Today, in an age of increasingly automated production, new sources of power, and the multiplication of technologies, the elimination of actual poverty seems within our grasp. But some writers are pointing to a new set of symptoms that are uniquely characteristic of man in our modern industrial society. These symptoms belong to man's inner life, his spirit, and indicate a profound change in the condition of man. In the age of science and technology, man's methods of work, his life style, and his values and culture are being drastically modified. While these changes are as important in the history of man as the discovery of fire or the development of agriculture, they are so different that no past age can serve as a model. Man now has limitless possibilities for re-creation or destruction of the environment and for the re-creation or destruction of himself. As Victor Ferkiss says, "At the deepest level of human existence man as we have known him is on the verge of becoming something else."[1]

The sheer rapidity and abundance of innovation and change are certainly a part of the new conditions with which we have to live. Obsolescence comes not only in the planned variety but seems to permanently threaten our individual knowledge and skills. Understanding the meaning of the continuing developments in science and technology seems beyond us. We are aware that profound changes are taking place that are severely affecting the way in which man communicates, educates, travels, works, loves, plays, worships, and makes war. Indeed, even death and the exhaustion of resources need not be inevitable when we can receive organ transplants, suspend the life of the body through freezing, and develop unheard of abundance in agriculture and the use of the sea.

These same opportunities also generate serious problems. Fundamental questions arise over the issue of who is to control these new powers and realize these new possibilities. How will we reconcile our present institutions and traditions to these new changes? The increasing mobility of the population raises questions about the survival of the family as a basic social unit. Global communication and increasing international economic interdependence raise questions about the survival of the nation as a basic political unit. Electronic surveillance devices raise moral and legal questions about the invasion of our physical privacy, as do the advent of truth drugs and the possibility of brain control in regard to our psychological privacy. The development of mass media and the need of expertise and centralization in running a complex technological society raise questions about the survival of democratic institutions as we know them.

But there are other problems more internal to man. Many people feel that the technological age provides man with too much personal freedom. The seemingly limitless possibilities and multiplication of choices can cause problems of personal adjustment and the loss of identity and sense of personal worth. In simpler societies, man knew who he was through his relationship to his family and traditions. Theodore Roszak describes what he feels is a growing strong reaction to a world more and more dominated by science and technology and its view of reality. This reaction to what he calls "technocracy" is expressed in the form of a counterculture that puts a premium on a simpler mode of life, a more personal vision of reality, and new modes of consciousness and feeling.[2]

The contemporary philosopher Herbert Marcuse is pessimistic regarding the survival of man's freedom in a technological society. Never merely a matter of means or techniques, technology has become, under the control of vested interests, totalitarian, restrictive of the individual's freedom, and repressive of man's realization of his true needs. It blinds man to the necessity of fundamental social and institutional changes. Fundamental changes are necessary because the present society, caught up in self-contradiction, increases productivity and promotes destruction, protects freedom and supports repression, accumulates wealth and preserves misery, and, in the name of rationality, becomes completely irrational.

We submit to these contradictions in our society because the mass media has sold us on the efficiency and rationality of our social organizations. The success of the economic-technological order in raising our standard of living has put it beyond all criticism. Through affluence, it has pacified the antagonism of the bourgeoisie and proletariat, merged them into members of a mass society, and taken away the chances for a revolution that would bring about a qualitatively different type of society. The technological society is here and ubiquitous. It has made Americans "happy" and satisfied with the institutional status quo. But, nevertheless, it is totalitarian.

For Marcuse, the result is a society which is one-dimensional, a culture which is one-dimensional, and a consciousness which is one-dimensional.

Potentially man is capable of new forms of existence, of realizing his real needs, and of criticizing his social order from a standpoint outside that order. But Marcuse is not optimistic about man's breaking a mold with which he is comfortable and which is increasingly strengthened by man's greatest productive tool, technology.

The New Forms of Control

A comfortable, smooth, reasonable, democratic unfreedom prevails in advanced industrial civilization, a token of technical progress. Indeed, what could be more rational than the suppression of individuality in the mechanization of socially necessary but painful performances; the concentration of individual enterprises in more effective, more productive corporations; the regulation of free competition among unequally equipped economic subjects; the curtailment of prerogatives and national sovereignties which impede the international organization of resources. That this technological order also involves a political and intellectual coordination may be a regrettable and yet promising development.

The rights and liberties which were such vital factors in the origins and earlier stages of industrial society yield to a higher stage of this society: they are losing their traditional rationale and content. Freedom of thought, speech, and conscience were—just as free enterprise, which they served to promote and protect—essentially *critical* ideas, designed to replace an obsolescent material and intellectual culture by a more productive and rational one. Once institutionalized, these rights and liberties shared the fate of the society of which they had become an integral part. The achievement cancels the premises.

To the degree to which freedom from want, the concrete substance of all freedom, is becoming a real possibility, the liberties which pertain to a state of lower productivity are losing their former content. Independence of thought, autonomy, and the right to political opposition are being deprived of their basic critical function in a society which seems increasingly capable of satisfying the needs of the individuals through the way in which it is organized. Such a society may justly demand acceptance of its principles and institutions, and reduce the opposition to the discussion and promotion of alternative policies *within* the status quo. In this respect, it seems to make little difference whether the increasing satisfaction of needs is accomplished by an authoritarian or a non-authoritarian system. Under the conditions of a rising standard of living, non-conformity with the system itself appears to be socially useless, and the more so when it entails tangible economic and political disadvantages and threatens the smooth operation of the whole. Indeed, at least in so far as the necessities of life are involved, there seems to be no reason why the production and distribution of goods and services should proceed through the competitive concurrence of individual liberties.

Freedom of enterprise was from the beginning not altogether a blessing. As the liberty to work or to starve, it spelled toil, insecurity, and fear for the vast majority of the population. If the individual were no longer compelled to prove himself on the market, as a free economic subject, the disappearance of this kind of freedom would be one of the greatest achievements of civilization. The technological processes of mechanization and standardization might release individual energy into a yet uncharted realm of freedom beyond necessity. The very structure of human existence would be altered; the individual would be liberated from the work world's imposing upon him alien needs and alien possibilities. The individual would be free to exert autonomy over a life that would be his own. If the productive apparatus could be organized and directed toward the satisfaction of the vital needs, its control might well be centralized; such control would not prevent individual autonomy, but render it possible.

This is a goal within the capabilities of advanced industrial civilization, the "end" of technological rationality. In actual fact, however, the contrary trend operates: the apparatus imposes its economic and political requirements for defense and expansion on labor time and free time, on the material and intellectual culture. By virtue of the way it has organized its technological base, contemporary industrial society tends to be totalitarian. For "totalitarian" is not only a terroristic political coordination of society, but also a nonterroristic economic-technical coordination which operates through the manipulation of needs by vested interests. It thus precludes the emergence of an effective opposition against the whole. Not only a specific form of government or party rule makes for totalitarianism, but also a specific system of production and distribution which may well be compatible with a "pluralism" of parties, newspapers, "countervailing powers," etc.

Today political power asserts itself through its power over the machine process and over the technical organization of the apparatus. The government of advanced and advancing industrial societies can maintain and secure itself only when it succeeds in mobilizing, organizing, and exploiting the technical, scientific, and mechanical productivity available to industrial civilization. And this productivity mobilizes society as a whole, above and beyond any particular individual or group interests. The brute fact that the machine's physical (only physical?) power surpasses that of the individual, and of any particular group of individuals, makes the machine the most effective political instrument in any society whose basic organization is that of the machine process. But the political trend may be reversed; essentially the power of the machine is only the stored-up and projected power of man. To the extent to which the work world is conceived of as a machine and mechanized accordingly, it becomes the *potential* basis of a new freedom for man.

Contemporary industrial civilization demonstrates that it has reached the stage at which "the free society" can no longer be adequately defined in the traditional terms of economic, political, and intellectual liberties, not because these liberties have become insignificant, but because they are too significant to be confined within the traditional forms. New modes of realization are needed, corresponding to the new capabilities of society.

Such new modes can be indicated only in negative terms because they would amount to the negation of the prevailing modes. Thus economic freedom would mean freedom *from* the economy—from being controlled by economic forces and relationships; freedom from the daily struggle for existence, from earning a living. Political freedom would mean liberation of the individuals *from* politics over which they have no effective control. Similarly, intellectual freedom would mean the restoration of individual thought now absorbed by mass communication and indoctrination, abolition of "public opinion" together with its makers. The unrealistic sound of these propositions is indicative, not of their utopian character, but of the strength of the forces which prevent their realization. The most effective and enduring form of warfare against liberation is the implanting of material and intellectual needs that perpetuate obsolete forms of the struggle for existence.

The intensity, the satisfaction and even the character of human needs, beyond the biological level, have always been preconditioned. Whether or not the possibility of doing or leaving, enjoying or destroying, possessing or rejecting something is seized as a *need* depends on whether or not it can be seen as desirable and necessary for the prevailing societal institutions and interests. In this sense, human needs are historical needs and, to the extent to which the society demands the repressive development of the individual, his needs themselves and their claim for satisfaction are subject to overriding critical standards.

We may distinguish both true and false needs. "False" are those which are superimposed upon the individual by particular social interests in his repression: the needs which perpetuate toil, aggressiveness, misery, and injustice. Their satisfaction might be most gratifying to the individual, but this happiness is not a condition which has to be maintained and protected if it serves to arrest the development of the ability (his own and others) to recognize the disease of the whole and grasp the chances of curing the disease. The result then is euphoria in unhappiness. Most of the prevailing needs to relax, to have fun, to behave and consume in accordance with the advertisements, to love and hate what others love and hate, belong to this category of false needs.

Such needs have a societal content and function which are determined by external powers over which the individual has no control; the development and satisfaction of these needs is heteronomous. No matter how much such needs may have become the individual's own, reproduced and fortified by the conditions of his existence; no matter how much he identifies himself with them and finds himself in their satisfaction, they continue to be what they were from the beginning—products of a society whose dominant interest demands repression.

The prevalence of repressive needs is an accomplished fact, accepted in ignorance and defeat, but a fact that must be undone in the interest of the happy individual as well as all those whose misery is the price of his satisfac-

tion. The only needs that have an unqualified claim for satisfaction are the vital ones—nourishment, clothing, lodging at the attainable level of culture. The satisfaction of these needs is the prerequisite for the realization of *all* needs, of the unsublimated as well as the sublimated ones.

For any consciousness and conscience, for any experience which does not accept the prevailing societal interest as the supreme law of thought and behavior, the established universe of needs and satisfactions is a fact to be questioned—questioned in terms of truth and falsehood. These terms are historical throughout, and their objectivity is historical. The judgment of needs and their satisfaction, under the given conditions, involves standards of *priority*—standards which refer to the optimal development of the individual, of all individuals, under the optimal utilization of the material and intellectual resources available to man. The resources are calculable. "Truth" and "falsehood" of needs designate objective conditions to the extent to which the universal satisfaction of vital needs and, beyond it, the progressive alleviation of toil and poverty, are universally valid standards. But as historical standards, they do not only vary according to area and stage of development, they also can be defined only in (greater or lesser) *contradiction* to the prevailing ones. What tribunal can possibly claim the authority of decision?

In the last analysis, the question of what are true and false needs must be answered by the individuals themselves, but only in the last analysis; that is, if and when they are free to give their own answer. As long as they are kept incapable of being autonomous, as long as they are indoctrinated and manipulated (down to their very instincts), their answer to this question cannot be taken as their own. By the same token, however, no tribunal can justly arrogate to itself the right to decide which needs should be developed and satisfied. Any such tribunal is reprehensible, although our revulsion does not do away with the question: how can the people who have been the object of effective and productive domination by themselves create the conditions of freedom?

The more rational, productive, technical, and total the repressive administration of society becomes, the more unimaginable the means and ways by which the administered individuals might break their servitude and seize their own liberation. To be sure, to impose Reason upon an entire society is a paradoxical and scandalous idea—although one might dispute the righteousness of a society which ridicules this idea while making its own population into objects of total administration. All liberation depends on the consciousness of servitude, and the emergence of this consciousness is always hampered by the predominance of needs and satisfactions which, to a great extent, have become the individual's own. The process always replaces one system of preconditioning by another; the optimal goal is the replacement of false needs by true ones, the abandonment of repressive satisfaction.

The distinguishing feature of advanced industrial society is its effective suffocation of those needs which demand liberation—liberation also from that which is tolerable and rewarding and comfortable—while it sustains and absolves the destructive power and repressive function of the affluent society. Here, the social controls exact the overwhelming need for the production and consumption of waste; the need for stupefying work where it is no longer a real necessity; the need for modes of relaxation which soothe and prolong this stupefication; the need for maintaining such deceptive liberties as free competition at administered prices, a free press which censors itself, free choice between brands and gadgets.

Under the rule of a repressive whole, liberty can be made into a powerful instrument of domination. The range of choice open to the individual is not the decisive factor in determining the degree of human freedom, but *what* can be chosen and what *is* chosen by the individual. The criterion for free choice can never be an absolute one, but neither is it entirely relative. Free election of masters does not abolish the masters or the slaves. Free choice among a wide variety of goods and services does not signify freedom if these goods and services sustain social controls over a life of toil and fear—that is, if they sustain alienation. And the spontaneous reproduction of superimposed needs by the individual does not establish autonomy; it only testifies to the efficacy of the controls.

Our insistence on the depth and efficacy of these controls is open to the objection that we overrate greatly the indoctrinating power of the "media," and that by themselves the people would feel and satisfy the needs which are now imposed upon them. The objection misses the point. The preconditioning does not start with the mass production of radio and television and with the centralization of their control. The people enter this stage as preconditioned receptacles of long standing; the decisive difference is in the flattening out of the contrast (or conflict) between the given and the possible, between the satisfied and the unsatisfied needs. Here, the so-called equalization of class distinctions reveals its ideological function. If the worker and his boss enjoy the same television program and visit the same resort places, if the typist is as attractively made up as the daughter of her employer, if the Negro owns a Cadillac, if they all read the same newspaper, then this assimilation indicates not the disappearance of classes, but the extent to which the needs and satisfactions that serve the preservation of the Establishment are shared by the underlying population.

Indeed, in the most highly developed areas of contemporary society, the transplantation of social into individual needs is so effective that the difference between them seems to be purely theoretical. Can one really distinguish between the mass media as instruments of information and entertainment, and as agents of manipulation and indoctrination? Between the automobile as nuisance and as convenience? Between the horrors and the comforts of functional architecture? Between the work for national defense and the work for corporate gain? Between the private pleasure and the commercial and political utility involved in increasing the birth rate?

We are again confronted with one of the most vexing aspects of advanced industrial civilization: the rational character of its irrationality. Its productivity and efficiency, its capacity to increase and spread comforts, to turn waste into need, and destruction into construction, the extent to which this civilization transforms the object world into an extension of man's mind and body makes the very notion of alienation questionable. The people recognize themselves in their commodities; they find their soul in their automobile, hi-fi set, split-level home, kitchen equipment. The very mechanism which ties the individual to his society has changed, and social control is anchored in the new needs which it has produced.

The prevailing forms of social control are technological in a new sense. To be sure, the technical structure and efficacy of the productive and destructive apparatus has been a major instrumentality for subjecting the population to the established social division of labor throughout the modern period. Moreover, such integration has always been accompanied by more obvious forms of compulsion: loss of livelihood, the administration of justice, the police, the armed forces. It still is. But in the contemporary period, the technological controls appear to be the very embodiment of Reason for the benefit of all social groups and interests—to such an extent that all contradiction seems irrational and all counteraction impossible.

No wonder then that, in the most advanced areas of this civilization, the social controls have been introjected to the point where even individual protest is affected at its roots. The in-

tellectual and emotional refusal "to go along" appears neurotic and impotent. This is the socio-psychological aspect of the political event that marks the contemporary period: the passing of the historical forces which, at the preceding stage of industrial society, seemed to represent the possibility of new forms of existence.

But the term "introjection" perhaps no longer describes the way in which the individual by himself reproduces and perpetuates the external controls exercised by his society. Introjection suggests a variety of relatively spontaneous processes by which a Self (Ego) transposes the "outer" into the "inner." Thus introjection implies the existence of an inner dimension distinguished from and even antagonistic to the external exigencies—an individual consciousness and an individual unconscious *apart from* public opinion and behavior.[3] The idea of "inner freedom" here has its reality: it designates the private space in which man may become and remain "himself."

Today this private space has been invaded and whittled down by technological reality. Mass production and mass distribution claim the *entire* individual, and industrial psychology has long since ceased to be confined to the factory. The manifold processes of introjection seem to be ossified in almost mechanical reactions. The result is, not adjustment but *mimesis:* an immediate identification of the individual with *his* society and, through it, with the society as a whole.

This immediate, automatic identification (which may have been characteristic of primitive forms of association) reappears in high industrial civilization; its new "immediacy," however, is the product of a sophisticated, scientific management and organization. In this process, the "inner" dimension of the mind in which opposition to the status quo can take root

3. [Footnotes 1 and 2 from original source have been omitted.—ED.] The change in the function of the family here plays a decisive role: its "socializing" functions are increasingly taken over by outside groups and media. See my *Eros and Civilization* (Boston: Beacon Press, 1955), p. 96 ff.

is whittled down. The loss of this dimension, in which the power of negative thinking—the critical power of Reason—is at home, is the ideological counterpart to the very material process in which advanced industrial society silences and reconciles the opposition. The impact of progress turns Reason into submission to the facts of life, and to the dynamic capability of producing more and bigger facts of the same sort of life. The efficiency of the system blunts the individuals' recognition that it contains no facts which do not communicate the repressive power of the whole. If the individuals find themselves in the things which shape their life, they do so, not by giving, but by accepting the law of things—not the law of physics but the law of their society.

I have just suggested that the concept of alienation seems to become questionable when the individuals identify themselves with the existence which is imposed upon them and have in it their own development and satisfaction. This identification is not illusion but reality. However, the reality constitutes a more progressive stage of alienation. The latter has become entirely objective; the subject which is alienated is swallowed up by its alienated existence. There is only one dimension, and it is everywhere and in all forms. The achievements of progress defy ideological indictment as well as justification; before their tribunal, the "false consciousness" of their rationality becomes the true consciousness.

This absorption of ideology into reality does not, however, signify the "end of ideology." On the contrary, in a specific sense advanced industrial culture is *more* ideological than its predecessor, inasmuch as today the ideology is in the process of production itself.[4] In a provocative form, this proposition reveals the political aspects of the prevailing technological rationality. The productive apparatus and the goods and services which it produces "sell" or impose the social system as a whole. The means of mass transportation and communication, the commodities of lodging, food, and clothing, the irresistible output of the entertainment and information industry carry with them prescribed attitudes and habits, certain intellectual and emotional reactions which bind the consumers more or less pleasantly to the producers and, through the latter, to the whole. The products indoctrinate and manipulate; they promote a false consciousness which is immune against its falsehood. And as these beneficial products become available to more individuals in more social classes, the indoctrination they carry ceases to be publicity; it becomes a way of life. It is a good way of life—much better than before —and as a good way of life, it militates against qualitative change. Thus emerges a pattern of *one-dimensional thought and behavior* in which ideas, aspirations, and objectives that, by their content, transcend the established universe of discourse and action are either repelled or reduced to terms of this universe. They are redefined by the rationality of the given system and of its quantitative extension.

The trend may be related to a development in scientific method: operationalism in the physical, behaviorism in the social sciences. The common feature is a total empiricism in the treatment of concepts; their meaning is restricted to the representation of particular operations and behavior. The operational point of view is well illustrated by P. W. Bridgman's analysis of the concept of length:[5]

We evidently know what we mean by length if we can tell what the length of any

4. Theodor W. Adorno, *Prismen. Kulturkritik und Gesellschaft.* (Frankfurt: Suhrkamp, 1955), p. 24 f.

5. P. W. Bridgman, *The Logic of Modern Physics* (New York: Macmillan, 1928), p. 5. The operational doctrine has since been refined and qualified. Bridgman himself has extended the concept of "operation" to include the "paper-and-pencil" operations of the theorist (in Philipp J. Frank, *The Validation of Scientific Theories* [Boston: Beacon Press, 1954], Chap. II). The main impetus remains the same: it is "desirable" that the paper-and-pencil operations "be capable of eventual contact, although perhaps indirectly, with instrumental operations."

and every object is, and for the physicist nothing more is required. To find the length of an object, we have to perform certain physical operations. The concept of length is therefore fixed when the operations by which length is measured are fixed: that is, the concept of length involves as much and nothing more than the set of operations by which length is determined. In general, we mean by any concept nothing more than a set of operations; *the concept is synonymous with the corresponding set of operations.*

Bridgman has seen the wide implications of this mode of thought for the society at large:[6]

To adopt the operational point of view involves much more than a mere restriction of the sense in which we understand 'concept,' but means a far-reaching change in all our habits of thought, in that we shall no longer permit ourselves to use as tools in our thinking concepts of which we cannot give an adequate account in terms of operations.

Bridgman's prediction has come true. The new mode of thought is today the predominant tendency in philosophy, psychology, sociology, and other fields. Many of the most seriously troublesome concepts are being "eliminated" by showing that no adequate account of them in terms of operations or behavior can be given. The radical empiricist onslaught (I shall subsequently, in chapters VII and VIII, examine its claim to be empiricist) thus provides the methodological justification for the debunking of the mind by the intellectuals—a positivism which, in its denial of the transcending elements of Reason, forms the academic counterpart of the socially required behavior.

Outside the academic establishment, the "far-reaching change in all our habits of thought" is

more serious. It serves to coordinate ideas and goals with those exacted by the prevailing system, to enclose them in the system, and to repel those which are irreconcilable with the system. The reign of such a one-dimensional reality does not mean that materialism rules, and that the spiritual, metaphysical, and bohemian occupations are petering out. On the contrary, there is a great deal of "Worship together this week," "Why not try God," Zen, existentialism, and beat ways of life, etc. But such modes of protest and transcendence are no longer contradictory to the status quo and no longer negative. They are rather the ceremonial part of practical behaviorism, its harmless negation, and are quickly digested by the status quo as part of its healthy diet.

One-dimensional thought is systematically promoted by the makers of politics and their purveyors of mass information. Their universe of discourse is populated by self-validating hypotheses which, incessantly and monopolistically repeated, become hypnotic definitions or dictations. For example, "free" are the institutions which operate (and are operated on) in the countries of the Free World; other transcending modes of freedom are by definition either anarchism, communism, or propaganda. "Socialistic" are all encroachments on private enterprises not undertaken by private enterprise itself (or by government contracts), such as universal and comprehensive health insurance, or the protection of nature from all too sweeping commercialization, or the establishment of public services which may hurt private profit. This totalitarian logic of accomplished facts has its Eastern counterpart. There, freedom is the way of life instituted by a communist regime, and all other transcending modes of freedom are either capitalistic, or revisionist, or leftist sectarianism. In both camps, non-operational ideas are non-behavioral and subversive. The movement of thought is stopped at barriers which appear as the limits of Reason itself.

6. P. W. Bridgman, *The Logic of Modern Physics*, loc. cit., p. 31.

Such limitation of thought is certainly not new. Ascending modern rationalism, in its speculative as well as empirical form, shows a striking contrast between extreme critical radicalism in scientific and philosophic method on the one hand, and an uncritical quietism in the attitude toward established and functioning social institutions. Thus Descartes' *ego cogitans* was to leave the "great public bodies" untouched, and Hobbes held that "the present ought always to be preferred, maintained, and accounted best." Kant agreed with Locke in justifying revolution *if and when* it has succeeded in organizing the whole and in preventing subversion.

However, these accommodating concepts of Reason were always contradicted by the evident misery and injustice of the "great public bodies" and the effective, more or less conscious rebellion against them. Societal conditions existed which provoked and permitted real dissociation from the established state of affairs; a private as well as political dimension was present in which dissociation could develop into effective opposition, testing its strength and the validity of its objectives.

With the gradual closing of this dimension by the society, the self-limitation of thought assumes a larger significance. The interrelation between scientific-philosophical and societal processes, between theoretical and practical Reason, asserts itself "behind the back" of the scientists and philosophers. The society bars a whole type of oppositional operations and behavior; consequently, the concepts pertaining to them are rendered illusory or meaningless. Historical transcendence appears as metaphysical transcendence, not acceptable to science and scientific thought. The operational and behavioral point of view, practiced as a "habit of thought" at large, becomes the view of the established universe of discourse and action, needs and aspirations. The "cunning of Reason" works, as it so often did, in the interest of the powers that be. The insistence on operational

and behavioral concepts turns against the efforts to free thought and behavior *from* the given reality and *for* the suppressed alternatives. Theoretical and practical Reason, academic and social behaviorism meet on common ground: that of an advanced society which makes scientific and technical progress into an instrument of domination.

"Progress" is not a neutral term; it moves toward specific ends, and these ends are defined by the possibilities of ameliorating the human condition. Advanced industrial society is approaching the stage where continued progress would demand the radical subversion of the prevailing direction and organization of progress. This stage would be reached when material production (including the necessary services) becomes automated to the extent that all vital needs can be satisfied while necessary labor time is reduced to marginal time. From this point on, technical progress would transcend the realm of necessity, where it served as the instrument of domination and exploitation which thereby limited its rationality; technology would become subject to the free play of faculties in the struggle for the pacification of nature and of society.

Such a state is envisioned in Marx's notion of the "abolition of labor." The term "pacification of existence" seems better suited to designate the historical alternative of a world which —through an international conflict which transforms and suspends the contradictions within the established societies—advances on the brink of a global war. "Pacification of existence" means the development of man's struggle with man and with nature, under conditions where the competing needs, desires, and aspirations are no longer organized by vested interests in domination and scarcity—an organization which perpetuates the destructive forms of this struggle.

Today's fight against this historical alternative finds a firm mass basis in the underlying population, and finds its ideology in the rigid orientation of thought and behavior to the given universe of facts. Validated by the accomplishments of science and technology, justified by its growing productivity, the status quo defies all transcendence. Faced with the possibility of pacification on the grounds of its technical and intellectual achievements, the mature industrial society closes itself against this alternative. Operationalism, in theory and practice, becomes the theory and practice of *containment*. Underneath its obvious dynamics, this society is a thoroughly static system of life: self-propelling in its oppressive productivity and in its beneficial coordination. Containment of technical progress goes hand in hand with its growth in the established direction. In spite of the political fetters imposed by the status quo, the more technology appears capable of creating the conditions for pacification, the more are the minds and bodies of man organized against this alternative.

The most advanced areas of industrial society exhibit throughout these two features: a trend toward consummation of technological rationality, and intensive efforts to contain this trend within the established institutions. Here is the internal contradiction of this civilization: the irrational element in its rationality. It is the token of its achievements. The industrial society which makes technology and science its own is organized for the ever-more-effective domination of man and nature, for the ever-more-effective utilization of its resources. It becomes irrational when the success of these efforts opens new dimensions of human realization. Organization for peace is different from organization for war; the institutions which served the struggle for existence cannot serve the pacification of existence. Life as an end is qualitatively different from life as a means.

Such a qualitatively new mode of existence can never be envisaged as the mere by-product of economic and political changes, as the more or less spontaneous effect of the new institutions which constitute the necessary prerequisite. Qualitative change also involves a change in the *technical* basis on which this society rests— one which sustains the economic and political institutions through which the "second nature" of man as an aggressive object of administration is stabilized. The techniques of industrialization are political techniques; as such, they prejudge the possibilities of Reason and Freedom.

To be sure, labor must precede the reduction of labor, and industrialization must precede the development of human needs and satisfactions. But as all freedom depends on the conquest of alien necessity, the realization of freedom depends on the *techniques* of this conquest. The highest productivity of labor can be used for the perpetuation of labor, and the most efficient industrialization can serve the restriction and manipulation of needs.

When this point is reached, domination—in the guise of affluence and liberty—extends to all spheres of private and public existence, integrates all authentic opposition, absorbs all alternatives. Technological rationality reveals its political character as it becomes the great vehicle of better domination, creating a truly totalitarian universe in which society and nature, mind and body are kept in a state of permanent mobilization for the defense of this universe.

Notes

1. Victor Ferkiss, *Technological Man: The Myth and the Reality* (New York: The New American Library, Inc., 1969), p. 31.

2. Theodore Roszak, *The Making of a Counter Culture* (New York: Doubleday & Co., Inc., 1969).

18 / Man Under Control
Skinner

B. F. Skinner, the psychologist, would agree with Marcuse that a new and improved social order is desperately needed. However, his solution to man's predicament is not to revolt against control, but to move toward more rational control and conditioning. The question is not, Should we allow ourselves to be controlled?; we are already being controlled by a complex of institutional and environmental factors. The question is, rather, How can we scientifically design a culture to do a better and more efficient job in controlling the conditions under which people live?

Government, industry, education, religion, the family, and other social institutions use modes of control that are, to varying degrees, successful in molding and controlling human behavior. Skinner believes that some modes of control, such as punishment, are inefficient and undesirable because they lead to modes of countercontrol that block the achievement of their intended ends. These should be discarded in favor of methods that use positive rather than negative reinforcement of behavior. Behavior that is reinforced is strengthened. This can be done either by removing aversive, i.e., unwanted stimuli (negative reinforcement), or by rewarding it by presenting attractive, i.e., wanted stimuli (positive reinforcement). Skinner approves of and advises only the latter in satisfactorily controlling human behavior.

Skinner's view of man results from a scientific study of human behavior. There is nothing spontaneous or mysterious about human behavior that makes it different from the behavior of other organisms and thus places it outside the domain of scientific methods and principles. To think of man as an autonomous agent who can do what he pleases is to ignore the factors that determine preferences and to posit a freedom of choice that is indefensible against the overwhelming evidence that all behavior is caused. If freedom and dignity must be discarded to make way for predictability and control, then the sooner we discard them the better.

Skinner has devoted a great deal of attention not only to a systematic and intensive study of operant conditioning, but also to the technology of teaching and to problems relating to cultural design and behavioral engineering.

He has also shown a keen interest in utopian speculation, planning, and experimentation. This interest is coupled with an awareness that utopias have usually failed in the past and that, at present, the design of a fully utopian cultural design may be premature. This does not mean, however, that he thinks we should stop trying to achieve it. At the very least, there can be a piecemeal improvement of cultural practices. The science of behavior is a science in the making. The possibility of a utopia is in direct proportion to the development of this science.

One can get an idea of how Skinner would envisage a totally planned society by reading his utopian novel, *Walden Two* (1948). Named in honor of Henry David Thoreau's original utopian experiment, Walden Two is a community of a thousand members planned and instituted by T. E. Frazier, a behavioral engineer. The affairs of the community are overseen by a Board of Planners and are carried out by the managers, workers, and scientists, all of whom work on a labor-credit system. There is communal ownership of property and collective sharing of the rights and responsibilities of membership. The cohesive community is virtually self-sufficient. Marriage of couples still exists but, as children are raised in community nurseries and cared for by all members of the utopia, the nuclear family has been replaced by the communal family. Leisure time is plentiful and filled with creative, educational activities. Religion is virtually nonexistent. Moral training is completed by the time a child is six, due to refined techniques of positive reinforcement. In such a carefully controlled community, democracy is considered superfluous because it rests upon the false assumption that man can choose freely and ignores the fact that, in actuality, the state determines man. But totalitarianism would be rejected equally, because it fails to be genuinely experimental, employs terror and brute force as means of control, and usually overpropagandizes. What is needed to achieve an ideal society, Frazier insists, is "a constantly experimental attitude" and the courage to develop and consistently apply a science of behavior for the good of mankind.

In a new preface to *Walden Two* written twenty years after its initial publication, Skinner reaffirmed his commitment to the ideal of a planned community similar to the one he had described in his earlier book.[1] An adequate and precise science of behavior will point the way to a transformation of man's cultural environment and thus man himself. Then we shall see at last, Skinner believes, "what man can make of man." In the following selection from his most controversial book, *Beyond Freedom and Dignity* (1970), Skinner sums up his view of human nature.

What Is Man?

It is in the nature of an experimental analysis of human behavior that it should strip away the functions previously assigned to autonomous man and transfer them one by one to the controlling environment. The analysis leaves less and less for autonomous man to do. But what about man himself? Is there not something about a person which is more than a living body? Unless something called a self survives, how can we speak of self-knowledge or self-control? To whom is the injunction "Know thyself" addressed?

It is an important part of the contingencies to which a young child is exposed that his own body is the only part of his environment which remains the same (*idem*) from moment to moment and day to day. We say that he discovers his *identity* as he learns to distinguish between his body and the rest of the world. He does this long before the community teaches him to call things by name and to distinguish "me" from "it" or "you."

A self is a repertoire of behavior appropriate to a given set of contingencies. A substantial part of the conditions to which a person is exposed may play a dominant role, and under other conditions a person may report, "I'm not myself today," or, "I couldn't have done what you said I did, because that's not like me." The identity conferred upon a self arises from the contingencies responsible for the behavior. Two or more repertoires generated by different sets

From *Beyond Freedom and Dignity,* by B. F. Skinner. Copyright © 1971 by B. F. Skinner. Reprinted by permission of Alfred A. Knopf, Inc.

of contingencies compose two or more selves. A person possesses one repertoire appropriate to his life with his friends and another appropriate to his life with his family, and a friend may find him a very different person if he sees him with his family or his family if they see him with his friends. The problem of identity arises when situations are intermngled, as when a person finds himself with both his family and his friends at the same time.

Self-knowledge and self-control imply two selves in this sense. The self-knower is almost always a product of social contingencies, but the self that is known may come from other sources. The controlling self (the conscience or superego) is of social origin, but the controlled self is more likely to be the product of genetic susceptibilities to reinforcement (the id, or the Old Adam). The controlling self generally represents the interests of others, the controlled self the interests of the individual.

The picture which emerges from a scientific analysis is not of a body with a person inside, but of a body which *is* a person in the sense that it displays a complex repertoire of behavior. The picture is, of course, unfamiliar. The man thus portrayed is a stranger, and from the traditional point of view he may not seem to be a man at all. "For at least one hundred years," said Joseph Wood Krutch, "we have been prejudiced in every theory, including economic determinism, mechanistic behaviorism, and relativism, that reduces the stature of man until he ceases to be man at all in any sense that the humanists of an earlier generation would recognize." Matson has argued that "the empirical behavioral scientist . . . denies, if only by implication, that a unique being, called Man, exists." "What is now under attack," said Maslow, "is the 'being' of man." C. S. Lewis put it quite bluntly: Man is being abolished.

There is clearly some difficulty in identifying the man to whom these expressions refer. Lewis cannot have meant the human species, for not only is it not being abolished, it is filling the earth. (As a result it may eventually abolish itself through disease, famine, pollution, or a nuclear holocaust, but that is not what Lewis meant.) Nor are individual men growing less effective or productive. We are told that what is threatened is "man *qua* man," or "man in his humanity," or "man as Thou not It," or "man as a person not a thing." These are not very helpful expressions, but they supply a clue. What is being abolished is autonomous man—the inner man, the homunculus, the possessing demon, the man defended by the literatures of freedom and dignity.

His abolition has long been overdue. Autonomous man is a device used to explain what we cannot explain in any other way. He has been constructed from our ignorance, and as our understanding increases, the very stuff of which he is composed vanishes. Science does not dehumanize man, it de-homunculizes him, and it must do so if it is to prevent the abolition of the human species. To man *qua* man we readily say good riddance. Only by dispossessing him can we turn to the real causes of human behavior. Only then can we turn from the inferred to the observed, from the miraculous to the natural, from the inaccessible to the manipulable.

It is often said that in doing so we must treat the man who survives as a mere animal. "Animal" is a pejorative term, but only because "man" has been made spuriously honorific. Krutch has argued that whereas the traditional view supports Hamlet's exclamation, "How like a god!," Pavlov, the behavioral scientist, emphasized "How like a dog!" But that was a step

forward. A god is the archetypal pattern of an explanatory fiction, of a miracle-working mind, of the metaphysical. Man is much more than a dog, but like a dog he is within range of a scientific analysis.

It is true that much of the experimental analysis of behavior has been concerned with lower organisms. Genetic differences are minimized by using special strains; environmental histories can be controlled, perhaps from birth; strict regimens can be maintained during long experiments; and very little of this is possible with human subjects. Moreover, in working with lower animals the scientist is less likely to put his own responses to the experimental conditions among his data, or to design contingencies with an eye to their effect on him rather than on the experimental organism he is studying. No one is disturbed when physiologists study respiration, reproduction, nutrition, or endocrine systems in animals; they do so to take advantage of very great similarities. Comparable similarities in behavior are being discovered. There is, of course, always the danger that methods designed for the study of lower animals will emphasize only those characteristics which they have in common with men, but we cannot discover what is "essentially" human until we have investigated nonhuman subjects. Traditional theories of autonomous man have exaggerated species differences. Some of the complex contingencies of reinforcement now under investigation generate behavior in lower organisms which, if the subjects were human, would traditionally be said to involve higher mental processes.

Man is not made into a machine by analyzing his behavior in mechanical terms. Early theories of behavior, as we have seen, represented man as a push-pull automaton, close to the nineteenth-century notion of a machine, but progress has been made. Man is a machine in the sense that he is a complex system behaving in lawful ways, but the complexity is extraordinary. His capacity to adjust to contingencies of reinforcement will perhaps be eventually simulated by machines, but this has not yet been done, and the living system thus simulated will remain unique in other ways.

Nor is man made into a machine by inducing him to use machines. Some machines call for behavior which is repetitious and monotonous, and we escape from them when we can, but others enormously extend our effectiveness in dealing with the world around us. A person may respond to very small things with the help of an electron microscope and to very large things with radiotelescopes, and in doing so he may seem quite inhuman to those who use only their unaided senses. A person may act upon the environment with the delicate precision of a micromanipulator or with the range and power of a space rocket, and his behavior may seem inhuman to those who rely only on muscular contractions. (It has been argued that the apparatus used in the operant laboratory misrepresents natural behavior because it introduces an external source of power, but men use external sources when they fly kites, sail boats, or shoot bows and arrows. They would have to abandon all but a small fraction of their achievements if they used only the power of their muscles.) People record their behavior in books and other media, and the use they make of the records may seem quite inhuman to those who can use only what they remember. People describe complex contingencies in the form of rules, and rules for manipulating rules, and they introduce them into electronic systems which "think" with a speed that seems quite inhuman to the unaided thinker. Human beings do all this with machines, and they would be less than human if they did not. What we now regard as machine-like behavior was, in fact, much commoner before the invention of these devices. The slave in the cotton field, the bookkeeper on his high stool, the student being drilled by a teacher—these were the machine-like men.

Machines replace people when they do what people have done, and the social consequences may be serious. As technology advances, machines will take over more and more of the functions of men, but only up to a point. We build machines which reduce some of the aversive features of our environment (grueling labor, for example) and which produce more positive reinforcers. We build them precisely because they do so. We have no reason to build machines to be reinforced by these consequences, and to do so would be to deprive ourselves of reinforcement. If the machines man makes eventually make him wholly expendable, it will be by accident, not design.

An important role of autonomous man has been to give human behavior direction, and it is often said that in dispossessing an inner agent we leave man himself without a purpose. As one writer has put it, "Since a scientific psychology must regard human behavior objectively, as determined by necessary laws, it must represent human behavior as unintentional." But "necessary laws" would have this effect only if they referred exclusively to antecedent conditions. Intention and purpose refer to selective consequences, the effects of which can be formulated in "necessary laws." Has life, in all the forms in which it exists on the surface of the earth, a purpose, and is this evidence of intentional design? The primate hand evolved *in order that* things might be more successfully manipulated, but its purpose is to be found not in a prior design but rather in the process of selection. Similarly, in operant conditioning the purpose of a skilled movement of the hand is to be found in the consequences which follow it. A pianist neither acquires nor executes the behavior of playing a scale smoothly because of a prior intention of doing so. Smoothly played scales are reinforcing for many reasons, and they select skilled movements. In neither the evolution of the human hand nor in the acquired use of the hand is any prior intention or purpose at issue.

The argument for purpose seems to be strengthened by moving back into the darker recesses of mutation. Jacques Barzun has argued that Darwin and Marx both neglected not only human purpose but the creative purpose responsible for the variations upon which natural selection plays. It may prove to be the case, as some geneticists have argued, that mutations are not entirely random, but nonrandomness is not necessarily the proof of a creative mind. Mutations will not be random when genetics explicitly design them in order that an organism will meet specific conditions of selection more successfully, and geneticists will then seem to be playing the role of the creative Mind in pre-evolutionary theory, but the purpose they display will have to be sought in their culture, in the social environment which has induced them to make genetic changes appropriate to contingencies of survival.

There is a difference between biological and individual purpose in that the latter can be felt. No one could have felt the purpose in the development of the human hand, whereas a person can in a sense feel the purpose with which he plays a smooth scale. But he does not play a smooth scale *because* he feels the purpose of doing so; what he feels is a by-product of his behavior in relation to its consequences. The relation of the human hand to the contingencies of survival under which it evolved is, of course, out of reach of personal observation; the relation of the behavior to contingencies of reinforcement which have generated it is not.

A scientific analysis of behavior dispossesses autonomous man and turns the control he has been said to exert over to the environment. The individual may then seem particularly vulnerable. He is henceforth to be controlled by the world around him, and in large part by other men. Is he not then simply a victim? Certainly men have been victims, as they have been victimizers, but the word is too strong. It implies despoliation, which is by no means an essential consequence of interpersonal control. But even under benevolent control is the individual not at best a spectator who may watch what happens but is helpless to do anything about it? Is he not "at a dead end in his long struggle to control his own destiny"?

It is only autonomous man who has reached a dead end. Man himself may be controlled by his environment, but it is an environment which is almost wholly of his own making. The physical environment of most people is largely man-made. The surfaces a person walks on, the walls which shelter him, the clothing he wears, many of the foods he eats, the tools he uses, the vehicles he moves about in, most of the things he listens to and looks at are human products. The social environment is obviously man-made—it generates the language a person speaks, the customs he follows, and the behavior he exhibits with respect to the ethical, religious, governmental, economic, educational, and psychotherapeutic institutions which control him. The evolution of a culture is in fact a kind of gigantic exercise in self-control. As the individual controls himself by manipulating the world in which he lives, so the human species has constructed an environment in which its members behave in a highly effective way. Mistakes have been made, and we have no assurance that the environment man has constructed will continue to provide gains which outstrip the losses, but man as we know him, for better or for worse, is what man has made of man.

This will not satisfy those who cry "Victim!" C. S. Lewis protested: ". . . the power of man to make himself what he pleases . . . means . . . the power of some men to make other men what they please." This is inevitable in the nature of cultural evolution. The controlling *self* must be distinguished from the controlled self, even when they are both inside the same skin, and when control is exercised through the design of an external environment, the selves are, with minor exceptions, distinct.

The person who unintentionally or intentionally introduces a new cultural practice is only one among possibly billions who will be affected by it. If this does not seem like an act of self-control, it is only because we have misunderstood the nature of self-control in the individual.

When a person changes his physical or social environment "intentionally"—that is, in order to change human behavior, possibly including his own—he plays two roles: one as a controller, as the designer of a controlling culture, and another as the controlled, as the product of a culture. There is nothing inconsistent about this; it follows from the nature of the evolution of a culture, with or without intentional design.

The human species has probably not undergone much genetic change in recorded time. We have only to go back a thousand generations to reach the artists of the caves of Lascaux. Features which bear directly on survival (such as resistance to disease) change substantially in a thousand generations, but the child of one of the Lascaux artists transplanted to the world of today might be almost indistinguishable from a modern child. It is possible that he would learn more slowly than his modern counterpart, that he could maintain only a smaller repertoire without confusion, or that he would forget more quickly; we cannot be sure. But we can be sure that a twentieth-century child transplanted to the civilization of Lascaux would not be very different from the children he met there, for we have seen what happens when a modern child is raised in an impoverished environment.

Man has greatly changed himself as a person in the same period of time by changing the world in which he lives. Something of the order of a hundred generations will cover the development of modern religious practices, and something of the same order of magnitude modern government and law. Perhaps no more than twenty generations will account for modern industrial practices, and possibly no more than four or five for education and psychotherapy. The physical and biological technologies which have increased man's sensitivity to the world around him and his power to change that world have taken no more than four or five generations.

Man has "controlled his own destiny," if that expression means anything at all. The man that man has made is the product of the culture man has devised. He has emerged from two quite different processes of evolution: the biological evolution responsible for the human species and the cultural evolution carried out by that species. Both of these processes of evolution may now accelerate because they are both subject to intentional design. Men have already changed their genetic endowment by breeding selectively and by changing contingencies of survival, and they may now begin to introduce mutations directly related to survival. For a long time men have introduced new practices which serve as cultural mutations, and they have changed the conditions under which practices are selected. They may now begin to do both with a clearer eye to the consequences.

Man will presumably continue to change, but we cannot say in what direction. No one could have predicted the evolution of the human species at any point in its early history, and the direction of intentional genetic design will depend upon the evolution of a culture which is itself unpredictable for similar reasons. "The limits of perfection of the human species," said Etienne Cabet in *Voyage en Icarie,* "are as yet unknown." But, of course, there are no limits. The human species will never reach a final state of perfection before it is exterminated— "some say in fire, some in ice," and some in radiation.

The individual occupies a place in a culture not unlike his place in the species, and in early evolutionary theory that place was hotly debated. Was the species simply a type of individual, and if so, in what sense could it evolve? Darwin himself declared species "to be purely subjective inventions of the taxonomist." A species has no existence except as a collection of individuals, nor has a family, tribe, race, nation, or class. A culture has no existence apart from the behavior of the individuals who maintain its practices. It is always an individual who behaves, who acts upon the environment and is changed by the consequences of his action, and who maintains the social contingencies which *are* a culture. The individual is the carrier of both his species and his culture. Cultural practices, like genetic traits, are transmitted from individual to individual. A new practice, like a new genetic trait, appears first in an individual and tends to be transmitted if it contributes to his survival as an individual.

Yet, the individual is at best a locus in which many lines of development come together in a unique set. His individuality is unquestioned. Every cell in his body is a unique genetic product, as unique as that classic mark of individuality, the fingerprint. And even within the most regimented culture every personal history is unique. No intentional culture can destroy that uniqueness, and, as we have seen, any effort to do so would be bad design. But the individual nevertheless remains merely a stage in a process which began long before he came into existence and will long outlast him. He has no ultimate responsibility for a species trait or a cultural practice, even though it was he who underwent the mutation or introduced the practice which became part of the species or culture. Even if Lamarck had been right in supposing that the individual could change his genetic structure through personal effort, we should have to point to the environmental circumstances re-

sponsible for the effort, as we shall have to do when geneticists begin to change the human endowment. And when an individual engages in the intentional design of a cultural practice, we must turn to the culture which induces him to do so and supplies the art or science he uses.

One of the great problems of individualism, seldom recognized as such, is death—the inescapable fate of the individual, the final assault on freedom and dignity. Death is one of those remote events which are brought to bear on behavior only with the aid of cultural practices. What we see is the death of others, as in Pascal's famous metophor: "Imagine a number of men in chains, all under sentence of death, some of whom are each day butchered in the sight of the others; those remaining see their own condition in that of their fellows, and looking at each other with grief and despair await their turn. This is an image of the human condition." Some religions have made death more important by picturing a future existence in heaven or hell, but the individualist has a special reason to fear death, engineered not by a religion but by the literatures of freedom and dignity. It is the prospect of personal annihilation. The individualist can find no solace in reflecting upon any contribution which will survive him. He has refused to act for the good of others and is therefore not reinforced by the fact that others whom he has helped will outlive him. He has refused to be concerned for the survival of his culture and is not reinforced by the fact that the culture will long survive him. In the defense of his own freedom and dignity he has denied the contributions of the past and must therefore relinquish all claim upon the future. . . .

Afterword / Perspective on Human Prospects

If we could represent these images of man in a pictorial way, we could include them in a time capsule for citizens of other planets or for future citizens of this planet. These images reflect man's self-image, or what he thinks he is. They also portray his hopes as to what he can be. Moreover, each reveals something of the historical period in which the portrait is drawn. In the traditional essentialist view of man as a rational animal or spiritual being, the portrait of man is clearer in outline, more definite in content. Descartes tried to reconcile the view of nature implied by the new physics with the older view of man as *essentially* a spiritual being. The result was his dual-substance theory. Man is composed of two independent substances: the spiritual and the material, or mind and body. Although a dualistic view of human nature goes back to at least the time of Socrates and Plato, it is still a prevalent view of human nature. For many of the ancient Greeks, man's rational nature, his capacity for thought and intelligence, put him in touch with a realm beyond nature. In the Medieval period, as a child of God, his soul put him in touch with the divine.

Yet this dualistic view of human nature raises serious difficulties. The arguments for the existence of a separate soul substance, or a mind, have become increasingly difficult to justify empirically. In his *Concept of Mind,* Gilbert Ryle asserts that it is a fundamental mistake to conceive of the activities of thinking, feeling, and sensing as nonphysical properties belonging to a spiritual substance inside the body. To think of consciousness in this way is to succumb to what he calls "the myth of the ghost in the machine."

Also, what Descartes thought were clear distinctions between mind-body, man-animal, and man-machine seem no longer clear. Whether or not the term "machine" should be applied to sophisticated electronic devices such as computers and robots, these devices perform more and more tasks (predicting, translating, playing chess, speaking) that once were thought to belong exclusively to man's capacity. Man is relying increasingly on these and other devices (e.g., heart pacers, artificial organs and limbs, and sensory units for the blind). The development of computers with sophisticated capacities for learning, self-improvement, memory, language, and the performance of a variety of tasks blurs some of the distinctions between man and machine. A favorite theme of science fiction is man's ambiguity about the difference between himself and the machine.

The materialistic view of man as simply a physiological organism, which was developed in opposition to Descartes' dual-substance theory by his contemporary Thomas Hobbes and others, is similar to the viewpoint of many writers today. Studies in neurosciences indicate a close correlation between the occurrences of mental events (e.g., thoughts and feelings) and the neural events in the brain. Recent experiments with drugs point to the close relationship between the chemical makeup of the brain and such psychological states as alertness and confidence. These investigations show the intimate way in which our behavior is bound up with the condition of our bodies. Descartes and Hobbes had rather limited views on the nature of the physical world and the biological organism. If the physical world is looked upon as a complex, relational system of energy, the distinctions between the living and the nonliving, the organic and the inorganic, may have to be revised. Likewise, mind and body might then be seen as two expressions of the same factor, energy, and man be totally explained within the new concept of nature—without the Cartesian additive "something more" or the reductive Hobbesian "something less."

Like the existentialists, Ortega y Gasset sees man through a totally different prism. By comparison to the essentialist image of man, his perspective seems much less definite in outline and content. Although Ortega's emphasis upon consciousness seems to return to the Cartesian starting point, he attempts to avoid any dualism between mind-body, man-world, or man-nature. Man is primarily consciousness, a being in and of the world. The lived experience that we know most intimately as ourselves is the central fact of what man is. Man's unique situation cannot be solved merely by changing his social conditions or his physiological makeup. He must first realize his unique condition and his dreadful freedom before he can realize his highest potentialities.

Because of Darwin's influence, we have come to accept the fact of man's evolution. The species man is not an eternally fixed essence. Because of Marx's influence, we have come to accept man as an active, productive, and, above all, a social animal. Today we are aware that our consciousness, language, and values are inseparable from our social context and social origins. We also tend to see and analyze our troubles—alienation, racism, poverty, crime, war—from a social point of view. Marcuse, like Marx, sees man as thoroughly social. His nature is bound to his social and cultural structure. Man has basic needs, but his nature is more or less plastic to social change. His transformation must come through social and political changes in the way in which he organizes his products and his relations to other men. If man's nature has been determined by his social structure and organization, it can be redetermined by redirecting and controlling these same means. But his essential freedom is more threatened today by that structure and by controls that were only hinted at in Marx. Marcuse sees man in a crisis situation. Unless he can overcome the totalitarian restraints of the industrial and technological society, he will end with a one-dimensional existence. Marcuse calls not for piecemeal compromise or reform but for radical social and cultural change. In his later writings, he sees some hope in the man of the counterculture who exhibits sensibilities to human possibilities that have been repressed by the technological establishment. He envisions a new society in which plan and work and reason and joy are merged into a new humanism.

From the perspective of the determinist B. F. Skinner, Marcuse's vision of a freer society and a liberated humanity places him, along with Ortega y Gasset, among those who continue to believe, despite all evidence to the contrary, in the freedom and dignity of a so-called "autonomous man." Skinner considers such an image of man to be not only illusory but pernicious. It is illusory because it assumes that man's essential controlling force is an inner free will, while in fact everything man does is determined by his external environment which, when controlled and manipulated, controls and manipulates him. The belief in autonomous man is pernicious to Skinner because it distracts from the pressing problem of finding better and more efficient modes of control and stands in the way of the development of what is urgently needed, a perfected science of human behavior.

Many people today have a sense of living in a world in which the old opposites are no longer clear: mind/body, man/society, man/nature. Along with this is the strong presentiment that everything can be changed—the physical environment, the biological organism, consciousness, society, culture, religion, art, and philosophy—in short, everything that has been thought fixed enough to yield a stable definition of man. The issue now is not primarily whether we initiate techniques for change upon the inner man or his external environment; in many ways this distinction between inner and outer no longer makes sense. The question today is the direction toward which the change is to take place. Thus we return to the question of the good and the issue of moral choice, which was outlined in Part IV.

Related Reading

(Works marked * are available in paperbound editions.)

*Anderson, H. R., ed. *Minds and Machines.* Englewood Cliffs, N. J.: Prentice-Hall, 1964.

*Ardrey, Robert. *African Genesis.* New York: Atheneum, 1961.

*Barrett, William. *Irrational Man.* New York: Doubleday & Co., Inc., 1962.

*Breisach, Ernst. *Introduction to Modern Existentialism.* New York: Grove Press, 1962.

Burtt, Edwin, ed. *The English Philosophers from Bacon to Mill.* New York: The Modern Library, 1939.

*Cassirer, Ernst. *Essay on Man: An Introduction to a Philosophy of Human Culture.* New York: Doubleday, 1953.

Comfort, Alex. *The Nature of Human Nature.* New York: Harper, 1967.

*Doney, Willis, ed. *Descartes: A Collection of Critical Essays.* New York: Doubleday & Co., Inc., 1967.

*Douglas, Jack D., ed. *Freedom and Tyranny: Social Problems in a Technological Society.* New York: Alfred A. Knopf, 1970.

Ellul, Jacques. *The Technological Society,* trans. J. Wilkinson. New York: Vintage Books, 1964.

*Ferkiss, Victor C. *Technological Man: The Myth and the Reality.* New York: The New American Library, Inc., 1969.

Ferrater Mora, José. *Ortega y Gasset: An Outline of his Philosophy.* New Haven: Yale University Press, 1957.

*Flew, Antony, ed. *Body, Mind, and Death.* New York: Collier Books, 1965.

*Frankl, Viktor E. *Man's Search for Meaning.* New York: Washington Square Press, 1963.

*Friedman, Maurice. *To Deny Our Nothingness: Contemporary Images of Man.* New York: Dell Publishing Co., 1967.

*Fromm, Erich. *Marx's Concept of Man.* New York: Frederick Ungar Pub. Co., 1961.

*Grene, Marjorie. *Introduction to Existentialism.* Chicago: University of Chicago Press, 1959.

*Hayek, F. A. *The Counter-Revolution of Science.* London: Collier-Macmillan Ltd., 1955.

*Hook, Sidney, ed. *Dimensions of Mind.* New York: New York University Press, 1960.

Kahn, Herman and A. J. Wiener. *The Year 2000.* New York: Macmillan Co., 1967.

*Kaufman, Walter, ed. *Existentialism from Dostoevsky to Sartre.* New York: Meridian Books, Inc., 1956.

*Kelley, W. L. and A. Tallon. *Readings in the Philospohy of Man.* New York: McGraw-Hill Book Co., 1967.

Kinkade, Kathleen. *A Walden Two Experiment: The First Five Years of Twin Oaks Community.* New York: Morrow, 1973.

Krutch, Joseph Wood. *The Measure of Man.* Indianapolis: Bobbs-Merrill, 1954.

Lamont, Corliss. *The Philosophy of Humanism,* 4th ed. New York: Philosophical Library, 1962.

*Lorenz, Konrad. *On Aggression.* New York: Harcourt, Brace & World, 1966.

Mann, Jesse A. and Gerald F. Kreyche, eds. *Reflections of Man.* New York: Harcourt, Brace & World, Inc., 1966.

*Marcuse, Herbert. *Reason and Revolution,* 2d ed. New York: Humanities Press, 1954.

*———. *Eros and Civilization.* New York: Alfred A. Knopf, Inc., 1955.

*May, Rollo. *Psychology and the Human Dilemma.* Princeton, N. J.: Van Nostrand, 1967.

*Medawar, P. B. *The Future of Man.* New York: New American Library, 1959.

*Mendel, Arthur P., ed. *Essential Works of Marxism.* New York: Bantam Books, Inc., 1961.

*Mumford, Lewis. *The Transformations of Man.* New York: Crowell-Collier Pub. Co., 1956.

*Niebuhr, Reinhold. *Marx and Engels on Religion.* New York: Schocken Books, 1964.

*Nielsen, H. A., ed. *The Visages of Adam.* New York: Random House, 1968.

*Odajnyk, Walter. *Marxism and Existentialism.* New York: Doubleday & Co., Inc., 1965.

Ortega y Gasset, José. *The Revolt of the Masses.* New York: W. W. Norton, 1932.

Platt, John R., ed. *New Views on the Nature of Man.* Chicago: University of Chicago Press, 1965.

———. *The Step to Man.* New York: John Wiley, 1966.

*Roszak, Theodore. *The Making of a Counter Culture.* New York: Doubleday & Co., Inc., 1969.

*Ryle, Gilbert. *The Concept of Mind.* New York: Barnes & Noble, Inc., 1949.

*Shaffer, Jerome A. *Philosophy of Mind.* Englewood Cliffs, N. J.: Prentice-Hall, 1963.

*Skinner, B. F. *Beyond Freedom and Dignity.* New York: Knopf, 1971.

*———. *Science and Human Behavior.* New York: Macmillan, 1953.

*———. *Walden Two.* New York: Macmillan, 1948.

*Slater, Philip. *The Pursuit of Loneliness: American Culture at the Breaking Point.* Boston: Beacon, 1970.

*Teilhard de Chardin, Pierre. *The Phenomenon of Man.* New York: Harper, 1959.

*White, Alan R. *The Philosophy of Mind.* New York: Random House, 1967.

PART SIX

Confrontation with Religious Experience:
Commitment to Faith

To see a World in a Grain of Sand
And a Heaven in a Wild Flower
Hold Infinity in the palm of your hand
And Eternity in an hour.
                              William Blake

Religion is morality tinged with emotion.
                              Matthew Arnold

Religion is what the individual does with his own
solitariness . . . if you are never solitary, you are never
religious.   Alfred North Whitehead

We are deprived of Truth by the energy
with which we immerse ourselves in *a
truth.*
                              Karl Barth

Neither faith nor doubt can be eliminated from man as
man.
                              Paul Tillich

Words have a power, a terrible power, of intruding
between man and God.
                              St. Ignatius

Religion — the opiate of the people.
                              Karl Marx

He who cleaveth firmly unto God is already
directed in the right way.
                              The Koran

Men overlook traces of divinity by reason of their
incredulity.
                              Heraclitus

Religious phenomena are to be understood only as the
model of the neurotic symptoms of the individual.
                              Sigmund Freud

When it comes to the question of life itself we cannot wait
for the ultimate solution to be offered by the intellect.
                              D. T. Suzuki

Introduction / Religion Revisited

Religions make a promise: a deeply moving encounter with the divine will transform human life and open the person to a totally new way of experiencing the world. But the encounter with religious experience is not confined to any one sect or any one culture or counterculture. Like the experience of falling in love, it can happen to the rich or poor, the moral or immoral, the brilliant or the not-so-brilliant.

Persons who have such an experience often come out of it with a different conception of themselves and of reality. Their entire life style may be transformed. The old commitments, values, daily habits, and friendships pale by comparison. The former life now seems stale and confused and concerned about the wrong things. The experience may have demanded a radical choice in the face of much personal anguish and soul searching. The new commitment often meets with hostility or smug silence from unsympathetic friends and relatives. Because the commitment to God can be so momentous, religious commitments have often served as models of what "total commitment" means.

Although there has been a weakening of the traditional forms and institutions of religion, confrontation with religious experience is just as moving and total religious commitment is just as difficult today as in the past. Converts feel the anguish and pain of moving into (and out of) the new religious revivals and movements. However, the revival of fundamentalism and the renewal of the beliefs and practices of the religions of the East are only a small part of a pervasive religious feeling. It seems to promise a new age—an age of liberation from the old and dying conceptions of life and human relationships; a new, more open life; a return to a more lyrical, simple, and childlike experience; a new sense of human potentiality and communal feeling—the Kingdom of God, the New Earth, a time when "we shall overcome."

We should be careful in calling apocalyptic moods and visions "religion." When we try to formulate a definition of religion that includes the wide variety of even such traditional religions as Greek polytheism and the many forms of Christianity, Buddhism, and Hinduism, it is difficult to find a common characteristic to express the unique nature of religion. We can look for a definition in its external manifestations, such as its institutions, ceremonies, forms of worship, and rituals. We can also look for a definition in terms of its more internal, psychological characteristics. The latter would include its attitudes, beliefs, emotions, special feelings of awe and reverence. One such definition, which emphasizes the internal and is perhaps as good a start as any, is the very inclusive definition given by Josiah Royce, the American philosopher. Royce defines religion as consisting of three interconnecting components.

> These three elements, then, go to constitute any religion. A religion must teach some moral code, must in some way inspire a strong feeling of devotion to that code, and in so doing must show something in the nature of things that answers to that code or that serves to reinforce the feeling. A religion is therefore practical, emotional, and theoretical; it teaches us to do, to feel, and to believe, and it teaches the belief as a means to its teaching of the action and of the feeling.[1]

Each of these components, when isolated from the others, is insufficient to define religion. A feeling is not religious merely because it is strong or "elevated." Nor is believing in a god or the supernatural sufficient in itself. A mere moral code is not religion either, although every religion does involve some form of "Thou shalt." All three factors interrelated through personal commitment are required. There must be a moral code, an emotional content which inspires devotion, and a view of reality that supports the first two factors.

Although any definition has its limitations, especially when the subject is as broad and complex as religion, we shall use Royce's definition as a point of departure for this part. Royce's definition emphasizes the moral and experiental components of religion. Religious belief, the "theoretical" religious component, seems only supportive in this definition. Yet religion has been identified with the assent to a set of propositions or truths about God and His nature.

In the first selection that follows, Ernest Nagel sketches and argues against the major arguments put forward for the existence of the God associated with the major Western religious world-view, theism. His own view of religion emphasizes the social and communal aspects of religion; the profession of creeds is only a minor aspect of religion. Nagel also denies the claim that mystical experience provides evidence for the existence of a deity and asserts that a secular, utilitarian ethics can be the basis for a perfectly adequate moral code for mankind.

In the next selection, Reinhold Niebuhr, using a Biblical-Christian interpretation of history, maintains that a purely secular ethics is inadequate. It evades some hard historical facts regarding the moral weakness of man. He rejects secularism, the idolatrous religions of nationalism and world communism, and mysticism as not providing a true account of man's search for meaning. Only a Biblical faith symbolizes and accounts for the trials of man in history and provides the basis for a genuine morality.

The third reading, a selection from Buddhist scriptures, supplies an excellent example of a religion in which the practical and experiential dominate the theoretical. Many regard Buddhism as simply a system of self-therapy and not a religion at all. The Buddha taught that life is suffering. Suffering has causes that are extinguishable by mental and spiritual discipline, through which the person can control his acts and intentions. Contrary to Niebuhr, the Buddhists deny the existence of a permanent self. Attachment to the illusory self leads to egoism, the craving for fame and fortune, and, hence, suffering and frustration. The young man Gautama Siddhartha became the Buddha (one who had attained *bodhi*, or enlightenment) by discipline that came to fruition in a religious experience. The attainment and experience of Nirvana is a focal part of all Buddhist teaching.

The fourth selection turns to the experiential aspect of the religious response and the central place mysticism has had in the history of religion. Huston Smith, a contemporary philosopher of religion, discusses the alleged differences between drug-induced experiences and mystical experiences, and the relation between drug experiences, religion, and the truth value of religious experience.

In the final selection, Paul Tillich attempts to redefine faith as the state of ultimate concern and as containing elements of risk, doubt, and uncertainty. His existential doubt attempts to go beyond the doubt discussed by Nagel. He defines faith so that it is not only compatible with reason and science but actually supplements the rational life. Tillich attempts to integrate the theoretical, practical, and experiential components of religion in a way that meets the requirements of man in a modern world.

Note

1. Josiah Royce, *The Religious Aspects of Philosophy* (Boston: Houghton Mifflin Co., 1885), p. 4.

The philosophy of religion is not in itself religion, nor need it entail a religious faith or commitment. It deals with the origin, nature, and function of religion and analyzes such central concepts as God, worship, creation, and revelation. Recently, it has shown a great deal of interest in analyzing religious language and assessing the special claims made regarding religious knowledge. Although religion is directly expressed in the worship, meditation, rituals, and practices of particular sects, it also has a doctrinal aspect. Its theoretical component, usually embodied in its doctrinal theology, accompanies and supports the experiential and moral components of a religion. Historically, the major interest of the philosopher in religion has been this theoretical component, in analyzing religious beliefs about the divine, man, and human destiny.

At the center of philosophical questions about religion are the classical arguments for the existence of God. These arguments differ in the strength of their claims and their mode of procedure. The ontological argument claims that the conclusion, God exists, has been deductively proven: given the concept of God as perfection, it must follow that He exists. The following selection refers to this argument as "purely dialectical" and "without appeal to empirical data." Other arguments claim that the premises show sufficient evidence to warrant the conclusion that God exists, although they are not sufficient to constitute strict proof. The argument for a first cause, the cosmological argument, is based upon cause-and-effect relationships in the world. The argument for a divine designer, the design argument, is based upon the fact of order in the world. Other arguments appeal to our moral nature or to mystical experience in order to justify the existence of God.

Ernest Nagel, the contemporary American philosopher (b. 1901), has made extensive and important contributions in the areas of logic and the philosophy of science. He has been a leading exponent of a system of beliefs called "naturalism." This view denies the existence of any realm that transcends nature. It also accepts the methods of the sciences as providing the only reliable way for man to obtain knowledge. In the following selection, Nagel outlines and argues against most of the classical arguments for the existence of God, expressing his scepticism regarding special avenues to religious truth that are claimed by some religious thinkers.

Western culture has understood religion within the context of the Judeo-Christian tradition and by means of a system of beliefs called theism. The central belief of theism is that one God, who is distinct from the world, is its creator and sustainer. Nagel is careful to state that his atheism is philosophical and directed against the concept of God and the religious view of the origin and nature of the world characteristic of theism. To ensure that we don't identify theism as a religion, Nagel refers to it as a "theological proposition." After pointing to what he considers inconsistencies in the theistic viewpoint, he goes on to discuss the positive doctrines of the atheistic position of naturalism.

A Defense of Atheism

The essays in this book are devoted in the main to the exposition of the major creeds of humanity. It is a natural expectation that this final paper, even though its theme is so radically different from nearly all of the others, will show how atheism belongs to the great tradition of religious thought. Needless to say, this expectation is difficult to satisfy, and did anyone succeed in doing so he would indeed be performing the neatest conjuring trick of the week. But the expectation nevertheless does cause me some embarrassment, which is only slightly relieved by an anecdote Bertrand Russell reports in his recent book, *Portraits from Memory.* Russell was imprisoned during the First World War for pacifistic activities. On entering the prison he was asked a number of customary questions about himself for the prison records. One question was about his religion. Russell explained that he was an agnostic. "Never heard of it," the warden declared. "How do you spell it?" When Russell told him, the warden observed "Well, there are many religions, but I suppose they all worship the same God." Russell adds that this remark kept him cheerful for about a week. Perhaps philosophical atheism is also a religion.

1.

I must begin by stating what sense I am attaching to the word "atheism," and how I am construing the theme of this paper. I shall understand by "atheism" a critique and a denial of the major claims of all varieties of theism.

And by theism I shall mean the view which holds, as one writer has expressed it, "that the heavens and the earth and all that they contain owe their existence and continuance in existence to the wisdom and will of a supreme, self-consistent, omnipotent, omniscient, righteous, and benevolent being, who is distinct from, and independent of, what he has created." Several things immediately follow from these definitions.

In the first place, atheism is not necessarily an irreligious concept, for theism is just one among many views concerning the nature and origin of the world. The denial of theism is logically compatible with a religious outlook upon life, and is in fact characteristic of some of the great historical religions. For as readers of this volume will know, early Buddhism is a religion which does not subscribe to any doctrine about a god; and there are pantheistic religions and philosophies which, because they deny that God is a being separate from and independent of the world, are not theistic in the sense of the word explained above.

The second point to note is that atheism is, not to be identified with sheer unbelief, or with disbelief in some particular creed of a religious group. Thus, a child who has received no religious instruction and has never heard about God, is not an atheist—for he is not denying

Ernest Nagel, "Philosophical Concepts of Atheism," *Basic Beliefs: The Religious Philosophies of Mankind,* ed. Johnson E. Fairchild (New York: Sheridan House, Inc., 1959), pp. 167–86 (with omissions). Reprinted by permission.

any theistic claims. Similarly in the case of an adult who, if he has withdrawn from the faith of his fathers without reflection or because of frank indifference to any theological issue, is also not an atheist—for such an adult is not challenging theism and is not professing any views on the subject. Moreover, though the term "atheist" has been used historically as an abusive label for those who do not happen to subscribe to some regnant orthodoxy (for example, the ancient Romans called the early Christians atheists, because the latter denied the Roman divinities), or for those who engage in conduct regarded as immoral it is not in this sense that I am discussing atheism.

One final word of preliminary explanation. I propose to examine some *philosophic* concepts of atheism, and I am not interested in the slightest in the many considerations atheists have advanced against the evidences for some particular religious and theological doctrine— for example, against the truth of the Christian story. What I mean by "philosophical" in the present context is that the views I shall consider are directed against any form of theism, in a comprehensive account of the world believed to be wholly intelligible without the adoption of a theistic hypothesis.

Theism as I conceive it is a theological proposition, not a statement of a position that belongs primarily to religion. On my view, religion as a historical and social phenomenon is primarily an institutionalized *cultus* or practice, which possesses identifiable social functions and which expresses certain attitudes men take toward their world. Although it is doubtful whether men ever engage in religious practices or assume religious attitudes without some more or less explicit interpretation of their ritual or some rationale for their attitude, it is still the case that it is possible to distinguish religion as a social and personal phenomenon from the theological doctrines which may be developed as justifications for religious practices. Indeed, in some of the great religions of

the world the profession of a creed plays a relatively minor role. In short, religion is a form of social communion, a participation in certain kinds of ritual (whether it be a dance, worship, prayer, or the like), and a form of experience (sometimes, though not invariably, directed to a personal confrontation with divine and holy things). Theology is an articulated and, at its best, a rational attempt at understanding these feelings and practices, in the light of their relation to other parts of human experience, and in terms of some hypothesis concerning the nature of things entire.

2.

As I see it, atheistic philosophies fall into two major groups: 1. those which hold that the theistic doctrine is meaningful, but reject it either on the ground that, (a) the positive evidence for it is insufficient, or (b) the negative evidence is quite overwhelming; and 2. those who hold the theistic thesis is not even meaningful, and reject it (a) as just nonsense or (b) as literally meaningless but interpreting it as a symbolic rendering of human ideals, thus reading the theistic thesis in a sense that most believers in theism would disavow. It will not be possible in the limited space at my disposal to discuss the second category of atheistic critiques; and in any event, most of the traditional atheistic critiques of theism belong to the first group.

But before turning to the philosophical examination of the major classical arguments for theism, it is well to note that such philosophical critiques do not quite convey the passion with which atheists have often carried on their analyses of theistic views. For historically, atheism has been, and indeed continues to be, a form of social and political protest, directed as much against institutionalized religion as against theistic doctrine. Atheism has been, in effect, a moral revulsion against the undoubted abuses of the secular power exercised by religious leaders and religious institutions.

Religious authorities have opposed the correction of glaring injustices, and encouraged politically and socially reactionary policies. Religious institutions have been havens of obscurantist thought and centers for the dissemination of intolerance. Religious creeds have been used to set limits to free inquiry, to perpetuate inhumane treatment of the ill and the underprivileged, and to support moral doctrines insensitive to human suffering.

These indictments may not tell the whole story about the historical significance of religion; but they are at least an important part of the story. The refutation of theism has thus seemed to many as an indispensable step not only towards liberating men's minds from superstition, but also towards achieving a more equitable reordering of society. And no account of even the more philosophical aspects of atheistic thought is adequate, which does not give proper recognition to the powerful social motives that actuate many atheistic arguments.

But however this may be, I want now to discuss three classical arguments for the existence of God, arguments which have constituted at least a partial basis for theistic commitments. As long as theism is defended simply as dogma, asserted as a matter of direct revelation or as the deliverance of authority, belief in the dogma is impregnable to rational argument. In fact, however, reasons are frequently advanced in support of the theistic creed, and these reasons have been the subject of acute philosophical critiques.

One of the oldest intellectual defenses of theism is the cosmological argument, also known as the argument from a first cause. Briefly put, the argument runs as follows. Every event must have a cause. Hence an event A must have as cause some event B, which in turn must have a cause C, and so on. But if there is no end to this backward progression of causes, the progression will be infinite; and in the opinion of those who use this argument, an infinite series of actual events is unintelligible and ab-

surd. Hence there must be a first cause, and this first cause is God, the initiator of all change in the universe.

The argument is an ancient one, and is especially effective when stated within the framework of assumptions of Aristotelian physics; and it has impressed many generations of exceptionally keen minds. The argument is nonetheless a weak reed on which to rest the theistic thesis. Let us waive any question concerning the validity of the principle that every event has a cause, for though the question is important its discussion would lead us far afield. However, if the principle is assumed, it is surely incongruous to postulate a first cause as a way of escaping from the coils of an infinite series. For if everything must have a cause, why does not God require one for His own existence? The standard answer is that He does not need any, because He is self-caused. But if God can be self-caused, why cannot the world be self-caused? Why do we require a God transcending the world to bring the world into existence and initiate changes in it? On the other hand, the supposed inconceivability and absurdity of an infinite series of regressive causes will be admitted by no one who has competent familiarity with the modern mathematical analysis of infinity. The cosmological argument does not stand up under scrutiny.

The second "proof" of God's existence is usually called the ontological argument. It too has a long history going back to early Christian days, though it acquired great prominence only in medieval times. The argument can be stated in several ways, one of which is the following. Since God is conceived to be omnipotent, he is a perfect being. A perfect being is defined as one whose essence or nature lacks no attributes (or properties) whatsoever, one whose nature is complete in every respect. But it is evident that we have an idea of a perfect being, for we have just defined the idea; and since this is so, the argument continues, God who is the perfect being must exist. Why must he? Because his existence follows from his defined nature. For if God lacked the attribute of existence, he would be lacking at least one attribute, and would therefore not be perfect. To sum up, since we have an idea of God as a perfect being, God must exist.

There are several ways of approaching this argument, but I shall consider only one. The argument was exploded by the eighteenth-century philosopher Immanuel Kant. The substance of Kant's criticism is that it is just a confusion to say that existence is an attribute, and that though the *word* "existence" may occur as the grammatical predicate in a sentence, no attribute is being predicted of a thing when we say that the thing exists or has existence. Thus, to use Kant's example, when we think of $100 we are thinking of the nature of this sum of money; but the nature of $100 remains the same whether we have $100 in our pocket or not. Accordingly, we are confounding grammar with logic if we suppose that some characteristic is being attributed to the nature of $100 when we say that a hundred dollar bill exists in someone's pocket.

To make the point clearer, consider another example. When we say that a lion has a tawny color, we are predicating a certain attribute of the animal, and similarly when we say that the lion is fierce or is hungry. But when we say the lion exists, all that we are saying is that something is (or has the nature of) a lion; we are not specifying an attribute which belongs to the nature of anything that is a lion. In short, the word "existence" does not signify any attribute, and in consequence no attribute that belongs to the nature of anything. Accordingly, it does not follow from the assumption that we have an idea of a perfect being that such a being exists. For the idea of a perfect being does not involve the attribute of existence as a constituent of that idea, since there is no such attribute. The ontological argument thus has a serious leak, and it can hold no water.

3.

The two arguments discussed thus far are purely dialectical, and attempt to establish God's existence without any appeal to empirical data. The next argument, called the argument from design, is different in character, for it is based on what purports to be empirical evidence. I wish to examine two forms of this argument.

One variant of it calls attention to the remarkable way in which different things and processes in the world are integrated with each other, and concludes that this mutual "fitness" of things can be explained only by the assumption of a divine architect who planned the world and everything in it. For example, living organisms can maintain themselves in a variety of environments, and do so in virtue of their delicate mechanisms which adapt the organisms to all sorts of environmental changes. There is thus an intricate pattern of means and ends throughout the animate world. But the existence of this pattern is unintelligible, so the argument runs, except on the hypothesis that the pattern has been deliberately instituted by a Supreme Designer. If we find a watch in some deserted spot, we do not think it came into existence by chance, and we do not hesitate to conclude that an intelligent creature designed and made it. But the world and all its contents exhibit mechanisms and mutual adjustments that are far more complicated and subtle than are those of a watch. Must we not therefore conclude that these things too have a Creator?

The conclusion of this argument is based on an inference from analogy: the watch and the world are alike in possessing a congruence of parts and an adjustment of means to ends; the watch has a watch-maker; hence the world has a world-maker. But is the analogy a good one? Let us once more waive some important issues, in particular the issue whether the universe is the unified system such as the watch admittedly is. And let us concentrate on the question, what is the ground for our assurance that watches do not come into existence except through the operations of intelligent manufacturers. The answer is plain. We have never run across a watch which has not been deliberately made by someone. But the situation is nothing like this in the case of the innumerable animate and inanimate systems with which we are familiar. Even in the case of living organisms, though they are generated by their parent organisms, the parents do not "make" their progeny in the same sense in which watchmakers make watches. And once this point is clear, the inference from the existence of living organisms to the existence of a supreme designer no longer appears credible.

Moreover, the argument loses all its force if the facts which the hypothesis of a divine designer is supposed to explain can be understood on the basis of a better supported assumption. And indeed, such an alternative explanation is one of the achievements of Darwinian biology. For Darwin showed that one can account for the variety of biological species, as well as for their adaptations to their environments, without invoking a divine creator and acts of special creation. The Darwinian theory explains the diversity of biological species in terms of chance variations in the structure of organisms, and of a mechanism of selection which retains those variant forms that possess some advantages for survival. The evidence for these assumptions is considerable; and developments subsequent to Darwin have only strengthened the case for a thoroughly naturalistic explanation of the facts of biological adaptation. In any event, this version of the argument from design has nothing to recommend it.

A second form of this argument has been recently revived in the speculations of some modern physicists. No one who is familiar with the facts can fail to be impressed by the success with which the use of mathematical methods has enabled us to obtain intellectual mastery of many parts of nature. But some thinkers have therefore concluded that since the book of nature is ostensibly written in mathematical language, nature must be the creation of a divine mathematician. However, the argument is most dubious. For it rests, among other things, on the assumption that mathematical tools can be successfully used only if the events of nature exhibit some special kind of order, and on the further assumption that if the structure of things were different from what they are mathematical language would be inadequate for describing such structure. But it can be shown that no matter what the world were like —even if it impressed us as being utterly chaotic —it would still possess some order, and would in principle be amenable to a mathematical description. In point of fact, it makes no sense to say that there is absolutely no pattern in any conceivable subject matter. To be sure, there are differences in complexities of structure, and if the patterns of events were sufficiently complex we might not be able to unravel them. But however that may be, the success of mathematical physics in giving us some understanding of the world around us does not yield the conclusion that only a mathematician could have devised the patterns of order we have discovered in nature.

4.

The inconclusiveness of the three classical arguments for the existence of God was already made evident by Kant, in a manner substantially not different from the above discussion....

One further type of argument, pervasive in much Protestant theological literature, deserves brief mention. Arguments of this type take their point of departure from the psychology of religious and mystical experience. Those who have undergone such experiences, often report that during the experience they feel themselves to be in the presence of the divine and holy, that they lose their sense of self-identity and become merged with some fundamental reality, or that they enjoy a feeling of total dependence upon some ultimate power. The overwhelming sense of transcending one's finitude which characterizes such vivid periods of life, and of coalescing with some ultimate source of all existence, is then taken to be compelling evidence for the existence of a supreme being. In a variant form of this argument, other theologians have identified God as the object which satisfies the commonly experienced need for integrating one's scattered and conflicting impulses into a coherent unity, or as the subject which is of ultimate concern to us. In short, a proof of God's existence is found in the occurrence of certain distinctive experiences.

It would be flying in the face of well-attested facts were one to deny that such experiences frequently occur. But do these facts constitute evidence for the conclusion based on them? Does the fact, for example, that an individual experiences a profound sense of direct contact with an alleged transcendent ground of all reality, constitute competent evidence for the experience? If well-established canons for evaluating evidence are accepted, the answer is surely negative. No one will dispute that many men do have vivid experiences in which such things as ghosts or pink elephants appear before them; but only the hopelessly credulous will without further ado count such experiences as establishing the existence of ghosts and pink elephants. To establish the existence of such things, evidence is required that is obtained under controlled conditions and that can be confirmed by independent inquirers. Again, though a man's report that he is suffering pain may be taken at face value, one cannot take at face value the claim, were he to make it, that it is the food he ate which is the cause (or a contributory cause) of his felt pain—not even if the man were to report a vivid feeling of abdominal disturbance. And similarly, an overwhelming feeling of being in the presence of the Divine is evidence enough for admitting the genuineness of such feeling; it is no evidence for the claim that a supreme being with a substantial existence independent of the experience is the cause of the experience....

5.

This last remark naturally leads to the question whether, apart from their polemics against theism, philosophical atheists have not shared a common set of positive views, a common set of philosophical convictions which set them off from other groups of thinkers. In one very clear sense of this query the answer is indubitably negative. For there never has been what one might call a "school of atheism," in the way in which there has been a Platonic school or even a Kantian school. In point of fact, atheistic critics of theism can be found among many of the conventional groupings of philosophical thinkers— even, I venture to add, among professional theologians in recent years who in effect preach atheism in the guise of language taken bodily from the Christian tradition.

Nevertheless, despite the variety of philosophic positions to which at one time or another in the history of thought atheists have subscribed, it seems to me that atheism is not simply a negative standpoint. At any rate, there is a certain quality of intellectual temper that has characterized, and continues to characterize, many philosophical atheists. (I am excluding from consideration the so-called "village atheist," whose primary concern is to twit and ridicule those who accept some form of theism, or for that matter those who have any religious convictions.) Moreover, their rejection of theism is based not only on the inadequacies they have found in the arguments for theism, but often also on the positive ground that atheism is a corollary to a better supported general outlook upon the nature of things. I want therefore to conclude this discussion with a brief enumeration of some points of positive doctrine to which by and large philosophical atheists seem to me to subscribe. These points fall into three major groups.

In the first place, philosophical atheists reject the assumption that there are disembodied spirits, or that incorporeal entities of any sort can exercise a causal agency. On the contrary, atheists are generally agreed that if we wish to achieve any understanding of what takes place in the universe, we must look to the operations of organized bodies. Accordingly, the various processes taking place in nature, whether animate or inanimate, are to be explained in terms of the properties and structures of identifiable and spatio-temporally located objects. Moreover, the present variety of systems and activities found in the universe is to be accounted for on the basis of the transformations things undergo when they enter into different relations with one another—transformations which often result in the emergence of novel kinds of objects. On the other hand, though things are in flux and undergo alteration, there is no all-encompassing unitary pattern of change. Nature is ineradicably plural, both in respect to the individuals occurring in it as well as in respect to the processes in which things become involved. Accordingly, the human scene and the human perspective are not illusory; and man and his works are no less and no more "real" than are other parts of phases of the cosmos. At the risk of using a possibly misleading characterization, all of this can be summarized by saying that an atheistic view of things is a form of materialism.

In the second place, atheists generally manifest a marked empirical temper, and often take as their ideal the intellectual methods employed in the contemporaneous empirical sciences. Philosophical atheists differ considerably on important points of detail in their account of how responsible claims to knowledge are to be established. But there is substantial agreement among them that controlled sensory observation is the court of final appeal in issues concerning matters of fact. It is indeed this commitment to the use of an empirical method which is the final basis of the atheistic critique of theism. For at bottom this critique seeks to show that we can understand whatever a theistic assumption is alleged to explain, through the use of the proved methods of the positive sciences and without the introduction of empirically unsupported *ad hoc* hypotheses about a Deity. It is pertinent in this connection to recall a familiar legend about the French mathematical physicist Laplace. According to the story, Laplace made a personal presentation of a copy of his now famous book on celestial mechanics to Napoleon. Napolean glanced through the volume, and finding no reference to the Diety asked Laplace whether God's existence played any role in the analysis. "Sire, I have no need for that hypothesis," Laplace is reported to have replied. The dismissal of sterile hypotheses characterizes not only the work of Laplace; it is the uniform rule in scientific inquiry. The sterility of the theistic assumption is one of the main burdens of the literature of atheism both ancient and modern.

And finally, atheistic thinkers have generally accepted a utilitarian basis for judging moral issues, and they have exhibited a libertarian attitude toward human needs and impulses. The conceptions of the human good they have advocated are conceptions which are commensurate with the actual capacities of mortal men, so that it is the satisfaction of the complex needs of the human creature which is the final standard for evaluating the validity of a moral ideal or moral prescription.

In consequence, the emphasis of atheistic moral reflection has been this-worldly rather than other-worldly, individualistic rather than authoritarian. The stress upon a good life that must be consummated in this world, has made atheists vigorous opponents of moral codes which seek to repress human impulses in the name of some unrealizable other-worldly ideal.

The individualism that is so pronounced a strain in many philosophical atheists has made them tolerant of human limitations and sensitive to the plurality of legitimate moral goals. On the other hand, this individualism has certainly not prevented many of them from recognizing the crucial role which institutional arrangements can play in achieving desirable patterns of human living. In consequence, atheists have made important contributions to the development of a climate of opinion favorable to pursuing the values of a liberal civilization and they have played effective roles in attempts to rectify social injustices.

Atheists cannot build their moral outlook on foundations upon which so many men conduct their lives. In particular, atheism cannot offer the incentives to conduct and the consolations for misfortune which theistic religions supply to their adherents. It can offer no hope of personal immortality, no threats of Divine chastisement, no promise of eventual recompense for injustices suffered, no blueprints to sure salvation. For on its view of the place of man in nature, human excellence and human dignity must be achieved within a finite life-span, or not at all, so that the rewards of moral endeavor must come from the quality of civilized living, and not from some source of disbursement that dwells outside of time. Accordingly, atheistic moral reflection at its best does not culminate in a quiescent ideal of human perfection, but is a vigorous call to intelligent activity —activity for the sake of realizing human potentialities and for eliminating whatever stands in the way of such realization. Nevertheless, though slavish resignation to remediable ills is not characteristic of atheistic thought, responsible atheists have never pretended that human effort can invariably achieve the heart's every legitimate desire. A tragic view of life is thus an uneliminable ingredient in atheistic thought. This ingredient does not invite or generally produce lugubrious lamentation. But it does touch the atheist's view of man and his place in nature with an emotion that makes the philosophical atheist a kindred spirit to those who, within the framework of various religious traditions, have developed a serenely resigned attitude toward the inevitable tragedies of the human estate.

Reinhold Niebuhr (1892–1971) was profoundly concerned and involved with many of the major political and social issues of his time. A theologian and clergyman, he was one of the most influential spokesmen for Neo-orthodoxy in contemporary Protestantism. He served as pastor in Detroit for thirteen years and then as professor of Christian Ethics at Union Theological Seminary in New York City.

In his major theological work, *The Nature and Destiny of Man* (1945), Niebuhr strongly disagreed with the view of man and human life as self-sufficing and as wholly within the sphere of nature.

> Man is an individual, but he is not self-sufficing. The law of his nature is love, a harmonious relation of life to life in obedience to the divine centre and source of his life. This law is violated when man seeks to make himself the centre and source of his own life. His sin is therefore spiritual and not carnal, though the infection of rebellion spreads from the spirit to the body and disturbs its harmonies also. Man, in other words, is a sinner not because he is one limited individual within a whole but rather because he is betrayed, by his very ability to survey the whole, to imagine himself the whole.[1]

Niebuhr takes a Biblical-Christian view that God is creator and judge of human existence. Only by this means can man's moral struggle and history adequately be interpreted. Biblical themes and myths, such as the Fall provide us with symbols that embody important truths to guide man's confrontation with life. Niebuhr spent his life spelling out the meaning of these myths and symbols for the modern world.

As indicated in the selection that follows, Niebuhr was critical of those who argue that a purely secular morality is adequate. No matter how objective the ethical system claims to be, it turns out to be a rationalization of man's own self-interest. A purely secular ethics is really the result of *hubris,* or pride, by which man asserts his own values and judgments as the highest.

Throughout history, man has placed himself, individually or collectively, at the center of the universe. His egoism is the root of the constant return of imperialism and cruelty. This is especially true in the modern world in which man has turned away from God and, through science, is willing to proclaim his own potential omnipotence. The brutal irony of modern history indicates that man has increased his power, but he has also increased his capacity for destructiveness. His newly won freedom from the forces of nature and the judgment of God has only shown what a frail and limited creature he is.

The moral crisis of modern man is a constant theme in Niebuhr's writings. A secular ethics evades some disturbing facts about the weakness of man, his failures, and his moral disorder. It is an abortive effort to overcome man's insecurity by his own power and to hide his own limitations. The theme is as old as the story of Adam. Man has yet to learn it. The best solution is to recognize that man is in dialogue with God. In mysticism, man is swallowed up in God; in a secular viewpoint, God is lost by virtue of man's usurpation of divine authority. In a Biblical faith, man keeps his relative autonomy, yet retains his vital relation to a personal God from whom his values are derived and by whom he is judged. The norms provided in revelation and through Jesus Christ still provide, Niebuhr believes, the core of the only adequate ethical code.

Note

1. Reinhold Niebuhr, *The Nature and Destiny of Man* (New York: Charles Scribner's Sons, 1945), pp. 16–17.

The Self and Its Search
for Ultimate Meaning

The task of penetrating the ultimate mystery prompts many responses, but they could all be placed into three general categories: (A) The first category embraces all religious responses in which the self seeks to break through a universal rational system in order to assert its significance ultimately. It may seek to do this individually, as in modern romantic and existentialist thought; or it may be so conscious of its finiteness as an individual that it finds no opportunity to assert the ultimate significance of itself in history except by asserting the significance of the collective self. This category, in short, embraces all the idolatrous religions of ancient history, including both primitive polytheism and the imperial religions of Egypt and Babylon, and (in more artificial terms) of Rome. Until a recent day this idolatry, in which the individual self finds the ultimate source of its meaning in the history of the collective self so much more imposing though also so much closer to the flux of nature, was thought to be a phase of history which was overcome by the rise of rigorously monotheistic religions and monistic philosophies. But the recrudescence of religious nationalism and the pseudo-universalistic Messianism of communism have instructed us that this idolatry, this worship of the collective self as if it were ul-

Excerpts from *The Self and the Dramas of History* by Reinhold Niebuhr are used by permission of Charles Scribner's Sons. Copyright 1955 Charles Scribner's Sons.

timate and not finite, is not merely due to the limits of a primitive imagination. It corresponds to a perennial desire in the human heart to eat one's cake and have it, too; to subordinate the finite self to something greater than it but not so great that the self may not participate in the exaltation of the finite value. Naturally this idolatrous religion must have baneful effects, not only because it complicates the problem of group relations by exaggerating the claims of contingent historical forces in competition with each other, but because the unconditioned commitment of the self to the collective self must rob it of its freedom; for the collective self is, though more imposing and more long-lived than the individual self, also so much more bound to nature and its necessities, so defective in organs of self-transcendence and therefore so much farther removed from the ultimate source of meaning, that the self debases itself by this uncritical devotion.

(B) The second alternative of explicit religious response has been defined by Aldous Huxley as "The Perennial Philosophy." He is right in asserting that it is a fairly universal response, but wrong in concluding that this universality guarantees its validity. This response, generally defined as "mysticism," stands at the opposite pole of idolatry. It is in fact an heroic effort to transcend all finite values and systems of meaning, including the self as particular existence, and to arrive at universality and "unconditioned" being. The persistence of this mystic tendency in the religions of the world is a telling proof of the ability of the self, in the ultimate reaches of its freedom and self-awareness, to discern some affinity between the mystery behind the observable phenomena and to find the key to universality in the joining of these two mysteries. This "perennial philosophy" embraces not only the systems, stemming from the thought of Plotinus, in the Western world but practically all religions of the Orient. It is expressed in the Brahman overtones of Hindu polytheism; in the Sufist tradition of Mohammedanism; in the Taoist tradition of Chinese culture and, most classically, in Buddhism. Here the search for undifferentiated being reaches the height of asserting a type of being as the goal of existence about which one can not be certain whether it is the fullness or the absence of being. It is certainly being bereft of all relationships and meanings.

(C) The third alternative, an explicitly religious answer to the self's search for the ultimate, embraces the two Biblical faiths of Judaism and Christianity. These faiths interpret the self's experience with the ultimate in the final reaches of its self-awareness as a dialogue with God. The idea of a dialogue between the self and God assumes the personality of God, an assumption which both rationalists and mystics find untenable, but to which Biblical faith clings stubbornly. Selfhood or personality is supposedly not attributable to God because the idea of personality is loaded with connotations of finiteness and therefore casts a suspicion of "anthropomorphism" upon Biblical faith. But it is significant that both mystics and rationalists have as much difficulty in ascribing personality to man as to God. This fact suggests that it is not the connotations of finiteness which create the difficulty but rather the fact that personality is characterized by both a basic structure and a freedom beyond structure. The rationalists can comprehend the structure within a system of rational cohesion; and the mystics are able to interpret the freedom as part of a system of undifferentiated potentiality. But neither is able

to comprehend the total fact of personality within its system.

The dialogue between self and God results in the conviction of the self, but not for reason of its finiteness. It is convicted rather of its pretension or "sin"; of claiming too much for its finiteness, and for the virtue and wisdom, which it achieves in its finiteness. The idea of such an encounter therefore permits the Biblical faiths both to affirm the life of the self in history and to challenge its achievements in any particular instance. "Enter not into judgment with thy servant, for in thy sight is no man living justified," declares the Psalmist. Kierkegaard sums up this theme of Biblical religions with the affirmation that "before God all men are in wrong." The fact that the self is judged for every inclination which affronts God's "majesty" by pride or lust for power is the religious dimension of sin. The prophets are however equally conscious of the social dimension which is the inclination of the self to take advantage of its fellow men. This "injustice" is never speculatively defined, as in Greek philosophy, but rigorously defined by reactions to injustice in particular situations.

The "severity" of God's judgment is matched by the "goodness" of His mercy. In the dialogue between the individual and God, this validates itself as the indeterminate possibilities of self-realization and fulfillment of the self's potentialities once it has ceased to seek fulfillment of life from the standpoint of itself. The problem of how the mercy of God is related to His justice is a perpetual problem in the Old Testament. The new Biblical faith of Christianity enters into history with the affirmation that the drama of Christ's life is in fact a final revelation, in which this problem is clarified by the assurance that God takes the demand of His justice upon Himself through Christ's suffering love and therefore "God was in Christ reconciling the world unto Himself."

The dying and rising again of Christ is the key to the self's possibilities in history. All of life is given this norm for the realization of self-hood. "I am crucified with Christ," declares St. Paul, "nevertheless I live." This theme is in perfect harmony with the words attributed to Jesus in the Johannine Gospel: "Except a corn of wheat fall into the ground and die, it abideth alone: but if it die, it bringeth forth much fruit." (John 12:24)

Thus the encounter of the self with God is defined in Biblical faith in terms of a norm which has been set by an historical "revelation." And this revelation is an historical event or series of events which are not essentially miraculous (miracles such as the "virgin birth" are afterthoughts) but are events in history which are discerned by faith to have revelatory power into the ultimate mystery. Both Biblical religions are covenant faiths, which organize covenant communities upon the basis of a common commitment of faith in the divine significance of these events. We must postpone until later, then, a consideration of the relation of revelation to the drama of history. In this connection it is necessary to observe that the discernment of ultimate significance of an historic event makes the Biblical religions seem primitive and unsophisticated in the eyes of both rationalists and mystics, who look for the ultimate or "unconditioned" in either the permanent structures of existence or in an undifferentiated ground of being. They may fail to note, however, that the Biblical presupposition is the only one of the three alternatives which asserts a discontinuity between the self and God. This discontinuity makes explicit faith indispensable in the ultimate dialogue; but it also prevents the self either from usurping the place of the divine for itself or from imagining itself merged with the divine. If we test these three alternative solutions for the self's search for the ultimate by the two tests of consistency or coherence with other truth, and by conformity with established facts subject to empirical tests, it will soon become apparent that the religions which tend to the exaltation of finite values and centers of mean-ing are most easily ruled out, as indeed they have been ruled out in principle for centuries. The collective self may be momentarily imposing; but its mortality is obvious and the perils to the individual self by its pretensions of divinity are very great.

It is however very significant that a religious solution which has been ruled out in principle for centuries should have so much practical force in our day, both in the version of a religious nationalism and in a pseudo-universalistic Messianic creed. These contemporary ventures into idolatry are proof of the difficulty of containing the collective self within any more general scheme of validity than its own interests. They prove that an affirmation of historical meaning as we have it in Western civilization is almost inevitably attended by pretentious efforts to close the system of meaning prematurely with some cherished value of the self at the center of the system.

It is equally significant that modern culture has generated less plausible and dangerous forms of individualistic pretention, in which the freedom and the uniqueness of the individual is asserted in defiance of any systems of consistency or universal meaning. The romantic revolt of the nineteenth century culminated in Nietzsche's effort to achieve the affirmation of unique vitality of the individual and his transcendence over the flux of history, thus seeking to combine classical with Hebraic attitudes toward time and eternity.

It must be apparent that modern existentialism is but another version of this romantic revolt. It has obviously learned from Biblical faith about the unique freedom of the individual and the distinction between the self's reason and personality. It is however unable to make the venture of faith of Biblical religion and therefore ends in the quasi-idolatrous attitude of making the individual his own creator and end. "Thus there is no human nature," declares the French existentialist Sartre, "because there is no God to conceive it. Man simply is. Not that he is simply what he conceives himself to be. But he is what he wills. . . . He is what he wills to be after that leap toward existence."*

Heidegger's concern for "authentic being," for the affirmation of the uniquely human freedom against the necessities of nature and the inevitability of death, is distantly related to Nietzsche's defiance of death. It is in the same category of quasi-idolatry. It may not make the self into its own God but it asserts the uniqueness of the self without reference to its relations to the community or to any general value.

If we rule out the idolatrous and quasi-idolatrous, the individualistic and collective forms of these idolatries, as valid answers to the self's quest for ultimate meaning even though we recognize that the popularity of such answers is not confined to past history but is an ever recurring phenomenon, we are left with the two alternatives of the Biblical faith and Mr. Huxley's "perennial philosophy" or the mystic answer to the problem.

The answer of Biblical faith embodies, as we have seen, several presuppositions and affirmations which the modern mind finds particularly difficult, not to say impossible: the personality of God; the definition of the relation between the self and God as a dialogue; and the determination of the form of that dialogue in terms of a previous historic "revelation," which is an event in past history, discerned by faith to give a key to the character and purpose of God and of His relationship to man. It is therefore understandable that when confronted with these two alternatives, sophisticated moderns who have become aware of a depth of selfhood which can not be comprehended within the limits of the self as a biological organism or the self as mind, are inclined to turn to the mystic alternative in preference to the Biblical one. It is even understandable that they should do this at the price of defying the very ethos of

their own life-affirming and history-affirming culture and choose an alternative which annuls every partial and particular meaning including the particular self. This is understandable in the sense that it proves how powerful are the compulsions to comprehend reality in a self-consistent scheme and to leave the mystery beyond the system of rational intelligibility unsolved.

Thus Professor Stace uttered a cry of despair some years ago because he became aware that the world which modern science explicated had no place for the human self or for any of the values which the self holds dear. Subsequently he published his considered answer to this problem in his *Time and Eternity*. He had accomplished his escape from the naturalistic prison by embracing the "perennial philosophy" of Mr. Huxley and the oriental mystics. He defined religion as the search for "the impossible, the unattainable and the inconceivable." Professor Stace thus bears testimony to the capacity of the self to reach for the ultimate; but he is sceptical of any venture of faith in an ultimate which would purify and complete the particular meanings of history. He finds it more acceptable to assert the pure mystery of the divine. He is impressed by the fact that the mystic approach arrives at the conclusion that God is both the fullness and the absence of being. Reporting on the account of divinity in the mystic tradition, he records that "God is non-Being, nothingness, emptiness, the void, the abyss . . . God is the great silence, the great darkness . . . yet God is also in the language of the medieval mystics, the supreme reality, the 'ens realissimum.'" "This supreme God," he declares, "is contrasted by the mystics with the worthlessness of the world . . . the world then is worthless trash. This is seen by all men more dimly or more clearly, but it is seen by the mystics with absolute clarity."**

Professor Stace refers frequently to the Hindu

---

*Existentialism and Humanism, p. 28.

**Time and Eternity, p. 126.

desire to achieve unity of the self and God, to realize the assurance that "Brahman and Atman are one." This seems to him to be pure religion in comparison with the religions of the Bible with their appreciation of particular selfhood. . . .

It will be regarded as futile by all pure "empiricists" to compare the Biblical and the mystic conceptions of the ultimate dimensions of selfhood and to judge between the thesis that the self is in "dialogue with God" and the thesis that the self on that level is in the process of merging with a universal divine consciousness. But if the evidence of introspection is accepted (though it is admittedly inexact), it cannot be too difficult to prove that the abstraction of the universal subject from the self as particular object is a futile procedure because the particular self always remains obtrusively in these exercises of introversion. There is furthermore the social evidence that mystics never succeed in eliminating particular selfhood or in transcending the self as a particular organism. The erotic overtones in the mystic visions of an absolute consciousness is a rather pathetic symbol of the futility of the self's attempt to escape from the "body" and time into an undifferentiated eternity.

In short, we are confronted with evidence that the thesis of Biblical faith, that the self is in dialogue with a God who must be defined as a "person" because He embodies both the structure of being and a transcendent freedom, is more valid than the alternative theses which find much greater favor among the sophisticated. The Biblical thesis requires a more explicit act of faith because it leaps a gap of discontinuity between man and God and because it dares to give a specific meaning to the divine, which is relevant to the partial and fragmentary meanings of hstory. It both fulfills and corrects these meanngs, loyalties and values, and therefore has a more valid attitude to the self's historic existence which the various rationalistic systems affirm too simply and the mystic thesis annuls too absolutely. This character of Biblical faith is therefore the crux of the question, why a faith which is more explicit than alternative ones should be more justified by actual experience than these. It gives a key to the seeming mystery of our whole cultural history. That mystery is why an allegedly "dogmatic" faith should be justified by the experiences of the human self more than the allegedly "empirical" approaches to selfhood, which obscure their potent, though implicit, dogmas within their prescriptions for empirical observation. . . .

21 / The Inward Way Out
The Buddha

Buddhism, one of the most profound answers to the search for the meaning of life, originated in the attempt of a young Hindu to come to grips with human suffering and to find an escape from it. Gautama Siddhartha Sakyamuni was a happy and wealthy Nepalese prince who lived in the sixth century B.C. and was protected from a realization of the painful aspects of human existence until, according to legend, while out taking rides he saw for the first time a decrepit old man, a disease-ridden body, and a decaying corpse. These three sights, along with the sight of a shaven-headed monk, brought on in the compassionate, intelligent young man what today would be called an existential crisis.

As a result, he renounced his luxurious life, left his family and possessions, and began to practice a life of rigorous asceticism in hopes of achieving liberation from the horror of existence. His agonizing confrontation with human suffering and his impassioned quest for liberation from selfish human cravings convinced Gautama that "what is dear to one brings hurt and misery, suffering, grief and despair which comes from what is dear." After a long and arduous period of self-mortification and meditation, he finally succeeded, while seated under the Bo tree, in achieving enlightenment. He was then able to diagnose the malady of the human condition and to prescribe the treatment that, he believed, would eventually cure it.

Gautama, now the Buddha or the Enlightened One, was concerned not with theory, but with practice. His cure for human suffering, summed up in his Four Noble Truths and the Eightfold Noble Way, is presented in the following sermon. Escape from selfish craving, which he believed lay at the root of human suffering, must be the focal point of all striving. To devote time to metaphysical speculations or controversy about religious dogmas when the basic moral problem of achieving salvation from suffering remains unsolved would be as foolish as to try to determine the cause of a fire in one's house when one should first be concerned with escaping from the threatening flames.

An agnostic himself, the Buddha apparently conceived of himself neither as a god nor as a holy guru, but rather as an experienced guide who, having achieved enlightenment, could help his fellow men and women with the urgent task of escaping from life's "existential predicament," the inevitability of suffering. In doing this, the Buddha turned his back on both asceticism and sensuous indulgence to practice and teach "the Middle Way." This path went between the dangerous extremes where one would either be lost in self-renunciation or in self-indulgence. This was the only way, he taught, which led safely to liberation from selfish craving and to the final extinction of all desiring, to the goal of Nirvana.

After the death of the Buddha, the meaning of Nirvana, the Buddhist salvation from suffering, and the ways of achieving it became subjects of controversy. Eventually, two different schools or denominations of Buddhism emerged and flourished: *Hinayana* ("Little Vehicle") or *Theravada* ("Way of the Elders") Buddhism, and *Mahayana* ("Greater Vehicle") Buddhism. Reflecting different cultural contexts and interpretations, many variations within these major divisions later developed. Despite the wide variety of doctrine and practice, however, the universal elements of Buddhism remained essentially the same: the belief in the Founder, the Way, and the Order of Monks.

Whether Buddhism is regarded as a philosophy or religion, much of its continuing appeal, especially in the West, rests upon the experience that its founder had under the Bo tree and which he transmitted, through his example and teaching, to his followers. That experience has often been considered a prime example of the truly mystical experience, the characteristics of which will be discussed in the selection by Huston Smith. Buddha said later that this experience came about only after a long and often agonizing and frustrating effort. It was not, however, the result of any kind of vigorous ascetic discipline nor was it, on the other hand, a miraculous gift. It was also ineffable—that is to say, ultimately indescribable in words—but it was supremely significant, genuine, real, and achievable by others following the way of the guide who had achieved or "seen" it. And, finally, it was a supremely valuable experience, the only truly worthwhile experience a human being can have. If one does have such an experience, and the Buddha suggested a way, the meaning of life becomes clear and one can live and act accordingly.

The result of this realization, however, will not be, the Buddhist believes, either pessimism or quietism (do-nothingism). Rather, it will be a peace of mind and serenity of spirit, a willingness to cooperate with the good and renounce the evil, and a deep and all-encompassing sense of compassion with all those beings, both animal and human, who perpetually suffer.

The Gospel of The Buddha

Enlightenment

Bôdhisattva having put to flight Mâra, gave himself up to meditation. All the miseries of the world, the evils produced by evil deeds and the sufferings arising therefrom passed before his mental eye, and he thought:

"Surely if living creatures saw the results of all their evil deeds, they would turn away from them in disgust. But selfhood blinds them, and they cling to their obnoxious desires.

"They crave for pleasure and they cause pain; when death destroys their individuality, they find no peace; their thirst for existence abides and their selfhood reappears in new births.

"Thus they continue to move in the coil and can find no escape from the hell of their own making. And how empty are their pleasures, how vain are their endeavors! Hollow like the plantain-tree and without contents like the bubble.

"The world is full of sin and sorrow, because it is full of error. Men go astray because they think that delusion is better than truth. Rather than truth they follow error, which is pleasant to look at in the beginning but causes anxiety, tribulation, and misery."

And Bôdhisattva began to expound the dharma. The dharma is the truth. The dharma is the sacred law. The dharma is religion. The dharma alone can deliver us from error, sin, and sorrow.

The Gospel of Buddha According to Old Records, 5th ed., ed. Paul Carus (Chicago: The Open Court Publishing Co., 1897), pp. 30–43 (with omissions).

270

Pondering on the origin of birth and death, the Enlightened One recognised that ignorance was the root of all evil; and these are the links in the development of life, called the twelve nidânas:

"In the beginning there is existence blind and without knowledge; and in this sea of ignorance there are appetences formative and organising. From appetences, formative and organising, rises awareness or feelings. Feelings beget organisms that live as individual beings. These organisms develop the six fields, that is, the five senses and the mind. The six fields come in contact with things. Contact begets sensation. Sensation creates the thirst of individualised being. The thirst of being creates a cleaving to things. The cleaving produces the growth and continuation of selfhood. Selfhood continues in renewed births. The renewed births of selfhood are the cause of suffering, old age, sickness, and death. They produce lamentation, anxiety, and despair.

"The cause of all sorrow lies at the very beginning; it is hidden in the ignorance from which life grows. Remove ignorance and you will destroy the wrong appetences that rise from ignorance; destroy these appetences and you will wipe out the wrong perception that rises from them. Destroy wrong perception and there is an end of errors in individualised beings. Destroy errors in individualised beings and the illusions of the six fields will disappear. Destroy illusions and the contact with things will cease to beget misconception. Destroy misconception and you do away with thirst. Destroy thirst and you will be free of all morbid cleaving. Remove the cleaving and you destroy the selfishness of selfhood. If the selfishness of selfhood is destroyed you will be above birth, old age, disease, and death, and you escape all suffering."

The Enlightened One saw the four noble truths which point out the path that leads to Nirvâna or the extinction of self:

"The first noble truth is the existence of sorrow. Birth is sorrowful, growth is sorrowful, illness is sorrowful, and death is sorrowful. Sad it is to be joined with that which we do not like. Sadder still is the separation from that which we love, and painful is the craving for that which cannot be obtained.

"The second noble truth is the cause of suffering. The cause of suffering is lust. The surrounding world affects sensation and begets a craving thirst, which clamors for immediate satisfaction. The illusion of self originates and manifests itself in a cleaving to things. The desire to live for the enjoyment of self entangles us in the net of sorrow. Pleasures are the bait and the result is pain.

"The third noble truth is the cessation of sorrow. He who conquers self will be free from lust. He no longer craves, and the flame of desire finds no material to feed upon. Thus it will be extinguished.

"The fourth noble truth is the eightfold path that leads to the cessation of sorrow. There is salvation for him whose self disappears before Truth, whose will is bent upon what he ought to do, whose sole desire is the performance of his duty. He who is wise will enter this path and make an end of sorrow.

"The eightfold path is (1) right comprehension; (2) right resolutions; (3) right speech; (4) right acts; (5) right way of earning a livelihood; (6) right efforts; (7) right thoughts; and (8) the right state of a peaceful mind."

This is the dharma. This is the truth. This is religion. And the Enlightened One uttered this stanza:

Long have I wandered! Long!
Bound by the chain of desire
Through many births,
Seeking thus long in vain,
Whence comes this restlessness in man?
Whence his egotism, his anguish?
And hard to bear is samsâra
When pain and death encompass us.
Found! it is found!
Author of selfhood,
No longer shalt thou build a house for me.
Broken are the beams of sin;
The ridge-pole of care is shattered,
Into Nirvâna my mind has passed,
The end of cravings has been reached at last.

There is self and there is truth. Where self is, truth is not. Where truth is, self is not. Self is the fleeting error of samsâra; it is individual separateness and that egotism which begets envy and hatred. Self is the yearning for pleasure and the lust after vanity. Truth is the correct comprehension of things; it is the permanent and everlasting, the real in all existence, the bliss of righteousness.

The existence of self is an illusion, and there is no wrong in this world, no vice, no sin, except what flows from the assertion of self.

The attainment of truth is possible only when self is recognised as an illusion. Righteousness can be practised only when we have freed our mind from the passions of egotism. Perfect peace can dwell only where all vanity has disappeared.

Blessed is he who has understood the dharma. Blessed is he who does no harm to his fellow-beings. Blessed is he who overcomes sin and is free from passion. To the highest bliss has he attained who has conquered all selfishness and vanity. He has become Buddha, the Perfect One, the Blessed One, the Holy One. . . .

Now the Blessed One thought: "To whom shall I preach the doctrine first? My old teachers are dead. They would have received the good news with joy. But my five disciples are still alive. I shall go to them, and to them shall I first proclaim the gospel of deliverance."

At that time the five bhikshus dwelt in the Deer Park at Benares, and the Blessed One not thinking of their unkindness in having left him at a time when he was most in need of their sympathy and help, but mindful only of the services which they had ministered unto him, and pitying them for the austerities which they practised in vain, rose and journeyed to their abode. . . .

The Sermon at Benares

The five bhikshus saw their old teacher approach and agreed among themselves not to salute him, nor to address him as a master, but by his name only. "For," so they said, "he has broken his vow and has abandoned holiness. He is no bhikshu but Gautama, and Gautama has become a man who lives in abundance and indulges in the pleasures of worldliness."

But when the Blessed One approached in a dignified manner, they involuntarily rose from their seats and greeted him in spite of their resolution. Still they called him by his name and addressed him as "friend."

When they had thus received the Blessed One, he said: "Do not call the Tathâgata by his name nor address him 'friend,' for he is Buddha, the Holy One. Buddha looks equally with a kind heart on all living beings and they therefore call him 'Father.' To disrespect a father is wrong; to despise him, is sin.

"The Tathâgata," Buddha continued, "does not seek salvation in austerities, but for that reason you must not think that he indulges in worldly pleasures, nor does he live in abundance. The Tathâgata has found the middle path.

"Neither abstinence from fish or flesh, nor going naked, nor shaving the head, nor wearing matted hair, nor dressing in a rough garment, nor covering oneself with dirt, nor sacrificing to Agni, will cleanse a man who is not free from delusions.

"Reading the Vêdas, making offerings to priests, or sacrifices to the gods, self-mortification by heat or cold, and many such penances performed for the sake of immortality, these do not cleanse the man who is not free from delusions.

"Anger, drunkenness, obstinacy, bigotry, deception, envy, self-praise, disparaging others, superciliousness, and evil intentions constitute uncleanness; not verily the eating of flesh.

"Let me teach you, O bhikshus, the middle path, which keeps aloof from both extremes. By suffering, the emaciated devotee produces confusion and sickly thoughts in his mind. Mortification is not conducive even to worldly knowledge; how much less to a triumph over the senses!

"He who fills his lamp with water will not dispel the darkness, and he who tries to light a fire with rotten wood will fail.

"Mortifications are painful, vain, and profitless. And how can any one be free from self by leading a wretched life if he does not succeed in quenching the fires of lust.

"All mortification is vain so long as self remains, so long as self continues to lust after either worldly or heavenly pleasures. But he in whom self has become extinct is free from lust; he will desire neither worldly nor heavenly pleasures, and the satisfaction of his natural wants will not defile him. Let him eat and drink according to the needs of the body.

"Water surrounds the lotus-flower, but does not wet its petals.

"On the other hand, sensuality of all kind is enervating. The sensual man is a slave of his passions, and pleasure-seeking is degrading and vulgar.

"But to satisfy the necessities of life is not evil. To keep the body in good health is a duty, for otherwise we shall not be able to trim the lamp of wisdom, and keep our mind strong and clear.

"This is the middle path, O bhikshus, that keeps aloof from both extremes."

And the Blessed One spoke kindly to his disciples, pitying them for their errors, and pointing out the uselessness of their endeavors, and the ice of ill-will that chilled their hearts melted away under the gentle warmth of the Master's persuasion.

Now the Blessed One set the wheel of the most excellent law a-rolling, and he began to preach to the five bhikshus, opening to them the gate of immortality, and showing them the bliss of Nirvâna.

And when the Blessed One began his sermon, a rapture thrilled through all the universes.

The dêvas left their heavenly abodes to listen to the sweetness of the truth; the saints that had parted from life crowded around the great teacher to receive the glad tidings; even the animals of the earth felt the bliss that rested upon the words of the Tathâgata: and all the creatures of the host of sentient beings, gods, men, and beasts, hearing the message of deliverance, received and understood it in their own language.

Buddha said:

"The spokes of the wheel are the rules of pure conduct; justice is the uniformity of their length; wisdom is the tire; modesty and thoughtfulness are the hub in which the immovable axle of truth is fixed.

"He who recognises the existence of suffering, its cause, its remedy, and its cessation has fathomed the four noble truths. He will walk in the right path.

"Right views will be the torch to light his way. Right aims will be his guide. Right words will be his dwelling-place on the road. His gait will be straight, for it is right behavior. His refreshments will be the right way of earning his livelihood. Right efforts will be his steps: right thoughts his breath; and peace will follow in his footprints."

And the Blessed One explained the instability of the ego.

"Whatsoever is originated will be dissolved again. All worry about the self is vain; the ego is like a mirage, and all the tribulations that touch it will pass away. They will vanish like a nightmare when the sleeper awakes.

"He who has awakened is freed from fear; he has become Buddha; he knows the vanity of all his cares, his ambitions, and also of his pains.

"It easily happens that a man, when taking a bath, steps upon a wet rope and imagines that it is a snake. Horror will overcome him, and he will shake from fear, anticipating in his mind all the agonies caused by the serpent's venomous bite. What a relief does this man experience when he sees that the rope is no snake. The cause of his fright lies in his error, his ignorance, his illusion. If the true nature of the rope is recognised, his tranquillity of mind will come back to him; he will feel relieved; he will be joyful and happy.

"This is the state of mind of one who has recognised that there is no self, that the cause of all his troubles, cares, and vanities is a mirage, a shadow, a dream.

"Happy is he who has overcome all selfishness; happy is he who has attained peace; happy is he who has found the truth.

"The truth is noble and sweet; the truth can deliver from evil. There is no saviour in the world except the truth.

"Have confidence in the truth, although you may not be able to comprehend it, although you may suppose its sweetness to be bitter, although you may shrink from it at first. Trust in the truth.

"The truth is best as it is. No one can alter it; neither can any one improve it. Have faith in the truth and live it.

"Errors lead astray; illusions beget miseries. They intoxicate like strong drinks; but they fade away soon and leave you sick and disgusted.

"Self is a fever; self is a transient vision, a

dream; but truth is wholesome, truth is sublime, truth is everlasting. There is no immortality except in truth. For truth alone abideth forever."

And when the doctrine was propounded, the venerable Kaundinya, the oldest one among the five bhikshus, discerned the truth with his mental eye, and he said: "Truly, O Buddha, our Lord, thou hast found the truth."

And the dêvas and saints and all the good spirits of the departed generations that had listened to the sermon of the Tathâgata, joyfully received the doctrine and shouted: "Truly, the Blessed One has founded the kingdom of righteousness. The Blessed One has moved the earth; he has set the wheel of Truth rolling, which by no one in the universe, be he god or man, can ever be turned back. The kingdom of Truth will be preached upon earth; it will spread; and righteousness, good-will, and peace will reign among mankind."

One of our dictionaries defines mysticism as "the doctrine or belief that direct knowledge of God, or spiritual truth, etc., is attainable through immediate experience or insight and in a way differing from ordinary sense perception or the use of logical reasoning."[1] In a facetious play on the word "mysticism," someone has said that "mysticism begins with 'misty' and ends with 'schism'." Mystics have claimed that direct knowledge of the Deity in their experience seemed to carry them beyond the bounds of ordinary sense experience. Their attempted description of the meaning of the experience has also carried them beyond the bounds of rational discourse. Many a sceptic has referred to them as "misty." Also, different doctrines and paths to enlightenment have been advocated by mystics throughout history. This diversity has generated schools and schisms.

However, the actual root of the term "mystic" is perhaps more revealing: the Greek *mu*, as in the Greek verb *muō* meaning "close" or "to be silent." (Our word "mum" as in "to keep mum" is from the same root.) Mystics have claimed that the experience does not admit of description. In analogy to human love, the experience is unique and is incomprehensible to anyone who has not experienced it. The mystic's focus is not upon doctrines and beliefs, but upon an experience, a mode of consciousness. The history of religion, East and West, is filled with accounts of this consciousness and the way in which it has transformed the lives of people. Although religions encompass a wide variety of practices, beliefs, and attitudes, mystical experiences are a part of the vitality of religion and religious life, whether as the Nirvana of the Buddhist, the encounter with the Oneness of all things of the Hindu mystic, or the Christian's joyful bliss in experiencing "the peace of God which passeth all understanding."

A mystical experience has been the most profound event in some people's lives. Yet understanding the experience presents several problems. The diversity of the reports of mystical experience in different parts of the world challenges us to devise an adequate description. Is the content of mystical experience wholly determined by the culture in which it occurs? How are we to evaluate the claim that some mystics make about their experiences? For example, some mystics claim that the existence of God is not an inference from some set of empirical facts, but is shown through our experience of Him in mystical ecstasy and absorption into His divine nature. To what extent can we take the reported experience as evidence for anything beyond the fact that the mystic has had the experience? Can we devise valid criteria to enable us to test the truth of these experiences? Should our assessment of the evidence be affected by the fact that the mystical experience was drug-induced?

Apart from the issue of the possibility of mystical knowledge, William James in his *Varieties of Religious Experience* pointed to the profound metaphysical issues generated by the drug-induced mystical experience. Do consciousness-changing substances allow us to understand more deeply the mystery of existence? Might these experiences reveal a dimension to things, an Other World, which lies beyond our normal waking consciousness—indeed, beyond the approaches and well-established canons of the sciences?

The selection that follows raises the question of the relationship of the drug experience to mystical experience and to the religious life. Huston Smith, a well-known contemporary philosopher and scholar of Oriental religions and cultures, cites evidence that there has been a close connection between religion and consciousness-changing substances, such as wine and hallucinogenic plants. He indicates that drug-induced religious experiences are descriptively indistinguishable from religious experiences that occur "naturally." The fact that a religious experience can be induced by drugs does not necessarily detract from the significance or veracity of the religious experience. Professor Smith ends his discussion by pointing out that, although drugs may be able to induce the necessary experiential component in all living religions, the religious experience is not the sum total of the religious life.

Note

1. Webster's New Collegiate Dictionary (Springfield, Mass.: G. & C. Merriam Co., 1960), p. 557.

Do Drugs Have Religious Import?

Until six months ago, if I picked up my phone in the Cambridge area and dialed KISS-BIG, a voice would answer, "If-if." These were coincidences: KISS-BIG happened to be the letter equivalents of an arbitrarily assigned telephone number, and I.F.I.F. represented the initials of an organization with the improbable name of the International Federation for Internal Freedom. But the coincidences were apposite to the point of being poetic. "Kiss big" caught the euphoric, manic, life-embracing attitude that characterized this most publicized of the organizations formed to explore the newly synthesized consciousness-changing substances; the organization itself was surely one of the "iffyest" phenomena to appear on our social and intellectual scene in some time. It produced the first firings in Harvard's history, an ultimatum to get out of Mexico in five days, and "the miracle of Marsh Chapel," in which, during a two-and-one-half-hour Good Friday service, ten theological students and professors ingested psilocybin and were visited by what they generally reported to be the deepest religious experiences of their lives.

Despite the last of these phenomena and its numerous if less dramatic parallels, students of religion appear by and large to be dismissing the psychedelic drugs that have sprung to our

From Huston Smith, "Do Drugs Have Religious Import?" *The Journal of Philosophy,* vol. LXI, no. 18 (October 1, 1964), pp. 517–30. Reprinted by permission.

attention in the '60s as having little religious relevance. The position taken in one of the most forward-looking volumes of theological essays to have appeared in recent years—*Soundings,* edited by A. R. Vidler[1]—accepts R. C. Zaehner's *Mysticism Sacred and Profane* as having "fully examined and refuted" the religious claims for mescalin which Aldous Huxley sketched in *The Doors of Perception.* This closing of the case strikes me as premature, for it looks as if the drugs have light to throw on the history of religion, the phenomenology of religion, the philosophy of religion, and the practice of the religious life itself.

1. Drugs and Religion Viewed Historically

In his trial-and-error life explorations man almost everywhere has stumbled upon connections between vegetables (eaten or brewed) and actions (yogi breathing exercises, whirling-dervish dances, flagellations) that alter states of consciousness. From the psychopharmacological standpoint we now understand these states to be the products of changes in brain chemistry. From the sociological perspective we see that they tend to be connected in some way with reli-

The emended version of a paper presented to The Woodrow Wilson Society, Princeton University, on May 16, 1964.
1. *Soundings: Essays concerning Christian Understandings,* A. R. Vidler, ed. (Cambridge: University Press, 1962). The statement cited appears on page 72, in H. A. William's essay on "Theology and Self-awareness."

gion. If we discount the wine used in Christian communion services, the instances closest to us in time and space are the peyote of The Native American [Indian] Church and Mexico's 2000-year-old "sacred mushrooms," the latter rendered in Aztec as "God's Flesh"—striking parallel to "the body of our Lord" in the Christian eucharist. Beyond these neighboring instances lie the *soma* of the Hindus, the *haoma* and hemp of the Zoroastrians, the Dionysus of the Greeks who "everywhere . . . taught men the culture of the vine and the mysteries of his worship and everywhere [was] accepted as a god,"[2] the *benzoin* of Southeast Asia, Zen's tea whose fifth cup purifies and whose sixth "calls to the realm of the immortals,"[3] the *pituri* of the Australian aborigines, and probably the mystic *kykeon* that was eaten and drunk at the climactic close of the sixth day of the Eleusinian mysteries.[4] There is no need to extend the list, as a reasonably complete account is available in Philippe de Félice's comprehensive study of the subject, *Poisons sacrés, ivresses divines.*

More interesting than the fact that consciousness-changing devices have been linked with religion is the possibility that they actually initiated many of the religious perspectives which, taking root in history, continued after their psychedelic origins were forgotten. Bergson saw the first movement of Hindus and Greeks toward "dynamic religion" as associated with the "divine rapture" found in intoxicating beverages;[5] more recently Robert Graves, Gordon Wasson, and Alan Watts have suggested that most religions arose from such chemically induced theophanies. Mary Barnard is the most explicit proponent of this thesis. "Which . . . was more likely to happen first," she asks,[6] "the

spontaneously generated idea of an afterlife in which the disembodied soul, liberated from the restrictions of time and space, experiences eternal bliss, or the accidental discovery of hallucinogenic plants that give a sense of euphoria, dislocate the center of consciousness, and distort time and space, making them balloon outward in greatly expanded vistas?" Her own answer is that "the [latter] experience might have had . . . an almost explosive effect on the largely dormant minds of men, causing them to think of things they had never thought of before. This, if you like, is direct revelation." Her use of the subjunctive "might" renders this formulation of her answer equivocal, but she concludes her essay on a note that is completely unequivocal: "Looking at the matter coldly, unintoxicated and unentranced, I am willing to prophesy that fifty theobotanists working for fifty years would make the current theories concerning the origins of much mythology and theology as out-of-date as pre-Copernican astronomy."

This is an important hypothesis—one which must surely engage the attention of historians of religion for some time to come. But as I am concerned here only to spot the points at which the drugs erupt onto the field of serious religious study, not to ride the geysers to whatever heights, I shall not pursue Miss Barnard's thesis. Having located what appears to be the crux of the historical question, namely the extent to which drugs not merely duplicate or simulate theologically sponsored experiences but generate or shape theologies themselves, I turn to phenomenology.

2. Drugs and Religion Viewed Phenomenologically

Phenomenology attempts a careful description of human experience. The question the drugs pose for the phenomenology of religion, there-

---

2. Edith Hamilton, *Mythology* (New York: Mentor, 1953), p. 55.
3. Quoted in Alan Watts, *The Spirit of Zen* (New York: Grove Press, 1958), p. 110.
4. George Mylonas, *Eleusis and the Eleusinian Mysteries* (Princeton, N.J.: Princeton Univ. Press, 1961), p. 284.
5. *Two Sources of Morality and Religion* (New York: Holt, 1935), pp. 206–212.

6. "The God in the Flowerpot," *The American Scholar* 32, 4 (Autumn, 1963): 584, 586.

fore, is whether the experiences they induce differ from religious experiences reached naturally, and if so how.

Even the Bible notes that chemically induced psychic states bear *some* resemblance to religious ones. Peter had to appeal to a circumstantial criterion—the early hour of the day—to defend those who were caught up in the Pentecostal experience against the charge that they were merely drunk: "These men are not drunk, as you suppose, since it is only the third hour of the day" (Acts 2:15); and Paul initiates the comparison when he admonishes the Ephesians not to "get drunk with wine . . . but [to] be filled with the spirit" (Ephesians 5:18). Are such comparisons, paralleled in the accounts of virtually every religion, superficial? How far can they be pushed?

Not all the way, students of religion have thus far insisted. With respect to the new drugs, Prof. R. C. Zaehner has drawn the line emphatically. "The importance of Huxley's *Doors of Perception*," he writes, "is that in it the author clearly makes the claim that what he experienced under the influence of mescalin is closely comparable to a genuine mystical experience. If he is right, . . . the conclusions . . . are alarming."[7] Zaehner thinks that Huxley is not right, but I fear that it is Zaehner who is mistaken.

There are, of course, innumerable drug experiences that have no religious feature; they can be sensual as readily as spiritual, trivial as readily as transforming, capricious as readily as sacramental. If there is one point about which every student of the drugs agrees, it is that there is no such thing as the drug experience *per se*— no experience that the drugs, as it were, merely secrete. Every experience is a mix of three ingredients: drug, set (the psychological make-up of the individual), and setting (the social and physical environment in which it is taken). But

given the right set and setting, the drugs can induce religious experiences indistinguishable from experiences that occur spontaneously. Nor need set and setting be exceptional. The way the statistics are currently running, it looks as if from one-fourth to one-third of the general population will have religious experiences if they take the drugs under naturalistic conditions, meaning by this conditions in which the researcher supports the subject but does not try to influence the direction his experience will take. Among subjects who have strong religious inclinations to begin with, the proportion of those having religious experiences jumps to three-fourths. If they take the drugs in settings that are religious too, the ratio soars to nine in ten.

How do we know that the experiences these people have really are religious? We can begin with the fact that they say they are. The "one-fourth to one-third of the general population" figure is drawn from two sources. Ten months after they had had their experiences, 24 per cent of the 194 subjects in a study by the California psychiatrist Oscar Janiger characterized their experiences as having been religious.[8] Thirty-two per cent of the 74 subjects in Ditman and Hayman's study reported, looking back on their LSD experience, that it looked as if it had been "very much" or "quite a bit" a religious experience; 42 per cent checked as true the statement that they "were left with a greater awareness of God, or a higher power, or ultimate reality."[9] The statement that three-fourths of subjects having religious "sets" will have religious experiences comes from the reports of sixty-nine religious professionals who took the drugs while the Harvard project was in progress.[10]

7. *Mysticism, Sacred and Profane* (New York: Oxford, 1961), p. 12.

8. Quoted in William H. McGlothlin, "Long-lasting Effects of LSD on Certain Attitudes in Normals," printed for private distribution by the RAND Corporation, May, 1962, p. 16.
9. *Ibid.*, pp. 45, 46.
10. Timothy Leary, "The Religious Experience: Its Production and Interpretation," *The Psychedelic Review*, 1, 3 (1964): 325.

In the absence of (a) a single definition of religious experience acceptable to psychologists of religion generally and (b) foolproof ways of ascertaining whether actual experiences exemplify any definition, I am not sure there is any better way of telling whether the experiences of the 333 men and women involved in the above studies were religious than by noting whether they seemed so to them. But if more rigorous methods are preferred, they exist; they have been utilized, and they confirm the conviction of the man in the street that drug experiences can indeed be religious. In his doctoral study at Harvard University, Walter Pahnke worked out a typology of religious experience (in this instance of the mystical variety) based on the classic cases of mystical experiences as summarized in Walter Stace's *Mysticism and Philosophy*. He then administered psilocybin to ten theology students and professors in the setting of a Good Friday service. The drug was given "double-blind," meaning that neither Dr. Pahnke nor his subjects knew which ten were getting psilocybin and which ten placebos to constitute a control group. Subsequently the reports the subjects wrote of their experiences were laid successively before three college-graduate housewives who, without being informed about the nature of the study, were asked to rate each statement as to the degree (strong, moderate, slight, or none) to which it exemplified each of the nine traits of mystical experience enumerated in the typology of mysticism worked out in advance. When the test of significance was applied to their statistics, it showed that "those subjects who received psilocybin experienced phenomena which were indistinguishable from, if not identical with . . . the categories defined by our typology of mysticism."[11]

11. "Drugs and Mysticism: An Analysis of the Relationship between Psychedelic Drugs and the Mystical Consciousness," a thesis presented to the Committee on Higher Degrees in History and Philosophy of Religion, Harvard University, June 1963.

With the thought that the reader might like to test his own powers of discernment on the question being considered, I insert here a simple test I gave to a group of Princeton students following a recent discussion sponsored by the Woodrow Wilson Society:

Below are accounts of two religious experiences. One occurred under the influence of drugs, one without their influence. Check the one you think *was* drug-induced.

I

Suddenly I burst into a vast, new, indescribably wonderful universe. Although I am writing this over a year later, the thrill of the surprise and amazement, the awesomeness of the revelation, the engulfment in an overwhelming feeling-wave of gratitude and blessed wonderment, are as fresh, and the memory of the experience is as vivid, as if it had happened five minutes ago. And yet to concoct anything by way of description that would even hint at the magnitude, the sense of ultimate reality . . . this seems such an impossible task. The knowledge which has infused and affected every aspect of my life came instantaneously and with such complete force of certainty that it was impossible, then or since, to doubt its validity.

II

All at once, without warning of any kind, I found myself wrapped in a flame-colored cloud. For an instant I thought of fire . . . the next, I knew that the fire was within myself. Directly afterward there came upon me a sense of exultation, of immense joyousness accompanied or immediately followed by an intellectual illumination impossible to describe. Among other things, I did not merely come to believe, but I saw that the universe is not composed of dead matter, but is, on the contrary, a living Presence; I became conscious in myself of eternal life.... I saw that all men are immortal: that the cosmic order is such that without any pre-adventure all things work together for the good of each and all; that the foundation principle of the world . . . is what we call love, and that the happiness of each and all is in the long run absolutely certain.

On the occasion referred to, twice as many students (46) answered incorrectly as answered correctly (23). I bury the correct answer in a footnote to preserve the reader's opportunity to test himself.[12]

Why, in the face of this considerable evidence, does Zaehner hold that drug experiences cannot be authentically religious? There appear to be three reasons:

1. His own experience was "utterly trivial." This of course proves that not all drug experiences are religious; it does not prove that no drug experiences are religious.

2. He thinks the experiences of others that appear religious to them are not truly so. Zaehner distinguishes three kinds of mysticism: nature mysticism, in which the soul is united with the natural world; monistic mysticism, in which the soul merges with an impersonal absolute; and theism, in which the soul confronts the living, personal God. He concedes that drugs can induce the first two species of mysticism, but not its supreme instance, the theistic. As proof, he analyzes Huxley's experience as recounted in *The Doors of Perception* to show that it produced at best a blend of nature and monistic mysticism. Even if we were to accept Zaehner's evaluation of the three forms of mysticism, Huxley's case, and indeed Zaehner's entire book, would prove only that not every mystical experience induced by the drugs is theistic. Insofar as Zaehner goes beyond this to imply that drugs do not and cannot induce theistic mysticism, he not only goes beyond the evidence but proceeds in the face of it. James Slotkin reports that the peyote Indians "see visions, which may be of Christ Himself. Sometimes they hear the voice of the Great Spirit. Sometimes they become aware of the presence of God and of those personal shortcomings which must be corrected if they are to do His will."[13] And G. M. Carstairs, reporting on the use of psychedelic *bhang* in India, quotes a Brahmin as saying, "It gives good bhakti. . . . You get a very good bhakti with bhang," *bhakti* being precisely Hinduism's theistic variant.[14]

3. There is a third reason why Zaehner might doubt that drugs can induce genuinely mystical experiences. Zaehner is a Roman Catholic, and Roman Catholic doctrine teaches that mystical rapture is a gift of grace and as such can never be reduced to man's control. This may be true; certainly the empirical evidence cited does not preclude the possibility of a genuine ontological or theological difference between natural and drug-induced religious experiences. At this point, however, we are considering phenomenology rather than ontology, description rather than interpretation, and on this level there is no

---

12. The first account is quoted anonymously in "The Issue of the Consciousness-expanding Drugs," *Main Currents in Modern Thought,* 20, 1 (September-October, 1963):10–11. The second experience was that of Dr. R. M. Bucke, the author of *Cosmic Consciousness,* as quoted in William James, *The Varieties of Religious Experience* (New York: Modern Library, 1902), pp. 390–391. The former experience occurred under the influence of drugs; the latter did not.

13. James S. Slotkin, *Peyote Religion* (New York: Free Press of Glencoe, 1956).

14. "Daru and Bhang," *Quarterly Journal of the Study of Alcohol,* 15 (1954): 229.

difference. Descriptively, drug experiences cannot be distinguished from their natural religious counterpart. When the current philosophical authority on mysticism, W. T. Stace, was asked whether the drug experience is similar to the mystical experience, he answered, "It's not a matter of its being *similar* to mystical experience; it *is* mystical experience."

What we seem to be witnessing in Zaehner's *Mysticism Sacred and Profane* is a reenactment of the age-old pattern in the conflict between science and religion. Whenever a new controversy arises, religion's first impulse is to deny the disturbing evidence science has produced. Seen in perspective, Zaehner's refusal to admit that drugs can induce experiences descriptively indistinguishable from those which are spontaneously religious is the current counterpart of the seventeenth-century theologians' refusal to look through Galileo's telescope or, when they did, their persistence on dismissing what they saw as machinations of the devil. When the fact that drugs can trigger religious experiences becomes incontrovertible, discussion will move to the more difficult question of how this new fact is to be interpreted. The latter question leads beyond phenomenology into philosophy.

3. Drugs and Religion Viewed Philosophically

Why do people reject evidence? Because they find it threatening, we may suppose. Theologians are not the only professionals to utilize this mode of defense. In his *Personal Knowledge,*[15] Michael Polanyi recounts the way the medical profession ignored such palpable facts as the painless amputation of human limbs, performed before their own eyes in hundreds of successive cases, concluding that the subjects were imposters who were either deluding their physicians or colluding with them. One phy-

sician, Esdaile, carried out about 300 major operations painlessly under mesmeric trance in India, but neither in India nor in Great Britain could he get medical journals to print accounts of his work. Polanyi attributes this closed-mindedness to "lack of a conceptual framework in which their discoveries could be separated from specious and untenable admixtures."

The "untenable admixture" in the fact that psychotomimetic drugs can induce religious experience is its apparent implicate: that religious disclosures are no more veridical than psychotic ones. For religious skeptics, this conclusion is obviously not untenable at all; it fits in beautifully with their thesis that *all* religion is at heart an escape from reality. Psychotics avoid reality by retiring into dream worlds of make-believe; what better evidence that religious visionaries do the same than the fact that identical changes in brain chemistry produce both states of mind? Had not Marx already warned us that religion is the "opiate" of the people?— apparently he was more literally accurate than he supposed. Freud was likewise too mild. He "never doubted that religious phenomena are to be understood only on the model of the neurotic symptoms of the individual."[16] He should have said "psychotic symptoms."

So the religious skeptic is likely to reason. What about the religious believer? Convinced that religious eperiences are not fundamentally delusory, can he admit that psychotomimetic drugs can occasion them? To do so he needs (to return to Polanyi's words) "a conceptual framework in which [the discoveries can] be separated from specious and untenable admixtures," the "untenable admixture" being in this case the conclusion that religious experiences are in general delusory.

One way to effect the separation would be to argue that, despite phenomenological similarities between natural and drug-induced religi-

---

15. Chicago: Univ. of Chicago Press, 1958.

16. *Totem and Taboo* (New York: Modern Library, 1938).

ous experiences, they are separated by a crucial *ontological* difference. Such an argument would follow the pattern of theologians who argue for the "real presence" of Christ's body and blood in the bread and wine of the Eucharist despite their admission that chemical analysis, confined as it is to the level of "accidents" rather than "essences," would not disclose this presence. But this distinction will not appeal to many today, for it turns on an essence-accident metaphysics which is not widely accepted. Instead of fighting a rear-guard action by insisting that if drug and non-drug religious experiences cannot be distinguished empirically there must be some transempirical factor that distinguishes them and renders the drug experience profane, I wish to explore the possibility of accepting drug-induced experiences as religious without relinquishing confidence in the truth-claims of religious experience generally.

To begin with the weakest of all arguments, the argument from authority: William James did not discount *his* insights that occurred while his brain chemistry was altered. The paragraph in which he retrospectively evaluates his nitrous oxide experiences has become classic, but it is so pertinent to the present discussion that it merits quoting once again.

One conclusion was forced upon my mind at that time, and my impression of its truth has ever since remained unshaken. It is that our normal waking consciousness, rational consciousness as we call it, is but one special type of consciousness, whilst all about it, parted from it by the filmiest of screens, there lie potential forms of consciousness entirely different. We may go through life without suspecting their existence; but apply the requisite stimulus, and at a touch they are there in all their completeness, definite types of mentality which probably somewhere have their field of application and adaptation. No account of the universe in its totality can be final

which leaves these other forms of consciousness quite disregarded. How to regard them is the question—for they are so discontinuous with ordinary consciousness. Yet they may determine attitudes though they cannot furnish formulas, and open a region though they fail to give a map. At any rate, they forbid a premature closing of our accounts with reality. Looking back on my own experiences, they all converge toward a kind of insight to which I cannot help ascribing some metaphysical significance (*op. cit.,* 378–379).

To this argument from authority, I add two arguments that try to provide something by ways of reasons. Drug experiences that assume a religious cast tend to have fearful and/or beatific features, and each of my hypotheses relates to one of these aspects of the experience. Beginning with the ominous, "fear of the Lord," awe-ful features, Gordon Wasson, the New York banker-turned-mycologist, describes these as he encountered them in his psilocybin experience as follows: "Ecstasy! In common parlance . . . ecstasy is fun. . . . But ecstasy is not fun. Your very soul is seized and shaken until it tingles. After all, who will choose to feel undiluted awe? . . . The unknowing vulgar abuse the word; we must recapture its full and terrifying sense."[17] Emotionally the drug experience can be like having forty-foot waves crash over you for several hours while you cling desperately to a life-raft which may be swept from under you at any minute. It seems quite possible that such an ordeal, like any experience of a close call, could awaken rather fundamental sentiments respecting life and death and destiny and trigger the "no atheists in foxholes" effect. Similarly, as the subject emerges from the trauma and realizes that he is not going to be insane as he had feared, there may come over him an

17. "The Hallucinogenic Fungi of Mexico: An Inquiry into the Origins of the Religious Idea among Primitive Peoples," *Harvard Botanical Museum Leaflets,* 19, 7 (1961).

intensified appreciation like that frequently reported by patients recovering from critical illness. "It happened on the day when my bed was pushed out of doors to the open gallery of the hospital," reads one such report:

> I cannot now recall whether the revelation came suddenly or gradually; I only remember finding myself in the very midst of those wonderful moments, beholding life for the first time in all its young intoxication of loveliness, in its unspeakable joy, beauty, and importance. I cannot say exactly what the mysterious change was. I saw no new thing, but I saw all the usual things in a miraculous new light—in what I believe is their true light. I saw for the first time how wildly beautiful and joyous, beyond any words of mine to describe, is the whole of life. Every human being moving across that porch, every sparrow that flew, every branch tossing in the wind, was caught in and was a part of the whole mad ecstasy of loveliness, of joy, of importance, of intoxication of life.[18]

If we do not discount religious intuitions because they are prompted by battlefields and *physical* crises; if we regard the latter as "calling us to our senses" more often than they seduce us into delusions, need comparable intuitions be discounted simply because the crises that trigger them are of an inner, *psychic* variety?

Turning from the hellish to the heavenly aspects of the drug experience, *some* of the latter may be explainable by the hypothesis just stated; that is, they may be occasioned by the relief that attends the sense of escape from high danger. But this hypothesis cannot possibly account for *all* the beatific episodes, for the simple reason that the positive episodes often come first, or to persons who experience no negative episodes

whatever. Dr. Sanford Unger of the National Institute of Mental Health reports that among his subjects "50 to 60% will not manifest any real disturbance worthy of discussion," yet "around 75% will have at least one episode in which exaltation, rapture, and joy are the key descriptions."[19] How are we to account for the drug's capacity to induce peak experiences, such as the following, which are *not* preceded by fear?

> A feeling of great peace and contentment seemed to flow through my entire body. All sound ceased and I seemed to be floating in a great, very very still void or hemisphere. It is impossible to describe the overpowering feeling of peace, contentment, and being a part of goodness itself that I felt. I could feel my body dissolving and actually becoming a part of the goodness and peace that was all around me. Words can't describe this. I feel an awe and wonder that such a feeling could have occurred to me.[20]

Consider the following line of argument. Like every other form of life, man's nature has become distinctive through specialization. Man has specialized in developing a cerebral cortex. The analytic powers of this instrument are a standing wonder, but the instrument seems less able to provide man with the sense that he is meaningfully related to his environment: to life, the world, and history in their wholeness. As Albert Camus describes the situation, "If I were . . . a cat among animals, this life would have a meaning, or rather this problem would not arise, for I should belong to this world. I would *be* this world to which I am now opposed

---

18. Margaret Prescott Montague, *Twenty Minutes of Reality* (St. Paul, Minn.: Macalester Park, 1947), pp. 15, 17.

19. "The Current Scientific Status of Psychedelic Drug Research," read at the Conference on Methods in Philosophy and the Sciences, New School for Social Research, May 3, 1964, and scheduled for publication in David Solomon, ed., *The Conscious Expanders* (New York: Putnam, fall of 1964).

20. Quoted by Dr. Unger in the paper just mentioned.

by my whole consciousness."[21] Note that it is Camus' consciousness that opposes him to his world. The drugs do not knock this consciousness out, but while they leave it operative they also activate areas of the brain that normally lie below its threshold of awareness. One of the clearest objective signs that the drugs are taking effect is the dilation they produce in the pupils of the eyes, and one of the most predictable subjective signs is the intensification of visual perception. Both of these responses are controlled by portions of the brain that lie deep, further to the rear than the mechanisms that govern consciousness. Meanwhile we know that the human organism is interlaced with its world in innumerable ways it normally cannot sense—through gravitational fields, body respiration, and the like: the list could be multiplied until man's skin began to seem more like a thoroughfare than a boundary. Perhaps the deeper regions of the brain which evolved earlier and are more like those of the lower animals—"If I were . . . a cat . . . I should belong to this world"—can sense this relatedness better than can the cerebral cortex which now dominates our awareness. If so, when the drugs rearrange the neurohumors that chemically transmit impulses across synapses between neurons, man's consciousness and his submerged, intuitive, ecological awareness might for a spell become interlaced. This is, of course, no more than a hypothesis, but how else are we to account for the extraordinary incidence under the drugs of that kind of insight the keynote of which James described as "invariably a reconciliation"? "It is as if the opposites of the world, whose contradictoriness and conflict make all our difficulties and troubles, were melted into one and the same genus, but *one of the species,* the nobler and better one, *is itself the genus and so soaks up and absorbs its opposites into itself*" (*op. cit.,* 379).

21. *The Myth of Sisyphus* (New York: Vintage, 1955), p. 38.

4. The Drugs and Religion Viewed "Religiously"

Suppose that drugs can induce experiences indistinguishable from religious experiences and that we can respect their reports. Do they shed any light, not (we now ask) on life, but on the nature of the religious life?

One thing they may do is throw religious experience itself into perspective by clarifying its relation to the religious life as a whole. Drugs appear able to induce religious experiences; it is less evident that they can produce religious lives. It follows that religion is more than religious experiences. This is hardly news, but it may be a useful reminder, especially to those who incline toward "the religion of religious experience"; which is to say toward lives bent on the acquisition of desired states of experience irrespective of their relation to life's other demands and components.

Despite the dangers of faculty psychology, it remains useful to regard man as having a mind, a will, and feelings. One of the lessons of religious history is that, to be adequate, a faith must rouse and involve all three components of man's nature. Religions of reason grow arid; religions of duty, leaden. Religions of experience have their comparable pitfalls, as evidenced by Taoism's struggle (not always successful) to keep from degenerating into quietism, and the vehemence with which Zen Buddhism has insisted that once students have attained *satori,* they must be driven out of it, back into the world. The case of Zen is especially pertinent here, for it pivots on an enlightenment experience—*satori,* or *kensho*—which some (but not all) Zennists say resembles LSD. Alike or different, the point is that Zen recognizes that unless the experience is joined to discipline, it will come to naught:

Even the Buddha . . . had to sit. . . . Without *joriki,* the particular power developed through *zazen* [seated meditation], the

vision of oneness attained in enlightenment
... in time becomes clouded and eventually
fades into a pleasant memory instead of
remaining an omnipresent reality shaping
our daily life. ... To be able to live in accordance with what the Mind's eye has
revealed through *satori* requires, like the
purification of character and the development of personality, a ripening period of
zazen.[22]

If the religion of religious experience is a
snare and a delusion, it follows that no religion
that fixes its faith primarily in substances that
induce religious experiences can be expected to
come to a good end. What promised to be a
short cut will prove to be a short circuit; what
began as a religion will end as a religion surrogate. Whether chemical substances can be helpful *adjuncts* to faith is another question. The
peyote-using Native American Church seems to
indicate that they can be; anthropologists give
this church a good report, noting among other
things that members resist alcohol and alcoholism better than do nonmembers.[23] The conclusion to which evidence currently points
would seem to be that chemicals *can* aid the
religious life, but only where set within a con-

text of faith (meaning by this the conviction
that what they disclose is true) and discipline
(meaning diligent exercise of the will in the
attempt to work out the implications of the
disclosures for the living of life in the everyday,
common-sense world).

Nowhere today in Western civilization are
these two conditions jointly fulfilled. Churches
lack faith in the sense just mentioned; hipsters
lack discipline. This might lead us to forget
about the drugs, were it not for one fact: the
distinctive religious emotion and the emotion
that drugs unquestionably can occasion—Otto's
*mysterium tremendum, majestas, mysterium
fascinans;* in a phrase, the phenomenon of
religious awe—seems to be declining sharply. As
Paul Tillich said in an address to the Hillel
Society at Harvard several years ago:

> The question our century puts before us
> [is]: Is it possible to regain the lost dimen-
> sion, the encounter with the Holy, the
> dimension which cuts through the world of
> subjectivity and objectivity and goes down
> to that which is not world but is the mystery
> of the Ground of Being?

Tillich may be right; this may be the religious
question of our century. For if (as we have
insisted) religion cannot be equated with religious experiences, neither can it long survive their
absence.

---

22. Philip Kapleau, *Zen Practice and Attainment,* a manuscript in process of publication.
23. Slotkin, *op. cit.*

23 / Faith as Ultimate Concern
Tillich

The arguments for the existence of God as outlined by Nagel are still debated. The discussion concerns not only whether or not they prove, or provide evidence for, the existence of God, but also it focuses upon them as arguments. Philosophers are interested in them as types of arguments and inferences. Historically, however, religion has been ambivalent about the significance of rational arguments for the existence of God and the place of reason in theology because of the elusiveness of the concept of God, the differing assessments of the value of human reason, and the difficulties in defining the limits of knowledge.

Many mystics hold that God is not an inferred entity at all. God is directly experienced. Others maintain that God's existence cannot be proven either by logical argument or by means of the mystical experience. Rather, God has disclosed himself through revelation, and man's acceptance of the truth of those revelations, his affirmative response to them through faith, provides the ground for religion.

The belief in, or assent to, religious doctrines or traditions is one meaning of the term "faith." This position is partly represented in the reading by Niebuhr.[1] One of the most recent and unique uses of the term "faith" is that of the German theologian, Paul Tillich (1886–1965). Faith is the state of man's being ultimately concerned or passionately preoccupied with the meaning and the basis for his existence. For Tillich, in one sense, all men have faith or ultimate concern; in another sense, it is misleading to speak of man as *having* faith because faith (and doubt) are a part of the human situation in which man shows ultimate concern. Likewise, all talk of the proofs for the existence of God in the debate between theists and atheists Tillich finds irrelevant to the central issue of religion. Arguing about God's existence assumes that God is a thing among other things; an object among other objects. "God" for Tillich is the name for that which concerns man ultimately.

Although the differences are perhaps more significant, Tillich has much in common with the existentialists. Like those philosophers, Tillich focuses on man's experience in the world and on the individual's searching questions about himself and the meaning of his existence. Man's personal involvement with what it means to be is the essence of what Tillich considers the religious life. As a professor, first in Germany and later in the United States, Tillich endeavored to make theology and religion speak to the human condition and to analyze human existence with its risks and doubts in a way that manifests the truths of theology. Like the existentialists, Tillich's portrait of modern man is a portrait of conflict, despair, and loneliness.

The man of today . . . is aware of the confusion of his inner life, the cleavage in his behavior, the demonic forces in his psychic and social existence. And he senses that not only his being but also his knowing is thrown into confusion, that he lacks ultimate truth. . . . In this situation in which most of the traditional values and forms of life are disintegrating, he is often driven to the abyss of complete meaninglessness, which is full of both horror and fascination.[2]

Another similarity between Tillich and the existentialists is his emphasis on the contrast between the objective, detached, public knowledge of science and the knowledge in which man's involvement and concern are an integral part of the situation—an "existential" truth in which the knowing subject "participates" in the object known. In one of Tillich's many autobiographical sketches, he says:

The spoken word is effective not only through the meaning of the sentences formulated, but also through the immediate impact of the personality behind these sentences. This is a temptation because one can use it for methods of mere persuasion. But it is also a benefit, because it agrees with what may be called "existential truth"; namely, a truth which lives in the immediate self-expression of an experience. This is not true of statements which have a merely objective character, which belong to the realm of "controlling knowledge"; but it is valid of statements which concern us in our very existence, and especially of theological statements which deal with that which concerns us ultimately.[3]

Religion is weakened, Tillich believes, when the revelation and myths of religion are taken literally. Myth is neither a kind of primitive science nor an irrational faith, belief "in spite of the evidence." The myths and stories of religion express symbolically the spiritual predicaments of man. Man's concern about his existence is a universal religious concern. It finds its highest expression in symbolic forms. By "loss of religion," Tillich does not mean the fall in attendance at church or temple, but the failure to raise the question of life's ultimate meaning. The inability or failure to raise, and demand an answer to, this central question is, for Tillich, one of the greatest dangers for contemporary man.

What Faith Is

Faith as Ultimate Concern

Faith is the state of being ultimately concerned: the dynamics of faith are the dynamics of man's ultimate concern. Man, like every living being, is concerned about many things, above all about those which condition his very existence, such as food and shelter. But man, in contrast to other living beings, has spiritual concerns—cognitive, aesthetic, social, political. Some of them are urgent, often extremely urgent, and each of them as well as the vital concerns can claim ultimacy for a human life or the life of a social group. If it claims ultimacy it demands the total surrender of him who accepts this claim, and it promises total fulfillment even if all other claims have to be subjected to it or rejected in its name. If a national group makes the life and growth of the nation its ultimate concern, it demands that all other concerns, economic well-being, health and life, family, aesthetic and cognitive truth, justice and humanity, be sacrificed. The extreme nationalisms of our century are laboratories for the study of what ultimate concern means in all aspects of human existence, including the smallest concern of one's daily life. Everything is centered in the only god, the nation—a god who certainly proves to be a demon, but who shows clearly the unconditional character of an ultimate concern.

But it is not only the unconditional demand

From pp. 1–4 and 16–21 in *Dynamics of Faith* by Paul Tillich. Copyright © 1957 by Paul Tillich. By permission of Harper & Row, Publishers, Inc.

made by that which is one's ultimate concern, it is also the promise of ultimate fulfillment which is accepted in the act of faith. The content of this promise is not necessarily defined. It can be expressed in indefinite symbols or in concrete symbols which cannot be taken literally, like the "greatness" of one's nation in which one participates even if one has died for it, or the conquest of mankind by the "saving race," etc. In each of these cases it is "ultimate fulfillment" that is promised, and it is exclusion from such fulfillment which is threatened if the unconditional demand is not obeyed.

An example—and more than an example—is the faith manifest in the religion of the Old Testament. It also has the character of ultimate concern in demand, threat and promise. The content of this concern is not the nation—although Jewish nationalism has sometimes tried to distort it into that—but the content is the God of justice, who, because he represents justice for everybody and every nation, is called the universal God, the God of the universe. He is the ultimate concern of every pious Jew, and therefore in his name the great commandment is given: "You shall love the Lord your God with all your heart, and with all your soul, and with all your might" (Deut 6:5). This is what ultimate concern means and from these words the term "ultimate concern" is derived. They state unambiguously the character of genuine faith, the demand of total surrender to the subject of ultimate concern. The Old Testament is full of commands which make the nature of this surrender concrete, and it is full of promises and threats in relation to it. Here also are the promises of symbolic indefiniteness, although they center around fulfillment of the national and individual life, and the threat is the exclusion from such fulfillment through national extinction and individual catastrophe. Faith, for the men of the Old Testament, is the state of being ultimately and unconditionally concerned about Jahweh and about what he represents in demand, threat and promise.

Another example—almost a counter-example, yet nevertheless equally revealing—is the ultimate concern with "success" and with social standing and economic power. It is the god of many people in the highly competitive Western culture and it does what every ultimate concern must do: it demands unconditional surrender to its laws even if the price is the sacrifice of genuine human relations, personal conviction, and creative *eros*. Its threat is social and economic defeat, and its promise—indefinite as all such promises—the fulfillment of one's being. It is the breakdown of this kind of faith which characterizes and makes religiously important most contemporary literature. Not false calculations but a misplaced faith is revealed in novels like *Point of No Return*. When fulfilled, the promise of this faith proves to be empty.

Faith is the state of being ultimately concerned. The content matters infinitely for the life of the believer, but it does not matter for the formal definition of faith. And this is the first step we have to make in order to understand the dynamics of faith.

Faith as a Centered Act

Faith as ultimate concern is an act of the total personality. It happens in the center of the personal life and includes all its elements. Faith is the most centered act of the human mind. It is not a movement of a special section or a special function of man's total being. They all are united in the act of faith. But faith is not the sum total of their impacts. It tran-

scends every special impact as well as the totality of them and it has itself a decisive impact on each of them. . . .

Faith and Doubt

We now return to a fuller description of faith as an act of the human personality, as its centered and total act. An act of faith is an act of a finite being who is grasped by and turned to the infinite. It is a finite act with all the limitations of a finite act, and it is an act in which the infinite partcipates beyond the limitations of a finite act. Faith is certain in so far as it is an experience of the holy. But faith is uncertain in so far as the infinite to which it is related is received by a finite being. This element of uncertainty in faith cannot be removed, it must be accepted. And the element in faith which accepts this is courage. Faith includes an element of immediate awareness which gives certainty and an element of uncertainty. To accept this is courage. In the courageous standing of uncertainty, faith shows most visibly its dynamic character.

If we try to describe the relation of faith and courage, we must use a larger concept of courage than that which is ordinarily used.[1] Courage as an element of faith is the daring self-affirmation of one's own being in spite of the powers of "nonbeing" which are the heritage of everything finite. Where there is daring and courage there is the possibility of failure. And in every act of faith this possibility is present. The risk must be taken. Whoever makes his nation his ultimate concern needs courage in order to maintain this concern. Only certain is the ultimacy as ultimacy, the infinite passion as infinite passion. This is a reality given to the self with his own nature. It is as immediate and as much beyond doubt as the self is to the self. It *is* the

1. Cf. Paul Tillich, *The Courage to Be.* Yale University Press.

self in its self-transcending quality. But there is not certainty of this kind about the content of our ultimate concern, be it nation, success, a god, or the God of the Bible: They all are contents without immediate awareness. Their acceptance as matters of ultimate concern is a risk and therefore an act of courage. There is a risk if what was considered as a matter of ultimate concern proves to be a matter of preliminary and transitory concern—as, for example, the nation. The risk to faith in one's ultimate concern is indeed the greatest risk man can run. For if it proves to be a failure, the meaning of one's life breaks down; one surrenders oneself, including truth and justice, to something which is not worth it. One has given away one's personal center without having a chance to regain it. The reaction of despair in people who have experienced the breakdown of their national claims is an irrefutable proof of the idolatrous character of their national concern. In the long run this is the inescapable result of an ultimate concern, the subject matter of which is not ultimate. And this is the risk faith must take; this is the risk which is unavoidable if a finite being affirms itself. Ultimate concern is ultimate risk and ultimate courage. It is not risk and needs no courage with respect to ultimacy itself. But it is risk and demands courage if it affirms a concrete concern. And every faith has a concrete element in itself. It is concerned about something or somebody. But this something or this somebody may prove to be not ultimate at all. Then faith is a failure in its concrete expression, although it is not a failure in the experience of the unconditional itself. A god disappears; divinity remains. Faith risks the vanishing of the concrete god in whom it believes. It may well be that with the vanishing of the god the believer breaks down without being able to re-establish his centered self by a new content of his ultimate concern. This risk cannot be taken away from any act of faith. There is only one point which is a matter not of risk but of immediate certainty and herein

lies the greatness and the pain of being human; namely, one's standing between one's finitude and one's potential infinity.

All this is sharply expressed in the relation of faith and doubt. If faith is understood as belief that something is true, doubt is incompatible with the act of faith. If faith is understood as being ultimately concerned, doubt is a necessary element in it. It is a consequence of the risk of faith.

The doubt which is implicit in faith is not a doubt about facts or conclusions. It is not the same doubt which is the lifeblood of scientific research. Even the most orthodox theologian does not deny the right of methodological doubt in matters of empirical inquiry or logical deduction. A scientist who would say that a scientific theory is beyond doubt would at that moment cease to be scientific. He may believe that the theory can be trusted for all practical purposes. Without such belief no technical application of a theory would be possible. One could attribute to this kind of belief pragmatic certainty sufficient for action. Doubt in this case points to the preliminary character of the underlying theory.

There is another kind of doubt, which we could call skeptical in contrast to the scientific doubt which we could call methodological. The skeptical doubt is an attitude toward all the beliefs of man, from sense experiences to religious creeds. It is more an attitude than an assertion. For as an assertion it would conflict with itself. Even the assertion that there is no possible truth for man would be judged by the skeptical principle and could not stand as an assertion. Genuine skeptical doubt does not use the form of an assertion. It is an attitude of actually rejecting any certainty. Therefore, it can not be refuted logically. It does not transform its attitude into a proposition. Such an attitude necessarily leads either to despair or cynicism, or to both alternately. And often, if this alternative becomes intolerable, it leads to indifference and the attempt to develop an attitude of complete unconcern. But since man is that being who is essentially concerned about his being, such an escape finally breaks down. This is the dynamics of skeptical doubt. It has an awakening and liberating function, but it also can prevent the development of a centered personality. For personality is not possible without faith. The despair about truth by the skeptic shows that truth is still his infinite passion. The cynical superiority over every concrete truth shows that truth is still taken seriously and that the impact of the question of an ultimate concern is strongly felt. The skeptic, so long as he is a serious skeptic, is not without faith, even though it has no concrete content.

The doubt which is implicit in every act of faith is neither the methodological nor the skeptical doubt. It is the doubt which accompanies every risk. It is not the permanent doubt of the scientist, and it is not the transitory doubt of the skeptic, but it is the doubt of him who is ultimately concerned about a concrete content. One could call it the existential doubt, in contrast to the methodological and the skeptical doubt. It does not question whether a special proposition is true or false. It does not reject every concrete truth, but it is aware of the element of insecurity in every existential truth. At the same time, the doubt which is implied in faith accepts this insecurity and takes it into itself in an act of courage. Faith includes courage. Therefore, it can include the doubt about itself. Certainly faith and courage are not identical. Faith has other elements besides courage and courage has other functions beyond affirming faith. Nevertheless, an act in which courage accepts risk belongs to the dynamics of faith. . . .

The Life of Faith

Faith and Courage

Everything said about faith in the previous chapters is derived from the experience of actual faith, of faith as a living reality, or in a metaphoric abbreviation, of the life of faith. This experience is the subject of our last chapter. The "dynamics of faith" are present not only in the inner tensions and conflicts of the content of faith, but also present in the life of faith, and of course the one is dependent on the other.

Where there is faith there is tension between participation and separation, between the faithful one and his ultimate concern. We have used the metaphor "being grasped" for describing the state of ultimate concern. And being grasped implies that he who is grasped and that by which he is grasped are, so to speak, at the same place. Without some participation in the object of one's ultimate concern, it is not possible to be concerned about it. In this sense every act of faith presupposes participation in that toward which it is directed. Without a preceding experience of the ultimate no faith in the ultimate can exist. The mystical type of faith has emphasized this point most strongly. Here lies its truth which no theology of "mere faith" can destroy. Without the manifestation of God in man the question of God and faith in God are not possible. There is no faith without participation!

From pp. 99–103 and 126–27 in *Dynamics of Faith* by Paul Tillich. Copyright © 1957 by Paul Tillich. By permission of Harper & Row, Publishers, Inc.

But faith would cease to be faith without separation—the opposite element. He who has faith is separated from the object of his faith. Otherwise he would possess it. It would be a matter of immediate certainty and not of faith. The "in-spite-of element" of faith would be lacking. But the human situation, its finitude and estrangement, prevents man's participation in the ultimate without both the separation and the promise of faith. Here the limit of mysticism becomes visible: it neglects the human predicament and the separation of man from the ultimate. There is no faith without separation.

Out of the element of participation follows the certainty of faith; out of the element of separation follows the doubt in faith. And each is essential for the nature of faith. Sometimes certainty conquers doubt, but it cannot eliminate doubt. The conquered of today may become the conqueror of tomorrow. Sometimes doubt conquers faith, but it still contains faith. Otherwise it would be indifference. Neither faith nor doubt can be eliminated, though each of them can be reduced to a minimum, in the life of faith. Since the life of faith is life in the state of ultimate concern and no human being can exist completely without such a concern, we can say: Neither faith nor doubt can be eliminated from man as man.

Faith and doubt have been contrasted in such a way that the quiet certainty of faith has been praised as the complete removal of doubt. There is, indeed, a serenity of the life in faith beyond the disturbing struggles between faith and doubt. To attain such a state is a natural and justified desire of every human being. But even if it is attained—as in people who are called saints or in others who are described as firm in their faith—the element of doubt, though conquered, is not lacking. In the saints it appears, according to holy legend, as a temptation which increases in power with the increase of saintliness. In those who rest on their unshakable faith, pharisaism and fanaticism are the unmistakable symptoms of doubt which has been repressed. Doubt is overcome not by repression but by courage. Courage does not deny that there is doubt, but it takes the doubt into itself as an expression of its own finitude and affirms the content of an ultimate concern. Courage does not need the safety of an unquestionable conviction. It includes the risk without which no creative life is possible. For example, if the content of someone's ultimate concern is Jesus as the Christ, such faith is not a matter of a doubtless certainty, it is a matter of daring courage with the risk to fail. Even if the confession that Jesus is the Christ is expressed in a strong and positive way, the fact that it is a confession implies courage and risk.

All this is said of living faith, of faith as actual concern, and not of faith as a traditional attitude without tensions, without doubt and without courage. Faith in this sense, which is the attitude of many members of the churches as well as of society at large, is far removed from the dynamic character of faith as described in this book. One could say that such conventional faith is the dead remnant of former experiences of ultimate concern. It is dead but it can become alive. For even nondynamic faith lives in symbols. In these symbols the power of original faith is still embodied. Therefore, one should not underestimate the importance of faith as a traditional attitude. It is not actual, not living faith; it is potential faith which can become actual. This is especially relevant for education. It is not meaningless to communicate to children or immature adults objective symbols of faith and with them expressions of the living faith of former generations. The danger of this method, of course, is that the faith, mediated in education, will remain a traditional attitude and never break through to a state of living faith. However, if this causes people to become hesitant about communicating any of the given symbols and to wait until independent questions about the meaning of life have arisen, it can lead to a powerful life of faith, but it also can lead to emptiness, to cynicism and, in reaction to it, to idolatrous forms of ultimate concern.

Living faith includes the doubt about itself, the courage to take this doubt into itself, and the risk of courage. There is an element of immediate certainty in every faith, which is not subject to doubt, courage and risk—the unconditional concern itself. It is experienced in passion, anxiety, despair, ecstasy. But it is never experienced in isolation from a concrete content. It is experienced in, with and through the concrete content, and only the analytic mind can isolate it theoretically. Such theoretical isolation is the basis of this whole book; it is the way to the definition of faith as ultimate concern. But the life of faith itself does not include such analytic work. Therefore, the doubt about the concrete content of one's ultimate concern is directed against faith in its totality, and faith as a total act must affirm itself through courage....

Conclusion: The Possibility and Necessity of Faith Today

Faith is real in every period of history. This fact does not prove that it is an essential possibility and necessity. It could be—like superstition—an actual distortion of man's true nature. This is what many people who reject faith believe. The question raised by this book is whether such belief is based on insight or on misunderstanding, and the answer is unambiguously that the rejection of faith is rooted in a complete misunderstanding of the nature of faith. Many forms of this misunderstanding, many misrepresentations and distortions of faith have been discussed. Faith is a concept—and a reality—which is difficult to grasp and to describe. Almost every word by which faith has been described —also on the preceding pages—is open to new misinterpretations. This cannot be otherwise, since faith is not a phenomenon beside others, but the central phenomenon in man's personal life, manifest and hidden at the same time. It is religious and transcends religion, it is universal and concrete, it is infinitely variable and always the same. Faith is an essential possibility of man, and therefore its existence is necessary and universal. It is possible and necessary also in our period. If faith is understood as what it centrally is, ultimate concern, it cannot be undercut by modern science or any kind of philosophy. And it cannot be discredited by its superstitions or authoritarian distortions within and outside churches, sects and movements. Faith stands upon itself and justifies itself against those who attack it, because they can attack it only in the name of another faith. It is the triumph of the dynamics of faith that any denial of faith is itself an expression of faith, of an ultimate concern.

Notes

1. Another meaning of the term "faith" in the sense of a volitional act of will, even though all the evidence is not in, is contained in Part II in the selection from William James's *The Will to Believe*.

2. Paul Tillich, *The Protestant Era* (Chicago: University of Chicago Press, 1948), p. 202.

3. C. W. Kegley and R. W. Bretall, eds. *The Theology of Paul Tillich* (New York: Macmillan, 1952), p. 16.

Afterword / Recovering the Lost Dimension

Huston Smith states that the phenomena of religious awe, the religious experience, is declining rapidly today and that Paul Tillich may be correct: the encounter with the Holy is a lost dimension in modern life. Since Huston Smith wrote his article, there has been some movement toward regaining the lost dimension. The interest in Jesus, the growth of evangelism and fundamentalism, and the study of mysticism are widespread. Among Jewish believers, there is the renewed interest in the mysteries of Hasidism; among Christians, a renewed interest in St. Theresa and Meister Eckhart. The Pentecostal movement has also introduced many Christians to a fresh encounter with the Holy Spirit.

A growing number of Westerners have turned to the East in search of this lost dimension. Followers of Krishna can be seen in almost any major American city. Tibetan Buddhists now have study and meditation communities in Colorado and Vermont, and Zen Buddhists have had a great number of adherents in the West for years.

Although Buddhism contains a wide variety of beliefs and practices, the selections we have included indicate what is unique to Buddhism and attractive to people in the Western world. As a faith, it is eminently practical and does not require an elaborate set of theological beliefs or a Biblical faith, which have to be defended against critics such as Nagel. Gautama himself was an agnostic. The simplicity of its teachings and practice can lead to an essentially religious attitude toward all living things. The Buddhist's middle way between self-renunciation and self-indulgence should be compared with Niebuhr's Biblical-Christian ethic. Insofar as the Buddhists emphasize the loss of the self in Nirvana, they would have to answer Niebuhr's critique of mysticism.

The return to the lost dimension may be the result of a strongly felt need to act and to feel differently and to try life styles that are deliberately out of step with our present culture, its pace, its values, and its technology. It is, perhaps, an attempt to bring some joy, some meaning, and some sense of control to what many feel is the grim, meaningless struggle in today's society. For whatever reason, there seems to be a renewed quest for the God of Western religions, the Nirvana of the Buddhists, and the divine Absolute of the Hindus.

Some individuals have refused to submit to the discipline or faith required by traditional religions and have looked for the lost dimension and the religious experience in drug-induced experiences. Science and technology have made possible the mass production of such chemicals as LSD. At the same time, they have also increased the number and kinds of available drugs that create euphoric states of consciousness and tranquilize or stimulate to various degrees. The use and control of new as well as old drugs raise serious questions. These questions not only confront biochemists, physicians, psychologists, legislators, and narcotics divisions of police departments; they also confront philosophers. The use of drugs for the purpose of birth control raises moral issues. The production, cost, and quality control of drugs raise serious public issues. The treatment of alcoholics and drug addicts are important and hotly debated social issues.

Drugs may someday be used effectively as a form of social control as were the "soma" pills in Aldous Huxley's *Brave New World*. Timothy Leary has suggested that drugs may also be used, not for the manipulation of man, but for his liberation. They could create a new political order, a "politics of ecstasy." A few years ago, some persons were suggesting seriously that LSD be placed in the water supply of large cities in order to change the conservative, bourgeois attitudes of the middle classes. Mind-expanding drugs could be used, they claimed, to break the bonds of sociopolitical ideologies and create a universal politics of love. Mankind would finally be united under this single drug-induced experience.

To many users, drug use is not associated with any political ideology. Rather, it is the source of an experience which breaks the crust of the ordinary, mundane life of modern man—a life which too often demands that enjoyment be delayed or put off permanently, a life which is devoid of spontaneity and play, and which lacks a sense of community. William James stated that alcohol "expands, unites, and says yes." Despite the possible harmful effects and legal consequences of using drugs, many people continue to seek a feeling of self-transcendence and ecstasy by means of them. Taking drugs represents an existential choice and a personal commitment to a life style.

 Huston Smith points out that mystical experience has two sides. It may open up a wider world or seduce us into delusion: it may lead to a fuller religious life or to a diabolical form of mysticism. Drugs may serve as a short cut to religion or shortcircuit our brains. Smith is sceptical that drugs alone will produce religious lives. Religious experiences need to be tested by their fruits: how they affect our attitudes and actions in everyday life.

Perhaps we have recovered some of the lost dimension of religion. But we still have difficulty squaring our beliefs about the world with this lost dimension. The issues surrounding the scientific-world view and the religious-world view have been with us at least since the Renaissance. Must the beliefs about reality which arise from religious experience be necessarily opposed to, or in defiance of, those which arise from science? Naturalists, such as Dewey and Nagel, believe that there is no necessary incompatibility between science and religion, but they would redefine religion in a very broad way. Tillich reconciles the two also, but within the context of a redefinition of faith as ultimate concern. The debate, however, involves not only differing beliefs about the world and man's place in it; it involves differences about how we test and arrive at our beliefs, questions which relate to the nature of doubt, knowledge, and truth. Nagel accepts the canons of the empirical sciences: his truth is of the propositional kind. For Tillich, faith is a human act which goes beyond these canons and includes a truth that is existential.

Related Reading

(Works marked * are available in paperbound editions.)

*Aaronson, Bernard, and Humphrey Osmond, eds. *Psychedelics: The Use and Implications of Hallucinogenic Drugs*. Garden City: Doubleday, 1970.

Abernathy, G. L. and T. A. Langford, eds. *Philosophy of Religion*. New York: Macmillan Co., 1962.

*Abramson, Harold, ed. *The Uses of LSD in Psychotherapy and Alcoholism*. New York: Bobbs-Merrill Co., 1967.

Alston, William D., ed. *Religious Belief and Philosophic Thought*. New York: Harcourt, Brace & World, 1963.

Bartley, W. W. *Morality and Religion*. New York: Macmillan Co., 1971.

*Bergson, Henri. *The Two Sources of Morality and Religion*. New York: Doubleday (Anchor Books), 1954.

*Buber, Martin. *I and Thou*, trans. R. G. Smith. Edinburgh: Clark, 1937.

*————. *Between Man and Man*. New York: Macmillan Co., 1947.

Cahn, Steven M., ed. *Philosophy of Religion*. New York: Harper & Row, 1970.

*DeRopp, Robert. *The Master Game: Pathways to Higher Consciousness Beyond The Drug Experience*. New York: Delta, 1968.

*Dewey, John. *A Common Faith*. New Haven: Yale University Press, 1934.

*Hick, John. *Philosophy of Religion*. Englewood Cliffs, N. J.: Prentice-Hall, Inc., 1963.

Hook, Sidney, ed. *Religious Experience and Truth*. New York: New York University Press, 1961.

*Hume, David. *Dialogues Concerning Natural Religion*. New York: Hafner, 1948.

Huxley, Aldous. *The Perennial Philosophy*. New York: Harper & Row, 1944.

*———. *The Doors of Perception* and *Heaven and Hell*. New York: Harper & Row, 1963.

*Huxley, Julian. *Religion without Revelation*. New York: Harper, 1957.

*Kant, Immanuel. *The Critique of Practical Reason*, trans. L. W. Beck. New York: Liberal Arts Press, 1956.

*Kaufman, Walter A. *Critique of Religion and Philosophy*. New York: Harper & Row, 1958.

*Kierkegaard, Soren. *Philosophical Fragments*, trans. David S. Swensen. Princeton, N. J.: Princeton University Press, 1936.

*Maslow, Abraham. *Religions, Values and Peak-Experiences*. Columbus: Ohio State University Press, 1964.

*Masters, R. E. L. and Jean Huston. *The Varieties of Psychedelic Experience*. New York: Holt, Rinehart, & Winston, 1966.

*McKelway, A. J. *The Systematic Theology of Paul Tillich*. New York: Dell Publishing Co., 1964.

*Mehta, Ved. *The New Theologian*. New York: Harper and Row, 1965.

*Miller, David. *Gods and Games: Toward a Theology of Play*. New York: Harper, 1970.

*Niebuhr, Reinhold. *Moral Man and Immoral Society*. New York: Charles Scribner's Sons, 1932.

Otto, Rudolf. *The Idea of the Holy*, 2d ed., trans. Harvey. Oxford: Oxford University Press, 1950.

*Plantuiga, Alvin, ed. *The Ontological Argument*. New York: Doubleday & Co., 1965.

*Russell, Bertrand. *Why I Am Not a Christian*, ed. P. Edwards. New York: Simon & Schuster, 1957.

*———. *Mysticism and Logic*. New York: Doubleday & Co., 1957.

St. Anselm. *Proslogium*, trans. Sidney Norton Deane. LaSalle, Ill.: Open Court Publishing Co., 1910.

St. Thomas Aquinas. *Summa Theologica*, ed. Anton C. Pegis. New York: Random House, 1945.

*Stace, Walter. *The Teachings of the Mystics*. New York: New American Library, 1960.

*Tillich, Paul. *The Shaking of the Foundations*. New York: Charles Scribner's Sons, 1948.

———. *Systematic Theology*. Chicago: University of Chicago Press, 1951.

*Watts, Alan. *The Joyous Cosmology*. New York: Pantheon Books, 1962.

Weil, Andrew. *The Natural Mind*. Boston: Houghton Mifflin, 1972.

*White, John, ed. *The Highest State of Consciousness*. New York: Doubleday & Co., 1972.

*Wieman, Henry Nelson. *Man's Ultimate Commitment*. Carbondale: Southern Illinois University Press, 1958.

*Zaehner, R. C. *Mysticism, Sacred and Profane*. New York: Oxford University Press, 1961.

PART SEVEN

Confrontation with Aesthetic Experience:
Commitment to Artistic Creation

Art alone expresses the inexpressible.
Etienne Souriau

When man creates he worships as surely
as he does when he kneels or sings a
psalm.
Paul Weiss

Art and Religion are two roads by which men escape from
circumstance to ecstasy.
Clive Bell

Life imitates art far more than art imitates life.
Oscar Wilde

The people who passionately love bad
music are much closer to good taste than
the wise men who love with good sense
and moderation the most perfect music
ever made.
Stendhal

Art is life seen through a temperament.
Emile Zola

The most immoral and disgraceful and dangerous thing
that anybody can do in the arts is knowingly to feed back
to the public its own ignorance and cheap tastes.
Edmund Wilson

Art imitates art more than it imitates
nature.
Jean Charbonneaux

To appreciate a work of art we need bring
with us nothing but a sense of form and
color and a knowledge of three-
dimensional space.
Clive Bell

Art comes to you proposing frankly to
give nothing but the highest quality to your
moments as they pass.
Walter Pater

There is no other way of making a reasonable being out
of a sensuous man than by making him first aesthetic.
Friedrich von Schiller

Introduction / Art, Imitation, and Life

For many people in our society, art is on the periphery of real living. It is an activity for leisure time or a product to be enjoyed when one feels the need to relax. As a result of this attitude, which places art in the same class as sports and games, artists in America usually have not been taken very seriously or honored for playing influential roles in the development of a better life. Yet this attitude toward art is by no means characteristic of all cultures, nor is it universal within our own society.

There have been societies in which art has been considered to be of importance to everyone and in which artists were not alienated from their fellow citizens. The creators of Greek drama, African sculpture, and Balinese dancing played vital roles in the religious life of whole communities. Their works aroused serious and enthusiastic response from the public for whom they were created. There have always been those for whom the arts are cultural frills and momentary diversions. But in the long run, as Confucius noted long ago, the extent to which the arts are developed and appreciated in a society will reveal the intrinsic qualities and lasting values of that society.

In the West, from Socrates on, philosophers have reflected upon art. What is art? How and why is it created? Of what value is it? Ought it to be unrestricted or controlled by the state? A branch of philosophy, aesthetics, developed in an effort to explain the nature of beauty and the process of creating and appreciating a work of art. In modern times, aesthetics has grown into a complex and rich discipline that embraces many fascinating and difficult problems, including those of explaining artistic expressiveness and of determining what is sense and nonsense in talk about art. As aestheticians, philosophers may choose to deal with only one part of the aesthetic domain—for example, with the definition of tragedy—or they may attempt generalizations of the broadest significance about art and beauty, as they do in the following selections.

Socrates and Plato dealt with problems that today would fall within the domain of aesthetics. Socrates is depicted by his admirer Xenophon as engaging in discussions about the nature of beauty, which he sometimes identified with the useful. A vase is beautiful, for example, if it fulfills efficiently the function for which it has been designed. Plato in his *Republic* uses Socrates to present what were probably his own views on art. Plato has Socrates define art as the imitation of nature. The artist, he says, holds up a mirror to nature and, like a mirror, merely reflects or copies what is already there. Because he conceives reality to be not what is material, but rather what is universal and ideal, Plato considers art to be only an imitative, second-rate activity. Unlike the philosopher who knows reality through reason, the artist sees only its reflection through the senses; unlike the artisan who at least creates actual objects, the artist only represents them. In light of his metaphysics, Plato tends to denigrate artists and places them under the supervision and control of the philosopher rulers of his ideal city-state. Art is to be strictly censored, and only those works are permitted that promote the general welfare, instill proper moral and aesthetic values in the minds of youth, and are useful for patriotic and religious purposes.

The view that art is an imitative process, that the work of art should copy or represent a real life model, is one of the earliest and most influential views in the history of aesthetics. Many interesting and difficult questions have been raised in the long discussion of the imitation theory. What exactly does the artist imitate? How does he go about imitating nature? How exact should his imitation be? After Plato, thinkers—Aristotle and Plotinus, for example—tended to reinterpret imitation or *mimesis*, and began a "retreat from likeness" in aesthetics. This tendency eventually gave rise to expressionist and formalist theories, which were radically different from the imitation theory as originally formulated.

Throughout the nineteenth century, however, several versions of the imitation theory were held. The sculptor Rodin said that there was no recipe for improving nature and urged his fellow artists to "copy what you see." The painter Courbet taught that beauty in nature was superior to beauty in art and extolled realism in painting. Émile Zola, famous for his naturalistic novels, compared the novelist to a scientist who accurately observes, analyzes, and truthfully reports actual phenomena. Today the imitation theory is by no means dead. Two of the most popular painters in America, Norman Rockwell and Andrew Wyeth, although quite different in their endowments, aims, and achievements, produced highly representational or realistic works of art. Many art schools stress "being true to the model." The public continues to demand a high degree of verisimilitude.

One of the most brilliant attacks on the view that art is an imitation of nature was delivered by Oscar Wilde, who builds a case for the very opposite view, namely, that it is life and nature that imitate art. Artistic creation is thus a higher and nobler activity than all others, including philosophy. Wilde's arguments led him to champion the cause of art for art's sake, a point of view that differed from Plato's and which the socialist William Morris challenged.

As a Marxian social philosopher, Morris vehemently opposed art that was isolated from material realities and from the interests of the working classes. While he did not advocate the extreme censorship and state control of art that Plato's moralism and, more recently, communist dogmatism have demanded, Morris was no less concerned with the relationship of art to each of the social institutions that make up the body politic. He was also concerned with finding ways of overcoming the sense of alienation that artists feel. Only a socialist reorganization, Morris believed, could solve the problems confronting artists in industrial society.

This proposed solution, as it is stated by Morris, would seem oversimplified to such a thinker as Albert Camus. He saw the problem as arising from the inner nature of man, his self-alienation, rather than solely from his relationship to external social processes and the means of production. Camus saw artistic creation as a kind of rebellion fraught with dangers and opportunities, but he stressed free and critically evaluated commitment.

Susanne Langer, a contemporary American philosopher of art, attempted to formulate a definition of art that would overcome the difficulties inherent in those of philosophers since Plato. Mrs. Langer probes deeply into the creative process to get at the relationship between feeling and form. At the same time, like Plato and the other thinkers here, she urges that art not be taken lightly but appreciated as one of man's highest and fullest achievements.

24 / Life as Imitation of Art
Wilde

As a witty defender of art for art's sake, the English playwright Oscar Wilde (1854–1900) went so far as to argue that art is superior to life even as a means of satisfying human needs. "Life! Life! Don't let us go to life for our fulfillment or our experience!" exclaims a character in one of his dialogues.[1] "Must we go, then to Art for everything?" asks another. "For everything," the first replies.[2] Wilde's character goes on to point out that, unlike life, art does not stir real emotions in us but, through a process of purgation and purification, creates emotions that are "exquisitely sterile." Life is, in Wilde's character's view, "a thing narrowed by circumstance, incoherent in its utterance, and without that fine correspondence of form and spirit which is the only thing that can satisfy the artistic and critical temperament."[3] In life there are always moral considerations. Real life emotion exists for the sake of action, whereas in the completely amoral realm of art, emotion exists for the sake of emotion and is represented solely for the sake of art.

Aesthetic contemplation is therefore of supreme value to Wilde, even though he recognizes that, to the so-called practical man, it may be considered to be the most useless, even the gravest sin a man can commit. "Society often forgives the criminal; it never forgives the dreamer," as one of Wilde's characters puts it.[4] The contemplative life, which puts a premium on aesthetic dreaming, has as its aim not doing but being. The aesthetic contemplator should never confuse the sphere of art and the sphere of ethics, for if he does he will appreciate neither. He should realize that art is not a matter of morality or of rationality but of passionate inspiration or, as Plato noted, of divine madness.

Above everything, Wilde emphasizes the individuality of activity that underlies all genuine creative effort. Art is, he believes, "the most intense mode of individualism that the world has known, and a work of art is always "the unique result of a unique temperament."[5] Art expresses the wants of the artist, not what is wanted by others. When the artist puts the expectations and needs of others above his own goals as an artist and stops creating for his own benefit alone, his role shifts from that of artist to that of craftsman. The public may want artists to produce works of art that cater to their tastes. But if the artist attempts to do this he will inevitably cheapen his works, his taste will deteriorate, and he will become a mere entertainer. "Art should never try to be popular," Wilde writes with his usual wit; rather, "the public should try to make itself artistic."[6]

Art is often viewed with suspicion by the public precisely because art is a mode of individualism and thus runs counter to the norms and popular values of the masses. In fact, art by its very nature is disturbing to ordinary sensibilities, threatening to the status quo, and subversive to dogmatism of every kind. Contrary to what many people may think, "the one thing the public dislikes is novelty."[7] For novelty, that which does not conform to the norm, is threatening, and people want to be amused, diverted, entertained by art, but not shaken in their convictions by seeing their favorite prejudices undermined. Yet art is of inestimable value to society, Wilde believes, because it is "a disturbing and disintegrating force."[8] Art is the enemy of "monotony to type," "slavery to custom," and "tyranny of habit." By opposing the mechanization of existence and the stereotyping of human beings, art is an innovative force that can recreate interest and revitalize life.

If it is to give expression to the individuality of the artist and, in so doing, bring benefits to society, art must be free of political and social interferences of any kind. Wilde defends the integrity and freedom of the artist against the demands of the spectator, the so-called "aesthetic consumer." "The work of art is to dominate the spectator: the spectator is not to dominate the work of art," he writes.[9] The spectator's function is, in Wilde's view, receptive or responsive: "the violin on which the master plays." A person perceiving a new work of art should not bring to the experience a fixed conception of what a work of art ought to be. Instead, he should try to clear his mind of all aesthetic and moral prejudices and give himself as fully as possible to the experience of the new work, realizing that whatever beauty it possesses will lie in its "being what art has never been."[10]

In discussing the relationship of art to different social philosophies and forms of government, Wilde takes the position that "the form of government that is most suitable to the artist is no government at all."[11] All kinds of authority are equally bad for the integrity of the artist and his work. Despotism, whether in the form of a prince, a pope, or a people must be opposed if the artist is to be free to pursue the goals of his art as only he himself can define them. However, Wilde does argue, somewhat paradoxically perhaps, that socialism can give birth to a new individualism and thus eventually bring about a new Renaissance in the arts.

The Decay of Lying

CYRIL (*coming in through the open window from the terrace*). My dear Vivian, don't coop yourself up all day in the library. It is a perfectly lovely afternoon. The air is exquisite. There is a mist upon the woods, like the purple bloom upon a plum. Let us go and lie on the grass, and smoke cigarettes, and enjoy Nature.

VIVIAN Enjoy Nature! I am glad to say that I have entirely lost that faculty. People tell us that Art makes us love Nature more than we loved her before; that it reveals her secrets to us; and that after a careful study of Corot and Constable we see things in her that had escaped our observation. My own experience is that the more we study Art, the less we care for Nature. What Art really reveals to us is Nature's lack of design, her curious crudities, her extraordinary monotony, her absolutely unfinished condition. Nature has good intentions, of course, but, as Aristotle once said, she cannot carry them out. When I look at a landscape I cannot help seeing all its defects. It is fortunate for us, however, that Nature is so imperfect, as otherwise we should have had no art at all. Art is our spirited protest, our gallant attempt to teach Nature her proper place. As for the infinite variety of Nature, that is a pure myth. It is not to be found in Nature herself. It resides in the imagination, or fancy, or cultivated blindness of the man who looks at her.

CYRIL Well, you need not look at the landscape. You can lie on the grass and smoke and talk.

VIVIAN But Nature is so uncomfortable. Grass is hard and lumpy and damp, and full of dreadful black insects. Why, even Morris' poorest workman could make you a more comfortable seat than the whole of Nature can. Nature pales before the furniture of "the Street which from Oxford has borrowed its name," as the poet you love so much once vilely phrased it. I don't complain. If Nature had been comfortable, mankind would never have invented architecture, and I prefer houses to the open air. In a house we all feel of the proportions. Everything is subordinated to us, fashioned for our use and our pleasure. Egotism itself, which is so necessary to a proper sense of human dignity, is entirely the result of indoor life. Out of doors one becomes abstract and impersonal. One's individuality absolutely leaves one. And then Nature is so indifferent, so unappreciative. Whenever I am walking in the park here, I always feel that I am no more to her than the cattle that browse on the slope, or the burdock that blooms in the ditch. Nothing is more evident than that Nature

From Oscar Wilde, "The Decay of Lying" in *Intentions and the Soul of Man* (London: Methuen & Co., 1908), pp. 1–57 (with omissions).

hates Mind. Thinking is the most unhealthy thing in the world, and people die of it just as they die of any other disease. Fortunately, in England at any rate, thought is not catching. Our splendid physique as a people is entirely due to our national stupidity. I only hope we shall be able to keep this great historic bulwark of our happiness for many years to come; but I am afraid that we are beginning to be overeducated; at least everybody who is incapable of learning has taken to teaching—that is really what our enthusiasm for education has come to. In the meantime, you had better go back to your wearisome uncomfortable Nature, and leave me to correct my proofs.

CYRIL   Writing an article! That is not very consistent after what you have just said.

VIVIAN   Who wants to be consistent? The dullard and the doctrinaire, the tedious people who carry out their principles to the bitter end of action, to the *reductio ad absurdum* of practice. Not I. Like Emerson, I write over the door of my library the word "Whim." Besides, my article is really a most salutary and valuable warning. If it is attended to, there may be a new Renaissance of Art.

CYRIL   What is the subject?

VIVIAN   I intend to call it "The Decay of Lying: a Protest."

CYRIL   Lying! I should have thought that our politicians kept up that habit.

VIVIAN   I assure you that they do not. They never rise beyond the level of misrepresentation, and actually condescend to prove, to discuss, to argue. How different from the temper of the true liar, with his frank, fearless statements, his superb irresponsibility, his healthy, natural disdain of proof of any kind! After all, what is a fine lie? Simply that which is its own evidence. If a man is sufficiently unimaginative to produce evidence in support of a lie, he might just as well speak the truth at once. No, the politicians won't do. Something may, perhaps, be argued on behalf of the Bar. The mantle of the Sophist has fallen on its members. Their feigned ardours and unreal rhetoric are delightful. They can make the worse appear the better cause, as though they were fresh from Leontine schools, and have been known to wrest from reluctant juries triumphant verdicts of acquittal for their clients, even when those clients, as often happens, were clearly and unmistakeably innocent. But they are briefed by the prosaic, and are not ashamed to appeal to precedent. In spite of their endeavours, the truth will out. Newspapers, even, have degenerated. They may now be absolutely relied upon. One feels it as one wades through their columns. It is always the unreadable that occurs. I am afraid that there is not much to be said in favour of either the lawyer or the journalist. Besides, what I am pleading for is the Lying in art. Shall I read you what I have written? It might do you a great deal of good.

CYRIL   Certainly, if you give me a cigarette. Thanks. By the way, what magazine do you intend it for?

VIVIAN   For the *Retrospective Review*. I think I told you that the elect had revived it.

CYRIL   Whom do you mean by "the elect"?

VIVIAN   Oh, The Tired Hedonists of course. It is a club to which I belong. We are supposed to wear faded roses in our button-holes when we meet, and to have a sort of cult for Domitian. I am afraid you are not eligible. You are too fond of simple pleasures.

CYRIL   I should be black-balled on the ground of animal spirits, I suppose?

VIVIAN Probably. Besides, you are a little too old. We don't admit anybody who is of the usual age.

CYRIL Well, I should fancy you are all a good deal bored with each other.

VIVIAN We are. That is one of the objects of the club. Now, if you promise not to interrupt too often, I will read you my article.

CYRIL You will find me all attention.

VIVIAN (*reading in a very clear, musical voice*). "THE DECAY OF LYING: A PRO-TEST.—One of the chief causes that can be assigned for the curiously commonplace character of most of the literature of our age is undoubtedly the decay of Lying as an art, a science, and a social pleasure. The ancient historians gave us delightful fiction in the form of fact; the modern novelist presents us with dull facts under the guise of fiction. The Blue-Book is rapidly becoming his ideal both for method and manner. He has his tedious '*document humain,*' his miserable little '*coin de la création,*' into which he peers with his microscope. He is to be found at the Librairie Nationale, or at the British Museum, shamelessly reading up on his subject. He has not even the courage of other people's ideas, but insists on going directly to life for everything, and ultimately, between encyclopaedias and personal experience, he comes to the ground, having drawn his types from the family circle or from the weekly washerwoman, and having acquired an amount of useful information from which never, even in his most meditative moments, can be thoroughly free himself.

"The loss that results to literature in general from this false ideal of our time can hardly be overestimated. People have a careless way of talking about a 'born liar,' just as they talk about a 'born poet.' But in both cases they are wrong. Lying and poetry are arts—arts, as Plato saw, not unconnected with each other—and they require the most careful study, the most disinterested devotion. Indeed, they have their technique, just as the more material arts of painting and sculpture have, their subtle secrets of form and colour, their craft-mysteries, their deliberate artistic methods. As one knows the poet by his fine music, so one can recognize the liar by his rich rhythmic utterance, and in neither case will the casual inspiration of the moment suffice. Here, as elsewhere, practice must precede perfection. But in modern days while the fashion of writing poetry has become far too common, and should, if possible, be discouraged, the fashion of lying has almost fallen into disrepute. Many a young man starts in life with a natural gift for exaggeration which, if nurtured in congenial and sympathetic surroundings, or by the imitation of the best models, might grow into something really great and wonderful. But, as a rule, he comes to nothing. He either falls into careless habits of accuracy—"

CYRIL My dear fellow!

VIVIAN Please don't interrupt in the middle of a sentence. "He either falls into careless habits of accuracy, or takes to frequenting the society of the aged and the well-informed. Both things are equally fatal to his imagination, as indeed they would be fatal to the imagination of anybody, and in a short time he develops a morbid and unhealthy faculty of truth-telling, begins to verify all statements made in his presence, has no hesitation in contradicting people who are much younger than himself, and often ends by writing novels which are so like life that no one can possibly believe in their probability. This is no isolated instance that we are giving. It is simply one example out of many; and if something cannot be done to check, or at least to modify, our monstrous worship of facts, Art will become sterile, and beauty will pass away from the land. . . ."

CYRIL   There is something in what you say, and there is no doubt that whatever amusement we may find in reading a purely modern novel, we have rarely any artistic pleasure in rereading it. And this is perhaps the best rough test of what is literature and what is not. If one cannot enjoy reading a book over and over again, there is no use reading it at all. But what do you say about the return to Life and Nature? This is the panacea that is always being recommended to us.

VIVIAN   I will read you what I say on that subject. The passage comes later on in the article, but I may as well give it to you now?—

"The popular cry of our time is 'Let us return to Life and Nature; they will recreate Art for us, and send the red blood coursing through her veins; they will shoe her feet with swiftness and make her hand strong!' But, alas! we are mistaken in our amiable and well-meaning efforts. Nature is always behind the age. And as for Life, she is the solvent that breaks up Art, the enemy that lays waste her house."

CYRIL   What do you mean by saying that Nature is always behind the age?

VIVIAN   Well, perhaps that is rather cryptic. What I mean is this. If we take Nature to mean natural simple instinct as opposed to self-conscious culture, the work produced under this influence is always old-fashioned, antiquated, and out of date. One touch of Nature may make the whole world kin, but two touches of Nature will destroy any work of Art. If, on the other hand, we regard Nature as a collection of phenomena external to man, people only discover in her what they bring to her. She has no suggestions of her own. Wordsworth went to the lakes, but he was never a lake poet. He found in stones the sermons he had already hidden there. He went moralizing about the district, but his good work was produced when he returned, not to Nature but to poetry. Poetry gave him "Laodamia" and the fine sonnets, and the great Ode, such as it is. Nature gave him "Martha Ray" and "Peter Bell" and the address to Mr. Wilkinson's spade.

CYRIL   I think that view might be questioned. I am rather inclined to believe in the "impulse from a vernal wood," though of course the artistic value of such an impulse depends entirely on the kind of temperament that receives it, so that the return to Nature would come to mean simply the advance to a great personality. You would agree with that, I fancy. However, proceed with your article.

VIVIAN   (reading) "Art begins with abstract decoration, with purely imaginative and pleasurable work dealing with what is unreal and non-existent. This is the first stage. Then Life becomes fascinated with this new wonder, and asks to be admitted into the charmed circle. Art takes life as part of her rough material, recreates it, and refashions it in fresh forms, is absolutely indifferent to fact, invests, imagines, dreams, and keeps between herself and reality the impenetrable barrier of beautiful style, of decorative or ideal treatment. The third stage is when Life gets the upper hand, and drives Art out into the wilderness. This is the true decadence, and it is from this that we are now suffering. . . .

"It was not always thus. We need not say anything about the poets, for they, with the unfortunate exception of Mr. Wordsworth, have been really faithful to their high mission, and are universally recognized as being absolutely unreliable. . . .

"Art finds her own perfection within, and not outside of, herself. She is not to be judged by any external standard of resemblance. She is a veil, rather than a mirror. She has flowers that no forests know of, birds that no woodland possesses. She makes and unmakes many worlds, and can draw the moon from heaven with a scarlet thread. Hers are the 'forms more real than living man,' and hers the great archetypes of which things that have existence are but unfinished copies. Nature has, in her eyes, no laws, no uniformity. She can work miracles at her will, and when she calls monsters from the deep they come. She can bid the almond tree blossom in winter, and send the snow upon the ripe cornfield. At her word the frost lays its silver finger on the burning mouth of June, and the winged lions creep out from the hollows of the Lydian hills. The dryads peer from the thicket as she passes by, and the brown fauns smile strangely at her when she comes near them. She has hawk-faced gods that worship her, and the centaurs gallop at her side."

CYRIL I like that. I can see it. Is that the end?

VIVIAN No. There is one more passage, but it is purely practical. It simply suggests some methods by which we could revive this lost art of Lying.

CYRIL Well, before you read it to me, I should like to ask you a question. What do you mean by saying that life, "poor, probable, uninteresting human life," will try to reproduce the marvels of art? I can quite understand your objection to art being treated as a mirror. You think it would reduce genius to the position of a cracked looking-glass. But you don't mean to say that you seriously believe that Life imitates Art, that life in fact is the mirror, and Art the reality?

VIVIAN Certainly I do. Paradox though it may seem—and paradoxes are always dangerous things—it is none the less true that Life imitates art far more than Art imitates life. We have all seen in our own day in England how a certain curious and fascinating type of beauty, invented and emphasized by two imaginative painters, has so influenced Life that whenever one goes to a private view or to an artistic salon one sees, here the mystic eyes of Rossetti's dream, the long ivory throat, the strange square-cut jaw, the loosened shadowy hair that he so ardently loved, there the sweet maidenhood of "The Golden Stair," the blossom-like mouth and weary loveliness of the "Laous Amoris," the passion-pale face of Andromeda, the thin hands and lithe beauty of the Vivien in "Merlin's Dream." And it has always been so. A great artist invents a type, and Life tries to copy it, to reproduce it in a popular form, like an enterprising publisher. Neither Holbein nor Vandyck found in England what they have given us. They brought their types with them, and Life with her keen imitative faculty set herself to supply the master with models. The Greeks, with their quick artistic instinct, understood this, and set in the bride's chamber the statue of Hermes or of Apollo, that she might bear children as lovely as the works of art that she looked at in her rapture or her pain. They knew that Life gains from Art not merely spirituality, depth of thought and feeling, soul-turmoil or soul-peace, but that she can form herself on the very lines and colours of art, and can reproduce the dignity of Pheidias as well as the grace of Praxiteles. Hence came their objection to realism. They disliked it on purely social grounds. They felt that it inevitably makes people ugly, and they were perfectly right. We try to improve the conditions of the race by means of good air, free sunlight, wholesome water, and hideous bare buildings for the better housing of the lower orders. But these things merely produce health, they do not produce beauty. For this, Art is required, and the true disciples of the great artist are not his studio-imitators, but those who become like his works of art, be they plastic as in the Greek days, or pictorial as in modern times; in a word, Life is Art's best, Art's only pupil.

As it is with the visible arts, so it is with literature. The most obvious and the vulgarest form in which this is shown is in the case of the silly boys who, after reading the adventures of Jack Sheppard or Dick Turpin, pillage the stalls of unfortunate apple-women, break into sweetshops at night, and alarm old gentlemen who are returning home from the city by leaping out on them in suburban lanes, with black masks and unloaded revolvers. This interesting phenomenon, which always occurs after the appearance of a new edition of either of the books I have alluded to, is usually attributed to the influence of literature on the imagination. But this is a mistake. The imagination is essentially creative and always seeks for a new form. The boy-

burglar is simply the inevitable result of life's imitative instinct. He is Fact, occupied as Fact usually is, with trying to reproduce Fiction, and what we see in him is repeated on an extended scale throughout the whole of life. Schopenhauer has analyzed the pessimism that characterizes modern thought, but Hamlet invented it. The world has become sad because a puppet was once melancholy. The Nihilist, that strange martyr who has no faith, who goes to the stake without enthusiasm, and dies for what he does not believe in, is a purely literary product. He was invented by Tourgénieff, and completed by Dostoieffski. Robespierre came out of the pages of Rousseau as surely as the People's Palace rose out of the *débris* of a novel. Literature always anticipates life. It does not copy it, but moulds it to its purpose. The nineteenth century, as we know it, is largely an invention of Balzac. Our Luciens de Rubempré, our Rastignacs, and De Marsays made their first appearance on the stage of the *Comédie Humaine....*

However, I do not wish to dwell any further upon individual instances. Personal experience is a most vicious and limited circle. All that I desire to point out is the general principle that Life imitates Art far more than Art imitates Life, and I feel sure that if you think seriously about it you will find that it is true. Life holds the mirror up to Art, and either reproduces some strange type imagined by painter or sculptor, or realizes in fact what has been dreamed in fiction. Scientifically speaking, the basis of life—the energy of life, as Aristotle would call it—is simply the desire for expression, and Art is always presenting various forms through which this expression can be attained. Life seizes on them and uses them, even if they be to her own hurt. Young men have committed suicide because Rolla did so, have died by their own hand because by his own hand Werther died. Think of what we owe to the imitation of Christ, of what we owe to the imitation of Caesar.

CYRIL   The theory is certainly a very curious one, but to make it complete you must show that Nature, no less than Life, is an imitation of Art. Are you prepared to prove that?

VIVIAN   My dear fellow, I am prepared to prove anything.

CYRIL   Nature follows the landscape painter then, and takes her effects from him?

VIVIAN   Certainly. Where, if not from the Impressionists, do we get those wonderful brown fogs that come creeping down our streets, blurring the gas-lamps and changing the houses into monstrous shadows? To whom, if not to them and their master, do we owe the lovely silver mists that brood over our river, and turn to faint forms of fading grace curved bridge and swaying barge? The extraordinary change that has taken place in the climate of London during the last ten years is entirely due to this particular school of Art. You smile. Consider the matter from a scientific or a metaphysical point of view, and you will find that I am right. For what is Nature? Nature is no great mother who has borne us. She is our creation. It is in our brain that she quickens to life. Things are because we see them, and what we see, and how we see it, depends on the Arts that have influenced us. To look at a thing is very different from seeing a thing. One does not see anything until one sees its beauty. Then, and then only, does it come into existence. At present, people see fogs, not because there are fogs, but because poets and painters have taught them the mysterious loveliness of such effects. There may have been fogs for centuries in London. I dare say there were. But no one saw them, and so we do not know anything about them. They did not exist till Art had invented them. Now, it must be admitted, fogs are carried to excess. They have become the mere mannerism of a clique, and the exaggerated realism of their method gives dull people bronchitis. Where the cultured catch an effect, the uncultured catch cold. And so, let us be humane, and invite Art to turn her wonderful eyes elsewhere. She has done so already, indeed. That white quivering sunlight that one sees now in France, with its strange blotches of mauve, and its restless violet shadows, is her latest fancy, and, on the whole, Nature reproduces it quite admirably. Where she used to give us Corots and Daubignys, she gives us now exquisite Monets and entrancing Pissarros. Indeed there are moments, rare, it is true, but still to be observed from time to time, when Nature becomes absolutely modern. Of course she is not always to be relied upon. The fact is that she is in this unfortunate position. Art creates an incomparable and unique effect, and, having done so, passes on to other things. Nature, upon the other hand, forgetting that imitation can be made the sincerest form of insult, keeps on repeating this effect until we all become absolutely wearied of it. Nobody of any real culture, for instance, ever talks now-a-days about the beauty of a sunset. Sunsets are quite old-fashioned. They belong to the time when Turner was the last note in art. To admire them is a distinct sign of provincialism of temperament. . . . But have I proved my theory to your satisfaction?

CYRIL You have proved it to my dissatisfaction, which is better. But even admitting this strange imitative instinct in Life and Nature, surely you would acknowledge that Art expresses the temper of its age, the spirit of its time, the moral and social conditions that surround it, and under whose influence it is produced.

VIVIAN Certainly not! Art never expresses anything but itself. This is the principle of my new aesthetics; and it is this, more than that vital connection between form and substance, on which Mr. Pater dwells, that makes music the type of all the arts. Of course, nations and individuals, with that healthy natural vanity which is the secret of existence, are always under the impression that it is of them that the Muses are talking, always trying to find in the calm dignity of imaginative art some mirror of their own turbid passions, always forgetting that the singer of life is not Apollo, but Marsyas. Remote from reality, and with her eyes turned away from the shadows of the cave, Art reveals her own perfection, and the wondering crowd that watches the opening of the marvellous, many-petalled rose fancies that it is its own history that is being told to it, its own spirit that is finding expression in a new form. But it is not so. The highest art rejects the burden of the human spirit, and gains more from a new medium or a fresh material than she does from any enthusiasm for art, or from any lofty passion, or from any great awakening of the human consciousness. She develops purely on her own lines. She is not symbolic of any age. It is the ages that are her symbols. . . . However, I must read the end of my article:—

"What we have to do, what at any rate it is our duty to do, is to revive this old art of Lying. Much of course may be done, in the way of educating the public, by amateurs in the domestic circle, at literary lunches, and at afternoon teas. But this is merely the light and graceful side of lying, such as was probably heard at Cretan dinner parties. There are many other forms. Lying for the sake of gaining some immediate personal advantage, for instance—lying with a moral purpose, as it is usually called—though of late it has been rather looked down upon, was extremely popular with the antique world. Athena laughs when Odysseus tells her 'his words of sly devising,' as Mr. William Morris phrases it, and the glory of mendacity illumines the pale brow of the stainless hero of Euripidean tragedy, and sets among the noble women of the past the young bride of one of Horace's most exquisite odes. Later on, what at first had been merely a natural instinct was elevated into a self-conscious science. Elaborate rules were laid down for the guidance of mankind, and an important school of literature grew up round the subject. Indeed, when one remembers the excellent philosophical treatise of Sanchez on the whole question, one cannot help regretting that no one has ever thought of publishing a cheap and condensed edition of the works of that great casuist. A short primer, 'When to Lie and How,' if brought out in an attractive and not too expensive a form, would no doubt command a large sale, and would prove of real practical service to many earnest and deep-thinking people. Lying for the sake of the improvement of the young, which is the basis of home education, still lingers amongst us, and its advantages are so admirably set forth in the early books of Plato's *Republic* that it is unnecessary to dwell upon them here. It is a mode of lying for which all good mothers have peculiar capabilities, but it is capable of still further development, and has been sadly overlooked by the School Board. Lying for the sake of a monthly salary is of course well known in Fleet Street, and the profession of a political leader-writer is not without its advantages. But it is said to be a somewhat dull occupation, and it certainly does not lead to much beyond a kind of ostentatious obscurity. The only form of lying that is absolutely beyond reproach is Lying for its own sake, and the highest development of this is, as we have already pointed out, Lying in Art. Just as those who do not love Plato more than Truth cannot pass beyond the threshold of the Academe, so those who do not love Beauty more than Truth never know the inmost shrine of Art. The solid stolid British intellect lies in the desert sands like the Sphinx in Flaubert's marvellous tale, and fantasy, *La Chimère,* dances round it, and calls to it with her false, flute-toned voice. It may not hear her now, but surely some day, when we are all bored to death with the commonplace character of modern fiction, it will hearken to her and try to borrow her wings.

"And when that day dawns, or sunset reddens how joyous we shall all be! Facts will be regarded as discreditable, Truth will be found mourning over her fetters, and Romance, with her temper of wonder, will return to the land. The very aspect of the world will change to our startled eyes. Out of the sea will rise Behemoth and Leviathan, and sail round the high-pooped galleys, as they do on the delightful maps of those ages when books on geography were actually readable. Dragons will wander about the waste places, and the phoenix will soar from her nest of fire into the air. We shall lay our hands upon the basilisk, and see the jewel in the toad's head. Champing his gilded oats, the Hippogriff will stand in our stalls, and over our heads will float the Blue Bird singing of beautiful and impossible things, of things that are lovely and that never happen, of things that are not and that should be. But before this comes to pass we must cultivate the lost art of Lying."

CYRIL   Then we must certainly cultivate it at once. But in order to avoid making any error I want you to tell me briefly the doctrines of the new aesthetics.

VIVIAN   Briefly, then, they are these. Art never expresses anything but itself. It has an independent life, just as Thought has, and develops purely on its own lines. It is not necessarily realistic in an age of realism, nor spiritual in an age of faith. So far from being the creation of its time, it is usually in direct opposition to it, and the only history that it preserves for us is the history of its own progress. Sometimes it returns upon its footsteps, and revives some antique form, as happened in the archaistic movement of late Greek Art, and in the pre-Raphaelite movement of our own day. At other times it entirely anticipates its age, and produces in one century work that it takes another century to understand, to appreciate, and to enjoy. In no case does it reproduce its age. To pass from the art of a time to the time itself is the great mistake that all historians commit.

The second doctrine is this. All bad art comes from returning to Life and Nature, and elevating them into ideals.

Life and Nature may sometimes be used as part of Art's rough material, but before they are of any real service to art they must be translated into artistic conventions. The moment Art surrenders its imaginative medium it surrenders everything. As a method Realism is a complete failure, and the two things that every artist should avoid are modernity of form and modernity of subject-matter. To us, who live in the nineteenth century, any century is a suitable subject for art except our own. The only beautiful things are the things that do not concern us. It is, to have the pleasure of quoting myself, exactly because Hecuba is nothing to us that her sorrows are so suitable a motive for a tragedy. Besides, it is only the modern that ever becomes old-fashioned. M. Zola sits down to give us a picture of the Second Empire. Who cares for the Second Empire now? It is out of date. Life goes faster than Realism, but Romanticism is always in front of Life.

The third doctrine is that Life imitates Art far more than Art imitates Life. This results not merely from Life's imitative instinct, but from the fact that the self-conscious aim of Life is to find expression, and that Art offers it certain beautiful forms through which it may realize that energy. It is a theory that has never been put forward before, but it is extremely fruitful, and throws an entirely new light upon the history of Art.

It follows, as a corollary from this, that external Nature also imitates Art. The only effects that she can show us are effects that we have already seen through poetry, or in paintings. This is the secret of Nature's charm, as well as the explanation of Nature's weakness.

The final revelation is that Lying, the telling of beautiful untrue things, is the proper aim of art. But of this I think I have spoken at sufficient length. And now let us go out on the terrace, where "droops the milk-white peacock like a ghost," while the evening star "washes the dusk with silver." At twilight nature becomes a wonderfully suggestive effect, and is not without loveliness, though perhaps its chief use is to illustrate quotations from the poets. Come! We have talked long enough.

Notes

1. Oscar Wilde, "The Critic as Artist, Part II" in *Intentions and The Soul of Man* (London: Methuen, 1908), p. 173.
2. Ibid., p. 174.
3. Ibid., p. 173.
4. Ibid., p. 175.
5. Ibid., p. 300.
6. Ibid., p. 301.
7. Ibid., p. 304.
8. Ibid.
9. Ibid., p. 317.
10. Ibid.
11. Ibid., p. 322.

25 / Art and Revolution
Morris

The English poet William Morris (1834–1896) was one of the most important critics of the values promoted by modern industrial society. He eloquently expressed his conviction that, under the impact of machine production, art and with it the appreciation of beauty were rapidly being destroyed. He accompanied this with an urgent warning that if civilized man allowed art and beauty to disappear, he would lose not merely cultural frills but activities essential to his well-being and to the civilization he had inherited. Art, Morris urged, is "no mere accident to human life, which people can take or leave as they choose, but a positive necessity of life, if we are to live as nature meant us to; that is, unless we are content to be less than men."[1]

Morris looked back nostalgically to the Middle Ages when art and society had been harmoniously conjoined. Then practical arts and crafts were permeated with vitality and pursued with enthusiasm, and artists were ordinary men who did what they did well and gladly. Artists thus expressed the life-promoting values which sustained them and their fellowmen. Art was then, Morris believed, something that was created for and belonged to all the people. It was something natural rather than artificial in everyday life. Works of art were at once useful, beautiful, and popular; they brought joy both to the maker and to the user. In modern times, according to Morris, all of this has changed. With the development of a capitalistic economy and machine production, artistic creation has declined and the quality of works of art has deteriorated. Ugliness has triumphed in man's everyday working environment, Morris believes, and everywhere there is evidence of the pollution resulting from the wastes of the industrial system. Unless a way is found to reconstruct society and to bring about a renewal of arts and crafts, the gap between art and the social order will widen and become even more difficult to bridge.

Morris's socialism and his utopian proposals offer a way, he believed, of solving the social and aesthetic problems faced by contemporary man. In his famous utopian novel, *News from Nowhere* (1891), he presented a vision of the new society that he would like to see replace the old. In Morris's utopia, irksome work is still done by machinery but other kinds of work have been made so pleasant that they are no longer drudgery but forms of artistic creation. Through careful planning, a balance is kept between supply and demand so that only what is wanted and needed is made and "whatever is made is good, and thoroughly fit for its function." In accord with Morris's favorite aesthetic maxim, the reconstructed English society values "art made by the people and for the people as a joy to the maker and to the user."[2] There is once more, as in medieval England, real art; art which is, as Morris puts it, "the expression by man of his pleasure in labour."[3] As in Plato's *Republic*, the material surroundings of the utopians are pleasant, simple, and beautiful, instilling in them at every moment of their lives, and in whatever they may be doing, an appreciation of beauty and art. Unlike their ancestors of the previous capitalistic era, the utopian citizens do not separate art from morality, politics, and religion. They believe that simplicity, justice, and truth are virtues that all of their activities have in common.

Like Plato, Morris refuses to separate the good, the useful, and the beautiful. "Nothing can be a work of art," he holds, "which is not useful, that is to say, which does not minister to the body when well under the command of the mind, or which does not amuse, soothe, or elevate the mind in a healthy state."[4] This belief permeated Morris's thinking on every topic related to art from ceramics and sculpture to poetry and music. "Have nothing in your houses," he advised his readers, "that you do not know to be useful, or believe to be beautiful."[5] Morris tried to fuse the practical with the aesthetically pleasing in everything that he did. Speaking of Morris's "new style of poetic prose," for example, an English critic characterized it as "a form of singular charm which steals upon the soul with music, dies off, and leaves it satisfied."[6]

Through his polemical prose and poetry as well as through his practical activities—as a designer of furniture and wallpaper and as a social reformer—Morris strived for a renewal in the arts of his time. He wanted this renaissance of the arts not for the sake of a select group of artists and critics, but for the benefit of all the people. As he said, "I do not want art for a few, any more than education for a few, or freedom for a few."[7] This view is clearly formulated in the following essay. It placed Morris in sharp opposition to the aesthetes and other defenders of art for art's sake of his time, especially to Walter Pater and Oscar Wilde who had very different proposals for the liberation of the arts.

The Aims of Art

In considering the Aims of Art, that is, why men toilsomely cherish and practise Art, I find myself compelled to generalize from the only specimen of humanity of which I know anything; to wit, myself. Now, when I think of what it is that I desire, I find that I can give it no other name than happiness. I want to be happy while I live; for as for death, I find that, never having experienced it, I have no conception of what it means, and so cannot even bring my mind to bear upon it. I know what it is to live; I cannot even guess what it is to be dead. Well, then, I want to be happy, and even sometimes, say generally, to be merry; and I find it difficult to believe that that is not the universal desire: so that, whatever tends towards that end I cherish with all my best endeavour. Now, when I consider my life further, I find out, or seem to, that it is under the influence of two dominating moods, which for lack of better words I must call the mood of energy and the mood of idleness: these two moods are now one, now the other, always crying out in me to be satisfied. When the mood of energy is upon me, I must be doing something, or I become mopish and unhappy; when the mood of idleness is on me, I find it hard indeed if I cannot rest and let my mind wander over the various pictures, pleasant or terrible, which my own experience or my communing with the thoughts of other men, dead or alive, have fashioned in

From William Morris, "The Aims of Art," in *Signs of Change* in *The Collected Works of William Morris,* ed. May Morris (New York: Russell and Russell, 1910–15), vol. 23, pp. 81–97.

it; and if circumstances will not allow me to cultivate this mood of idleness, I find I must at the best pass through a period of pain till I can manage to stimulate my mood of energy to take its place and make me happy again. And if I have no means wherewith to rouse up that mood of energy to do its duty in making me happy, and I have to toil while the idle mood is upon me, then am I unhappy indeed, and almost wish myself dead, though I do not know what that means.

Furthermore, I find that while in the mood of idleness memory amuses me, in the mood of energy hope cheers me; which hope is sometimes big and serious, and sometimes trivial, but that without it there is no happy energy. Again, I find that while I can sometimes satisfy this mood by merely exercising it in work that has no result beyond the passing hour—in play, in short—yet that it presently wearies of that and gets languid, the hope therein being too trivial, and sometimes even scarcely real; and that on the whole, to satisfy my master the mood, I must either be making something or making believe to make it.

Well, I believe that all men's lives are compounded of these two moods in various proportions, and that this explains why they have always, with more or less toil, cherished and practised art.

Why should they have touched it else, and so added to the labour which they could not choose but do in order to live? It must have been done for their pleasure, since it has only been in very elaborate civilizations that a man could get men to keep him alive merely to produce works of art, whereas all men that have left any signs of their existence behind them have practised art.

I suppose, indeed, that nobody will be inclined to deny that the end proposed by a work of art is always to please the person whose senses are to be made conscious of it. It was done *for* some one who was to be made happier by it; his idle or restful mood was to be amused by it, so that the vacancy which is the besetting evil of that mood might give place to pleased contemplation, dreaming, or what you will; and by this means he would not so soon be driven into his workful or energetic mood: he would have more enjoyment, and better.

The restraining of restlessness, therefore, is clearly one of the essential aims of art, and few things could add to the pleasure of life more than this. There are, to my knowledge, gifted people now alive who have no other vice than this of restlessness, and seemingly no other curse in their lives to make them unhappy: but that is enough; it is "the little rift within the lute." Restlessness makes them hapless men and bad citizens.

But granting, as I suppose you all will do, that this is a most important function for art to fulfil, the question next comes, at what price do we obtain it? I have admitted that the practice of art has added to the labour of mankind, though I believe in the long run it will not do so; but in adding to the labour of man has it added, so far, to his pain? There always have been people who would at once say yes to that question; so that there have been and are two sets of people who dislike and condemn art as an embarrassing folly. Besides the pious ascetics, who look upon it as a worldly entanglement which prevents men from keeping their minds fixed on the chances of their individual happiness or misery in the next world; who, in short, hate art, because they think that it adds to man's earthly happiness—besides these, there are also people who, looking on the struggle of life from the most reasonable point that they

know of, condemn the arts because they think that they add to man's slavery by increasing the sum of his painful labour: if this were the case, it would still, to my mind, be a question whether it might not be worth the while to endure the extra pain of labour for the sake of the extra pleasure added to rest; assuming, for the present, equality of condition among men. But it seems to me that it is not the case that the practice of art adds to painful labour; nay more, I believe that, if it did, art would never have arisen at all, would certainly not be discernible, as it is, among peoples in whom only the germs of civilization exist. In other words, I believe that art cannot be the result of external compulsion; the labour which goes to produce it is voluntary, and partly undertaken for the sake of the labour itself, partly for the sake of the hope of producing something, which, when done, shall give pleasure to the user of it. Or, again, this extra labour, when it *is* extra, is undertaken with the aim of satisfying that mood of energy by employing it to produce something worth doing, and which, therefore, will keep before the worker a lively hope while he is working; and also by giving it work to do in which there is absolute immediate pleasure. Perhaps it is difficult to explain to the non-artistic capacity that this definite sensuous pleasure is always present in the handiwork of the deft workman when he is working successfully, and that it increases in proportion to the freedom and individuality of the work. Also you must understand that this production of art, and consequent pleasure in work, is not confined to the production of matters which are works of art only, like pictures, statues, and so forth, but has been and should be a part of all labour in some form or other: so only will the claims of the mood of energy be satisfied.

Therefore the Aim of Art is to increase the happiness of man, by giving them beauty and interest of incident to amuse their leisure, and prevent them wearying even of rest, and by giving them hope and bodily pleasure in their work; or, shortly, to make man's work happy and his rest fruitful. Consequently, genuine art is an unmixed blessing to the race of man.

But as the word "genuine" is a large qualification, I must ask leave to attempt to draw some practical conclusions from this assertion of the Aims of Art, which will, I suppose, or indeed hope, lead us into some controversy on the subject; because it is futile indeed to expect anyone to speak about art, except in the most superficial way, without encountering those social problems which all serious men are thinking of, since art is and must be, either in its abundance or its barrenness, in its sincerity or its hollowness, the expression of the society amongst which it exists.

First, then, it is clear that, at the present time, those who look widest at things and deepest into them are quite dissatisfied with the present state of the arts, as they are also with the present condition of society. This I say in the teeth of the supposed revivification of art which has taken place of late years: in fact, that very excitement about the arts amongst a part of the cultivated people of today does but show on how firm a basis the dissatisfaction above mentioned rests. Forty years ago there was much less talk about art, much less practice of it, than there is now; and that is specially true of the architectural arts, which I shall mostly have to speak about now. People have consciously striven to raise the dead in art since that time, and with some superficial success. Nevertheless, in spite of this conscious effort, I must tell you that England, to a person who can feel and understand beauty, was a less grievous place to live in then than it is now; and we who feel what art means know well, though we do not often dare to say so, that forty years hence it will be a more grievous place to us than it is now if we still follow up the road we are on. Less than forty years ago—about thirty—I first saw the city of Rouen, then still in its outward aspect a piece of the Middle Ages: no words can tell you how its mingled beauty, history,

and romance took hold on me: I can only say that, looking back on my past life, I find it was the greatest pleasure I have ever had: and now it is a pleasure which no one can ever have again: it is lost to the world for ever. At that time I was an undergraduate of Oxford. Though not so astounding, so romantic, or at first sight so mediaeval as the Norman city, Oxford in those days still kept a great deal of its earlier loveliness: and the memory of its grey streets as they then were has been an abiding influence and pleasure in my life, and would be greater still if I could only forget what they are now—a matter of far more importance than the so-called learning of the place could have been to me in any case, but which, as it was, no one tried to teach me, and I did not try to learn. Since then the guardians of this beauty and romance so fertile of education, though professedly engaged in "the higher education" (as the futile system of compromises which they follow is nicknamed), have ignored it utterly, have made its preservation give way to the pressure of commercial exigencies, and are determined apparently to destroy it altogether. There is another pleasure for the world gone down the wind; here, again, the beauty and romance have been uselessly, causelessly, most foolishly thrown away.

These two cases are given simply because they have been fixed in my mind; they are but types of what is going on everywhere throughout civilization: the world is everywhere growing uglier and more commonplace, in spite of the conscious and very strenuous efforts of a small group of people towards the revival of art, which are so obviously out of joint with the tendency of the age that, while the uncultivated have not even heard of them, the mass of the cultivated look upon them as a joke, and even that they are now beginning to get tired of.

Now, if it be true, as I have asserted, that genuine art is an unmixed blessing to the world, this is a serious matter; for at first sight it seems to show that there will soon be no art at all in the world, which will thus lose an unmixed blessing; it can ill afford to do that, I think.

For, art, if it has to die, has worn itself out, and its aim will be a thing forgotten; and its aim was to make work happy and rest fruitful. Is all work to be unhappy, all rest unfruitful, then? Indeed, if art is to perish, that will be the case, unless something is to take its place —something at present unnamed, undreamed of.

I do not think that anything will take the place of art; not that I doubt the ingenuity of man, which seems to be boundless in the direction of making himself unhappy, but because I believe the springs of art in the human mind to be deathless, and also because it seems to me easy to see the causes of the present obliteration of the arts.

For we civilized people have not given them up consciously, or of our free will; we have been *forced* to give them up. Perhaps I can illustrate that by the detail of the application of machinery to the production of things in which artistic form of some sort is possible. Why does a reasonable man use a machine? Surely to save his labour. There are some things which a machine can do as well as a man's hand, *plus* a tool, can do them. He need not, for instance, grind his corn in a handquern; a little trickle of water, a wheel, and a few simple contrivances will do it all perfectly well, and leave him free to smoke his pipe and think, or to carve the handle of his knife. That, so far, is unmixed gain in the use of a machine —always, mind you, supposing equality of condition among men; no art is lost, leisure or time for more pleasurable work is gained. Perhaps a perfectly reasonable and free man would stop there in his dealings with machinery; but such reason and freedom are too much to expect, so let us follow our machine-inventor a step farther. He has to weave plain cloth, and finds doing so dullish on the one hand, and

on the other that a power-loom will weave the cloth nearly as well as a hand-loom, and foregoes the small advantage of the little extra art in the cloth. But so doing, as far as the art is concerned, he has not got a pure gain; he has made a bargain between art and labour, and got a makeshift as a consequence. I do not say that he may not be right in so doing, but that he has lost as well as gained. Now, this is as far as a man who values art and is reasonable would go in the matter of machinery *as long as he was free*—that is, was not *forced* to work for another man's profit; so long as he was living in a society *that had accepted equality of condition*. Carry the machine used for art a step farther, and he becomes an unreasonable man, if he values art and is free. To avoid misunderstanding, I must say that I am thinking of the modern machine, which is as it were alive, and to which the man is auxiliary, and not of the old machine, the improved tool, which is auxiliary to the man, and only works as long as his hand is thinking; though I will remark, that even this elementary form of machine has to be dropped when we come to the higher and more intricate forms of art. Well, as to the machine proper used for art, when it gets to the stage above dealing with a necessary production that has accidentally some beauty about it, a reasonable man with a feeling for art will only use it when he is *forced* to. If he thinks he would like ornament, for instance, and knows that the machine cannot do it properly, and does not care to spend the time to do it properly, why should he do it at all? He will not diminish his leisure for the sake of making something he does not want unless some man or band of men force him to it; so he will either go without the ornament, or sacrifice some of his leisure to have it genuine. There will be a sign that he wants it very much, and that it will be worth his trouble: in which case, again, his labour on it will not be mere trouble, but will interest and please him by satisfying the needs of his mood of energy.

This, I say, is how a reasonable man would act if he were free from man's compulsion; not being free, he acts very differently. He has long passed the stage at which machines are only used for doing work repulsive to an average man, or for doing what could be as well done by a machine as a man, and he instinctively expects a machine to be invented whenever any product of industry becomes sought after. He is the slave to machinery; the new machine *must* be invented, and when invented he *must* —I will not say use it, but be used by it, whether he likes it or not.

But why is he the slave to machinery? Because he is the slave to the system for whose existence the invention of machinery was necessary.

And now I must drop, or rather have dropped, the assumption of the equality of condition, and remind you that, though in a sense we are all the slaves of machinery, yet that some men are so directly without any metaphor at all, and that these are just those on whom the great body of the arts depends—the workmen. It is necessary for the system which keeps them in their position as an inferior class that they should either be themselves machines or be the servants to machines, in no case having any interest in the work which they turn out. To their employers they are, so far as they are workmen, a part of the machinery of the workshop or the factory; to themselves they are proletarians, human beings working to live that they may live to work: their part of craftsmen, of makers of things by their own free will, is played out.

At the risk of being accused of sentimentality, I will say that since this is so, since the work which produces the things that should be matters of art is but a burden and a slavery, I exult in this at least, that it cannot produce art; that all it can do lies between stark utilitarianism and idiotic sham.

Or indeed is that merely sentimental? Rather, I think, we who have learned to see the connection between industrial slavery and the degradation of the arts have learned also to hope for a future for those arts; since the day will certainly come when men will shake off the yoke, and refuse to accept the mere artificial compulsion of the gambling market to waste their lives in ceaseless and hopeless toil; and when it does come, their instincts for beauty and imagination set free along with them, will produce such art as they need; and who can say that it will not as far surpass the art of past ages as that does the poor relics of it left us by the age of commerce?

A word or two on an objection which has often been made to me when I have been talking on this subject. It may be said, and is often, You regret the art of the Middle Ages (as indeed I do), but those who produced it were not free; they were serfs, or gild-craftsmen surrounded by brazen walls of trade restrictions; they had no political rights, and were exploited by their masters, the noble caste, most grievously. Well, I quite admit that the oppression and violence of the Middle Ages had its effect on the art of those days, its shortcomings are traceable to them; they repressed art in certain directions, I do not doubt that; and for that reason I say, that when we shake off the present oppression as we shook off the old, we may expect the art of the days of real freedom to rise above that of those old violent days. But I do say that it was possible then to have social, organic, hopeful progressive art; whereas now such poor scraps of it as are left are the result of individual and wasteful struggle, are retrospective and pessimistic. And this hopeful art was possible amidst all the oppression of those days, because the instruments of that oppression were grossly obvious, and were external to the work of the craftsman. They were laws and customs obviously intended to rob him, and open violence of the highway-robbery kind. In short, industrial production was not the instrument used in that honourable profession. The mediaeval craftsman was free in his work, therefore he made it as amusing to himself as he could; and it was his pleasure and not his pain that made all things beautiful that were made, and lavished treasures of human hope and thought on everything that man made, from a cathedral to a porridge-pot. Come, let us put it in the way least respectful to the mediaeval craftsman, most polite to the modern "hand": the poor devil of the fourteenth century, his work was of so little value that he was allowed to waste it by the hour in pleasing himself— and others; but our highly-strung mechanic, his minutes are too rich with the burden of perpetual profit for him to be allowed to waste one of them on art; the present system will not allow him—cannot allow him—to produce works of art.

So that there has arisen this strange phenomenon, that there is now a class of ladies and gentlemen, very refined indeed, though not perhaps as well informed as is generally supposed, and of this refined class there are many who do really love beauty and incident—i.e., art, and would make sacrifices to get it; and these are led by artists of great manual skill and high intellect, forming altogether a large body of demand for the article. And yet the supply does not come. Yes, and moreover, this great body of enthusiastic demanders are no mere poor and helpless people, ignorant fisher-peasants, half-mad monks, scatter-brained sans-culottes—none of those, in short, the expression of whose needs has shaken the world so often before, and will do yet again. No, they are of the ruling classes, the masters of men, who can live without labour, and have abundant leisure to scheme out the fulfilment of their desires; and yet I say they cannot have the art which they so much long for, though they hunt it about the world so hard, sentimentalizing the sordid lives of the miserable peasants of Italy and the starving proletarians of her towns, now that all the picturesqueness has departed from the poor devils of our own country-side,

and of our own slums. Indeed, there is little of reality left them anywhere, and that little is fast fading away before the needs of the manufacturer and his ragged regiment of workers, and before the enthusiasm of the archaeological restorer of the dead past. Soon there will be nothing left except the lying dreams of history, the miserable wreckage of our museums and picture-galleries, and the carefully guarded interiors of our aesthetic drawing-rooms, unreal and foolish, fitting witnesses of the life of corruption that goes on there, so pinched and meagre and cowardly, with its concealment and ignoring, rather than restraint of, natural longings; which does not forbid the greedy indulgence in them if it can but be decently hidden.

The art then is gone, and can no more be "restored" on its old lines than a mediaeval building can be. The rich and refined cannot have it though they would, and though we will believe many of them would. And why? Because those who could give it to the rich are not allowed by the rich to do so. In one word, slavery lies between us and art.

I have said as much as that the aim of art was to destroy the curse of labour by making work the pleasurable satisfaction of our impulse towards energy, and giving to that energy hope of producing something worth its exercise.

Now, therefore, I say, that since we cannot have art by striving after its mere superficial manifestation, since we can have nothing but its sham by so doing, there yet remains for us to see how it would be if we let the shadow take care of itself and try, if we can, to lay hold of the substance. For my part I believe, that if we try to realize the aims of art without much troubling ourselves what the aspect of the art itself shall be, we shall find we shall have what we want at last: whether it is to be called art or not, it will at least be *life;* and, after all, that is what we want. It may lead us into new splendours and beauties of visible art; to architecture with manifolded magnificence free from the curious incompleteness and fail-

ings of that which the older times have produced—to painting, uniting to the beauty which
mediaeval art attained the realism which modern art aims at; to sculpture, uniting the beauty
of the Greek and the expression of the Renaissance with some third quality yet undiscov-
ered, so as to give us the images of men and
women splendidly alive, yet not disqualified
from making, as all true sculpture should, architectural ornament. All this it may do; or, on
the other hand, it may lead us into the desert,
and art may seem to be dead amidst us; or
feebly and uncertainly to be struggling in a
world which has utterly forgotten its old
glories.

For my part, with art as it now is, I cannot
bring myself to think that it much matters
which of these dooms awaits it, so long as
each bears with it some hope of what is to
come; since here, as in other matters, there is
no hope save in Revolution. The old art is no
longer fertile, no longer yields us anything save
elegantly poetical regrets; being barren, it has
to die, and the matter of moment now is, as to
how it shall die, whether *with* hope or *without*
it.

What is it, for instance, that has destroyed
the Rouen, the Oxford of *my* elegant poetic
regret? Has it perished for the benefit of the
people, either slowly yielding to the growth
of intelligent change and new happiness? or has
it been, as it were, thunderstricken by the tragedy which mostly accompanies some great new
birth? Not so. Neither phalangstere nor dyna-
mite has swept its beauty away, its destroyers
have not been either the philanthropist or the
Socialist, the co-operator or the anarchist. It
has been sold, and at a cheap price indeed:
muddled away by the greed and incompetence
of fools who do not know what life and pleasure mean, who will neither take them themselves nor let others have them. That is why
the death of that beauty wounds us so: no man
of sense or feeling would dare to regret such
losses if they had been paid for by new life and

happiness for the people. But there is the
people still as it was before, still facing for its
part the monster who destroyed all that beauty,
and whose name is Commercial Profit.

I repeat, that every scrap of genuine art will
fall by the same hands if the matter only goes
on long enough, although a sham art may be
left in its place, which may very well be carried on by *dilettanti* fine gentlemen and ladies
without any help from below; and, to speak
plainly, I fear that this gibbering ghost of the
real thing would satisfy a great many of those
who now think themselves lovers of art;
though it is not difficult to see a long vista of
its degradation till it shall become at last a
mere laughing-stock; that is to say, if the thing
were to go on: I mean, if art were to be for
ever the amusement of those whom we now
call ladies and gentlemen.

But for my part I do not think it will go on
long enough to reach such depths as that; and
yet I should be hypocritical if I were to say
that I thought that the change in the basis of
society, which would enfranchise labour and
make men practically equal in condition, would
lead us by a short road to the splendid new
birth of art which I have mentioned, though I
feel quite certain that it would not leave what
we now call art untouched, since the aims of
that revolution do include the aims of art—viz.,
abolishing the curse of labour.

I suppose that this is what is likely to happen;
that machinery will go on developing, with the
purpose of saving men labour, till the mass of
the people attain real leisure enough to be
able to appreciate the pleasure of life; till, in
fact, they have attained such mastery over Nature that they no longer fear starvation as a
penalty for not working more than enough.
When they get to that point they will doubtless
turn themselves and begin to find out what it
is that they really want to do. They would
soon find out that the less work they did (the
less work unaccompanied by art, I mean), the
more desirable a dwelling-place the earth would

be; they would accordingly do less and less work, till the mood of energy, of which I began by speaking, urged them on afresh: but by that time Nature relieved by the relaxation of man's work, would be recovering her ancient beauty, and be teaching men the old story of art. And as the Artificial Famine, caused by men working for the profit of a master, and which we now look upon as a matter of course, would have long disappeared, they would be free to do as they chose, and they would set aside their machines in all cases where the work seemed pleasant or desirable for handiwork; till in all crafts where production of beauty was required, the most direct communication between a man's hand and his brain would be sought for. And there would be many occupations also, as the processes of agriculture, in which the voluntary exercise of energy would be thought so delightful, that people would not dream of handing over its pleasure to the jaws of a machine.

In short, men will find out that the men of our days were wrong in first multiplying their needs, and then trying, each man of them, to evade all participation in the means and processes whereby those needs are satisfied; that this kind of division of labour is really only a new and wilful form of arrogant and slothful ignorance, far more injurious to the happiness and contentment of life than the ignorance of the processes of Nature, of what we sometimes call *science,* which men of the earlier days unwittingly lived in.

They will discover, or rediscover rather, that the true secret of happiness *lies in the taking a genuine interest in all the details of daily life,* in elevating them by art instead of handing the performance of them over to unregarded drudges, and ignoring them; and that in cases where it was impossible either so to elevate them and make them interesting, or to lighten them by the use of machinery, so as to make the labour of them trifling, that should be taken

as a token that the supposed advantages gained by them were not worth the trouble and had better be given up. All this to my mind would be the outcome of men throwing off the burden of Artificial Famine, supposing, as I cannot help supposing, that the impulses which have from the first glimmerings of history urged men on to the practice of Art were still at work in them.

Thus and thus only *can* come about the new birth of Art, and I think it *will* come about thus. You may say it is a long process, and so it is; but I can conceive of a longer. I have given you the Socialist or Optimist view of the matter. Now for the Pessimist view.

I can conceive that the revolt against Artificial Famine or Capitalism, which is now on foot, may be vanquished. The result will be that the working class—the slaves of society—will become more and more degraded; that they will not strive against overwhelming force, but, stimulated by that love of life which Nature, always anxious about the perpetuation of the race, has implanted in us, will learn to bear everything—starvation, overwork, dirt, ignorance, brutality. All these things they will bear, as, alas! they bear them too well even now; all this rather than risk sweet life and bitter livelihood, and all sparks of hope and manliness will die out of them.

Nor will their masters be much better off: the earth's surface will be hideous everywhere, save in the uninhabitable desert; Art will utterly perish, as in the manual arts so in literature, which will become, as it is indeed speedily becoming, a mere string of orderly and calculated ineptitudes and passionless ingenuities; Science will grow more and more one-sided, more incomplete, more wordy and useless, till at last she will pile herself up into such a mass of superstition, that beside it the theologies of old time will seem mere reason and enlightenment. All will get lower and lower, till the heroic struggles of the past to realize hope from year to year, from century to century, will be utterly forgotten, and man will be an indescribable being—hopeless, desireless, lifeless.

And will there be deliverance from this even? Maybe: man may, after some terrible cataclysm, learn to strive towards a healthy animalism, may grow from a tolerable animal into a savage, from a savage into a barbarian, and so on; and some thousands of years hence he may be beginning once more those arts which we have now lost, and be carving interlacements like the New Zealanders, or scratching forms of animals on their cleaned blade-bones, like the prehistoric men of the drift.

But in any case, accordng to the pessimistic view, which looks upon revolt against Artificial Famine as impossible to succeed, we shall wearily trudge the circle again, until some accident, some unforeseen consequence of arrangement, makes an end of us altogether.

That pessimism I do not believe in, nor, on the other hand, do I suppose that it is altogether a matter of our wills as to whether we shall further human progress or human degradation; yet, since there are those who are impelled towards the Socialist or Optimistic side of things, I must conclude that there is some hope of its prevailing, that the strenuous efforts of many individuals imply a force which is thrusting them on. So that I believe that the "Aims of Art" will be realized, though I know that they

cannot be, so long as we groan under the tyranny of Artificial Famine. Once again I warn you against supposing, you who may specially love art, that you will do any good by attempting to revivify art by dealing with its dead exterior. I say it is the *aims of art* that you must seek rather than the *art itself;* and in that search we may find ourselves in a world blank and bare, as the result of our caring at least this much for art, that we will not endure the shams of it.

Anyhow, I ask you to think with me that the worst which can happen to us is to endure tamely the evils that we see; that no trouble or turmoil is so bad as that; that the necessary destruction which reconstruction bears with it must be taken calmly; that everywhere—in State, in Church, in the household—we must be resolute to endure no tyranny, accept no lie, quail before no fear, although they may come before us disguised as piety, duty, or affection, as useful opportunity and good-nature, as prudence or kindness. The world's roughness, falseness, and injustice will bring about their natural consequences, and we and our lives are part of those consequences; but since we inherit also the consequences of old resistance to those curses, let us each look to it to have our fair share of that inheritance also, which, if nothing else come of it, will at least bring to us courage and hope; that is, eager life while we live, which is above all things the Aim of Art.

Notes

1. A. H. R. Ball, ed. *Selections from the Prose Works of William Morris* (Cambridge, England: University Press, 1931), p. 81.

2. Ibid., p. 84.

3. Ibid., p. 117.

4. Ibid., p. 145.

5. Ibid., p. 157.

6. Ball, op. cit., xxxiv.

7. Ibid., p. 169.

Instead of focusing on beauty or on some other general category as so many previous aesthetic philosophers have done, Susanne K. Langer, an American, developed an aesthetic theory by reflecting on the problem of artistic creation. In her major treatment of the arts, *Form and Feeling* (1953), she interpreted artistic creation as a process of finding significant forms for the expression of feeling. Expressing feeling does not mean, in her view, revealing the artist's states of mind or manifesting his personality, but rather creating nondiscursive symbols to serve as analogues for the feeling. Music thus "sounds the way feelings feel" because the pattern of sounds is tonally analogous to the composer's (and the listener's) emotive life. But as the feelings are not expressed through words or discursive symbols but through sounds, that is, through nondiscursive symbols, we should refer not to the music's meaning, but rather to its "vital import," which is expressed sensuously through its dynamic structure or significant form.

Having defined art as "the creation of forms symbolic of feeling,"[1] Mrs. Langer explains the significance of the various art forms, each of which creates a "purely virtual" (i.e., illusory) object, an image or semblance through which aesthetic feeling can be expressed. Painting expresses the semblance of a virtual three-dimensional space, an illusion of scene. Sculpture makes tactual space visible by creating the semblance of living forms, the import of vital functions; it is essentially "the image of kinetic volume in sensory space."[2] Architecture creates a different semblance of space, that which Mrs. Langer calls "an ethnic domain" or "a virtual place."[3] Such, in brief, is the nature of the plastic arts.

Turning next to arts of time or the "occurrent arts"—music, dance, literature and drama—Mrs. Langer points out that the elements which make up music are not tones, chords, and measured beats, but something virtual: the semblance of motion. The image of lived or experienced time is made sensuously audible through the dynamic structures which the composer creates and the performers recreate for the listener. Further, the art of the dance, contrary to previous interpretations, is neither musical nor plastic nor dramatic. Like the other arts, dance creates an illusory realm, which in its case is an imaginary realm of power. Through virtual movements or gestures, dancers express not themselves but the semblance of self-expression and vital force. Poetry creates the semblance of life by creating illusory events, experiences not actually lived through and felt, but recreated through expressive forms, symbols of feeling. Like the poet, but by different devices, the novelist, the short story writer, and the biographer use language to create virtual life or history, an illusory experience of things past which has been clarified, intensified, and objictified in and through aesthetic forms. Finally, drama creates an imaginary future by projecting the image of life in the mode of dramatic action. Unlike literature, which gives us a history in retrospect, drama gives us a history in prospect. For this reason, Mrs. Langer calls it "the mode of Destiny."[4]

From the following essay, the reader can discover why Mrs. Langer considers art to be of such great importance not just to artists but to all those who want to have life more abundantly. In her view, every work of art has a social intent, a public (real or imagined) for whom the artist creates his symbol of feeling. When the observer or auditor experiences the work of art, he does not enter into a direct relation with the artist, but rather intuits or directly apprehends the structure and texture of the work of art, which immediately reveals its feeling import. A person cannot understand and appreciate art unless he has good taste in the sense of keen aesthetic responsiveness. This cannot be taught, but it can operate more freely, when one has clarified his conceptions of what art is and knows what to expect of it and of himself in fully experiencing it.

Since art can reveal to us our innermost life, the feelings which lie at the very core of our being, its importance can scarcely be overestimated. For without art, our experience would lack that coherence, that completeness of form, which art alone can discover in it and make visible or audible. The significance of feeling would not and could not be apparent without aesthetic form. The artist molds forms that are the symbols of feelings and these forms, in turn, mold actual feelings. This is the fundamental basis of all aesthetic education. Like John Dewey, Mrs. Langer opposes the view that sees art as merely "a cultural veneer" or as "a beauty parlor of civilization." Also, like John Dewey and Herbert Read, Mrs. Langer believes that the arts offer far more than merely diversion, entertainment, and escape from everyday life. A culture that views the world of art as a kind of Disneyland will never see in it what Mrs. Langer sees, namely, a valuable "school of feeling," a source of exaltation, and a defense against inner and outer chaos.

The Cultural Importance
of Art

Every culture develops some kind of art as surely as it develops language. Some primitive cultures have no real mythology or religion, but all have some art—dance, song, design (sometimes only on tools or on the human body). Dance, above all, seems to be the oldest elaborated art.

The ancient ubiquitous character of art contrasts sharply with the prevalent idea that art is a luxury product of civilization, a cultural frill, a piece of social veneer.

It fits better with the conviction held by most artists, that art is the epitome of human life, the truest record of insight and feeling, and that the strongest military or economic society without art is poor in comparison wih the most primitive tribe of savage painters, dancers, or idol carvers. Wherever a society has really achieved culture (in the ethnological sense, not the popular sense of "social form") it has begotten art, not late in its career, but at the very inception of it.

Art is, indeed, the spearhead of human development, social and individual. The vulgarization of art is the surest symptom of ethnic decline. The growth of a new art or even a great and radically new style always bespeaks a young and vigorous mind, whether collective or single.

From Susanne K. Langer, "The Cultural Importance of the Arts" in M. F. Andrews, *Aesthetic Form and Education,* Syracuse University Press, 1958. Reprinted by permission.

What sort of thing is art, that it should play such a leading role in human development? It is not an intellectual pursuit, but is necessary to intellectual life; it is not religion, but grows up with religion, serves it, and in large measure determines it.

We cannot enter here on a long discussion of what has been claimed as the essence of art, the true nature of art, or its defining function; in a single lecture dealing with one aspect of art, namely its cultural influence, I can only give you by way of preamble my own definition of art, with categorical brevity. This does not mean that I set up this definition in a categorical spirit, but only that we have no time to debate it; so you are asked to accept it as an assumption underlying these reflections.

Art, in the sense here intended—that is, the generic term subsuming painting, sculpture, architecture, music, dance, literature, drama, and film—may be defined as the practice of creating perceptible forms expressive of human feeling. I say "perceptible" rather than "sensuous" forms because some works of art are given to imagination rather than to the outward senses. A novel, for instance, usually is read silently with the eye, but is not made for vision, as a painting is; and though sound plays a vital part in poetry, words even in poetry are not essentially sonorous structures like music. Dance requires to be seen, but its appeal is to deeper centers of sensation. The difference between dance and mobile sculpture makes this immediately apparent. But all works of art are purely perceptible forms that seem to embody some sort of feeling.

"Feeling" as I am using it here covers much more than it does in the technical vocabulary of psychology, where it denotes only pleasure and displeasure, or even in the shifting limits of ordinary discourse, where it sometimes means sensation (as when one says a paralyzed limb has no feeling in it), sometimes sensibility (as we speak of hurting someone's feelings), sometimes emotion (e.g., as a situation is said to harrow your feelings, or to evoke tender feeling), or a directed emotional attitude (we say we feel strongly *about* something), or even our general mental or physical condition, feeling well or ill, blue, or a bit above ourselves. As I use the word, in defining art as the creation of perceptible forms expressive of human feeling, it takes in all those meanings; it applies to everything that may be felt.

Another word in the definition that might be questioned is "creation." I think it is justified, not pretentious, as perhaps it sounds, but that issue is slightly beside the point here; so let us shelve it. If anyone prefers to speak of the "making" or "construction" of expressive forms, that will do here just as well.

What does have to be understood is the meaning of "form," and more particularly "expressive form"; for that involves the very nature of art and therefore the question of its cultural importance.

The word "form" has several current uses; most of them have some relation to the sense in which I am using it here, though a few, such as "a form to be filled in for tax purposes" or "a mere matter of form," are fairly remote, being quite specialized. Since we are speaking of art, it might be good to point out that the meaning of stylistic pattern—"the sonata form," "the sonnet form"—is not the one I am assuming here.

I am using the word in a simpler sense, which it has when you say, on a foggy night, that you see dimly moving forms in the mist; one of them emerges clearly, and is the form of a man. The trees are gigantic forms; the rills of rain trace sinuous forms on the windowpane. The rills are not fixed things; they are forms of motion. When you watch gnats weaving in the air, or flocks of birds wheeling overhead, you see dynamic forms—forms made by motion.

It is in this sense of an apparition given to our perception that a work of art is a form. It may be a permanent form like a building or a vase or a picture, or a transient, dynamic form like a melody or a dance, or even a form given to imagination, like the passage of purely imaginary, apparent events that constitutes a literary work. But it is always a perceptible, self-identical whole; like a natural being, it has a character of organic unity, self-sufficiency, individual reality. And it is thus, as an appearance, that a work of art is good or bad or perhaps only rather poor—as an appearance, not as a comment on things beyond it in the world, or as a reminder of them.

This, then, is what I mean by "form"; but what is meant by calling such forms "expressive of human feeling"? How do apparitions "express" anything—feeling or anything else? First of all, let us ask just what is meant here by "express," what sort of "expression" we are talking about.

The word "expression" has two principal meanings. In one sense it means self-expression—giving vent to our feelings. In this sense it refers to a symptom of what we feel. Self-expression is a spontaneous reaction to an actual, present situation, an event, the company we are in, things people say, or what the weather does to us; it bespeaks the physical and mental state we are in and the emotions that stir us.

In another sense, however, "expression" means the presentation of an idea, usually by the proper and apt use of words. But a device for presenting an idea is what we call a symbol, not a symptom. Thus a word is a symbol, and so is a meaningful combination of words.

A sentence, which is a special combination of

words, expresses the idea of some state of affairs, real or imagined. Sentences are complicated symbols. Language will formulate new ideas as well as communicate old ones, so that all people know a lot of things that they have merely heard or read about. Symbolic expression, therefore, extends our knowledge beyond the scope of our actual experience.

If an idea is clearly conveyed by means of symbols we say it is well expressed. A person may work for a long time to give his statement the best possible form, to find the exact words for what he means to say, and to carry his account or his argument most directly from one point to another. But a discourse so worked out is certainly not a spontaneous reaction. Giving expression to an idea is obviously a different thing from giving expression to feelings. You do not say of a man in a rage that his anger is well expressed. The symptoms just are what they are; there is no critical standard for symptoms. If, on the other hand, the angry man tries to tell you what he is fuming about, he will have to collect himself, curtail his emotional expression, and find words to express his ideas. For to tell a story coherently involves "expression" in quite a different sense: this sort of expression is not "self-expression," but may be called "conceptual expression."

Language, of course, is our prime instrument of conceptual expression. The things we can say are in effect the things we can think. Words are the terms of our thinking as well as the terms in which we present our thoughts, because they present the objects of thought to the thinker himself. Before language communicates ideas, it gives them form, makes them clear, and in fact makes them what they are. Whatever has a name is an object for thought. Without words, sense experience is only a flow of impressions, as subjective as our feelings; words make it objective, and carve it up into *things* and *facts* that we can note, remember, and think about. Language gives outward experience its form, and makes it definite and clear.

There is, however, an important part of reality that is quite inaccessible to the formative influence of language: that is the realm of so-called "inner experience," the life of feeling and emotion. The reason why language is so powerless here is not, as many people suppose, that feeling and emotion are irrational; on the contrary, they seem irrational because language does not help to make them conceivable, and most people cannot conceive anything without the logical scaffolding of words. The unfitness of language to convey subjective experience is a somewhat technical subject, easier for logicians to understand than for artists; but the gist of it is that the form of language does not reflect the natural form of feeling, so that we cannot shape any extensive concepts of feeling with the help of ordinary, discursive language. Therefore the words whereby we refer to feeling only name very general kinds of inner experience—excitement, calm, joy, sorrow, love, hate, and so on. But there is no language to describe just how one joy differs, sometimes radically, from another. The real nature of feeling is something language as such —as discursive symbolism—cannot render.

For this reason, the phenomena of feeling and emotion are usually treated by philosophers as irrational. The only pattern discursive thought can find in them is the pattern of outward events that occasion them. There are different degrees of fear, but they are thought of as so many degrees of the same simple feeling.

But human feeling is a fabric, not a vague mass. It has an intricate dynamic pattern, possible combinations and new emergent phenomena. It is a pattern of organically interdependent and interdetermined tensions and resolutions, a pattern of almost infinitely complex activation and cadence. To it belongs the whole gamut of our sensibility—the sense of straining thought, all mental attitude and motor set. Those are the deeper reaches that underlie the surface waves of our emotion, and make human life a life of feeling instead of an unconscious metabolic existence interrupted by feelings.

It is, I think, this dynamic pattern that finds its formal expression in the arts. The expressiveness of art is like that of a symbol, not that of an emotional symptom; it is as a formulation of feeling for our conception that a work of art is properly said to be expressive. It may serve somebody's need of self-expression besides, but that is not what makes it good or bad art. In a special sense one may call a work of art a symbol of feeling, for, like a symbol, it formulates our ideas of inward experience, as discourse formulates our ideas of things and facts in the outside world. A work of art differs from a genuine symbol—that is, a symbol in the full and usual sense—in that it does not point beyond itself to something else. Its relation to feeling is a rather special one that we cannot undertake to analyze here; in effect, the feeling it expresses appears to be directly given with it—as the sense of a true metaphor, or the value of a religious myth—and is not separable from its expression. We speak of the feeling *of*, or the feeling *in*, a work of art, not the feeling it means. And we speak truly; a work of art presents something like a direct vision of vitality, emotion, subjective reality.

The primary function of art is to objectify feeling so that we can contemplate and understand it. It is the formulation of so-called "inward experience," the "inner life," that is impossible to achieve by discursive thought, because its forms are incommensurable with the forms of language and all its derivatives (e.g., mathematics, symbolic logic). Art objectifies the sentience and desire, self-consciousness and world-consciousness, emotions and moods, that are generally regarded as irrational because words cannot give us clear ideas of them. But the premise tacitly assumed in such a judgment —namely, that anything language cannot express is formless and irrational—seems to me to be an error. I believe the life of feeling is not irrational; its logical forms are merely very different from the structures of discourse. But they are so much like the dynamic forms of art that art is their natural symbol. Through plastic works, music, fiction, dance, or dramatic forms we can conceive what vitality and emotion feel like.

This brings us, at last, to the question of the cultural importance of the arts. Why is art so apt to be the vanguard of cultural advance, as it was in Egypt, in Greece, in Christian Europe (think of Gregorian music and Gothic architecture), in Renaissance Italy—not to speculate about ancient cavemen, whose art is all that we know of them? One thinks of culture as economic increase, social organization, the gradual ascendancy of rational thinking and scientific control of nature over superstitious imagination and magical practices. But art is not practical; it is neither philosophy nor science; it is not religion, morality, or even social comment (as many drama critics take comedy to be). What does it contribute to culture that could be of major importance?

It merely presents forms—sometimes intangible forms—to imagination. Its direct appeal is to that faculty, or function, that Lord Bacon considered the chief stumbling block in the way of reason, and that enlightened writers like Stuart Chase never tire of condemning as the source of all nonsense and bizarre erroneous beliefs. And so it is; but it is also the source of all insight and true beliefs. Imagination is probably the oldest mental trait that is typically human—older than discursive reason; it is probably the common source of dream, reason, religion, and all true general observation. It is this primitive human power—imagination—that engenders the arts and is in turn directly affected by their products.

Somewhere at the animalian starting line of human evolution lie the beginnings of that supreme instrument of the mind—language. We think of it as a device for communication among the members of a society. But communication is only one, and perhaps not even the first, of its functions. The first thing it does is to break up what William James called the "blooming, buzzing confusion" of sense perception into units and groups, events and chains of events—things and relations, causes and effects. All these patterns are imposed on our experience by language. We think, as we speak, in terms of objects and their relations.

But the process of breaking up our sense experience in this way, making reality conceivable, memorable, sometimes even predictable, is a process of imagination. Primitive conception is imagination. Language and imagination grow up together in a reciprocal tutelage.

What discursive symbolism—language in its literal use—does for our awareness of things about us and our own relation to them, the arts do for our awareness of subjective reality, feeling and emotion; they give form to inward experiences and thus make them conceivable. The only way we can really envisage vital movement, the stirring and growth and passage of emotion, and ultimately the whole direct sense of human life, is in artistic terms. A musical person thinks of emotions musically. They cannot be discursively talked about above a very general level. But they may nonetheless be known—objectively set forth, publicly known—and there is nothing necessarily confused or formless about emotions.

As soon as the natural forms of subjective experience are abstracted to the point of symbolic presentation, we can use those forms to imagine feeling and understand its nature. Self-knowledge, insight into all phases of life and mind, springs from artistic imagination. That is the cognitive value of the arts.

But their influence on human life goes deeper than the intellectual level. As language actually gives form to our sense experience, grouping our impressions around those things which have names, and fitting sensations to the qualities that have adjectival names, and so on, the arts we live with—our picture books and stories and the music we hear—actually form our emotive experience. Every generation has its styles of feeling. One age shudders and blushes and faints, another swaggers, still another is godlike in a universal indifference. These styles in actual emotion are not insincere. They are largely unconscious—determined by many social causes, but *shaped* by artists, usually popular artists of the screen, the jukebox, the shop-window, and the picture magazine. (That, rather than incitement to crime, is my objection to the comics.) Irwin Edman remarks in one of his books that our emotions are largely Shakespeare's poetry.

This influence of art on life gives us an indication of why a period of efflorescence in the arts is apt to lead a cultural advance: it formulates a new way of feeling, and that is the beginning of a cultural age. It suggests another matter for reflection, too—that a wide neglect of artistic education is a neglect in the education of feeling. Most people are so imbued with the idea that feeling is a formless, total organic excitement in men as in animals that the idea of educating feeling, developing its scope and quality, seems odd to them, if not absurd. It is really, I think, at the very heart of personal education.

There is one other function of the arts that benefits not so much the advance of culture as its stabilization—an influence on individual lives. This function is the converse and complement of the objectification of feeling, the driving force of creation in art: it is the education of vision that we receive in seeing, hearing, reading works of art—the development of the artist's eye, that assimilates ordinary sights (or sounds, motions, or events) to inward vision, and lends expressiveness and emotional import to the world. Wherever art takes a motif from actuality—a flowering branch, a bit of landscape, a historic event, or a personal memory, any model or theme from life—it transforms it into a piece of imagination, and imbues its image with artistic vitality. The result is an impregnation of ordinary reality with the significance of created form. This is the subjectification of nature that makes reality itself a symbol of life and feeling.

The arts objectify subjective reality, and subjectify outward experience of nature. Art education is the education of feeling, and a society that neglects it gives itself up to formless emotion. Bad art is corruption of feeling. This is a large factor in the irrationalism which dictators and demagogues exploit.

Notes

1. Susanne K. Langer, *Philosophical Sketches* (New York: New American Library, 1962), p. 76.
2. Susanne K. Langer, *Feeling and Form* (New York: Charles Scribner's Sons, 1959), p. 92.
3. Ibid., p. 95.
4. Ibid., p. 307.

27 / Creation as Commitment
Camus

The French writer Albert Camus (1913–1960) believed that the artist in today's world cannot avoid being committed when he is confronted with tyranny. In the past, when tyrannies were less efficient in suppressing unorthodox works and in curtailing artistic creativity, artists could perhaps remain detached and silent. Today, to be silent or neutral under tyranny is often as dangerous as to oppose it. "One has to take a stand, be either for or against," Camus wrote.[1] Camus was proudly against tyranny.

Some artists hold that as artists they must avoid interfering in the affairs of the world. As artists they may be right, Camus admitted, but as men they must interfere.

Because of his profound interest in and sympathy for the sufferings, the humiliations, and the triumphs of ordinary human beings, Camus was attracted to the problems of everyday life. However, despite his social concern, or perhaps because of it, he was unwilling to cease being an artist and to become only a social propagandist. Is the artist to serve the values of creativity or the values of humanity? Neither can be separated from the other, Camus believed. In trying to balance the demands of both kinds of values, the artist sets up a tension in himself that inevitably has repercussions on his life, his work, and his world. "We must simultaneously serve suffering and beauty," he asserted.[2] Artists who withdraw into ivory towers are no different than those who seek refuge in a formula for social salvation. Both are choosing forms of resignation rather than confronting the world in all its absurdity and searching courageously for solutions to human problems. Bitterness must be rejected, but dangers must be accepted. "The era of chairbound artists is over," Camus writes.[3] "Commit thyself" must be the new artistic maxim.

While Camus stressed the importance of artistic commitment, which, as he viewed it, certainly did not mean making one's art subservient to an ideology, he also stressed the importance of maintaining artistic detachment, or what the English psychologist Edward Bullough called "aesthetic distance." The artist must throw himself into the historical arena, sharing in the misfortunes of his time and seeking to alleviate them; otherwise he can never "insert his art into its time." But he must also withdraw sufficiently from the action if he is to evaluate and recreate it. "Every work presupposes a content of reality and a creator who shapes the container," Camus pointed out.[4] The artist, then, cannot understand the content of action unless he has been a part of it—that is, unless he has been involved in and committed to it— yet he cannot give it form unless he has been able to tear himself away from it long enough to see it, in Spinoza's phrase, "under the form of eternity."

It is a symptom of the sickness and derangement of our times, Camus believed, that the artist has to be reminded that he is, after all, only another human being. Like the ordinary man, he gropes his way in the dark and longs for the things that other men long for—solitude, justice, help, pleasure, friendship, love, admiration, freedom, and hope. Hope to Camus was particularly important. By means of hope he was able to reject nihilism, concentrate on the idea of fecundity, and remain committed to his role of artist. In the very process of negating, of criticizing and defying the world in which he lived, Camus noted that to negate is also to affirm. Even when he was depicting the sordidness and absurdity of life, he recognized that he was also paying "homage to the wretched and magnificent life of ours."[5]

Camus also realized that he was paying homage to the value that he prized above all others in art and in life, the value of freedom. "The aim of art, the aim of life can only be to increase the sum of freedom and responsibility to be found in every man and in the world."[6] An artist who uses his art as a means of expressing his hatred of life and his contempt for human beings is like the artist who uses his works as disguised tracts for converting his readers to a cause to which the artist is committed. Neither kind of artist will succeed in creating works with lasting value as their works will add nothing to the understanding and appreciation of freedom. In the contemporary world, Camus was convinced that "the force of resistance, together with the value of freedom gives us new reasons for living."[7]

Notes

1. Albert Camus, "The Artist and His Time" in *The Myth of Sisyphus and Other Essays* (New York: Vintage Books, 1955), p. 207.
2. Ibid., p. 212.
3. Ibid.
4. Albert Camus, *Resistance, Rebellion and Death* (New York: Modern Library, Random House, 1963), p. 182.
5. Ibid., p. 183.
6. Ibid., p. 184.
7. Ibid., p. 185.

Create Dangerously

An Oriental wise man always used to ask the divinity in his prayers to be so kind as to spare him from living in an interesting era. As we are not wise, the divinity has not spared us and we are living in an interesting era. In any case, our era forces us to take an interest in it. The writers of today know this. If they speak up, they are criticized and attacked. If they become modest and keep silent, they are vociferously blamed for their silence.

In the midst of such din the writer cannot hope to remain aloof in order to pursue the reflections and images that are dear to him. Until the present moment, remaining aloof has always been possible in history. When someone did not approve, he could always keep silent or talk of something else. Today everything is changed and even silence has dangerous implications. The moment that abstaining from choice is itself looked upon as a choice and punished or praised as such, the artist is willy-nilly impressed into service. "Impressed" seems to me a more accurate term in this connection than "committed." Instead of signing up, indeed, for voluntary service, the artist does his compulsory service. Every artist today is embarked on the contemporary slave galley. He has to resign himself to this even if he considers that the galley reeks of its past, that the slavedrivers are really too numerous, and, in addition, that the steering is badly

handled. We are on the high seas. The artist, like everyone else, must bend to his oar, without dying if possible—in other words, go on living and creating.

To tell the truth, it is not easy, and I can understand why artists regret their former comfort. The change is somewhat cruel. Indeed, history's amphitheater has always contained the martyr and the lion. The former relied on eternal consolations and the latter on raw historical meat. But until now the artist was on the sidelines. He used to sing purposely, for his own sake, or at best to encourage the martyr and make the lion forget his appetite. But now the artist is in the amphitheater. Of necessity, his voice is not quite the same; it is not nearly so firm.

It is easy to see all that art can lose from such a constant obligation. Ease, to begin with, and that divine liberty so apparent in the work of Mozart. It is easier to understand why our works of art have a drawn, set look and why they collapse so suddenly. It is obvious why we have more journalists than creative writers, more boy scouts of painting than Cézannes, and why sentimental tales or detective novels have taken the place of *War and Peace* or *The Charterhouse of Parma*. Of course, one can always meet that state of things with a humanistic lamentation and become what Stepan Trofimovich in *The Possessed* insists upon being: a living reproach. One can also have, like him, attacks of patriotic melancholy. But such melancholy in no way changes reality. It is better, in my opinion, to give the era its due,

From Albert Camus, "Create Dangerously" in *Resistance, Rebellion and Death* trans. Justin O'Brien. Copyright © 1960 by Alfred A. Knopf, Inc. Reprinted by permission of the publisher.

since it demands this so vigorously, and calmly admit that the period of the revered master, of the artist with a camellia in his buttonhole, of the armchair genius is over. To create today is to create dangerously. Any publication is an act, and that act exposes one to the passions of an age that forgives nothing. Hence the question is not to find out if this is or is not prejudicial to art. The question, for all those who cannot live without art and what it signifies, is merely to find out how, among the police forces of so many ideologies (how many churches, what solitude), the strange liberty of creation is possible.

It is not enough to say in this regard that art is threatened by the powers of the State. If that were true, the problem would be simple: the artist fights or capitulates. The problem is more complex, more serious too, as soon as it becomes apparent that the battle is waged within the artist himself. The hatred for art, of which our society provides such fine examples, is so effective today only because it is kept alive by artists themselves. The doubt felt by the artists who preceded us concerned their own talent. The doubt felt by artists of today concerns the necessity of their art, hence their very existence. Racine in 1957 would make excuses for writing *Bérénice* when he might have been fighting to defend the Edict of Nantes.

That questioning of art by the artist has many reasons, and only the loftiest need be considered. Among the best explanations is the feeling the contemporary artist has of lying or of indulging in useless words if he pays no attention to history's woes. What characterizes our time, indeed, is the way the masses and their wretched condition have burst upon contemporary sensibilities. We now know that they exist, whereas we once had a tendency to forget them. And if we are more aware, it is not because our aristocracy, artistic or otherwise, has become better—no, have no fear—it is because the masses have become stronger and keep people from forgetting them.

There are still other reasons, and some of them less noble, for this surrender of the artist. But, whatever those reasons may be, they all work toward the same end: to discourage free creation by undermining its basic principle, the creator's faith in himself. "A man's obedience to his own genius," Emerson said magnificently, "is faith in its purest form." And another American writer of the nineteenth century added: "So long as a man is faithful to himself, everything is in his favor, government, society, the very sun, moon, and stars." Such amazing optimism seems dead today. In most cases the artist is ashamed of himself and his privileges, if he has any. He must first of all answer the question he has put to himself: is art a deceptive luxury?

I

The first straightforward reply that can be made is this: on occasion art may be a deceptive luxury. On the poop deck of slave galleys it is possible, at any time and place, as we know, to sing of the constellations while the convicts bend over the oars and exhaust themselves in the hold; it is always possible to record the social conversation that takes place on the benches of the amphitheater while the lion is crunching the victim. And it is very hard to make any objections to the art that has known such success in the past. But things have changed somewhat, and the number of convicts and martyrs has increased amazingly over the surface of the globe. In the face of so much suffering, if art insists on being a luxury, it will also be a lie.

Of what could art speak, indeed? If it adapts itself to what the majority of our society wants, art will be a meaningless recreation. If it blindly rejects that society, if the artist makes up his mind to take refuge in his dream, art will express nothing but a negation. In this way we shall have the production of entertainers or of formal grammarians, and in both cases this leads to an art cut off from living reality. For about a century we have been living in a society that is not even the society of money (gold can arouse carnal passions) but that of the abstract symbols of money. The society of merchants can be defined as a society in which things disappear in favor of signs. When a ruling class measures its fortunes, not by the acre of land or the ingot of gold, but by the number of figures corresponding ideally to a certain number of exchange operations, it thereby condemns itself to setting a certain kind of humbug at the center of its experience and its universe. A society founded on signs is, in its essence, an artificial society in which man's carnal truth is handled as something artificial. There is no reason for being surprised that such a society chose as its religion a moral code of formal principles and that it inscribes the words "liberty" and "equality" on its prisons as well as on its temples of finance. However, words cannot be prostituted with impunity. The most misrepresented value today is certainly the value of liberty. Good minds (I have always thought there were two kinds of intelligence—intelligent intelligence and stupid intelligence) teach that it is but an obstacle on the path of true progress. But such solemn stupidities were uttered because for a hundred years a society of merchants made an exclusive and unilateral use of liberty, looking upon it as a right rather than as a duty, and did not fear to use an ideal liberty, as often as it could, to justify a very real oppression. As a result, is there anything surprising in the fact that such a society asked art to be, not an instrument of liberation, but an inconsequential exercise and a mere entertainment? Consequently, a fashionable society in which all troubles were money troubles and all worries were sentimental worries was satisfied for decades with its society novelists and with the most futile art in the world, the one about which Oscar Wilde, thinking of himself before he knew prison, said that the greatest of all vices was superficiality.

In this way the manufacturers of art (I did not say the artists) of middle-class Europe, before and after 1900, accepted irresponsibility because responsibility presupposed a painful break with their society (those who really broke with it are named Rimbaud, Nietzsche, Strindberg, and we know the price they paid). From that period we get the theory of art for art's sake, which is merely a voicing of that irresponsibility. Art for art's sake, the entertainment of a solitary artist, is indeed the artificial art of a factitious and self-absorbed society. The logical result of such a theory is the art of little cliiques or the purely formal art fed on affectations and abstractions and ending in the destruction of all reality. In this way a few works charm a few individuals while many coarse inventions corrupt many others. Finally art takes shape outside society and cuts itself off from its living roots. Gradually the artist, even if he is celebrated, is alone or at least is known to his nation only through the intermediary of the popular press or the radio, which will provide a convenient and simplified idea of him. The more art specializes, in fact, the more necessary popularization becomes. In this way millions of people will have the feeling of knowing this or that great artist of our time because they have learned from the newspapers that he raises canaries or that he never stays married more than six months. The greatest renown today consists in being admired or hated without having been read. Any artist who goes in for being famous in our society must know that it is not he who will become famous, but someone else under his name, someone who will eventually escape him and perhaps someday will kill the true artist in him.

Consequently, there is nothing surprising in the fact that almost everything worthwhile created in the mercantile Europe of the nineteenth and twentieth centuries—in literature, for instance—was raised up against the society of its time. It may be said that until almost the time of the French Revolution current literature was, in the main, a literature of consent. From the moment when middle-class society, a result of the revolution, became stabilized, a literature of revolt developed instead. Official values were negated, in France, for example, either by the bearers of revolutionary values, from the Romantics to Rimbaud, or by the maintainers of aristocratic values, of whom Vigny and Balzac are good examples. In both cases the masses and the aristocracy—the two sources of all civilization —took their stand against the artificial society of their time.

But this negation, maintained so long that it is now rigid, has become artificial too and leads to another sort of sterility. The theme of the exceptional poet born into a mercantile society (Vigny's *Chatterton* is the finest example) has hardened into a presumption that one can be a great artist only against the society of one's time, whatever it may be. Legitimate in the beginning when asserting that a true artist could not compromise with the world of money, the principle became false with the subsidiary belief that an artist could assert himself only by being against everything in general. Consequently, many of our artists long to be exceptional, feel guilty if they are not, and wish for simultaneous applause and hisses. Naturally, society, tired or indifferent at present, applauds and hisses only at random. Consequently, the intellectual of today is always bracing himself stiffly to add to his height. But as a result of rejecting everything, even the tradition of his art, the contemporary artist gets the illusion that he is creating his own rule and eventually takes himself for God. At the same time he thinks he can create his reality himself. But, cut off from his society, he will create nothing but formal or abstract works, thrilling as experiences but devoid of the fecundity we associate with true art, which is called upon to unite. In short, there will be as much difference between the contemporary subtleties or abstractions and the work of a Tolstoy or a Molière as between an anticipatory draft on invisible wheat and the rich soil of the furrow itself.

II

In this way art may be a deceptive luxury. It is not surprising, then, that men or artists wanted to call a halt and go back to truth. As soon as they did, they denied that the artist had a right to solitude and offered him as a subject, not his dreams, but reality as it is lived and endured by all. Convinced that art for art's sake, through its subjects and through its style, is not understandable to the masses or else in no way expresses their truth, these men wanted the artist instead to speak intentionally about and for the majority. He had only to translate the sufferings and happiness of all into the language of all and he will be universally understood. As a reward for being absolutely faithful to reality, he will achieve complete communication among men.

This ideal of universal communication is indeed the ideal of any great artist. Contrary to the current presumption, if there is any man who has no right to solitude, it is the artist. Art cannot be a monologue. When the most solitary and least famous artist appeals to posterity, he is merely reaffirming his fundamental vocation. Considering a dialogue with deaf or inattentive contemporaries to be impossible, he appeals to a more far-reaching dialogue with the generations to come.

But in order to speak about all and to all, one has to speak of what all know and the reality common to us all. The sea, rains, necessity, desire, the struggle against death—these are the things that unite us all. We resemble one another in what we see together, in what we suffer together. Dreams change from individual to individual, but the reality of the world is common to us all. Striving toward realism is therefore legitimate, for it is basically related to the artistic adventure.

So let's be realistic. Or, rather, let's try to be so, if this is possible. For it is not certain that the world has a meaning; it is not certain that realism, even if it is desirable, is possible in art. If we believe the declarations of the nineteenth-century naturalists, it is the exact reproduction of reality. Therefore it is to art what photography is to painting: the former reproduces and the latter selects. But what does it reproduce and what is reality? Even the best of photographs, after all, is not a sufficiently faithful reproduction, is not yet sufficiently realistic. What is there more real, for instance, in our universe than a man's life, and how can we hope to preserve it better than in a realistic film? But under what conditions is such a film possible? Under purely imaginary conditions. We should have to presuppose, in fact, an ideal camera focused on the man day and night and constantly registering his every move. The very projection of such a film would last a lifetime and could be seen only by an audience of people willing to waste their lives in watching someone else's life in great detail. Even under such conditions, such an unimaginable film would not be realistic for the simple reason that the reality of a man's life is not limited to the spot in which he happens to be. It lies also in other lives that give shape to his—lives of people he loves, to begin with, which would have to be filmed too, and also lives of unknown people, influential and insignificant, fellow citizens, policemen, professors, invisible comrades from the mines and foundries, diplomats and dictators, religious reformers, artists who create myths that are decisive of our conduct—humble representatives, in short, of the sovereign chance that dominates the most routine existences. Consequently, there is but one possible realistic film: the one that is constantly shown us by an invisible camera on the world's screen. The only realistic artist, then, is God, if he exists. All other artists are, *ipso facto*, unfaithful to reality.

As a result, the artists who reject bourgeois society and its formal art, who insist on speaking of reality, and reality alone, are caught in a painful dilemma. They must be realistic and yet cannot be. They want to make their art subservient to reality, and reality cannot be described without effecting a choice that makes it subservient to the originality of an art. The beautiful and tragic production of the early years of the Russian Revolution clearly illustrates this torment. What Russia gave us then with Blok and the great Pasternak, Maiakovski and Essenine, Eisenstein and the first novelists of cement and steel, was a splendid laboratory of forms and themes, a fecund unrest, a wild enthusiasm for research. Yet it was necessary to conclude and to tell how it was possible to be realistic even though complete realism was impossible. Dictatorship, in this case as in others, went straight to the point: in its opinion realism was first necessary and then possible so long as it was deliberately socialistic. What is the meaning of this decree?

As a matter of fact, such a decree frankly admits that reality cannot be reproduced without exercising a selection, and it rejects the theory of realism as it was formulated in the nineteenth century. The only thing needed, then, is to find a principle of choice that will give shape to the world. And such a principle is found, not in the reality we know, but in the reality that will be—in short, the future. In order to reproduce properly what is, one must depict also what will be. In other words, the true object of socialistic realism is precisely what has not reality yet.

The contradiction is rather beautiful. But, after all, the very expression of socialistic realism was contradictory. How, indeed, is a socialistic realism possible when reality is not altogether socialistic? It is not socialistic, for example, either in the past or altogether in the present. The answer is easy: we shall choose in the reality of today or of yesterday what announces and serves the perfect city of the future. So we shall devote ourselves, on the one hand, to negating and condemning whatever aspects of reality are not socialistic and, on the other hand, to glorifying what is or will become so. We shall inevitably get a propaganda art with its heroes and its villains—an edifying literature, in other words, just as remote as formalistic art is from complex and living reality. Finally, that art will be socialistic insofar as it is not realistic.

This aesthetic that intended to be realistic therefore becomes a new idealism, just as sterile for the true artist as bourgeois idealism. Reality is ostensibly granted a sovereign position only to be more readily thrown out. Art is reduced to nothing. It serves and, by serving, becomes a slave. Only those who keep from describing reality will be praised as realists. The others will be censured, with the approval of the former. Renown, which in bourgeois society consisted in not being read or in being misunderstood, will in a totalitarian society consist in keeping others from being read. Once more, true art will be distorted or gagged and universal communication will be made impossible by the very people who most passionately wanted it.

The easiest thing, when faced with such a defeat, would be to admit that so-called socialist realism has little connection with great art and that the revolutionaries, in the very interest of the revolution, ought to look for another aesthetic. But it is well known that the defenders of the theory described shout that no art is possible outside it. They spend their time shouting this. But my deep-rooted conviction is that they do not believe it and that they have decided, in their hearts, that artistic values must be subordinated to the values of revolutionary action. If this were clearly stated, the discussion would be easier. One can respect such great renunciation on the part of men who suffer too much from the contrast between the unhappiness of all and the privileges sometimes associated with an artist's lot, who reject the unbearable distance separating those whom poverty gags and those whose vocation is rather to express themselves constantly. One might then understand such men, try to carry on a dialogue with them, attempt to tell them, for instance, that suppressing creative liberty is perhaps not the right way to overcome slavery and that until they can speak for all it is stupid to give up the ability to speak for a few at least. Yes, socialist realism ought to own up to the fact that it is the twin brother of political realism. It sacrifices art for an end that is alien to art but that, in the scale of values, may seem to rank higher. In short, it suppresses art temporarily in order to establish justice first. When justice exists, in a still indeterminate future, art will resuscitate. In this way the golden rule of contemporary intelligence is applied to matters of art—the rule that insists on the impossibility of making an omelet without breaking eggs. But such overwhelming common sense must not mislead us. To make a good omelet it is not enough to break thousands of eggs, and the value of a cook is not judged, I believe, by the number of broken eggshells. If the artistic cooks of our time upset more baskets of eggs than they intended, the omelet of civilization may never again come out right, and art may never resuscitate. Barbarism is never temporary. Sufficient allowance is never made for it, and, quite naturally, from art barbarism extends to morals. Then the suffering and blood of men give birth to insignificant literatures, an ever-indulgent press, photographed portraits, and sodality plays in which hatred takes the place of religion. Art culminates thus in forced optimism, the worst of luxuries, it so happens, and the most ridiculous of lies.

How could we be surprised? The suffering of mankind is such a vast subject that it seems no one could touch it unless he was like Keats so sensitive, it is said, that he could have touched pain itself with his hands. This is clearly seen when a controlled literature tries to alleviate that suffering with official consolations. The lie of art for art's sake pretended to know nothing of evil and consequently assumed responsibility for it. But the realistic lie, even though managing to admit mankind's present unhappiness, betrays that unhappiness just as seriously by making use of it to glorify a future state of happiness, about which no one knows anything, so that the future authorizes every kind of humbug.

The two aesthetics that have long stood opposed to each other, the one that recommends a complete rejection of real life and the one that claims to reject anything that is not real life, end up, however, by coming to agreement, far from reality, in a single lie and in the suppression of art. The academicism of the Right does not even acknowledge a misery that the academicism of the Left utilizes for ulterior reasons. But in both cases the misery is only strengthened at the same time that art is negated.

III

Must we conclude that this lie is the very essence of art? I shall say instead that the attitudes I have been describing are lies only insofar as they have but little relation to art. What, then, is art? Nothing simple, that is certain. And it is even harder to find out amid the shouts of so many people bent on simplifying everything. On the one hand, genius is expected to be splendid and solitary; on the other hand, it is called upon to resemble all. Alas, reality is more complex. And Balzac suggested this in a sentence: "The genius resembles everyone and no one resembles him." So it is with art, which is nothing without reality and without which reality is insignificant. How, indeed, could art get along without the real and how could art be subservient to it? The artist chooses his object as much as he is chosen by it. Art, in a sense, is a revolt against everything fleeting and unfinished in the world. Consequently, its only aim is to give another form to a reality that it is nevertheless forced to preserve as the source of its emotion. In this regard, we are all realistic and no one is. Art is neither complete rejection nor complete acceptance of what is. It is simultaneously rejection and acceptance, and this is why it must be a perpetually renewed wrenching apart. The artist constantly lives in such a state of ambiguity, incapable of negating the real and yet eternally bound to question it in its eternally unfinished aspects. In order to paint a still life, there must be confrontation and mutual adjustment between a painter and an apple. And if forms are nothing without the world's lighting, they in turn add to that lighting. The real universe which, by its radiance, calls forth bodies and statues receives from them at the same time a second light that determines the light from the sky. Consequently, great style lies midway between the artist and his object.

There is no need of determining whether art must flee reality or defer to it, but rather what precise dose of reality the work must take on as ballast to keep from floating up among the clouds or from dragging along the ground with weighted boots. Each artist solves this problem according to his lights and abilities. The greater an artist's revolt against the world's reality, the greater can be the weight of reality to balance that revolt. But the weight can never stifle the artist's solitary exigency. The loftiest work will always be, as in the Greek tragedians, Melville, Tolstoy, or Molière, the work that maintains an equilibrium between reality and man's rejection of that reality, each forcing the other upward in a ceaseless overflowing, characteristic of life itself at its most joyous and heart-rending extremes. Then, every once in a while, a new world appears, different from the everyday world and yet the same, particular but universal, full of innocent insecurity —called forth for a few hours by the power and longing of genius. That's just it and yet that's not it; the world is nothing and the world is everything—this is the contradictory and tireless cry of every true artist, the cry that keeps him on his feet with eyes ever open and that, every once in a while, awakens for all in this world asleep the fleeting and insistent image of a reality we recognize without ever having known it.

Likewise, the artist can neither turn away from his time nor lose himself in it. If he turns away from it, he speaks in a void. But, conversely, insofar as he takes his time as his object, he asserts his own existence as subject and cannot give in to it altogether. In other words, at the very moment when the artist chooses to share the fate of all, he asserts the individual he is. And he cannot escape from this ambiguity. The artist takes from history what he can see of it himself or undergo himself, directly or indirectly—the immediate event, in other words, and men who are alive today, not the relationship of that immediate event to a future that is invisible to the living artist. Judging contemporary man in the name of a man who does not yet exist is the function of prophecy. But the artist can value the myths that are offered him only in relation to their repercussion on living people. The prophet, whether religious or political, can judge absolutely and, as is known, is not chary of doing so. But the artist cannot. If he judged absolutely, he would arbitrarily divide reality into good and evil and thus indulge in melodrama. The aim of art, on the contrary, is not to legislate or to reign supreme, but rather to understand first of all. Sometimes it does reign supreme, as a result of understanding. But no work of genius has ever been based on hatred and contempt. This is why the artist, at the end of his slow advance, absolves instead of condemning. Instead of being a judge, he is a justifier. He is the perpetual advocate of the living creature, because it is alive. He truly argues for love of one's neighbor and not for that love of the remote stranger which debases contemporary humanism until it becomes the catechism of the law court. Instead, the great work eventually confounds all judges. With it the artist simultaneously pays homage to the loftiest figure of mankind and bows down before the worst of criminals. "There is not," Wilde wrote in prison, "a single wretched man in this wretched place along with me who does not stand in symbolic relation to the very secret of life." Yes, and that secret of life coincides with the secret of art.

For a hundred and fifty years the writers belonging to a mercantile society, with but few exceptions, thought they could live in happy irresponsibility. They lived, indeed, and then died alone, as they had lived. But we writers of the twentieth century shall never again be alone. Rather, we must know that we can never escape the common misery and that our only justification, if indeed there is a justification, is to speak up, insofar as we can, for those who cannot do so. But we must do so for all those who are suffering at this moment, whatever may be the glories, past or future, of the States and parties oppressing them: for the artist there are no privileged torturers. This is why beauty, even today, especially today, cannot serve any party; it cannot serve, in the long or short run, anything but men's suffering or their liberty. The only really committed artist is he who, without refusing to take part in the combat, at least refuses to join the regular armies and remains a freelance. The lesson he then finds in beauty, if he draws it fairly, is a lesson not of selfishness but rather of hard brotherhood. Looked upon thus, beauty has never enslaved anyone. And for thousands of years, every day, at every second, it has instead assuaged the servitude of millions of men and, occasionally, liberated some of them once and for all. After all, perhaps the greatness of art lies in the perpetual tension between beauty and pain, the love of man and the madness of creation, unbearable solitude and the exhausting crowd, rejection and consent. Art advances between two chasms, which are frivolity and propaganda. On the ridge where the great artist moves forward, every step is an adventure, an extreme risk. In that risk, however, and only there, lies the freedom of art. A difficult freedom that is more like an ascetic discipline? What artist would deny this? What artist would dare to claim that he was equal to such a ceaseless task? Such freedom presupposes health of body and mind, a style that reflects strength of soul, and a patient defiance. Like all freedom, it is a perpetual risk, an exhausting adventure, and this is why people avoid the risk today, as they avoid liberty with its exacting demands, in order to accept any kind of bondage and achieve at least comfort of soul. But if art is not an adventure, what is it and where is its justification? No, the free artist is no more a man of comfort than is the free man. The free artist is the one who, with great effort, creates his own order. The more undisciplined what he must put in order, the stricter will be his rule and the more he will assert his freedom. There is a remark of Gide that I have always approved although it may be easily misunderstood: "Art lives on constraint and dies of freedom." That is true. But it must not be interpreted as meaning that art can be controlled. Art lives only on constraints it imposes on itself; it dies of all others. Conversely, if it does not constrain itself, it indulges in ravings and becomes a slave to mere shadows. The freest art and the most rebellious will therefore be the most classical; it will reward the greatest effort. So long as a society and its artists do not accept this long and free effort, so long as they relax in the comfort of amusements or the comfort of conformism, in the games of art for art's sake or the preachings of realistic art, its artists are lost in nihilism and sterility. Saying this amounts to saying that today the rebirth depends on our courage and our will to be lucid.

Yes, the rebirth is in the hands of all of us. It is up to us if the West is to bring forth any anti-Alexanders to tie together the Gordian Knot of civilization cut by the sword. For this purpose, we must assume all the risks and labors of freedom. There is no need of knowing whether, by pursuing justice, we shall manage to preserve liberty. It is essential to know that, without liberty, we shall achieve nothing and that we shall lose both future justice and ancient beauty. Liberty alone draws men from their isolation; but slavery dominates a crowd of solitudes. And art, by virtue of that free essence I have tried to define, unites whereas tyranny separates. It is not surprising, there-fore, that art should be the enemy marked out by every form of oppression. It is not surprising that artists and intellectuals should have been the first victims of modern tyrannies, whether of the Right or of the Left. Tyrants know there is in the work of art an emancipatory force, which is mysterious only to those who do not revere it. Every great work makes the human face more admirable and richer, and this is its whole secret. And thousands of concentration camps and barred cells are not enough to hide this staggering testimony of dignity. This is why it is not true that culture can be, even temporarily, suspended in order to make way for a new culture. Man's unbroken testimony as to his suffering and his nobility cannot be suspended; the act of breathing cannot be suspended. There is no culture without legacy, and we cannot and must not reject anything of ours, the legacy of the West. Whatever the works of the future may be, they will bear the same secret, made up of courage and freedom, nourished by the daring of thousands of artists of all times and all nations. Yes, when modern tyranny shows us that, even when confined to his calling, the artist is a public enemy, it is right. But in this way tyranny pays its respects, through the artist, to an image of man that nothing has ever been able to crush.

My conclusion will be simple. It will consist of saying, in the very midst of the sound and the fury of our history: "Let us rejoice." Let us rejoice, indeed, at having witnessed the death of a lying and comfort-loving Europe and at being faced with cruel truths. Let us rejoice as men because a prolonged hoax has collapsed and we see clearly what threatens us. And let us rejoice as artists, torn from our sleep and our deafness, forced to keep our eyes on destitution, prisons, and bloodshed. If, faced with such a vision, we can preserve the memory of days and of faces, and if, conversely, faced with the world's beauty, we manage not to forget the humiliated, then Western art will gradually recover its strength and its sovereignty. To be sure, there are few examples in history of artists confronted with such hard problems. But when even the simplest words and phrases cost their weight in freedom and blood, the artist must learn to handle them with restraint. Danger makes men classical, and all greatness, after all, is rooted in risk.

The time of irresponsible artists is over. We shall regret it for our little moments of bliss. But we shall be able to admit that this ordeal contributes meanwhile to our chances of authenticity, and we shall accept the challenge. The freedom of art is not worth much when its only purpose is to assure the artist's comfort. For a value or a virtue to take root in a society, there must be no lying about it; in other words, we must pay for it every time we can. If liberty has become dangerous, then it may cease to be prostituted. And I cannot agree, for example, with those who complain today of the decline of wisdom. Apparently they are right. Yet, to tell the truth, wisdom has never declined so much as when it involved no risks and belonged exclusively to a few humanists buried in libraries. But today, when at last it has to face real dangers, there is a chance that it may again stand up and be respected.

It is said that Nietzsche after the break with Lou Salomé, in a period of complete solitude, crushed and uplifted at the same time by the perspective of the huge work he had to carry on without any help, used to walk at night on the mountains overlooking the gulf of Genoa and light great bonfires of leaves and branches which he would watch as they burned. I have often dreamed of those fires and have occasionally imagined certain men and certain works in front of those fires, as a way of testing men and works. Well, our era is one of those fires whose unbearable heat will doubtless reduce many a work to ashes! But as for those which remain, their metal will be intact, and, looking at them, we shall be able to indulge without restraint in the supreme joy of the intelligence which we call "admiration."

One may long, as I do, for a gentler flame, a respite, a pause for musing. But perhaps there is no other peace for the artist than what he finds in the heat of combat. "Every wall is a door," Emerson correctly said. Let us not look for the door, and the way out, anywhere but in the wall against which we are living. Instead, let us seek the respite where it is—in the very thick of the battle. For in my opinion, and this is where I shall close, it *is* there. Great ideas, it has been said, come into the world as gently as doves. Perhaps then, if we listen attentively, we shall hear, amid the uproar of empires and nations, a faint flutter of wings, the gentle stirring of life and hope. Some will say that this hope lies in a nation; others, in a man. I believe rather that it is awakened, revived, nourished by millions of solitary individuals whose deeds and works every day negate frontiers and the crudest implications of history. As a result, there shines forth fleetingly the ever-threatened truth that each and every man, on the foundation of his own sufferings and joys, builds for all.

Afterword / Art and the Re-creation of Man

The writers included in Part Seven agree on one point: to understand ourselves and reach our highest fulfillment as human beings we must give serious attention to art. Man is an art-producing animal. Through his art he sometimes imitates nature, and through the influence of art he sometimes sees nature as imitating art. Further, as Mrs. Langer emphasizes, he also values art because only through it can he create forms expressive of feeling. Art is essential to the fulfillment of human life because it enables us to fully comprehend our feelings.

Wilde's discussion, aside from its delightful irony and breezy paradoxes, points to something about the nature of art that previous aestheticians neglected or ignored. Following Aristotle rather than Plato, Wilde emphasizes the genuinely creative aspect of artistic production. The artist can bring to satisfying completion what nature can only start. He proceeds the way nature would if nature had artistic consciousness. Artistic production is not a mere copying; it is a unique creative process whereby matter is formed and transformed. In the process, life itself is given higher significance.

As Mrs. Langer conceives of it, art is "form expressive of feeling." Life appears to be imitating art, as Wilde noted, because our modes of perception have been remolded, reeducated by the instrument of art. We have learned to see the world through the eyes of the artist, whether he be impressionist or surrealist. Thus we are able to feel what he feels, notice what he notices, appreciate what he appreciates. Art can cleanse and polish the windows of perception.

William Morris and Albert Camus put a greater emphasis upon the social significance of art and upon the revolutionary role of the artist. Morris commits himself to a Marxian program of revolutionary reconstruction that would liberate artists and allow art to play an important role in the creation of a classless society. But Morris would probably strenuously object to the restrictions imposed on art in the name of a socialist revolution in Russia and China in our century. Art, to him, was above all an essentially free and spontaneous activity.

Both socialist realism and abstract formalism were rejected as extremes by Albert Camus, because he, too, stressed the importance of free, unhampered, and even dangerous creation. In order to create, the artist must at times be willing to negate, to destroy. But this destruction is not, according to Camus, to be undertaken lightly or simply in order to create a sensation, as when a frenetic rock musician smashes a guitar or a dada artist blows up a machine he has built only to destroy. While the artist can attain through his work, at least temporarily, a sense of wholeness and of liberation as well as a feeling of meaningful involvement in his times, he can never escape the awareness of the absurdity and, ultimately, the futility of his efforts. Like Sisyphus, his efforts will finally, for himself at least, come to nothing. But in the meantime, there are situations to be confronted and commitments to be decided upon. Man is called to action, to create himself through his art.

Related Reading

(Works marked * are available in paperbound editions.)

Art and Confrontation: The Arts in an Age of Change. Greenwich, Conn.: New York Graphic Society, 1968.

Baxandall, Lee, ed. *Radical Perspectives in the Arts.* Baltimore: Penguin, 1972.

*Breé, Germaine. *Camus,* rev. ed. New York: Harcourt, Brace and World, 1964.

*Camus, Albert. *The Rebel: An Essay on Man in Revolt,* trans. by Justin O'Brien. New York: Vintage Books, 1956.

*Dewey, John. *Art as Experience.* New York: Putnam's, 1934.

*Fallico, A. G. *Art and Existentialism.* Englewood Cliffs, N. J.: Prentice-Hall, 1962.

*Friedman, Maurice. *To Deny our Nothingness: Contemporary Images of Man.* New York: Delta, 1967.

Fry, Edward F., ed. *On the Future of Art.* New York: Viking Press, 1970.

*Gotshalk, D. W. *Art and the Social Order,* 2d ed. New York: Dover, 1962.

Henderson, Philip. *William Morris: His Life, Work and Friends.* New York: McGraw-Hill, 1968.

Hunter, Howard, ed. *Humanities, Religion and the Arts Tomorrow.* New York: Holt, Rinehart & Winston, 1972.

Jarrett, James L. *The Quest for Beauty.* Englewood Cliffs, N. J.; Prentice-Hall, 1957.

*Langer, Susanne K. *Feeling and Form: A Theory of Art.* New York: Charles Scribner's Sons, 1953.

*———. *Problems of Art.* New York: Charles Scribner's Sons, 1957.

Lodge, Rupert C. *Plato's Theory of Art.* London: Routledge and Regan Paul, 1953.

Mead, Hunter. *An Introduction to Aesthetics.* New York: Ronald, 1952.

Nettleship, Richard L. *Lectures on the Republic of Plato.* London: Macmillan and Co., 1937.

Rader, Melvin. *A Modern Book of Esthetics,* 3d ed. New York: Holt, Rinehart, 1953.

*Rand, Ayn. *The Romantic Manifesto.* New York: Signet, 1971.

*Read, Herbert. *The Forms of Things Unknown: Essays Towards an Aesthetic Philosophy.* New York: Meridian Books, 1960.

————. *Art and Alienation.* New York: Horizon Press, 1967.

*Richter, Peyton E., ed. *Perspectives in Aesthetics: Plato to Camus.* New York: Odyssey Press, 1967.

Rosenberg, Harold. *The De-definition of Art.* New York: Horizon, 1972.

Sartre, Jean Paul. *Situations,* trans. Benita Eisler. New York: Fawcett, 1966.

Sparshott, F. H. *The Structure of Aesthetics.* Toronto: University of Toronto Press, 1963.

Stolnitz, Jerome. *Aesthetics and Philosophy of Art Criticism.* Boston: Houghton Mifflin, 1960.

Thompson, Paul. *The Work of William Morris.* New York: Viking Press, 1968.

Warry, J. G. *Greek Aesthetic Theory.* New York: Barnes and Noble, 1962.

*Wilde, Oscar. *The Artist as Critic: Critical Writings of Oscar Wilde,* ed. Richard Ellman. New York: Vintage Books, 1968.

PART EIGHT

Confrontation with the Future:
Commitment to the Present

Today as never before we need a multiplicity of visions,
dreams, and prophecies — images of potential tomorrows.
Alvin Toffler

The future cannot be predicted, but
futures can be invented.
Dennis Gabor

If you have built castles in the air, your work need not be
lost; that is where they should be. Now put foundations
under them.
Henry D. Thoreau

To predict the future we need logic; but we also need faith
and imagination which can sometimes defy logic itself.
Arthur C. Clarke

I hold that man is in the right who is
most closely in league with the future.
Henrik Ibsen

Every intelligent and active-minded person
is to some degree a utopian.
Arthur E. Morgan

Change in the climate of the imagination is the
precursor of the changes that affect more than the details
of life.
John Dewey

All living things act to anticipate the future; this is what
distinguishes them from lifeless things.
Jacob Bronowski

It has usually been lack of imagination, rather than excess
of it, that caused unfortunate decisions and missed
opportunities.
Herman Kahn and Anthony Wiener

Introduction / Present Strain; Future Shock?

There are as many criteria for choosing readings for a philosophy anthology as there are philosophical viewpoints. Viewing philosophy as an instrument of an ideology, Marxist editors would include material on the class struggle, alienation under capitalism, revolution, and the vision of the Marxist reorganization of society. Commited to a conception of philosophy as concerned reflection, existentialists would choose readings that illustrate the ambiguity and anguish of human existence and focus upon the importance and necessity of human choice. Followers of St. Thomas Aquinas would see philosophy as a handmaiden to Christian theology and would include readings that speak to the issues of theology, the relation of reason to faith, the natural to the supernatural world. Logical positivists, viewing philosophy as an adjunct to the sciences, would concentrate on the linguistic and methodological problems that arise from scientific thought. They would perhaps give little attention to religious beliefs except to discuss them within the context of the methods used in the verification of scientific beliefs.

We have chosen "confrontation and commitment" as our underlying theme in order to present philosophy as an activity in which the individual encounters problematic situations that demand resolution. These problems challenge our analytic capabilities and require our total involvement. Philosophy has grown out of man's attempt to understand a mysterious universe and to give some meaning to his existence in it. It has thus addressed itself to the human condition and has guided individuals in their search for more reliable beliefs, for freedom, for the better life, for a deeper understanding of themselves, and for something of ultimate concern and of aesthetic worth. Philosophers have tried to make intelligent, defensible commitments using the approach that John Stuart Mill identified as the spirit of philosophy:

> To question all things;—never to turn away from any difficulty; to accept no doctrine either from ourselves or from other people without a rigid scrutiny by negative criticism; letting no fallacy, or incoherence, or confusion of thought, step by unperceived; above all, to insist upon hav-

ing the meaning of a word clearly understood before using it, and the meaning of a proposition before assenting to it....[1]

While confronting human problems, philosophical thinking has attempted to replace obscurity with clarity, fragmentation with coherence, partial understanding with one which is more complete. Although Mill described the critical spirit of philosophy, Alfred North Whitehead gave us a beautiful statement of the wider effects it may have on human life:

> Philosophy begins in wonder. And, at the end, when philosophic thought has done its best, the wonder remains. There have been added, however, some grasp of the immensity of things, some purification of emotion by understanding.[2]

The Paradigms: Profiles in Courage

The twentieth century presents us with unique social conditions associated with rapid social change, which require new analyses and commitments. Many people think that we must look to the present and future rather than to the past in order to discover the wisdom we so desperately need. Socrates offers no advice on how to deal with an impersonalized and computerized bureaucratic government. Descartes does not help us to understand cybernetics. Marx is silent on eugenics. Epicurus was unaware of psychoanalysis. Thoreau never dreamed of an ecological crisis of today's gigantic proportions. The solutions to twentieth-century problems are more likely to be found in contemporary "think tanks," it is argued, than in the so-called "wisdom of the ages."

Yet the editors believe that comparisons between past and present problems of mankind are useful and that the gifts of insight and foresight of our paradigmatic thinkers are relevant to the modern age. Philosophy, like history, has its profiles in courage: Socrates and Hume, courage to doubt; James and Tillich, courage to believe; Thoreau and Tolstoy, courage to act; and Camus and Sartre, courage to create. These profiles have not lost their relevance. As in the time of the Buddha, human suffering, psychological conflict, and the raw fact of death are very much in evidence. Although Mill and Marx condemned and sought to overcome them, social injustice, class hatred, and human exploitation have continued. In twentieth-century China, Mao Tse-tung found himself confronting many social changes and administrative problems that would have seemed familiar to Confucius.

Uniqueness of the Present

Although social change is not new, the accelerative rate of change today presents us with conditions that strain many of the analogies between present and past societies. It is not surprising that such a thinker as B. F. Skinner discouraged the study of history in his utopia, or that followers of Marshall McLuhan denigrate historical perspective as only a kind of rear-mirror vision. Few would deny that we face grave and unprecedented challenges today and possibly inescapable calamities tomorrow. Our situation is like that of the race driver: the faster the rate of speed, the more momentous each little decision becomes. For our national leaders, today's commitments are of overwhelming significance for the future of man: for world peace or nuclear holocaust, for ecological balance or destruction, for social justice or continued social violence.

Our rapidly changing society and social institutions also affect the individual's inner life. His sanity depends upon his ability to cope with, to some degree of adequacy, a complex, ever-changing world. Alvin Toffler's *Future Shock* points to the social and psychological consequences of rapid change in an advanced technological society—the disruption of government; the breakdown of family, community, and identity; the fragmentation of cultures; and the increased sense of alienation. All of this places an overload of demands upon individuals. We constantly face the obsolescence of our skills and training, our moral and religious values, and even many of the everyday expressions of our language. The proliferation of goods, services, and life styles challenges our abilities to absorb the innovations and threatens our very concept of self. Because of the multiplicity of innovations and alternative values, commitments based upon a thorough assessment do not come easily, but they are still required of us. Facing such dilemmas, many have commited themselves to the radical alternatives of revolt or of retreat: revolt against a society increasingly out of the individual's control, or retreat to an approximation of an imagined past, a time when human conditions were simpler and life's commitments more steady. Marx and Thoreau have their corollaries in the revolutionists and communards of the present day.

Fragmentation and Uncertainty

Our intellectual world seems likewise fragmented. This fragmentation is apparent in the specialized terminology of the separate academic disciplines that C. P. Snow discussed in *The Two Cultures*. It is also apparent in the changing attitudes toward science and the search for absolutely certain knowledge. Modern philosophy got its start in the quest for certainty undertaken by thinkers such as Descartes, who optimistically believed that the new methods so successfully employed in the new sciences offered the key to the resolution of all philosophical problems. Many philosophers today consider the quest for certainty futile and the optimism regarding science premature. Earlier in this century, John Dewey argued persuasively that well-warranted beliefs will do. We do not need the type of certainty modeled after that of mathematics. More recently, philosophers such as Roderick

Chisholm in his *Theory of Knowledge* have made similar points in analyzing such expressions as "knowing" and "evidence." Also, developments in the theoretical sciences have dimmed the hopes of discovering that indubitable principle or theory which would completely and finally explain the structure of the physical world. Flux, fragmentation, and tentativeness rather than stability, order, and certainty seem to be characteristic of our times.

The early optimism regarding science, which was expressed so eloquently by the English philosophers Thomas Hobbes and Francis Bacon, has faded long ago. Although science and its "younger brother" technology have provided the greatest abundance and varieties of goods and services mankind has ever known, wars and social upheavals have continued up to the present. Scientific and technological methods have not yet been successful in solving the most pressing problems of human existence. Like Tolstoy in the throes of his existential crisis, modern man is at the apex of his powers, yet experiences fear and trembling in face of the possible meaninglessness of modern life. Lewis Mumford in his *Technics and Civilization* describes the ways in which technology and machinery have permeated our life and culture. The continuous and extensive use of the machine—the model of precision, calculation, impersonality, and objectivity—has conditioned the ways in which man approaches all his problems, personal as well as technological. These techniques have proven to be tragically inadequate in dealing with man's uniquely human problems and have narrowed and distorted his vision of himself and his environment.

Although philosophy, at least since the time of the Renaissance, has been busily analyzing questions in the area of epistemology, the theory of knowledge, no criteria of truth or meaning have yet received undebatable assent by philosophers. Modern man confronts, not the unity of one perspective, but a plurality of intellectual viewpoints and criteria for reliable belief. The Marxists, existentialists, Thomists, and logical positivists disagree not only on their views of man and the world, but in their language, their methods, and the criteria by which they justify their differing conclusions. We moderns have the freedom to choose the method of reaching the beliefs that are to receive our intellectual allegiance. Our choice carries with it the responsibility of defending the adequacy of that method. To confront the future is to be drawn into this debate regarding reliable beliefs.

28 / Confronting the Future with Equanimity

Whitehead

In *Future Shock* Alvin Toffler stresses the importance of envisaging and examining alternative futures by utopian speculation, futuristic games playing, and other means. An examination of alternatives is valuable to the reflective person for several reasons. It prepares him, at least partially, for what he can expect to happen. Even if the expectation fails, he will be better able to cope than someone who is caught unaware. Examination of alternatives can also call attention to paths of action that might have been overlooked in more hasty commitment to action. Finally, such examination supports the habit of openmindedness and comprehensiveness of investigation without which one cannot be either rational or reasonable. The challenge of future shock, as Toffler graphically depicts it, can only be met if we confront it with "a dramatically new, a more deeply rational response toward change."[3] To do this is to confront its challenge philosophically in the way that Socrates confronted death, as the Buddha met the challenge of suffering, and as Confucius and Marx met the challenge of radical social change.

But whether or not this "more deeply rational response toward change" is ever something really new is open to question. History is "more or less bunk," as Henry Ford once described it, only to those who refuse to recreate it imaginatively in the present and fail to contemplate its implications for the future. We cannot profit from knowledge of the past by viewing it as something dead. As Alfred North Whitehead stressed, "the great achievements of the past were the great adventures of the past."[4] Without a sense of adventure, one can never share in the achievement of the past, the opportunity of the present, or face the challenge of the future. Philosophers are "adventurers in the world of thought." Their courage, as Nietzsche reminded us, lies not in their having convictions, but in their being willing to examine their convictions.

Whitehead exemplified this adventuring in the world of thought when, in the final chapter of his *Science and the Modern World,* he turned to a consideration of "the reaction of science upon some problems confronting civilized societies." Here we can see how one of the greatest philosophers of the twentieth century looked back upon the past to get his bearings in the present, and looked forward, courageously and hopefully, to a future fraught with danger and opportunity.

Requisites for Social Progress

The general conceptions introduced by science into modern thought cannot be separated from the philosophical situation as expressed by Descartes. I mean the assumption of bodies and minds as independent individual substances, each existing in its own right apart from any necessary reference to each other. Such a conception was very concordant with the individualism which had issued from the moral discipline of the Middle Ages. But, though the easy reception of the idea is thus explained, the derivation in itself rests upon a confusion, very natural but none the less unfortunate. The moral discipline had emphasized the intrinsic value of the individual entity. This emphasis had put the notions of the individual and of its experiences into the foreground of thought. At this point the confusion commences. The emergent individual value of each entity is transformed into the independent substantial existence of each entity, which is a very different notion.

I do not mean to say that Descartes made this logical, or rather illogical transition, in the form of explicit reasoning. Far from it. What he did, was first to concentrate upon his own conscious experiences, as being facts within the independent world of his own mentality. He was led to speculate in this way by the current emphasis upon the individual value of his

Reprinted with permission of Macmillan Publishing Co., Inc. from *Science and the Modern World* by Alfred North Whitehead. Copyright 1925 by Macmillan Publishing Co., Inc. renewed 1953 by Evelyn Whitehead.

total self. He implicitly transformed this emergent individual value, inherent in the very fact of his own reality, into a private world of passions, or modes, of independent substance.

Also the independence ascribed to bodily substances carried them away from the realm of values altogether. They degenerated into a mechanism entirely valueless, except as suggestive of an external ingenuity. The heavens had lost the glory of God. This state of mind is illustrated in the recoil of Protestantism from aesthetic effects dependent upon a material medium. It was taken to lead to an ascription of value to what is in itself valueless. This recoil was already in full strength antecedently to Descartes. Accordingly, the Cartesian scientific doctrine of bits of matter, bare of intrinsic value, was merely a formulation, in explicit terms, of a doctrine which was current before its entrance into scientific thought or Cartesian philosophy. Probably this doctrine was latent in the scholastic philosophy, but it did not lead to its consequences till it met with the mentality of northern Europe in the sixteenth century. But science, as equipped by Descartes, gave stability and intellectual status to a point of view which has had very mixed effects upon the moral presuppositions of modern commmunities. Its good effects arose from its efficiency as a method for scientific researches within those limited regions which were then best suited for exploration. The result was a general clearing of the European mind away from the stains left upon it by the hysteria of remote barbaric ages. This was all to the good, and was most completely exemplified in the eighteenth century.

But in the nineteenth century, when society was undergoing transformation into the manufacturing system, the bad effects of these doctrines have been very fatal. The doctrine of minds, as independent substances, leads directly not merely to private worlds of experience, but also to private worlds of morals. The moral intuitions can be held to apply only to the strictly private world of psychological experience. Accordingly, self-respect, and the making the most of your own individual opportunities, together constituted the efficient morality of the leaders among the industrialists of that period. The western world is now suffering from the limited moral outlook of the three previous generations.

Also the assumption of the bare valuelessness of mere matter led to a lack of reverence in the treatment of natural or artistic beauty. Just when the urbanisation of the western world was entering upon its state of rapid development, and when the most delicate, anxious consideration of the aesthetic qualities of the new material environment was requisite, the doctrine of the irrelevance of such ideas was at its height. In the most advanced industrial countries, art was treated as a frivolity. A striking example of this state of mind in the middle of the nineteenth century is to be seen in London where the marvellous beauty of the estuary of the Thames, as it curves through the city, is wantonly defaced by the Charing Cross railway bridge, constructed apart from any reference to aesthetic values.

The two evils are: one, the ignoration of the true relation of each organism to its environment; and the other, the habit of ignoring the intrinsic worth of the environment which must be allowed its weight in any consideration of final ends.

Another great fact confronting the modern world is the discovery of the method of training professionals, who specialise in particular regions of thought and thereby progressively add to the sum of knowledge within their respective limitations of subject. In consequence of the success of this professionalising of knowledge, there are two points to be kept in mind, which differentiate our present age from the past. In the first place, the rate of progress is such that an individual human being, of ordinary length of life, will be called upon to face novel situations which find no parallel in his past. The fixed person for the fixed duties, who in older societies was such a godsend, in the future will be a public danger. In the second place, the modern professionalism in knowledge works in the opposite direction so far as the intellectual sphere is concerned. The modern chemist is likely to be weak in zoölogy, weaker still in his general knowledge of the Elizabethan drama, and completely ignorant of the principles of rhythm in English versification. It is probably safe to ignore his knowledge of ancient history. Of course I am speaking of general tendencies; for chemists are no worse than engineers, or mathematicians, or classical scholars. Effective knowledge is professionalised knowledge, supported by a restricted acquaintance with useful subjects subservient to it.

This situation has its dangers. It produces minds in a groove. Each profession makes progress, but it is progress in its own groove. Now to be mentally in a groove is to live in contemplating a given set of abstractions. The groove prevents straying across country, and the abstraction abstracts from something to which no further attention is paid. But there is no groove of abstractions which is adequate for the comprehension of human life. Thus in the modern world, the celibacy of the medieval learned class has been replaced by a celibacy of the intellect which is divorced from the concrete contemplation of the complete facts. Of course, no one is merely a mathematician, or merely a lawyer. People have lives outside their professions or their businesses. But the point is the restraint of serious thought within a groove. The remainder of life is treated superficially, with the imperfect categories of thought derived from one profession.

The dangers arising from this aspect of professionalism are great, particularly in our democratic societies. The directive force of reason is weakened. The leading intellects lack balance. They see this set of circumstances, or that set; but not both sets together. The task of coördination is left to those who lack either the force or the character to succeed in some definite career. In short, the specialised functions of the community are performed better and more progressively, but the generalised direction lacks vision. The progressiveness in detail only adds to the danger produced by the feebleness of coördination.

This criticism of modern life applies throughout, in whatever sense you construe the meaning of a community. It holds if you apply it to a nation, a city, a district, an institution, a family, or even to an individual. There is a development of particular abstractions, and a contraction of concrete appreciation. The whole is lost in one of its aspects. It is not necessary for my point that I should maintain that our directive wisdom, either as individuals or as communities, is less now than in the past. Perhaps it has slightly improved. But the novel pace of progress requires a greater force of direction if disasters are to be avoided. The point is that the discoveries of the nineteenth century were in the direction of professionalism, so that we are left with no expansion of wisdom and with greater need for it.

Wisdom is the fruit of a balanced development. It is this balanced growth of individuality which it should be the aim of education to secure. The most useful discoveries for the immediate future would concern the furtherance of this aim without detriment to the necessary intellectual professionalism.

My own criticism of our traditional educational methods is that they are far too much occupied with intellectual analysis, and with the acquirement of formularised information. What I mean is, that we neglect to strengthen habits of concrete appreciation of the individual facts in their full interplay of emergent values, and that we merely emphasize abstract formulations which ignore this aspect of the interplay of diverse values.

In every country the problem of the balance of the general and specialist education is under consideration. I cannot speak with firsthand knowledge of any country but my own. I know that there, among practical educationalists, there is considerable dissatisfaction with the existing practice. Also, the adaptation of the whole system to the needs of a democratic community is very far from being solved. I do not think that the secret of the solution lies in terms of the antithesis between thoroughness in special knowledge and general knowledge of a slighter character. The make-weight which balances the thoroughness of the specialist intellectual training should be of a radically different kind from purely intellectual analytical knowledge. At present our education combines a thorough study of a few abstractions, with a slighter study of a larger number of abstractions. We are too exclusively bookish in our scholastic routine. The general training should aim at eliciting our concrete apprehensions, and should satisfy the itch of youth to be doing something. There should be some analysis even here, but only just enough to illustrate the ways of thinking in diverse spheres. In the Garden of Eden Adam saw the animals before he named them: in the traditional system, children named the animals before they saw them.

There is no easy single solution of the practical difficulties of education. We can, however, guide ourselves by a certain simplicity in its general theory. The student should concentrate within a limited field. Such concentration should include all practical and intellectual acquirements requisite for that concentration. This is the ordinary procedure; and, in respect to it, I should be inclined even to increase the facilities for concentration rather than to diminish them. With the concentration there are associated certain subsidiary studies, such as languages for science. Such a scheme of professional training should be directed to a clear end congenial to the student. It is not necessary to elaborate the qualifications of these statements. Such a training must, of course, have the width requisite for its end. But its design should not be complicated by the consideration of other ends. This professional training can only touch one side of education. Its centre of gravity lies in the intellect, and its chief tool is the printed book. The centre of gravity of the other side of training should lie in intuition without an analytical divorce from the total environment. Its object is immediate apprehension with the minimum of eviscerating analysis. The type of generality, which above all is wanted, is the appreciation of variety of value. I mean an aesthetic growth. There is something between the gross specialized values of the mere practical man, and the thin specialised values of the mere scholar. Both types have missed something; and if you add together the two sets of values, you do not obtain the missing elements. What is wanted is an appreciation of the infinite variety of vivid values achieved by an organism in its proper environment. When you understand all about the sun and all about the atmosphere and all about the rotation of the earth, you may still miss the radiance of the sunset. There is no substitute for the direct perception of the concrete achievement of a thing in its actuality. We want concrete fact with a high light thrown on what is relevant to its preciousness.

What I mean is art and aesthetic education. It is, however, art in such a general sense of the term that I hardly like to call it by that name. Art is a special example. What we want is to draw out habits of aesthetic apprehension. According to the metaphysical doctrine which I have been developing, to do so is to increase the depth of individuality. The analysis of reality indicates the two factors, activity emerging into individualised aesthetic value. Also the emergent value is the measure of the individual-

isation of the activity. We must foster the creative initiative towards the maintenance of objective values. You will not obtain the apprehension without the initiative, or the initiative without the apprehension. As soon as you get towards the concrete, you cannot exclude action. Sensitiveness without impulse spells decadence, and impulse without sensitiveness spells brutality. I am using the word 'sensitiveness' in its most general signification, so as to include apprehension of what lies beyond oneself; that is to say, sensitiveness to all the facts of the case. Thus 'art' in the general sense which I require is any selection by which the concrete facts are so arranged as to elicit attention to particular values which are realisable by them. For example, the mere disposing of the human body and the eyesight so as to get a good view of a sunset is a simple form of artistic selection. The habit of art is the habit of enjoying vivid values.

But, in this sense, art concerns more than sunsets. A factory, with its machinery, its community of operatives, its social service to the general population, its dependence upon organising and designing genius, its potentialities as a source of wealth to the holders of its stock is an organism exhibiting a variety of vivid values. What we want to train is the habit of apprehending such an organism in its completeness. It is very arguable that the science of political economy, as studied in its first period after the death of Adam Smith (1790), did more harm than good. It destroyed many economic fallacies, and taught how to think about the economic revolution then in progress. But it riveted on men a certain set of abstractions which were disastrous in their influence on modern mentality. It dehumanised industry. This is only one example of a general danger inherent in modern science. Its methodological procedure is exclusive and intolerant, and rightly so. It fixes attention on a definite group of abstractions, neglects everything else, and elicits every scrap of information and theory which is relevant to what it has retained. This method is triumphant, provided that the abstractions are judicious. But, however triumphant, the triumph is within limits. The neglect of these limits leads to disastrous oversights. The anti-rationalism of science is partly justified, as a a preservation of its useful methodology; it is partly mere irrational prejudice. Modern professionalism is the training of minds to conform to the methodology. The historical revolt of the seventeenth century, and the earlier reaction towards naturalism, were examples of transcending the abstractions which fascinated educated society in the Middle Ages. These early ages had an ideal of rationalism, but they failed in its pursuit. For they neglected to note that the methodology of reasoning requires the limitations involved in the abstract. Accordingly, the true rationalism must always transcend itself by recurrence to the concrete in search of inspiration. A self-satisfied rationalism is in effect a form of anti-rationalism. It means an arbtrary halt at a particular set of abstractions. This was the case with science.

There are two principles inherent in the very nature of things, recurring in some particular embodiments whatever field we explore—the spirit of change, and the spirit of conservation. There can be nothing real without both. Mere change without conservation is a passage from nothing to nothing. Its final integration yields mere transient non-entity. Mere conservation without change cannot conserve. For after all, there is a flux of circumstance, and the freshness of being evaporates under mere repetition. The character of existent reality is composed of organisms enduring through the flux of things. The low type of organisms have achieved a self-identity dominating their whole physical life. Electrons, molecules, crystals, belong to this type. They exhibit a massive and complete sameness. In the higher types, where life appears, there is greater complexity. Thus, though there is a complex, enduring pattern, it has retreated into deeper recesses of the total fact. In a sense, the self-identity of a human being

is more abstract than that of a crystal. It is the life of the spirit. It relates rather to the individualisation of the creative activity; so that the changing circumstances received from the environment are differentiated from the living personality, and are thought of as forming its perceived field. In truth, the field of perception and the perceiving mind are abstractions which, in the concrete, combine into the successive bodily events. The psychological field, as restricted to sense-objects and passing emotions, is the minor permanence, barely rescued from the nonentity of mere change; and the mind is the major permanence, permeating that complete field, whose endurance is the living soul. But the soul would wither without fertilisation from its transient experiences. The secret of the higher organisms lies in their two grades of permanences. By this means the freshness of the environment is absorbed into the permanence of the soul. The changing environment is no longer, by reason of its variety, an enemy to the endurance of the organism. The pattern of the higher organism has retreated into the recesses of the individualised activity. It has become a uniform way of dealing with circumstances; and this way is only strengthened by having a proper variety of circumstances to deal with.

This fertilisation of the soul is the reason for the necessity of art. A static value, however serious and important, becomes unendurable by its appalling monotony of endurance. The soul cries aloud for release into change. It suffers the agonies of claustrophobia. The transitions of humour, wit, irreverence, play, sleep, and—above all—of art are necessary for it. Great art is the arrangement of the environment so as to provide for the soul vivid, but transient, values. Human beings require something which absorbs them for a time, something out of the routine which they can stare at. But you cannot subdivide life, except in the abstract analysis of thought. Accordingly, the great art is more than a transient refreshment. It is something which adds to the permanent richness of the soul's self-attainment. It justifies itself both by its immediate enjoyment, and also by its discipline of the inmost being. Its discipline is not distinct from enjoyment, but by reason of it. It transforms the soul into the permanent realisation of values extending beyond its former self. This element of transition in art is shown by the restlessness exhibited in its history. An epoch gets saturated by the masterpieces of any one style. Something new must be discovered. The human being wanders on. Yet there is a balance in things. Mere change before the attainment of adequacy of achievement, either in quality or output, is destructive of greatness. But the importance of a living art, which moves on and yet leaves its permanent mark, can hardly be exaggerated.

In regard to the aesthetic needs of civilised society the reactions of science have so far been unfortunate. Its materialistic basis has directed attention to *things* as opposed to *values*. The antithesis is a false one, if taken in a concrete sense. But it is valid at the abstract level of ordinary thought. This misplaced emphasis coalesced with the abstractions of political economy, which are in fact the abstractions in terms of which commercial affairs are carried on. Thus all thought concerned with social organisation expressed itself in terms of material things and of capital. Ultimate values were excluded. They were politely bowed to, and then handed over to the clergy to be kept for Sundays. A creed of competitive business morality was evolved, in some respects curiously high; but entirely devoid of consideration for the value of human life. The workmen were conceived as mere hands, drawn from the pool of labour. To God's question, men gave the answer of Cain—'Am I my brother's keeper?'; and they incurred Cain's guilt. This was the atmosphere in which the industrial revolution was accomplished in England, and to a large extent elsewhere. The internal history of England during the last half century has been an

endeavour slowly and painfully to undo the evils wrought in the first stage of the new epoch. It may be that civilisation will never recover from the bad climate which enveloped the introduction of machinery. This climate pervaded the whole commercial system of the progressive northern European races. It was partly the result of aesthetic errors of Protestantism and partly the result of scientific materialism, and partly the result of the natural greed of mankind, and partly the result of the abstractions of political economy. An illustration of my point is to be found in Macaulay's Essay criticising Southey's *Colloquies on Society*. It was written in 1830. Now Macaulay was a very favourable example of men living at that date, or at any date. He had genius; he was kindhearted, honourable; and a reformer. This is the extract:—'We are told, that our age has invented atrocities beyond the imagination of our fathers; that society has been brought into a state compared with which extermination would be a blessing; and all because the dwellings of cotton-spinners are naked and rectangular. Mr. Southey has found out a way he tells us, in which the effects of manufactures and agriculture may be compared. And what is this way? To stand on a hill, to look at a cottage and a factory, and to see which is the prettier.'

Southey seems to have said many silly things in his book; but, so far as this extract is concerned, he could make a good case for himself if he returned to earth after the lapse of nearly a century. The evils of the early industrial system are now a commonplace of knowledge. The point which I am insisting on is the stone-blind eye with which even the best men of that time regarded the importance of aesthetics in a nation's life. I do not believe that we have as yet nearly achieved the right estimate. A contributory cause, of substantial efficacy to produce this disastrous error, was the scientific creed that matter in motion is the one concrete reality in nature; so that aesthetic values form an adventitious, irrelevant addition.

There is another side to this picture of the possibilities of decadence. At the present moment a discussion is raging as to the future of civilisation in the novel circumstances of rapid scientific and technological advance. The evils of the future have been diagnosed in various ways, the loss of religious faith, the malignant use of material power, the degradation attending a differential birth rate favouring the lower types of humanity, the suppression of aesthetic creativeness. Without doubt, these are all evils, dangerous and threatening. But they are not new. From the dawn of history, mankind has always been losing its religious faith, has always suffered from the malignant use of material power, has always suffered from the infertility of its best intellectual types, has always witnessed the periodical decadence of art. In the reign of the Egyptian king, Tutankhamen, there was raging a desperate religious struggle between Modernists and Fundamentalists; the cave pictures exhibit a phase of delicate aesthetic achievement as superseded by a period of comparative vulgarity; the religious leaders, the great thinkers, the great poets and authors, the whole clerical caste in the Middle Ages, have been notably infertile; finally, if we attend to what actually has happened in the past, and disregard romantic visions of democracies, aristocracies, kings, generals, armies, and merchants, material power has generally been wielded with blindness, obstinacy and selfishness, often with brutal malignancy. And yet, mankind has progressed. Even if you take a tiny oasis of peculiar excellence, the type of modern man who would have most chance of happiness in ancient Greece at its best period is probably (as now) an average professional heavy-weight boxer, and not an average Greek scholar from Oxford or Germany. Indeed, the main use of the Oxford scholar would have been his capability of writing an ode in glorification of the boxer. Nothing does more harm in unnerving men for their duties in the present, than the attention devoted to the points of excellence in the past as compared with the average failure of the present day.

But, after all, there have been real periods of decadence; and at the present time, as at other epochs, society is decaying, and there is need for preservative action. Professionals are not new to the world. But in the past, professionals have formed unprogressive castes. The point is that professionalism has now been mated with progress. The world is now faced with a self-evolving system, which it cannot stop. There are dangers and advantages in this situation. It is obvious that the gain in material power affords opportunity for social betterment. If mankind can rise to the occasion, there lies in front a golden age of beneficent creativeness. But material power in itself is ethically neutral. It can equally well work in the wrong direction. The problem is not how to produce great men, but how to produce great societies. The great society will put up the men for the occasions. The materialistic philosophy emphasized the given quantity of material, and thence derivatively the given nature of the environment. It thus operated most unfortunately upon the social conscience of mankind. For it directed almost exclusive attention to the aspect of struggle for existence in a fixed environment. To a large extent the environment is fixed, and to this extent there is a struggle for existence. It is folly to look at the universe through rose-tinted spectacles. We must admit the struggle. The question is, who is to be eliminated. In so far as we are educators, we have to have clear ideas upon that point; for it settles the type to be produced and the practical ethics to be inculcated.

But during the last three generations, the exclusive direction of attention to this aspect of things has been a disaster of the first magnitude. The watchwords of the nineteenth century have been, struggle for existence, competition, class warfare, commercial antagonism between nations, military warfare. The struggle for existence has been construed into the gospel of hate. The full conclusion to be drawn from a philosophy of evolution is fortunately of a more balanced character. Successful organisms modify their environment. Those organisms are successful which modify their environments so as to assist each other. This law is exemplified in nature on a vast scale. For example, the North American Indians accepted their environment, with the result that a scanty population barely succeeded in maintaining themselves over the whole continent. The European races when they arrived in the same continent pursued an opposite policy. They at once coöperated in modifying their environment. The result is that a population more than twenty times that of the Indian population now occupies the same territory, and the continent is not yet full. Again, there are associations of different species which mutually coöperate. This differentiation of species is exhibited in the simplest physical entities, such as the association between electrons and positive nuclei, and in the whole realm of animate nature. The trees in a Brazilian forest depend upon the association of various species of organisms, each of which is mutually dependent on the other species. A single tree by itself is dependent upon all the adverse chances of shifting circumstances. The wind stunts it: variations in temperature check its foliage: the rains denude its soil: its leaves are blown away and are lost for the purpose of fertilisation. You may obtain individual specimens of fine trees either in exceptional circumstances, or where human cultivation has intervened. But in nature the normal way in which trees flourish is by their association in a forest. Each tree may lose something of its individual perfection of growth, but they mutually assist each other in preserving the conditions for survival. The soil is preserved and shaded; and the microbes necessary for its fertility are neither scorched, nor frozen, nor washed away. A forest is the triumph of the organisation of mutually dependent species. Further a species of microbes which kills the forest, also exterminates itself. Again the two sexes exhibit the same advantage of differentiation. In the history of the world, the prize has not gone to those species which specialised in methods of violence, or even in defensive armour. In fact, nature began with producing animals encased in hard shells for defence against the ills of life. It also experimented in size. But smaller animals, without external armour, warm-blooded, sensitive, and alert, have cleared these monsters off the face of the earth. Also, the lions and tigers are not the successful species. There is something in the ready use of force which defeats its own object. Its main defect is that it bars coöperation. Every organism requires an environment of friends, partly to shield it from violent changes, and partly to supply it with its wants. The Gospel of Force is incompatible with a social life. By *force,* I mean *antagonism* in its most general sense.

Almost equally dangerous is the Gospel of Uniformity. The differences between the nations and races of mankind are required to preserve the conditions under which higher development is possible. One main factor in the upward trend of animal life has been the power of wandering. Perhaps this is why the armour-plated monsters fared badly. They could not wander. Animals wander into new conditions. They have to adapt themselves or die. Mankind has wandered from the trees to the plains, from the plains to the seacoast, from climate to climate, from continent to continent, and from habit of life to habit of life. When man ceases to wander, he will cease to ascend in the scale of being. Physical wandering is still important, but greater still is the power of man's spiritual adventures—adventures of thought, adventures of passionate feeling, adventures of aesthetic experience. A diversification among human communities is essential for the provision of the incentive and material for the Odyssey of the human spirit. Other nations of different habits are not enemies: they are godsends. Men require of their neighbours something sufficiently akin to be understood, something sufficiently different to provoke attention, and something great enough to command admiration. We must not expect, however, all the virtues. We should even be satisfied if there is something odd enough to be interesting.

Modern science has imposed on humanity the necessity for wandering. Its progressive thought and its progressive technology make the transition through time, from generation to generation, a true migration into uncharted seas of adventure. The very benefit of wandering is that it is dangerous and needs skill to avert evils. We must expect, therefore, that the future will disclose dangers. It is the business of the future to be dangerous; and it is among the merits of science that it equips the future for its duties. The prosperous middle classes, who ruled the nineteenth century, placed an excessive value upon placidity of existence. They refused to face the necessities for social reform imposed by the new industrial system, and they are now refusing to face the necessities for intellectual reform imposed by the new knowledge. The middle class pessimism over the future of the world comes from a confusion between civilisation and security. In the immediate future there will be less security than in the immediate past, less stability. It must be admitted that there is a degree of instability which is inconsistent with civilisation. But, on the whole, the great ages have been unstable ages.

I have endeavoured in these lectures to give a record of a great adventure in the region of thought. It was shared in by all the races of western Europe. It developed with the slowness of a mass movement. Half a century is its unit of time. The tale is the epic of an episode in the manifestation of reason. It tells how a particular direction of reason emerges in a race by the long preparation of antecedent epochs, how after its birth its subject-matter gradually unfolds itself, how it attains its triumphs, how its influence moulds the very springs of action of mankind, and finally how at its moment of supreme success its limitations disclose themselves and call for a renewed exercise of the creative imagination. The moral of the tale is the power of reason, its decisive influence on the life of humanity. The great conquerors, from Alexander to Caesar, and from Caesar to Napoleon, influenced profoundly the lives of subsequent generations. But the total effect of this influence shrinks to insignificance, if compared to the entire transformation of human habits and human mentality produced by the long line of men of thought from Thales to the present day, men individually powerless, but ultimately the rulers of the world.

Notes

1. Francis W. Garforth, ed., *John Stuart Mill on Education* (New York: Teachers College Press, 1971), p. 177.

2. Alfred North Whitehead, *Modes of Thought* (New York: Macmillan Co., 1938), p. 232.

3. Alvin Toffler, *Future Shock* (New York: Random House, 1970), p. 429.

4. Alfred North Whitehead, *Adventures in Ideas* (New York: Macmillan Co., 1933), p. 279.

Afterword / In Quest of Utopia

Whitehead's discussion brings into clear focus most of the topics with which this book has been concerned—reliable beliefs, freedom, the nature of man, moral choice, religious experience, and artistic creation. It also shows how a man in the twentieth century can find a philosophical frame of orientation to which he is freely committed and which gives him a source of inspiration and hope. If history, as H. G. Wells once said, is becoming more and more a race between education and catastrophe, it is urgent that we, as Socrates and Whitehead advised, get on with our education, not just by accumulating knowledge and technique but by examining our present commitments and looking into our ultimate concerns. Whitehead defined civilization as consisting of "the five qualities of Truth, Beauty, Adventure, Art, and Peace,"[1] which he hoped that education would help to promote. He recognized, however, that no one can be educated and civilized until these abstract ideas have become consciously experienced present realities by effort, involvement, and commitment. The aim of life should be dynamic process instead of static perfection. Thus neither the past nor the future should take precedence over the present.

As the philosopher Schopenhauer pointed out, just as no one ever lives in the past, no one will ever live in the future. We live always in the present; it is the present only which we possess. Yet we try by our planning and actions to influence future developments; we imagine in the present what it will be like to live in the future. For the future, when it *is* the present, will have grown out of our actions, attitudes, beliefs, and fantasies as to what it might be.

Man the Time-Binder

The psychologist Carl Jung believed that if we could probe into the mind of a young person daydreaming, we would find that his or her fantasies would be concerned mainly with the future. Most fantasies, Jung claimed, consist of anticipations. They are "preparatory acts," "psychic exercises for dealing with certain future realities."[2] Ortega told his students that life is preoccupation; we are constantly being compelled to decide what we are going to do, what we are going to be, how we are going to occupy ourselves in anticipation, *pre-occupying* ourselves. The great semanticist Alfred Korzybski distinguished man from other animals by his "time-bound capacity" —his capacity to use past knowledge in the present to plan for the future. Morris L. Ernst wrote in *Utopia 1976* that "possibly our distinguishing trait is that no other animal expects, or dreams about, a tomorrow."[3] William Pepperell Montague called this peculiar trait "man's self-transcending capacity," the capacity by which he retrospectively, logically, spatially, and prospectively rises above the present moment to be master (at least imaginatively) of all he surveys. Man's life is a never-ending process of decision-making, of confronting alternatives and choosing among them, and of committing one's self to one rather than to another. This process of decision-making is, as the existentialists never tire of reminding us, simply another name for self-making or destiny-making.

Of course, as John Dewey pointed out, one can live too much in anticipation of the future and miss the intrinsic satisfactions that lie in the present, just as one can be so preoccupied with the past that one can forget to live for the present moment. Friedrich Nietzsche recognized the latter danger when he wrote in *The Use and Abuse of History* that "the knowledge of the past is desired only for the service of the future and the present, not to weaken the present or undermine a living future."[4] One needs a sense of retrospect as well as prospect, nostalgia as well as hope, to savor and appreciate fully a present moment. As Rollo May put it, "the past has meaning as it lights up the present, and the future as it makes the present richer and more profound."[5]

Confronting *Le Fin de Siècle* — Utopian Speculation

As the end of this century approaches, people are giving more attention to the future. Conferences are being held on prospects to be looked forward to (or dreaded) in the new century; masses of data are being gathered; philosophers and scientists are making predictions; and academic courses are paying more attention to what is now called "futurology." Prognostication has become a popular pastime, indulged in not just by the practitioners of occult sciences, but by business, industry, and government.

As one might expect in an age that has produced manned flights to the moon, a great deal of attention is being directed toward future scientific and technological advancements. In *Profiles of the Future*, Arthur C. Clarke, the author of the movie script and novel *2001: A Space Odyssey,* paints a glowing picture of this future world. Planetary landings and colonizations, interstellar probes and flights, contact and meetings with extra-terrestrials are conceivable within the next one hundred and fifty years. Artificial life and intelligence; telesensory devices; robots and cyborgs; control of weather, climate, gravity, and heredity; and space mining are some of the achievements that Clarke envisages as possible by 2100. For an encyclopedic treatment of possible and probable scientific and technological advances, as well as for a myriad scenarios of possible future developments, one can go to Herman Kahn and Anthony Wiener's *The Year 2000: A Framework for Speculation about the Future.*

Meanwhile, in today's world many people, especially those in the so-called counterculture, have shown increasing disillusionment with the widespread idea that "science and technology can save us." Actual wars and threats of war, environmental pollution and senseless waste, violence and crime, and racism and social inequality have driven many to seek alternatives to the present organization of the technological society. Communes of almost every conceivable variety have sprung up throughout this country (there are about three thousand, according to a recent estimate) and in many parts of the world as attempts to perform "experiments in living." *Utopia or Oblivion,* the title of a recent book by the utopian thinker F. Buckminster Fuller, is a reoccurring theme in discussions of the perennial question, What is to be done?

Contrary to popular misconceptions, utopian proposals are not necessarily impractical and useless or a waste of time. Presented either in fictional form or in a program for action, utopias have often served as designs for actual reform, as blueprints for new societies, and as beacons to guide human affairs. To say that utopian thinkers are mere visionaries and that utopias are irrelevant to the actual world is to ignore the tremendous impact that thinkers, such as Jesus, Confucius, and Marx, have had on human thought and action and to discount the continuing influence of utopian works, such as Plato's *Republic,* More's *Utopia,* Bellamy's *Looking Backward* and, more recently, Skinner's *Walden Two.* As Oscar Wilde wrote, "A map of the world that does not include Utopia is not worth even glancing at, for it leaves out the one country at which Humanity is always landing. And when Humanity lands there, it looks out, and seeing a better country, sets sail. Progress is the realisation of Utopias."[6]

Following is a guide that you may wish to use, either alone or with a group, in engaging in utopian speculation. It includes questions of freedom, the good, human nature, and other major topics which we have discussed. We hope that this book is of some help in your own venture toward the future.

Philosophy . . . is the most effective of all the intellectual pursuits. It builds cathedrals before the workmen have moved a stone, and it destroys them before the elements have worn down their arches. It is the architect of the buildings of the spirit, and it is also their solvent.[7]

Notes

1. Alfred North Whitehead, *Adventures in Ideas* (New York: Macmillan Company, 1933), p. 274.

2. Carl Jung, "The Soul and Death" in Herman Feifel, ed. *The Meaning of Death* (New York: McGraw–Hill, 1959), pp. 9–10.

3. Morris L. Ernst, *Utopia 1976* (New York: Rinehart & Co., 1955), p. 4.

4. Friedrich Nietzsche, *The Use and Abuse of History* (Indianapolis: Bobbs-Merrill, 1957), p. 22.

5. Rollo May, *Man's Search for Himself* (New York: Signet, 1953), p. 227.

6. Oscar Wilde, *Intentions and the Soul of Man* (London: Methuen, 1908), p. 299.

7. Alfred North Whitehead, *Science and the Modern World* (New York: Macmillan Co., 1925), pp. viii–ix.

Related Reading

(Works marked * are available in paperbound editions.)

Bell, Daniel, ed. *Toward the Year 2000.* Boston: Houghton Mifflin, 1968.

*Bellamy, Edward. *Looking Backward.* New York: Appleton Century Co., 1897.

Berneri, Mary Louise. *Journey Through Utopia.* London: Routledge and Kegan Paul, 1950.

*Calder, Nigel, ed. *The World in 1984.* Baltimore: Penguin Books, 1965, 2 vols.

*Chase, Stuart. *The Most Probable World.* New York: Harper & Row, 1968.

*Clarke, Arthur C. *Profiles of the Future.* New York: Harper and Row, 1963.

*Dunstan, Maryjane and Patricia W. Garlan, eds. *Worlds in the Making: Probes for Students of the Future.* Englewood Cliffs, N. J.: Prentice-Hall, 1970.

*Goodman, Paul. *Utopian Essays and Practical Proposals.* New York: Random House, 1964.

*Hedgepeth, William and Dennis Stock. *The Alternative: Communal Life in New America.* New York: Collier Books, 1970.

*Holloway, Mark. *Heavens on Earth: Utopian Communities in America.* New York: Dover Publications, 1966.

*Houriet, Robert. *Getting Back Together.* New York: Avon, 1971.

*Huxley, Aldous. *Brave New World.* New York: Bantam Books, 1931.

*———. *Brave New World Revisited.* New York: Bantam Books, 1958.

Kahn, Herman and Anthony J. Weiner. *The Year 2000: A Framework for Speculation on the Next Thirty-Three Years.* New York: Macmillan Co., 1967.

*Kanter, Rosabeth M. *Communes: Commitment and Community.* Cambridge: Harvard University Press, 1972.

Kateb, George. *Utopia and its Enemies.* New York: Free Press of Glencoe, 1963.

King-Hele, Desmond. *The End of the Twentieth Century.* New York: St. Martin's, 1970.

Kostelanetz, Richard, ed. *Social Speculations: Visions for Our Time.* New York: Morrow, 1971.

Manuel, Frank E., ed. *Utopias and Utopian Thought.* Boston: Houghton Mifflin, 1966.

*McHale, John. *The Future of the Future.* New York: Braziller, 1969.

Morgan, Arthur. *Nowhere was Somewhere.* Chapel Hill, N. C.: University of North Carolina Press, 1946.

*Mumford, Lewis. *The Story of Utopias.* New York: Viking Press, 1962.

*Negley, Glenn R. and J. Max Patrick. *The Quest for Utopia: An Anthology of Imaginary Societies.* Garden City, N.Y.: Doubleday & Co., 1962.

*Orwell, George. 1984. New York: Harcourt Brace and Company, 1948.

*Ozmon, Howard. *Utopias and Education.* Minneapolis: Burgess Publishing Co., 1968.

*Richter, Peyton E., ed. *Utopias: Social Ideals and Communal Experiments.* Boston: Holbrook Press, 1971.

*Roberts, Ron E. *The New Communes: Coming Together in America.* Englewood Cliffs, N. J.: Prentice-Hall, 1971.

Russell, Bertrand. *Has Man a Future?* Baltimore: Penguin, 1961.

*Skinner, B. F. *Walden Two.* New York: Macmillan Co., 1948.

Theobald, Robert. *Futures Conditional.* Indianapolis: Bobbs-Merrill, 1972.

*Toffler, Alvin. *Future Shock.* New York: Bantam, 1970.

"The Utopian Urge: You Make the Future Today," Harper's Wraparound, *Harper's,* March, 1973.

Walsh, Chad. *From Utopia to Nightmare.* New York: Harper and Row, 1962.

*Wells, H. G. *A Modern Utopia.* London: Chapman and Hall, 1905.

Appendix

A Utopia Project:
Confronting the Future Today

Utopian speculation is often used in stimulating people to confront social and philosophical problems and to commit themselves to imaginative solutions to them. It can also help to bring various fields of knowledge into meaningful relationships, affording new perspectives from which to view past, present, and future experience. When the speculation takes place in small groups of people working together to design an imaginary commune or intentional community, it can contribute to the understanding and tolerance of divergent points of view and foster fellowship, cooperation, and compromise in reaching group decisions. In any case, utopian speculation, individual or collective, is usually engrossing, provocative, and fun.

The following directions may be useful as guidelines:

1. Your utopia may be written alone or with a group of fellow students. If with a group, discuss all questions together, keep notes, then assign different parts to be written by different persons. Finally, edit and integrate the various parts into a unified paper.

2. It may be written in the form of a dialogue, a report, an essay, a diary, letters, a short story, a novelette, a scrapbook, or in some other form you may think appropriate. For different successful approaches, see Plato's *Republic*, Thomas More's *Utopia*, Edward Bellamy's *Looking Backward*, H. G. Wells's *A Modern Utopia*, Aldous Huxley's *Island*, and B .F. Skinner's *Walden Two*.

3. Try to be feasible rather than fantastic. Attempt to explain how your utopia could come about and why it might succeed. Construct arguments for your solutions to problems rather than state the solutions dogmatically. Throughout your presentation, aim at coherence, clarity, consistency, and plausibility.

4. You may decide to write a dystopia or anti-utopia, in which case your task will be harder but even more challenging. You'll soon discover that you have to keep both your social criticism and your implied utopian solution or alternative simultaneously in mind if you expect your dystopia to be effective. For examples of successful dystopias, see Ignatius Donnelly's *Caesar's Column*, Eugene Zamiatin's *We*, Aldous Huxley's *Brave New World*, George Orwell's *1984*, and Ayn Rand's *Anthem* and *Atlas Shrugged*.

5. The papers should be typed, double-spaced and with ample margins. Illustrations, clippings, diagrams, charts, and photographs will help bring it to life. As for length, individually written papers should be from ten to twenty pages long and group papers, a minimum of thirty pages long in light of the extensive list of questions.

6. For a source book containing extensive bibliographies on utopian speculation, see Peyton E. Richter, ed. *Utopias: Social Ideals and Communal Experiments* (Boston: Holbrook Press, 1971). Other relevant books are listed in the Related Readings within this book, especially the one that precedes. The titles by Garlan and Dunstan, Kanter, King-Hele, Roberts, and Theobald should be especially helpful.

Guide to Constructing a Utopia

I. Education, Methods and Beliefs

1. What are the purposes of education in your utopia?
2. Who will be educated Why? How?
3. Describe your ideal school system—its goals, methodology, and curriculum.
4. What will be the ideal characteristics of your teachers, students, and administrators?
5. Would only one view of the nature of ultimate reality be taught in your educational system? If so, what will it be and how will its truth be justified?
6. What is the definition and test of truth in your utopia?
7. What would be the relationship between your educational system and the state? How free would your educational approaches be?
8. How might your utopian education deal with:
   a. racial prejudices and conflicts; b. drug taking; c. sex education; d. political activists among students and faculty; e. exceptional students; f. boundary situations (guilt, suffering, struggle, death)?

II. Politics, Authority, and Freedom

1. What will be the form of government of your utopia? Justify your choice.
2. Will you have a written constitution? Why, or why not?
3. If your society has governing officials, how will they be selected, changed, or removed?
4. How will abuses of political power be avoided or dealt with?
5. What will be the rights and responsibilities of citizenship in your utopia?
6. What is the relative importance of freedom and authority in your utopia? Of innovation and tradition?
7. How will your political system deal with:
   a. racial discrimination; b. internal and external defense; c. differences between the sexes; d. civil disobedience; e. religious differences?

III. The Good Life

A. *Physical Plan*

1. Where will your utopia be located? Why?
2. Describe its distinctive geographical features and natural resources.
3. Describe or sketch examples of its physical appearance—kinds and styles of buildings, community or city plans, transportation systems, disposal systems, etc. (Be as concrete and detailed as you wish.)

B. *Economics*

1. How are problems of production and distribution to be solved in your utopia?
2. Explain the relative importance of agriculture, handicrafts, and industrial production in your utopia.
3. How much economic planning and control will there be in your utopia?
4. Who will do the "dirty work" in your utopia? Why?
5. How will your economic system deal with:
   a. possible depressions; b. waste and pollution; c. trade; d. class conflicts; e. vested interests or power cliques; f. incentives; g. loafers?

C. *Human Relations and Morality*

1. What are the size and characteristics (racial, ethnic, age, etc.) of your utopia's population?
2. Are members of your utopia to be selected, or is there open-admission to all? Why?
3. What moral virtues are you trying to promote? How do your utopian institutions promote these virtues?
4. What is your utopian criterion for judging action to be morally right or wrong? Give several examples of how the criterion would be applied.
5. How are deviants from your social norms to be dealt with? Justify.
6. What mechanisms will operate in your society to keep it unified and cohesive yet diversified and flexible?
7. Will the nuclear family be retained? Why, or why not?
8. How will your utopians spend their leisure time?
9. How will conflicts among members or groups be avoided or resolved?

10. What will be your society's attitude toward and treatment of:
    a. marriage; b. premarital and extra-marital sex; c. divorce; d. mental illness and emotional problems; e. old age; f. funeral rites?

IV. Human Nature, Science, and Technology

1. What assumptions about human nature are you making in constructing your utopia? Justify.
2. How important are science and technology in bringing about and maintaining your utopia?
3. What is the attitude of your utopians toward machines and machine production?
4. How much applied and pure scientific research would there be in your utopia? How would it be subsidized?
5. Would scientific education be stressed in schools? Why or why not? What would be the relationship between the sciences and the humanities in your education?
6. How would scientists be selected, trained, and rewarded in your utopia?
7. What would be the relationship or relevance of science and technology to these problems in your utopia:
    a. warfare or peace-keeping; b. over-population; c. weather-control; d. feeding, sheltering, and clothing people; e. ecological problems; f. eugenics; g. behavioral engineering?

V. Religion

1. How would religion be defined in your ideal society?
2. What would be its functions?
3. In your utopia, would there be religious institutions with officials, creeds, rites, rituals, and other collective activities? If so, what would they be, why would they exist, and how would they function?
4. What would be the relationship between religion and other aspects of your society—e.g., the state, science, education, morality, and art? What conflicts might arise between these and how would they be avoided or resolved?
5. Do your utopians believe in God? Why or why not? Do they believe in personal survival after death or some other form of immortality? Why, or why not?
6. What would be your utopian religion's stand (if any) on these:
    a. euthanasia; b. abortion; c. suicide; d. drug-induced mystical experiences; e. messianic individuals; f. religious schisms; g. premarital and extra-marital sex; h. divorce; i. atheism; j. miracles?

VI. Art, Beauty, and Creativity

1. How would art and beauty be defined in your utopia?
2. What roles would art play in the everyday life of inhabitants of your utopia?
3. Would any organized or official attempt be made to nurture and reward creative artists in your society? Why, or why not?
4. Would your utopians allow censorship of art? If so, for what reason and by whom?
5. Would your schools be engaged in "aesthetic education" for everyone? If so, describe it.
6. Would tragedy, comedy, and satire continue to exist in your utopia? Why, or why not?
7. Do you think great art, artistic geniuses, and creative rebels would exist in your utopia? Why, or why not?

Notes

This brief syllabus is similar to, but not identical with, a larger syllabus for a utopia project developed by Peyton E. Richter and other members of the Division of Humanities at Boston University College of Basic Studies in the early 1950s (see James A. Fisher and Peyton E. Richter, "Education for Citizenship: A Utopian Approach to General Education," *Journal of Higher Education* XXVIII, April 1957, pp. 220–24). Professor Glenn R. Negley at Duke University had already instituted a similar project in his course in Social Philosophy and Utopian Ideals. For an example of a student-written utopia, see Glenn R. Negley and J. Max Patrick, eds. *The Quest for Utopia: An Anthology of Imaginary Societies,* (Garden City, N.Y.: Doubleday and Co., 1962), Appendix.

Index